CONTENTS

PREFACE

In 1986, just after the publication of my first musical-theatre book, *The British Musical Theatre*, I was commissioned by the London publisher The Bodley Head to compile a musical-theatre companion to their celebrated *Kobbé's Complete Book of Opera*. What they blush-makingly called *Gänzl's Book of the Musical Theatre* came out in 1988. It was (and is) a fairly sizeable tome, some 1,350 pages filled with synopses and production details for around three hundred musical plays of all shapes, sizes, and eras: Parisian *opéra-bouffe* and *opérette*, two centuries' worth of Austro-Hungarian *Operette*, Spanish zarzuela, turn-of-the-century and 1920s musical comedy and romantic musical plays from both sides of the Atlantic, and, of course, many an example of the "musical" of our own postwar days.

Simultaneously with its British appearance, *Gänzl's Book of the Musical Theatre* was published in the United States by Schirmer Books. A few years down the line, Schirmer came up with the idea of putting out a new and updated version, a rather less compendious (and less expensive) volume than the original, and one that concentrated on the best of Broadway, rather than on the farther-flung corners of the musical stage of earlier centuries. And so, *Gänzl's Book of the Broadway Musical* went into the making.

I've written and/or compiled a number of books on the musical theatre in recent years, and I've discovered, on the way, that the one thing that is inclined to ruffle certain readers (not to mention writers) quite disproportionately is what one chooses to put into a book like this. Or, perhaps more pertinently, what one chooses—often unwillingly—to leave out. I think, in the past, I've managed not to provoke too many gross indignations by my choices—when choices had to be made—but I really had to put on my surgical gown when Richard-my-editor came through to me with the brief for this one: seventy-five shows, with the accent on the most modern.

Seventy-five! From all the great shows of the past, and—with emphasis—the present! How to choose? For once, I decided that this wasn't a job I was willing to tackle on my own. Even Miss World and the president of the truckers union get elected by some kind of committee. So I cravenly suggested to Richard-my-editor: "Why don't you send me a list of suggestions and we'll go on from there?" He started. We started. Faxes ricocheted back and forth between New York and St. Paul de Vence, France. It's the "Broadway" musical, so let's forget the off-Broadway hits (goodbye *Fantasticks* and *Little Shop of Horrors* and *Threepenny Opera*). No one-acters (forget *Trial by Jury*). No musical pasticcio or scissors-and-paste musicals (farewell *Kismet*, *Crazy for You*, *Blossom Time*). Oh, heck, let's have only English-language musicals (nix *The Merry Widow*, *Die Fledermaus*, and *Irma la douce*, but reprieve *Les Misérables* on account of its English rebirth). And when the bell rang at the end of round one, we actually agreed on sixty-three out of seventy-five. Not bad. Not bad.

Then I leaned firmly backward (*Robin Hood*, *Naughty Marietta*, *Oh, Boy!*, *Rose Marie*, and so forth). Richard-my-editor leaned firmly forward (the recently revived *Damn Yankees*, *She Loves Me*, *Bye Bye Birdie*, and so on). We had seventy-three, at which stage he said magnanimously to me, "Go on, put your particular favorites in the last two spots." So I did. And that's how we got *On the Twentieth Century* and *Little Me*. Sorry *Irene*, *Barnum*, *The New Moon*, *The Boy Friend*, *Half a Sixpence*, *Chess*, *Wonderful Town*, *The Most Happy Fella*, *Going Up*, *Once Upon a Mattress*, *The Prince of Pilsen*, *Do I Hear a Waltz?*, and all my other favorites. But seventy-five is seventy-five. And if it had been twenty-five or two hundred and fifty, the job would have been just as tricky. There would still have been many marvellous shows left on the bank.

Hopefully, the ones we've chosen, strung together on a silk-strong sliver of Broadway history, are a judicious mixture of old and new. When my colleague, Andrew Lamb, and I were going through the same process, at the outset of planning *Gänzl's Book of the Musical Theatre*, we decided that a good yardstick was, 'Is the musical still being played today, either by professional or amateur groups?' Looking down our list of seventy-five shows, I'm pleased to see that there is only a handful among them that I've not had the opportunity to see in one kind of production or another. And, as the passion for revivals of classic musicals rises indomitably to a height unheard of in recent decades, I'll look forward to seeing those ones back on the stage—hopefully in a not-too-fiddled-about shape—before very long.

Some of the shows that are described here have been through more than one version during their long (or even not so long) lives. Libretti and song schedules for some older shows have been overhauled in line with what are considered "modern tastes," or simply to boost the role of a particular performer, when revivals have been mounted. Sometimes this has resulted in an improvement to the piece, often it hasn't. And in modern times, with the virtual abolition of the old-time out-of-town tryout, many a major show has gone through alterations after its official opening night, after its cast recording, and even after its first run. *Dreamgirls*, *Cats*, and *Sunset Boulevard* are three that come to mind. In each case where the original Broadway text hasn't been followed, I've indicated what version I've used for my synopsis and pointed out major alterations.

With regard to the headers describing each show, you'll notice that I've included only Broadway productions, on the grounds that that is what our book's about. However, when a show—from *H.M.S. Pinafore* to *Sunset Boulevard*—has had its initial production (pre-Broadway tryouts not counted) somewhere else, that production is noted. Film versions are only described when the film has been made up very largely of, and from the original book and score of, the stage show.

Our photos are in the same case. I've always, in my earlier illustrated books, tried not to use that same handful of much-reproduced pictures that have already been seen so many times before. But this time around it's different. We're on Broadway, and Broadway pictures—much recycled or not—it has to be. It's been much, much harder to be original, but I have tried as well as I know how.

Instead of including a record appendix, as I did in the earlier book, I've decided to move with the times and provide you with an appendix of compact discs relating to the shows in this book. However, because my shelves hold about 3,000 records and something like thirty CDs, I've pretty much put this delicate question of recordings into the hands of the two most outstanding collectors of show albums that I know, Mr. Rexton S. Bunnett of London, and Mr. Bradley S. Bennett of Los Angeles. I'm quite sure that if these two don't know about or have a disc, then it doesn't exist. Thanks, fellers.

One last point. It's a point that probably won't strike those of you who know me already through *The British Musical Theatre*, *Blackwell's Guide to Musical Theatre on Record*, *Gänzl's Book of the Musical Theatre*, or *The Encyclopedia of the Musical Theatre*. This is a book about the American stage, published by an American publisher. Yet, for the most part, it's written in English English . . . give or take a few colors and favors and ardors and the occasional while. And not only did Richard-my-editor let me put in *On the Twentieth Century* and *Little Me*, he also—almost—let me write the way I write. And insisted I tell you that the rest is not his fault.

Merry musical theatregoing to you.

Kurt Gänzl
St. Paul de Vence
June 1994

INTRODUCTION

The Broadway musical. It's an expression that sets all kinds of pictures and sounds bubbling up in your mind and in your memory. Sometimes it's a 1930s picture or sound—one that comes courtesy, perhaps, of getting-on-for-venerable age, but more often thanks to an old record, late-night television, or to the fin-de-this-siècle video industry. Naturally, it's a black-and-white picture. One of a platoon of banged or crimped maidens of indeterminate age, kitted out in what look like gym frocks and rock-climbing bootlets, dancing to the tune of a lithe little ditty, all the way from Smalltown, America, to the one-hundred-strong front line of the chorus of "a Broadway show." And, of course, eventually to fame, wealth, and the hand of the American equivalent of a fairy prince. Those sometimes tongue-in-cheekily oversized film versions of what were meant to be stage shows, purveyed to us piecemeal by Hollywood as the not-very-far-in-the-background to a tiny tale of showbiz romance, have left an enduring mark. To many folk, all around the world, who've been nowhere near Broadway, nor even America, nor even a theatre, a "Broadway musical" is one with Ruby Keeler and Dick Powell and hundreds of choristers in matching costumes, stretched across a stage that just goes on and on and on.

Sometimes, on the other hand, the "Broadway musical" that we'll think of has the full-color look and sound of a Rodgers and Hammerstein show: the handsomely distributed and decorated features of the romantic musical plays of those postwar years when America was the center of the musical-theatre universe. Even in the face of the many changes that have overcome the theatre in the past decades, those of us who grew up with *South Pacific* and *The King and I*, on the stage and/or on the cinema screen, are inclined to think first and foremost of those shows, their fellows, and their followers, when the words "Broadway musical" dance into the conversation. And not without good reason. These manufactured-in-America musicals of 1950s and 1960s Broadway were, give or take a *Boy Friend*, an *Oliver!*, or an *Irma la douce*, the most important popular musical plays of an era that the graying half of our graying world remembers gratefully. Less fluffy, less flighty, less ingenuous, and maybe a bit less happily foolish fun than the 1920s musical comedies of which Hollywood had shown us such extravagant versions, they've proved themselves to be every bit as memorable, and remain loved and played from one end of the English-speaking world to the other.

On other occasions, the picture or the sound that comes to us isn't one of the past, but rather one of the present. For to the theatregoer of today, and particularly the younger theatregoer, the words "Broadway musical" call up a third and more contemporary picture. The frilly, funny musical comedy and the handsome, romantic musical play both survive now virtually as if in a slice of theatrical aspic, but we've moved into an era where the theatre-bent world is luxuriating in a variegated wave of lushly scenic, dramatically spectacular, knee-tremblingly orchestrated and amplified, high-tech musical shows, many of which—by their powerful content and proportions—verge on completing a full circle with the nineteenth-century days when romantic opera was one of the most popular of musical-theatre entertainments. Unlike the favorite musicals of the fifties and sixties, most of the more favored among these dietarily-dangerous shows are no longer homemade pieces having their first outings on Broadway before continuing on around the world. They're reproductions of shows initially produced overseas. This change in provenance isn't, of course, any more significant than it was in the days when Gilbert and Sullivan or *The Merry Widow* really ruled the stage. No matter from whence the shows of today have sprung, they belong on, and to Broadway, just as their 150 years worth of predecessors did. No one except those very few whose xenophobia overrides their love of the theatre perceives them as any the less "Broadway" just because of an accident of birth.

For, you see, "Broadway" is more than just one dog-legged high-street slicing its way across one particular island in one particular American city. That Broadway exists, of course, a constantly changing thoroughfare, buried down in a crevasse of towering and time-pocked buildings. But our Broadway isn't the noun, the physical fact of the street, it's the adjective. The adjective as in "Broadway musical," "Broadway show," "Broadway song," as in "Broadway hit" and "Broadway flop." The adjective with its intimations of fantasy and fribble, the adjective that calls up all those images we have just been talking about. For when the word "Broadway" turned terminally from being a proper noun into its new existence as an effervescently improper adjective, it got hijacked by the theatre world. Right or wrong, today you can't use the word anywhere around this planet without its provoking some kind of theatrical image. And most particularly an image of the musical theatre: Those tap-dancing tootsies from Smalltown, Pa.; the hills that are alive with the sound of music; the Argentina that mustn't cry for Eva Peron; or a litter of terpsichorean cats.

The mind and the memory are, of course, always inclined to deliver us impressions that are a meli-mélange of a hundred different sights and sounds, rather than a series of precise pictures put together with historical fidelity. So we really have to look a bit further than this tiny if colorful handful of happy stage "snapshots" if we want to take in a full and proper panorama of the world of the musical theatre from the days of Broadway as it was, to those of Broadway as it is. It's a look that's worth the taking, for the history of the world's musical stage and its entertainments has been a fascinating one, one that takes us from one side of the globe to the other and back again. And, in the twentieth century part of that history, Broadway has played an extremely important part.

Virtually all of America's earliest theatrical entertainments—musical or not—were imported ready-made, and even well-used, from the countries that the American colonists had left behind them. The interesting word in that statement is the plural, "countries." America differed from the other major colonial outposts of the British Empire in that its people, the new Americans of the eighteenth and nineteenth centuries, didn't all—or nearly all—come from the so-called motherland. They came from a whole range of countries, including some where the English language was not the native tongue. So, in contrast to a colony such as Australia, which, with a largely ex-British population, set up what would become its theatre establishment simply as an extension of the British one, nineteenth-century America found itself blessed with an English-language stage, a French-language stage, and a German-language stage all coexisting one alongside the other. This multilingual setup meant that the America of this period was open to receive a much wider and richer selection of theatre, including a good deal of musical theatre, than virtually any other country in the world. And there is no doubt that it took advantage of that opportunity.

In the 1860s and 1870s, America—along with the rest of the world—caught the craze for the French opéra-bouffe, the new species of comical musical play that set off what is generally regarded as the modern era of musical theatre. Americans, and New Yorkers in particular, were able to see this groundbreaking product of the Parisian stage performed not only by French performers in its original language, but in German adaptations at the German-language theatres, and, of course, in a whole variety of English-speaking productions—productions mounted originally in San Francisco, in Boston, in London, or in New York itself. But, at the same time, the French companies also supplied Manhattanites with a whole further range of Parisian musical plays, from opéra-comique to vaudeville, while the German theatres turned out an amazingly full list of productions of the best Austrian and German imitations of the French models, as well as a goodly supply of Possen and Schwänke mit Gesang und Tanz, those genuine "musical comedies" that were such an important part of the entertainment on German-language stages. As for the English-language musical theatre, when it wasn't delivering anglicized *opéra-bouffe* or *Operette*, it drew deeply on the produce of London. The British theatre provided the colonial stage with a vast consignment of pasticcio burlesques, extravaganzas, and new and nearly new comic operas, until the time when Gilbert and Sullivan's original English *opéra-bouffe*, *H.M.S. Pinafore*, arrived to launch the biggest musical-theatre craze since the first fine French flush and give a witty send-off to a new, made-in-English era of musical theatre.

During these midcentury years, New York, although it was the home of a thriving three-language theatre scene that was crosspollinating happily, wasn't yet the overwhelming center of the American theatre that it has since become. Musicals didn't, by and large, install themselves at a Broadway house for a long run as the virtual be-all and end-all of their existence. Most shows were made for traveling, and their New York season was just one part—albeit an important part—of that touring life. Chicago, Boston, Philadelphia, San Francisco, and other such centers could be just as lucrative dates for a theatre company as New York was, and there was plenty of money to be mined in stays in the secondary cities as well. Often, a musical company would travel—as the opera companies had long done—not with just one piece to present, but with a repertoire of up to a dozen shows. In this way, a company could extend its stay in a seemingly minor date much longer than it might have been able to had it played the same piece at every performance. Theatregoers returned night after night to see the different musicals, with consequent benefit to the box office. Thus, in these years, touring musical companies of all kinds and all qualities—and several languages— proliferated, prospered, and stayed on the road for years at a time, returning episodically to central or suburban New York theatres for longer or shorter stays as items in their operation. The first American-made musical of any significance, Ben Woolf's and Julius Eichberg's *The Doctor of Alcantara*, was born under these conditions. It first saw stagelight not on Broadway, but in the theatrical and musical hotspot that was 1862 Boston. Its appearances in New York were as part of the repertoire of a touring company and, although it appeared thereafter all around the world, it was never played in New York for what might have constituted a run.

As the nineteenth century ran through its last two decades, the thriving theatres of Broadway overflowed with French *opéras-comiques*, German musical plays and *Operetten*, British comic operas, new burlesques, and, above all, versions of the musical comedies and romantic musical plays produced by George Edwardes and his colleagues in London. New, homemade works got a look in too, but the often rather rough-and-ready successes of the native American musical theatre were to be found as often on the road as in New York City. Boston's Edward Rice brought out the burlesque extravaganzas *Evangeline* and *Adonis* with great success, and like J. K. Emmet and his German musico-comico-weepie *Fritz, Our Cousin German*, these shows traipsed cities and towns throughout the country for years. Charles Hoyt's semipasticcio musical play, *A Trip to Chinatown*—a loose-limbed piece full of variety turns and comical acts, which, like the Chicago-born *Adonis*, ultimately proved one of the longest-running Broadway musicals up to its time—took something like a year to get itself to the Great White Way. It had been busy doing the road rounds for which it had been constructed, and its first visit to New York was not to Broadway, but for a short stand at the suburban Harlem Opera House.

There were, naturally, successful new pieces produced in and specifically for New York as well. The 1866 *The Black Crook*, a cobbled together bit of Germanic fairy melodrama and borrowed music, relied more on its parades, its not-overclad dancing girls, and its scenery than on its written content to win a year's run at Niblo's Gardens. A grotesque descendant of the *opéra-bouffe* called *Wang*, written by the facile author of *Evangeline*, proved a happy vehicle for comic-opera star De Wolf Hopper, who turned it into a road perennial after its New York run. However, neither of these successful but distinctly imitative pieces had the heart or the individual personality of the series of musical "farce-comedies" produced and played at their New York base by the favorite musical-comedy team of Ned Harrigan and Tony Hart. These colorful, low-brow pieces—pieces with a distinct flavor of the *Lokalpossen* or *Charakterbilden* regularly seen in New York's German theatres—drew long and loud audiences for many years. Their popular-song-filled tales, peopled by new-American character types—negro, Irish, Jewish—so broadly drawn as to be almost burlesqued, became an institution in the Broadway theatre.

In fact, American authors and songwriters of this period had got the provincial/popular taste down to a tee, and while Harrigan and Hoyt and others of their ilk kept a flow of vigorously, cheerfully unpretentious musical plays coming on to the home stages, some such American-bred shows went even further afield. *Fritz*, ex-Australian Willie Gill's *My Sweetheart*, George Fawcett Rowe's and Johnnie Sheridan's musical comedy oddity *Fun on the Bristol*, and the ever-changing *A Trip to Chinatown* all traveled beyond Columbia's shores, but there, as at home, they rarely found acceptance in what passed for sophisticated theatres and circles. And not without reason, for their audience—like much of their content—was a music hall one rather than a polite play one: the Bowery rather than brownstone.

It was 1890 before the native American theatre turned out its first really durable success in the field of what was, rather antiquatedly by this time, called "comic opera": a romantic-cum-comic musical play sporting a substantial original light-operatic score, as opposed to those handfuls of jolly songs, old and/or new, that had been and were used to illustrate the farce-comedies. Once again, as in the cases of *The Doctor of Alcantara*, *Adonis*, and *A Trip to Chinatown*, this landmark piece did not owe its existence to the New York theatre. *Robin Hood*, a reasonably adept, if not noticeably original comic opera, built to standard English, mid-nineteenth century dimensions, was produced by the Boston Ideal Opera Company, a much-admired troupe that played Continental and British comic opera and *opéra-bouffe* on a regular touring basis. It was given its first showing as part of that company's repertoire in Chicago, and didn't put in an appearance on the Broadway stage until fifteen months later, after it had already been mounted in London!

All this time, however, New York was gradually making itself a reputation as the single place that mattered most, the place where a good reception and/or run could set your show up as a potentially profitable hit to take on to those years and years of touring round the rest of the country. As a result, those folk who were interested in producing plays and—of course—musical plays started to center themselves on New York. Gradually, more and more musical plays were given their first, or virtual first, and/or most important showings to New York audiences. The New York theatre land was expanding and, with the associated restaurants, cafés, and general nightlife that merged with the theatres to make up that phenomenon that was known as "Broadway," it was moving further and further uptown toward the area that is now the city's theatrical heart. Broadway, as we know it, was getting itself together, in more ways than one.

Robin Hood became a genuine comic-opera favorite, on an altogether bigger scale than *The Doctor of Alcantara*. It survived into repeated revivals for half a century—the first homegrown show to do so—and, unlike its predecessor, it provoked some significant follow-up. Through the last decade of the century and the early years of the new one, a regular run of solidly made homemade musicals began to appear, strolling in with different degrees of success to share Broadway's stages with the continuing flood of imported shows, a flood fronted by the all-conquering musicals of the new English "musical-comedy" tradition. *Robin Hood* librettist Harry Bache Smith wrote a series of pieces with composer Reginald De Koven, some of which did reasonably well on Broadway and on the road, but it was his collaboration with another composer that set the American romantic musical play tradition more surely on its way. In 1895, Smith combined with the Irish-born Victor Herbert on a fine burlesque piece called *The Wizard of the Nile*, which went on from its Broadway production to be played in Britain and in Europe. The pair followed this quickly with *The Serenade* (1897) and *The Fortune Teller* (1898), and although both of these European-style light operas were again written for touring troupes that made only the usual tour-stop in New York, the career of Broadway's most successful (new-) American composer to date was launched.

Victor Herbert was to provide the scores for all kinds of Broadway musicals over the next quarter of a century. In the course of those years, without in any way dominating the scene, he became the grand old man of the American musical, a focal point of a growing native musical-theatrical scene that was steadily gaining in confidence, style, and quality. Whilst he turned out the music for pieces such as the nursery-tale spectacular *Babes in Toyland* (1903), the Frenchified comic operetta *Mlle. Modiste* (1905), and the farcical Yankees-in-Europe piece *The Red Mill* (1906), Gustave Luders and Frank Pixley had international hits with two further Americans-abroad shows, the splendidly funny and melodious Boston musical *The Prince of Pilsen* (1902) and the comical, Chicago-born *The Sho-Gun* (1904), George M. Cohan was turning out the first and liveliest of his series of jolly, all-American star-vehicles in the long-touring *Little Johnny Jones* (1904) and *Forty-five Minutes from Broadway* (1906), and others were attempting, though without the same success, to follow up the surprising worldwide triumph of the Casino Theatre's try at a homemade imitation of a Gaiety musical, *The Belle of New York* (1897).

The American musical stage of the turn of the century decades simply sang with all sorts of shapes and sizes of shows, and the variegated selection of entertainments that was to be found in New York theatre land—whether born of Broadway, or brought thence from Boston, Britain, or Berlin—was as magnificently rich in variety as it was in quality. Broadway was booming. And—as ever—Broadway was moving. Mostly, and most interestingly, it was moving toward what can only be called a more coherent kind of modern musical play. By and large, musical libretti had, in the nineteenth century, been either rather stilted comic-opera ones—the descendants of the marquis-meets-milkmaid pieces of earlier days—with their period and/or foreign settings, unlikely disguises, and conventional situations and character-types repeated in show after show; or flung together in the manner of the rumbustious, very loosely constructed, inevitably improbable, and decidedly unsophisticated farce comedies, extravaganzas, burlesques, and star-vehicles that were so popular in touring houses. If you'd removed the songs and dances from all but the very best of either kind of show, there'd have been pretty little of worth left.

During the last years of the old century, however, there began a trend toward the use of versions of properly made plays as the libretti for musicals on the English-language stage. This kind of legitimate "musical comedy" was, of course, nothing new. The Germanic theatre had had its *Possen*, *Schwänke*, and other musical-play-with-songs variants for years. Vienna, in particular, had long plundered the French stage for comic plays of quality to use in the fabrication of its *Operette* libretti. The native French comedy-with-numbers tradition, the vaudeville, also went back to time immemorial, and it had moved memorably up, in the 1870s and 1880s, from sporting a time-honored scissors-and-paste musical part to being illustrated with custom-composed score. But the more or less sophisticated comedy—rather than burlesque—libretto had, so far, been a rare thing in the English language.

Given the high profile of the German and French stages in New York, it was no coincidence that most of the earliest examples of such strong-backed musical plays on the American stage should have had a European background. Adolf Philipp, the German actor–manager who was the biggest star of the New York German theatre of his time, saw his Yiddish comedy *Der Corner Grocer aus der Avenue A* made over by others as a Broadway musical called *About Town* (1894). The celebrated French vaudeville *Niniche*, already played on Broadway in several English and German versions, got recycled as a full-scale musical comedy called *The Merry Countess* (1895) and later again as *The Little Duchess* (1901). *Wang* librettist Cheever Goodwin—who'd pilfered many a French *opérette* text to do over for American audiences in his time—made a successful musical comedy called *Lost, Strayed or Stolen* (1896) out of Eugène Grangé and Victor Bernard's 1873 Palais-Royal farce *Le Baptême du petit Oscar*. Pieces such as the Viennese hit *Heisses Blut* (*A Dangerous Girl*, 1898), Jean

Kren's Berlin *Im Himmelshof* (*Hodge, Podge & Co*, 1900) or the Parisian vaudeville-opérettes *Le Jockey malgré lui* (*The Office Boy*, 1903), and *Toto* (*The West Point Cadet*, 1904) were remade as American musical plays, equipped with replacement scores of locally made songs.

The British, too, had begun to lean in this same direction. The "musical comedies" of the Gaiety Theatre variety, with their paperweight star-opportunity libretti and elastic scores, which had been for years the joy of Broadway as of London, started to make way for pieces such as the musical comedy megahit *The Girl from Kays* (a musicalization of Gandillot's play *La Mariée recalcitrante*), the long-enduring *The Duchess of Dantzic* (based on Sardou's *Madame Sans-Gêne*), or the Gaiety's own first play-based musical *The Spring Chicken* (on *Coquin de printemps*). The well-made play with songs was invading the area previously the province of the songs-dances-and-dresses-stuck-together-with-dialogue type of show.

Then, suddenly, before this agreeable trend had yet had the time to develop to its full, musical theatre land was knocked sideways by a new craze that swept all before it, the fourth craze in four decades. After the French *opéra-bouffe*, English comic opera, and George Edwardesian musical comedy, came the new generation of Austrian musical plays. And at their fore was the Viennese show that had already taken London, *The Merry Widow*. The landmark "musical-comedy" hit that it had seemed would soon come, had come, but it had come from outside the English-language theatre, and its remade comedy script was attached to a score of a different flavor to those being written for adapted French comedies in America and England. For, yes, *The Merry Widow* was, like *Lost, Strayed and Stolen* or *The Girl from Kays*, a musicalization of a French play, *L'Attaché d'ambassade*.

While the flash flood of Austrian musicals that followed *The Merry Widow* onto Broadway took its place at the top of the town's list of entertainments, English-language attempts to turn out something in a similar (if usually less musically ambitious) vein rather withered under the heat of the competition. But slowly the homemade musical comedies began to resurface. Richard Carle turned the French *Madame Mongodin* into the touring *Mary's Lamb* (1908), and Otto Hauerbach re-adapted a French libretto that had been made into a German musical as the successful *Madame Sherry* (1910), before Broadway welcomed its first really significant homemade musical comedies. One of these actually came from no less a fellow than the Adolf Philipp who'd been in at the start of all this with *Der Corner Grocer* back in 1894. His "vaudeville" *Alma, wo wohnst du?* (1909/10) was, again, first played in New York's German theatre, but it soon found its translated way to Broadway and, as *Alma, Where Do You Live?*, was a full-scale musical comedy triumph. Close behind Philipp came Belgian–British composer Ivan Caryll, longtime purveyor of tunes to the London Gaiety, and his preferred librettist C. M. S. McLellan. It was their versions of the Parisian plays *Le Satyre* (*The Pink Lady*, 1911) and *La Grimpette* (*Oh! Oh! Delphine*, 1912) that, more than any other single pieces, put the seal on the new style. Modern musical comedy, American musical comedy, real musical comedy in the sense of both of those words, had well and truly arrived on Broadway.

In the years that followed, Broadway blossomed as never before as a breeding ground for this new type and weight of musical play. The other American production centers saw their portion of significant new shows shrink to nearly nothing as they became, at best, tryout dates for the now up-and-striding New York musical theatre, where the best native efforts were now very often musical comedies made from real plays—or at least with libretti that were built to be more than just song-and-dance cement stuck through with jokes. These were light, bright modern comic pieces, equipped with songs built around the kind of bouncy dance rhythms and melodies that were the rage of the age—the foxtrot, the shimmy, the one-step, the Boston, the tango.

At first, most authors—following the lead of *The Merry Widow* and the most successful local man of the day, composer and wheeler-dealer Ivan Caryll—went to France for their texts. France, at that time, was still the snappiest supplier of superior farcical comedies to the world's stages. But all kinds of local material soon found its way into the libretto-makers' hands as well, and pieces such as Charles Gebest's dramatic *The Red Widow* (1911), Jerome Kern's lightsome *Very Good Eddie* (1915), Earl Carroll's saucy wife-swapping *So Long, Letty* (1915), Kern's college-days *Leave It to Jane* (1917), Rudolf Friml's *Kitty Darlin'* (1917), Louis Hirsch's crazy airplane musical *Going Up* (1917), and Harry Tierney's triumphant bit of Cinderellary, *Irene* (1919), bore witness to the rising interest in and the effectiveness of putting together Broadway musical comedies that had their bases in Broadway comedies. This lively list—supported by a handful of hits (notably Guy Bolton's text to Kern's *Oh, Boy!*, 1917) written to original or quasi-original texts—included a number of shows that not only made good on Broadway and around America, but even found their way to full-scale success abroad. The made-on-Broadway musical had hit its first fine peak and won its first solid body of recognition not only at home, but beyond both the left-hand and right-hand oceans.

The list of top musical-comedy songsmiths who furnished these happy shows with their musical part was a fine mixture of old and new. If Caryll and Kern were veterans of the musical stage—the one with little time left, the other with half his enormous career still ahead of him—musicians such as young Czech immigrant Friml, launched as a possible successor to Herbert as the country's most exciting composer of romantic musicals with his score for *The Firefly* (1912), and the ineffably tuneful Hirsch, who had just helped introduce London theatre land to the joys of modern American dance music, were both much newer to the scene. Herbert, himself, was still around, and still turning out a whole sample book of Broadway music in almost the latest style, but the days of his earliest triumphs and of his most wholly successful romantic musical of recent years, *Naughty Marietta* (1910), were never to be equalled. *Naughty Marietta* and *The Firefly* would, in fact, remain the most successful American romantic musicals for a decade, during an era in which America turned out its own exportable musical comedies by the dozen, but still mostly imported its romantic "operettas."

The musical comedies in which Broadway—and much of the rest of the world—reveled during the 1920s were a deliciously light-footed bunch, bright, merry, fast-stepping, and feather-headed, with the farcical fun only rarely overladen with spectacle, dance specialties, and low-comedian low jinks, to the detriment—if that's the right word—of the show's story and its songs. Needless to say, not all these pieces were created to an identical image. Musical comedy came in several strains. There were those shows that followed the path established by the most widely popular American musical of the 1910s, *Irene*, and which told such a simplistic tale of poor-girl-(eventually) marries-rich 'n' handsome-hero that they became known, even in their time, as "Cinderella" shows. But if musicals such as *Mary, Sally, Sunny, Little Nellie Kelly, Tip-Toes*, and all their smuts-to-silver sisters may have been almost Gaiety-thin in their books, they were happy-hearted, dance-and-song filled evenings that even a wide-awake businessman could enjoy. There were other more staunchly made shows that, like *Irene*, continued to take established plays as their bases. These stayed sometimes closer and sometimes not close at all to their variously worthy originals, but by and large, shows like *No, No, Nanette, Mercenary Mary*, the French-based *Oh, Kay!, Kitty's Kisses, Hit the Deck, Queen High*, and the taken-from-Twain *A Connecticut Yankee* were much more substantial and less conventional in their plotting than the "Cinderella" shows. Following on behind the happy example of *Oh, Boy!*, there was also an increasing number of original musical-comedy texts, and if many of these were simply clumsy, star-serving, and/or thin, some—such as Harlan Thompson's *Little Jessie James* or Fred Thompson and Guy Bolton's *Lady, Be Good!*—were lively examples of straightforward farcical comedy writing.

The musical side of these shows combined happily with their love-and-laughter libretti, and, indeed, it was very often the songs and their allied dances that proved the highlights of the 1920s musicals. The successful songmakers of the 1910s—Hirsch, Friml, Kern, George M. Cohan—found a whole host of other merry music-makers to help them illustrate this jauntily dancing era of musical plays: Vincent Youmans, Harry Archer, George Gershwin, Con Conrad, Bert Kalmar and Harry Ruby, De Sylva, Brown and Henderson, Rodgers and Hart, or such folk as the lower-profiled but occasionally bulls-eyed Lew Gensler and Monte Carlo and Alma Sanders. And their songs, having done their duty on Broadway, went on to become the ballroom and barroom favorites of an era. Not just at home, either. American popular music and its short-skirted dance rhythms had been making serious inroads into established popular-music cultures all around the world for the past decade or two. By the 1920s, both those song-styles and dance-steps were established as utterly *à la mode* from Hobart to Hamburg. On the wings of the fashion for anything that shimmied or Bostonned, many a song that began its life in a Broadway show of the 1920s became known from one side of the world to another.

Sometimes they even took their shows with them, for these dance-and-laughter–based musicals found their way to every corner of the English-speaking theatre world, and occasionally even further afield. They were, however, far from being the only overseas ambassadors of the American musical stage in the 1920s. Alongside this shower of singing and dancing comedy musicals, Broadway turned out an equally effective series of romantic musical plays, a group fit to challenge the flow of imported "operettas," which had for a decade and more, dominated this side of the musical stage.

The two most important and prolific musicians working in this area were, like Eichberg and Herbert in particular before them, new Americans of continental origin. One was the same Rudolf Friml who had already made his name with *The Firefly* before trying his hand at musical comedy; the other was Sigmund Romberg, a musician from Nagykanizsa, Hungary, whose first decade of Broadway work had mostly been as a musical pieceworker, making over other folks' musicals for what the prolific Shubert brothers' organization considered "American tastes." Romberg found fame with a musical version of the perennial German play *Alt Heidelberg* called *The Student Prince* in 1924, the same year that Friml won a Kewpie doll with his score to Otto Harbach and Oscar Hammerstein II's Canadian rockies melodrama *Rose Marie*. He then went on to follow up that first hit with two pieces that would become standards of the American romantic musical repertoire, *The Desert Song* (1926) and *The New Moon* (1928), whilst Friml confirmed his first big hit with two shows written around dramas culled from French sources, *The Vagabond King* (1925) and *The Three Musketeers* (1928).

The final romantic musical hit of the era also came from the pen of *Rose Marie* and *Desert Song* colibrettist Hammerstein, but its score was composed by Jerome Kern, here abandoning the musical comedy for lusher things in the shape of a long-term love story set on the riverbanks and musical stages of bygone America. *Show Boat* (1927) has become accepted, in the later years of the twentieth century, as the landmark American "operetta" of this first great period of Broadway musicals in the same way that *No, No, Nanette* now represents the musical comedy of the time. But although *Nanette* was and always has been the most internationally famous piece of its time and type, *Show Boat* has risen in the popularity polls through the years, now taking preference over such pieces as *Rose Marie* or *The Desert Song*, which were more successful in their time.

These first boom years on musical Broadway faded away at about the same time that prosperity hid itself away around the corner. The 1930s were no more a prime time for musical theatre than they were for anything else, anywhere in the world. With very few exceptions, the best products of the Austro–Hungarian stage had been and gone, the dazzling series of French *années folles* musical comedies, which had run parallel to, and with no less toe-tapping success than, the American ones were virtually a thing of the past, and London existed largely on a menu of star-vehicles and spectaculars, which, profitable enough at home, never aroused much interest outside Britain.

And on Broadway? Somehow, the essential gaiety of the last twenty years of Broadway musicals did not work its way through into the 1930s, and a strange kind of vacuum appeared in, most noticeably, the lighter side of the musical theatre. Youmans failed to rise again to his heights of earlier years, Kern preferred to turn his hand to an imitation of sentimental continental styles, and Gershwin left the merry milieux of musical comedy to tackle political burlesque in *Of Thee I Sing* (1931) before moving away altogether from the light musical theatre to, at last, compose his folk opera *Porgy and Bess*. Archer, who had never got "fashionable," faded away, Conrad abandoned the theatre and, like De Sylva, Brown, and Henderson, headed for Hollywood. Only songwriter Cole Porter and his librettists, with the rumbustious, yet stylish, *Anything Goes* (1934), and the team of Rodgers and Hart—in an up-and-down run of shows, which, nevertheless, pleased only the home market—followed and occasionally recaptured the style of the best of the twenties musicals.

Otherwise, while tinselly, revusical shows proliferated, too many Broadway writers followed an inexplicable urge to turn away from the kind of light comic and romantic musicals that they had previously created with such success. It was a turning that all went very wrong. The result was not happy innovation, but a decade in which the mediocre and the pretentious were often in evidence, and durable and/or international success almost nonexistent. Since overseas didn't have much to contribute either, the 1930s on Broadway proved to be its least worthwhile era in a long, long time. But when its nighttime on one side of town, the sun is always shining somewhere else. All the merry meantime, across the continent, in the sunny purlieus of Hollywood, California, the films that would mean "Broadway" or "the American musical" to so many people, so far in the future, were being rolled on to reels of film, putting down the styles and songs of the great years just passed for posterity.

In the early 1940s a handful of pieces was produced on Broadway that pleased for a while, and certainly pleased as well as anything else that was being produced anywhere else at the time did, but the musical stage, all around the world, still seemed to be in nothing, more or less, than a kind of a creative doldrums. And there appeared to be no fair winds abaft that might provoke an escape from this sad situation. But those appearances were wrong. Propelled by two men who had long been part of the Broadway establishment, librettist and lyricist Oscar Hammerstein II and musician Richard Rodgers, the American musical theatre was soon to scud out of those doldrums, sailing straight into a second and even more important period of international prominence, a period of some thirty years in which Broadway was the crucible of the world's most popular musicals.

What was this new kind of musical with which two veterans of the musical theatre—with a total of fifty-three shows between them already to their credit—suddenly reinvigorated Broadway? Why, it wasn't new at all. It was nothing more nor less than the good, old-fashioned romantic musical play, decorated with all the good, old staple bits of musical-stage tradition, from ballet girls and love duets to soubretteries and villaineries, low comedy and high jinks. But *Oklahoma!* (1943) came at the right moment. Its chocolate-box cowboys and daintier-than-dimity love story, its quaint and never low-comedy out-west soubrettes, and its hat-waving praise of the pioneer, all decorated with a series of thoroughly singable melodies, were just the ticket for their time. The moment for the nifty dance-and-laughter shows of the twenties had come and gone. Now, again, the mood was right for the classic romantic musical play of the Daly's Theatre variety to put in a reappearance. It was no coincidence that, on the other side of the Atlantic, the other most memorable manufacturer of 1920s musical comedy, France, turned at virtually the same moment to a new run of successful musicals built on exactly these same principles.

After the Great War, people had demanded witty and preferably sexy fun allied with dance-bandable songs tailored for the new kind of close-together dances. After the Depression and the Second World War, they wanted not new freedoms but the good old days, and good old days romance in all its forms. Later, as postwar America grew in strength and confidence about its present, the comfortable good old days were supplemented and even almost wholly replaced by the comfortable good new days. But, in the beginning of these new bonanza years on Broadway came Oscar Hammerstein II and Richard Rodgers, leading the way back to the sound tenets of the classical musical play. And over the next sixteen years, with a fidelity to attractive plot, character, and staging, and with a sure touch for the most appealing and immediate, yet durable, in music and lyrics, they together turned out five of the most enduring romantic musicals of the century. The first two were versions of plays, one American (*Oklahoma!*) and one Hungarian (*Carousel*), the other three sprung initially from the printed page (*South Pacific, The King and I,* and *The Sound of Music*), and the five, amongst them, provided and provide still a solid core to a theatrical period that turned out as many memorable shows as any other era in the musical theatre.

The body of musical theatre work that was produced on Broadway in the twenty years after *Oklahoma!* was one that had a firm and ever more contemporary American identity to it. Like some of the better shows of the years just past, many of the most successful and attractive pieces took twentieth-century American settings and subjects for their material. Such shows as *On the Town, Wonderful Town, Guys and Dolls* and *West Side Story, The Most Happy Fella, How to Succeed in Business Without Really Trying, The Pajama Game, Damn Yankees, Kiss Me, Kate, Gentlemen Prefer Blondes, Bells Are Ringing, Call Me Madam,* and the thoroughly up-to-date *Bye Bye Birdie* made up a wide-ranging selection of hereish and nowish musicals to set triumphantly alongside the more period Americana of *The Music Man, Annie Get Your Gun,* or *Paint Your Wagon.* These shows took all kinds of recognizable areas of modern American life as the bases for their action, whether of the lightest comedy as in *Wonderful Town,* or of considerable drama and real romance as in *West Side Story.* Hometown setting, once only considered good for the lowbrow farce-comedy type of entertainment, had now become, if not a sine qua non, at very least the norm.

However, the outstanding musicals of this period were not, despite some setting similarities of time and place, by any means cast in the same mold. Alan Jay Lerner and Frederick Loewe, one of the quickest and most outstanding teams to follow where Rodgers and Hammerstein led, ranged from virile period hokum in *Paint Your Wagon* to pretty romantic fantasy in the Scottish-set (but American hero-ed) *Brigadoon* and to the lines of classical literature in *My Fair Lady,* one time pop-song writer Frank Loesser switched from tongue-in-cheek Runyonisms in *Guys and Dolls* to full-throated musical romance in *The Most Happy Fella* and the most briskly modern comedy in *How to Succeed,* while Leonard Bernstein's score of spirited New York songs for the ultralight *On the Town* could not have been more different to his powerful *West Side Story* music and the brave and brilliant fireworks of the modern *opéra-bouffe, Candide.*

Alongside such finely made and thoroughly composed examples of the musical play, there was still a place for other varieties. The songwriters' shows, with their unashamedly movable musical parts, were less in evidence, but the songwriters were still there, Cole Porter and Irving Berlin at their head. Only now their shows—from Porter's backstage (and onstage) *Kiss Me, Kate* and Americo-Parisian *Can-Can* to Berlin's sharpshooting *Annie Get Your Gun* and *Call Me Madam* with its American-in-Ruritania heroine—featured much more solidly romantic libretti than had been usual in the last decades, and left less chance for the irrelevant interpolated number of old times. Amongst all this fresh and exciting new writing, there was still even a place for the pasticcio musical, a form that might have been expected to have had its day. Fortunately it hadn't, for the era turned up two of the most skilled pasticcio-makers in history. Robert Wright's and George Forrest's *Song of Norway* and *Kismet* (featuring the music of Grieg and Borodin, respectively) joined the list of the most successful pasticcio shows of all time.

In retrospect, it is perhaps Loesser's very particular *Guys and Dolls* that has emerged from the era as the most remarkable, classic combination of all the elements of light musical theatre, and, along with *My Fair Lady, West Side Story, Annie Get Your Gun,* and the five triumphant Rodgers and Hammerstein musicals, it has survived the ensuing decades on the world's stages with a vigor that some other successful, but less durable, shows of the time have lacked. It is a fair bet that most of this group of musicals—and maybe others—will still be played in some kind of whatever-by-then-passes-for-a-theatre, half a century and even a century on, in the same way that those nineteenth-century hits *Orphée aux enfers* and *The Mikado* are still played today.

Few of the writers and musicians who had made this era of the Broadway musical theatre so prodigious continued to work in the field in the 1960s and, of those who did, rare were those who equalled their former successes. However, the light musical theatre, with its now clearly perceived high standards and with its obvious rewards, had proven attractive to younger authors, composers, and songwriters, and there was a significant group of new writers waiting to take over the positions abandoned by Hammerstein, Loewe, Berlin, Loesser, and Bernstein. So, the new Broadway shows kept coming, and amongst those shows kept on coming up handfuls of aces.

It was noticeable, however, that during these years a kind of harshness became evident in some Broadway music and some Broadway shows. Now there was less carefree fun and Laurey-loves-Curly romance in the stories, and more brashness and shiny heartlessness in the presentation. Shows such as *Hello, Dolly!*, *Gypsy*, *Mame*, *Applause*, *Cabaret*, and *Funny Girl* with their overwhelming, often brassy and/or loud heroines, and their slick, vigorous staging became a feature of the period. These qualities and the performances that contained them were ones that didn't necessarily displease contemporary taste, and there were plenty of other fine shows to entertain those whose preferences didn't run in the direction of such modern equivalents of the old Broadway coon shouters and the shows made to carry them.

There was comedy and even wittily made burlesque to be found in such shows as *Little Me* (1962), *A Funny Thing Happened on the Way to the Forum* (1962), and *Once Upon a Mattress* (1959); there was sentimental drama of the most endearing kind in the vastly popular Russo-Jewish *Fiddler on the Roof* (1964) and in the Don Quixote variant *Man of La Mancha* (1965); comedy for today in such screenplay-to-stage musical comedies as *Sweet Charity* (1965) and *Promises, Promises* (1968); a surprisingly effective history lesson to music called *1776* (1969); and even flower-power in the pubescently orientated *Hair* (1967). Names such as those of Cy Coleman, Michael Stewart, Jerry Herman, Stephen Sondheim, Charles Strouse, and John Kander, and Fred Ebb became foremost in the creative credits of a thriving Broadway system that was beginning to produce ever larger, more lavish, more technically sophisticated, and more expensive musicals for a public that had feasted for twenty years and was yet eager for bigger and better and more. And more. And more.

These same men were still the principal figures of the musical theatre in the seventies and even the eighties, and each of them was to bring forth further successes. Coleman created another outstanding piece of musical burlesque, *On the Twentieth Century*, one of the most traveling Broadway shows of the period in the circusy *Barnum* (with Stewart), as well as the songs for the most dazzling American musical comedy of years in Larry Gelbart's gumshoe-burlesque *City of Angels*. Strouse composed the songs for the ultimate children-and-animals musical, *Annie*, Kander and Ebb crafted the light-and-darkly satirical *Chicago*, Stewart gave Broadway *Barnum* and a stage version of the film *42nd Street*, and Herman adapted *La Cage aux folles*, the famous French comedy, to the musical stage. Even though each of these was, in itself, a fine and successful piece, it was, however, worryingly noticeable that such pieces were getting fewer. The list of hits per season—even of shows per season—was getting slimmer and slimmer. And, most worrying of all, as in Britain in the 1920s, and in Vienna and Berlin after the war, the relay was not being taken up from the threatening-to-be-veterans by a new and effective generation of writers and producers.

This is not to say that there were no successful new Broadway pieces produced in these years that came from the pens of new writers, but many of those that did appear were one-off novelty hits, as *Hair* had been: the Gospels in teeny-talk as purveyed in *Godspell* (1971); the record-breaking 1950s parody *Grease* (1972); the orange-oathed country-and-western show *The Best Little Whorehouse in Texas* (1977); the girl-group showbiz musical *Dreamgirls* (1981); and the Huckleberry Finnish *Big River* (1985). Sometimes a team or writer managed a pair of successes, raising hopes that a new name might be added to the pantheon and ensure its self-reproduction. Gary Geld and Peter Udell turned out the exuberant *Purlie* (1970) and the winningly sentimental *Shenandoah* (1975), but then faded away on the heels of a failure. Film composer Marvin Hamlisch, who evoked wild enthusiasm with his music for the remarkable slice-of-stagelife musical *A Chorus Line* (1975) and his zingy songs for the bright and bristling lovestory to pop-music, *They're Playing Our Song* (1979), failed to repeat his early successes in his rare returns to Broadway.

Undoubtedly the great hope for a new explosion of exciting Broadway shows in the 1980s and 1990s lay in Stephen Sondheim, the young lyricist of *West Side Story, A Funny Thing Happened on the Way to the Forum*, and *Do I Hear a Waltz?*, who had confirmed himself as a major personality on Broadway with his scores for the revusical *Company* and *Follies*, and then as a composer of brilliance in the wryly humorous *A Little Night Music* (1973). Working as both lyricist and composer, Sondheim has wandered through a vast spectrum of subjects and styles in the twenty years since his masterpiece, ranging from melodramatic light opera in *Sweeny Todd*, to fairy tales for the psychoanalyzable in *Into the Woods*, to one-act musical with one-act commentary in *Sunday in the Park with George*, in what seem to be a series of attempts to come up with a format or a genre to replace the established ideal of the "well-made musical play." Mostly, his pieces have wandered too far into textual opaqueness at the expense of audience comprehension and enjoyment, and into academically constructed music at the expense of melody, and, as a result, his works have become extravagantly popular with a minority audience and with subsidized directors and companies, but rarely commercially or generally successful.

The growing gap that Sondheim and other new writers might have been hoped to at least partly fill in the Broadway musical theatre of the past two decades did not, however, remain the kind of gap that nature is said to abhor. Just as the doubled-headed group of Broadway musicals of the years after the Great War had rushed in to fill the theatrical black hole left by the fading Edwardian British tradition, that same British stage, renascent after decades spent in the shadow of the all-consuming musicals of post-(second World)-war Broadway, now moved in to share the spotlight with New York's handful of long-running hits and that sadly meager ration of new ones. With this change in orientation came the new and changed conception of what makes a for-our-days Broadway musical. Not the musical that's made on or even made for Broadway, but the musical that's *played on* Broadway: *Jesus Christ Superstar, Evita, Cats, The Phantom of the Opéra*, and *Les Misérables*. "New," is of course the wrong word to use when talking about the international provenance of many of today's most successful Broadway musicals. We have, after all, been here before, time and time again over the century and a half of the modern musical theatre. It is nothing so very remarkable. All that has happened is that the pendulum has swung—as it persists in doing—and, for the moment, much of the most effective creativity in the musical theatre happens to be happening outside the Broadway establishment. But that kind of coming-and-going will always happen. Musicals will be born wherever the talented writers and producers of the moment are, where the circumstances and influences are the most favorable to the production of new shows, wherever the financial, theatrical, labor, and critical climates are the healthiest.

But, in the end, most of the best of those musicals—wherever they start out, and whatever they are—will make their way to that magic circle of theatres that goes by the name of Broadway. They, too, will be Broadway musicals. Please, may there be many, many more of them. Of all shapes and of all sizes. From any country or a mixture of many. With all kinds of music and all kinds of bands. Funny ones, pretty ones, romantic ones, dramatic ones, happy ones, silly ones and clever ones, singing ones and dancing ones, and even incoherent, overproduced, overamplified, and overpretentious ones. Because someone must like them, and I don't want to be selfish. I'll take them all. Just as long as we always have the Broadway musical.

GÄNZL'S
BOOK OF THE
BROADWAY
MUSICAL

1879

H.M.S. PINAFORE

OR *THE LASS THAT LOVED A SAILOR*, A COMIC OPERA IN TWO ACTS by W. S. Gilbert. Lyrics by W. S. Gilbert. Music by Arthur Sullivan.

Produced at the Standard Theatre, New York, 15 January 1879, with Thomas Whiffen (Sir Joseph), Eugene Clarke (Corcoran), Henri Laurent (Ralph), Eva Mills (Josephine), and Blanche Galton (Little Buttercup). Produced at innumerable Broadway theatres in the years that followed, notably by D'Oyly Carte at the Fifth Avenue Theatre, 1 December 1879, with J. H. Ryley, J. Furneaux Cook, Hugh Talbot, Blanche Roosevelt, and Alice Barnett. Produced at the Casino Theatre, 29 May 1911, with Henry E. Dixey, George J. Macfarlane, Arthur Aldridge, Louise Gunning, and Alice Brady with De Wolf Hopper as Dick, Eugene Cowles as Bill, Marie Cahill as Hebe, and Christine Nielsen as Tom. Produced at the New York Hippodrome, 9 April 1914, with William G. Gordon, Bertram Peacock, John Bardesley, Helen Heinemann, and Marie Horgan, and at the Century Theatre, 6 April 1926, with John E. Hazzard, Marion Green, Tom Burke, Marguerite Namara, and Fay Templeton.

Originally produced at the Opera Comique, London, 25 May 1878. First American production at the Boston Museum, Boston, MA, 25 November 1878, in a pirated version.

"Never mind the why and wherefore . . . "
Johnnie D'Auban's dance routine for
Josephine Corcoran, her papa, and Sir Joseph Porter
was one of this show's comic highlights.
White Studios, photographers.
Courtesy Performing Arts Research Center,
New York Public Library at Lincoln Center.

CHARACTERS

Rt. Hon. Sir Joseph Porter KCB,
First Lord of the Admiralty

Captain Corcoran, *commanding*
H.M.S Pinafore

Ralph Rackstraw, *able seaman*

Dick Deadeye, *able seaman*

Bill Bobstay, *boatswain's mate*

Bob Becket, *carpenter's mate*

Tom Tucker, *midshipmate*

Josephine, *the captain's daughter*

Hebe, *Sir Joseph's first cousin*

Mrs. Cripps (Little Buttercup),
a Portsmouth bumboat woman

Act 1

The quarter deck of Her Majesty's ship, Pinafore, at anchor in Portsmouth harbour, is alive with its complement of exceedingly able seamen splicing, polishing, scrubbing, and generally indulging in anything and everything nautical ("We Sail the Ocean Blue") when one of the local bumboat women arrives on board with her basket full of good things calculated to separate the lads from their pay ("I'm Called Little Buttercup"). In spite of her rosy cheeks and jolly comportment, Little Buttercup is not a wholly happy lady, for she confides that there is within her "a cankers worm that is slowly but surely eating its way into one's very heart." There are all sorts of cankers only too evident, on the other hand, in the appropriately named Dick Deadeye, a seaman of repellent aspect and minimal popularity, who earns from his crewmates a welcome of a very different style to that reserved for the popular Buttercup.

But hark! Our hero comes. On faltering feet, the smartest lad in all the fleet (the tenor Ralph Rackstraw) appears, moodily sighing of unrequited love ("The Nightingale Sighed for the Moon's Bright Ray"/"A Maiden Fair to See"). He has pretensions to the heart of no less a maiden than Josephine, his Captain's daughter, pretensions that run up against the very principles of the social order. Captain Corcoran is a child of the peerage who, nevertheless, can actually comprehend the basics of seamanship. He is hardly ever sick at sea, almost never loses his self-control to the extent of using "a big, big D," and is as popular with his crew as is allowed by their respective stations in life ("I Am the Captain of the *Pinafore*").

Captain Corcoran has arranged a most advantageous marriage for his daughter with the First Lord of the Admiralty, Sir Joseph Porter, but Josephine is sadly unimpressed by this *coup de mariage* and droops into a plaintive ballad at the thought ("Sorry Her Lot"). The truth is that she has fallen in love—oh, horror!—with a mere able seaman on her father's own ship but, true to her breeding, she stifles such improper yearnings and prepares herself bravely to meet her destined husband who even now is floating across the stretch of sea separating quayside from ship ("Over the Bright Blue Sea").

Piped aboard the poop deck, Sir Joseph, surrounded by a protective gaggle of sisters, cousins, and aunts, introduces himself with a *curriculum vitae* in song ("I Am the Monarch of the Sea"/"When I Was a Lad"). Sir Joseph has a curious idea or two on social order and informs Corcoran importantly that "a British sailor is any man's equal, excepting mine," requiring him to leaven his commands to his crew with such politenesses as "if you please." He advocates the learning of hornpipes as a democratic and characteristic occupation and, to illustrate his morale-supporting precepts, he has composed a glee ("A British Tar"), which the crew are required to con.

Josephine's good intentions are undergoing a true trial. Although she does her best to appreciate Sir Joseph's qualities, which he has personally detailed to her in the most helpful fashion, she yearns for her sailor. And now, as she pines alone on deck, who should appear before her but that very sailor—Ralph Rackstraw. To her delight he expresses himself in passionate terms but, remembering her position, she repulses him haughtily ("Refrain, Audacious Tar"). In despairing tones, Ralph determines on suicide and, taking the pistol helpfully proffered by the boatswain, is cocked for action when Josephine rushes on to stop him with an admission of her love ("Oh Joy, Oh Rapture Unforeseen"). Encouraged by the sailors and Sir Joseph's female relations, the lovers plan to steal ashore that very night to find a clergyman to regularize their attachment ("This Very Night with Bated Breath").

Act 2   That same evening the Captain is found on deck, perplexedly serenading the moon to the accompaniment of his guitar ("Fair Moon to Thee I Sing") and watched by a lovelorn Little Buttercup. Things are not going well for him, his plans are not prospering, and he feels alone and unappreciated. Buttercup offers her support but he moderates what would, in other circumstances, have been his expressions of fond thanks with due regard to the difference in their social standing. Buttercup hints broadly that "Things Are Seldom What They Seem" and the Captain answers in kind without understanding what she is getting at. His problems are compounded when Sir Joseph comes to complain that Josephine is not responding as required to his official utterances on the subject of his heart. Of course she isn't. She's outside her cabin soliloquizing on her position ("The Hours Creep on Apace") and the wealth and comfort she is about to give up for an alliance with physical attractiveness.

The Captain attempts to excuse his daughter's cool behaviour toward Sir Joseph by suggesting that she is dazzled by his superior rank. He and Sir Joseph tackle the young lady in the trio "Never Mind the Why and Wherefore," explaining pointedly that love levels all ranks. Little do they know that they are simply pleading the case of the First Lord's rival, and that their song and dance serve only to convince Josephine she is doing the right thing in running off with Ralph.

But nemesis is lurking in the shrouds in the form of Dick Deadeye. Shunned by his fellow seamen, he gets his revenge by enlightening the Captain about the forthcoming elopement ("Kind Captain, I've Important Information") and, as the lovers prepare their flight, escorted by the entire chorus ("Carefully on Tiptoe Stealing"), the Captain intervenes dramatically. Ralph throws Sir Joseph's precepts in his superior officer's face, and the sailors chorus in support that "He Is an Englishman." Exasperated out of his manners, the Captain underlines his exclamations with "a big, big D" and is overheard by Sir Joseph. There is never, never any excuse for bad language, and the Captain is ordered to be confined to quarters. But when the First Lord discovers the cause of the Captain's breach of etiquette, he does more than swear. Ralph's incredible presumption earns him a sentence to the ship's dungeon cell.

As the lovers sing their last, prior to parting ("Farewell, My Own"), Little Buttercup steps forward to elucidate the mysterious hints she has been spreading about throughout the evening. Once upon a time she was a baby farmer and she looked after a little lordling and a little plebeian at one and the same time. Unfortunately, she mixed them up. "The well-born babe was Ralph, your Captain was the other!" Yes, Ralph is the patrician of the pair and Captain Corcoran is a person of no breeding at all. Since breeding is paramount, this means that Ralph must be the Captain of the *Pinafore* and Corcoran reduced to the rank of Able Seaman. Sir Joseph of course cannot consider marriage with the daughter of a tar—love certainly does not level ranks that much—so the way is clear for Captain Ralph to be united with his Josephine, while Corcoran finds his way into the arms of the comfy Buttercup, and the First Lord is left to the tender but aristocratic mercies of Hebe, the most pressing of his sisters, cousins, and aunts.

The Pirates of Penzance

OR *THE SLAVE OF DUTY*, A COMIC OPERA IN TWO ACTS by W. S. Gilbert. Lyrics by W. S. Gilbert. Music by Arthur Sullivan.

Produced at the Fifth Avenue Theatre, New York, 31 December 1879, with J. H., Ryley (Major General), Hugh Talbot (Frederick), Sgr. Broccolini (Pirate King), Fred Clifton (Sergeant), Blanche Roosevelt (Mabel), and Alice Barnett (Ruth). Produced at the Plymouth Theatre, 6 December 1926, with Ernest Lawford, William Williams, John Barclay, William G. Gordon, Ruth Thomas, and Vera Ross. Produced at the Uris Theatre, 8 January 1981, and the Minskoff Theatre, 12 August 1981, with George Rose, Rex Smith, Kevin Kline, Tony Azito, Linda Ronstadt, and Estelle Parsons.

Played at the Bijou Theatre, Paignton, England, for copyright purposes, 30 December 1879.

A film of the 1981 version was produced by Universal in 1982 with Rose, Smith, Kline, Ronstadt, and Angela Lansbury.

CHARACTERS

Major General Stanley

The Pirate King

Samuel, *his lieutenant*

Frederic, *his pirate apprentice*

Sergeant of Police

Mabel

Kate

Isobel

Edith

General Stanley's daughters

Ruth, *a pirate maid-of-all-work*

With a fine disregard for the plot, the Pirate King (Kevin Kline) poses snuggishly with heroine Miss Mabel Stanley (Linda Ronstadt) on the set of the show's 1981 revival. Photograph © Martha Swope.

Act 1

Off the rocky coast of Cornwall, a pirate ship is anchored while its captain and crew partake of liquid refreshment on the seashore ("Pour, Oh Pour the Pirate Sherry"). This day the pirate apprentice, Frederic, comes to the end of his indentured period, and the Pirate King gladly tells him that he can consider himself a full-blown member of their buccaneering band. But Frederic has a sad surprise for his employer. Now that his apprenticeship is complete, he must leave the pirate life forever. He was never intended for it, and was bound to his indentures through an error. His old nurse, Ruth, who has spent the years of his apprenticeship skivvying for the pirate ship as a maid-of-all-work, confesses that her incipient deafness was the cause of the mistake. She should have apprenticed the boy to a pilot but got it a little wrong ("When Frederic Was a Little Lad").

So, though he dearly loves all his shipmates individually, Frederic has to admit that as a species he finds them atrocious and, now that his duty to them is done, he will be bound in duty to devote himself heart and soul to their extermination. However, since he is till midnight one of them, he is obliged to divulge to them their weak point. They are too tenderhearted. It suffices for a captive to plead to being an orphan, and he is immediately released. This bit of intelligence has clearly got around in nautical circles, for now it seems that the entire mercantile marine is crewed only by orphans.

If Frederic is to leave the pirate band, the question arises as to what shall become of Ruth. Neither Frederic nor the Pirate King wishes to deprive the other of her, but she is all for staying at the side of her young charge. Frederic, who has never seen another woman, is not quite sure how Ruth rates in feminine terms, and, although she assures him she compares (apart from a slight cold) very well, he clearly has suspicions that someone thirty years younger would make him a more suitable wife.

As the time comes for Frederic to depart, he tries to persuade the pirates to return with him to civilization, but the Pirate King refuses. His profession may not be the best but, contrasted with respectability, it is comparatively honest ("Oh, Better Far to Live and Die"). The pirates head back to their ship, leaving Frederic and the undetachable Ruth on the shore. Just as Frederic is assuring Ruth that if, as she says, she is truly an example of a beautiful woman that her age shall be no bar to their union, the voices of young girls are heard. Ruth is lost! One glimpse at the bevy of beautiful maidens that is approaching ("Climbing Over Rocky Mountains") and Frederic renounces her reproachfully ("You Told Me You Were Fair as Gold") and hides among the rocks to win a closer look at genuine femininity.

The girls have just begun to take off their shoes and stockings to paddle in the sea when Frederic emerges, throwing them into a delicious panic. The panic is eased by the fact that he is very beautiful but, when he begs that one of them should take pity on his unfortunate position ("Oh, Is There Not One Maiden Breast") and love him, they each and every one of them correctly refuse until a roulade of coloratura introduces a late arrival.

Like all the best prima donnas, Mabel has delayed her entrance. She now offers to reclaim the "Poor Wandering One" in a showy song, while her sisters wonder pointedly whether she would have shown quite such charity had the man in question not been so obviously attractive. In a selfless display of sisterly solidarity, however, they decide to talk about the weather ("How Beautifully Blue the Sky") while the two young people initiate their romance ("Did Ever Maiden Wake").

Suddenly Frederic recalls that they are on dangerous ground: there are pirates about! He is too late. Before they can retreat, the pirates are upon them, declaring delightedly "Here's a first rate opportunity of getting married with impunity." Their hasty marital ambitions are checked, however, by the arrival of the girls' father, Major-General Stanley ("I Am the Very Model of a Modern Major-General"), who wins the pirates' submission and his daughters' salvation by declaring untruthfully that he is an orphan ("Oh, Men of Dark and Dismal Fate"). There will be no weddings today.

Act 2   In a ruined gothic chapel on his estate, a sleepless General Stanley sits in his nightgown surrounded by his solicitous daughters ("Oh, Dry the Glistening Tear"). Nothing can calm the General's conscience or his fears over the lie he has told the pirates. Frederic tells him that he need not be afraid for, this very night, at the head of a stout band of police, he is to set out to apprehend the pirate band and put an end to their plundering of Penzance. The apparently ferocious Sergeant of Police ("When the Foeman Bares His Steel") and his men receive the extravagantly dramatic farewells of General Stanley's daughters ("Go Ye Heroes, Go to Glory"), which put an unpleasant emphasis on death and not returning. When Frederic is left alone to prepare his adventure, he receives an unexpected pair of visitors, the Pirate King and Ruth.

His old friends have an awkward piece of news for the reformed pirate ("When You Had Left Our Pirate Fold"): he is not yet free from his indentures. His apprenticeship papers state that he shall be apprenticed up to his twenty-first birthday and, although he has lived twenty-one years, he was actually born on 29 February and has so far had only five birthdays. Placed before this irrefutable recall to duty, Frederic is bound to tell the pirates what he knows—

General Stanley is no orphan. Piratical blood boils ("Away, Away! My Heart's on Fire") and the King swears revenge on the man who has thus taken advantage of his noble nature.

Mabel, returning, finds Frederic in tears ("All Is Prepared, Your Gallant Crew Awaits You"). When he explains what has happened, she bids him to ignore what is clearly an illegal claim ("Stay, Frederic, Stay!") but his sense of duty will not allow him to do so. Sadly they part ("Ah, Leave Me Not to Pine Alone"), and Mabel informs the policemen that the Sergeant will have to take over the direction of the operation. The Sergeant is a kindly chap who does not like depriving fellow creatures of their liberty but, after all, a job's a job and it has to be fulfilled ("When A Felon's Not Engaged in His Employment"). As he hits his final bottom note, the pirates' voices are heard approaching. They are coming already to take their dreadful revenge.

The policemen hide as the pirates burst into the chapel ("With Cat-like Tread"), and the pirates hide in their turn at the approach of Stanley, muffled up in his dressing-gown and carrying a candle. As he tossed on his sleepless bed, he thought he heard a noise ("Tormented with the Anguish Dread"), but now it seems there is nothing, only the wind in the trees ("Sighing Softly to the River"). The girls appear, tiptoeing in their nightgowns in search of their wandering father ("Now What Is This and What Is That"), and this is the cue for the pirates to leap from their cover.

Mabel calls on Frederic to help her father as he kneels under the Pirate King's blade but, duty-bound, Frederic cannot. The policemen can though. They jump out from their hiding places and a fearsome battle ensues from which the pirates emerge victorious. There will be none of the "orphan" trick this time. Their victims are well and truly doomed. But the police have the ultimate weapon. They charge the pirates to yield in the name of Queen Victoria.

That does it, of course. No British pirate can fail to respond to the name of his glorious monarch. Their swords are dropped and their collars grabbed, but Ruth has the last say: these are no ordinary pirates, they are all aristocratic striplings who have been indulging in too much youthful exuberance. Well, "peers will be peers and youth will have its fling," so all the naughty noblemen are pardoned and there are just enough Stanley daughters to go around as the "Poor Wandering Ones" are welcomed back to civilized living and matrimony.

The 1981 production included in its score the *HMS Pinafore* song "Sorry Her Lot" and the patter trio, "My Eyes Are Fully Open" from *Ruddigore*.

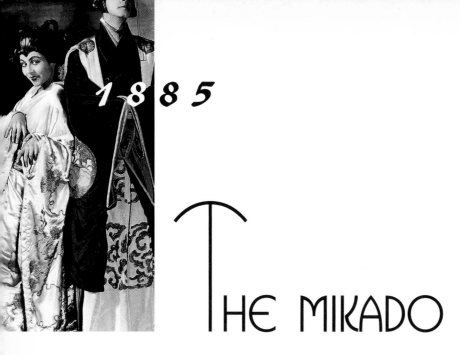

1885

THE MIKADO

OR *THE TOWN OF TITIPU*, A COMIC OPERA IN TWO ACTS by W. S. Gilbert. Lyrics by W. S. Gilbert. Music by Arthur Sullivan.

Produced at the Fifth Avenue Theatre, New York, 19 August 1885, with George Thorne (Ko-Ko), Fred Federici (Mikado), Geraldine Ulmar (Yum-Yum), Courtice Pounds (Nanki-Poo), Fred Billington (Pooh-Bah), and Elsie Cameron (Katisha). Produced at the Standard Theatre, 20 August 1885, with J. H. Ryley, William H. Hamilton, Verona Jarbeau, Harry S. Hilliard, Thomas Whiffen, and Zelda Seguin. Produced at the Madison Square Roof Garden, 14 July 1902. Produced at the Casino Theatre, 30 May 1910, with Jefferson de Angelis, William Danforth, Fritzi Scheff, Andrew Mack, William Pruette, Josephine Jacobs, Christie MacDonald (Pitti-Sing), and Christine Nielson (Peep-Bo). Produced at the Royale Theatre, 17 September 1927, with Fred Wright as Ko-Ko. Played at the Virginia Theatre, 2 April 1987, with Eric Donkin, Marie Baron, John Keane, and Arlene Meadows.

Originally produced at the Savoy Theatre, London, 14 March 1885.

First American production at the Museum, Chicago, 6 July 1885, and the Union Square Theatre, New York, 20 July 1885, in a pirated version.

A film version was produced in 1939 by G & S Films with Martyn Green as Ko-Ko, Jean Colin as Yum-Yum, and Kenny Baker as Nanki-Poo, and another in 1967 by British Home Entertainments with John Reed (Ko-Ko) and Valerie Masterton (Yum-Yum). A 1963 film, *The Cool Mikado*, featuring Frankie Howerd, Stubby Kaye, and Jill Mai Meredith, was based on *The Mikado*.

CHARACTERS

The Mikado of Japan

Nanki-Poo, *his son, disguised as a wandering minstrel and in love with Yum-Yum*

Ko-Ko, *Lord High Executioner of Titipu*

Pooh-Bah, *Lord High Everything Else*

Pish-Tush, *a noble Lord*

Yum-Yum

Pitti-Sing

Peep-Bo

three sisters—wards of Ko-Ko

Katisha, *an elderly lady, in love with Nanki-Poo*

Go-To

"The criminal cried as he dropped him down . . . "
Ko-Ko, Pooh-Bah, and Pitti-Sing make up a terrible tale
for the benefit of the local potentate.
White Studios, photographers.
Courtesy Performing Arts Research Center,
New York Public Library at Lincoln Center.

Act 1

In the courtyard of the palace of Ko-Ko, Lord High Executioner of Titipu, the local gentry are posing in Japanese attitudes reminiscent of popular pottery designs ("If You Want to Know Who We Are") when their pattern is intruded upon by a tattered young fellow with a stringed instrument. The young man, Nanki-Poo by name, describes his profession in a ballad ("A Wandering Minstrel I") and inquires as to the whereabouts of a young lady called Yum-Yum. He has, it appears, fallen in love with Yum-Yum but, until now, has quashed his passion under the knowledge that the young lady in question is engaged to be married to her guardian, the tailor Ko-Ko.

Hearing, in his self-imposed exile, that the said Ko-Ko had been condemned to death for the capital crime of flirting, he has hastily returned to Titipu. But bad news awaits him, for the noble Lord, Pish-Tush, after a dissertation on the laws against flirting ("Our Great Mikado, Virtuous Man") tells him that Ko-Ko has been reprieved and, indeed, promoted to the post of Lord High Executioner on the reasoning that since he was next in line for execution, he can't cut off anyone else's head until he's cut off his own. Thus, in Titipu, is the end of the law against flirting (and a good deal of other laws) sidestepped.

Ko-Ko's promotion has caused chaos in the Titipu hierarchy, for all the other notables have resigned en masse rather than serve with an extailor, and all their posts have been unhesitatingly accepted by the lofty but opportunistic Pooh-Bah, a paragon of anguished corruptibility. As far as Yum-Yum is concerned, Pooh-Bah gives Nanki-Poo no hope ("Young Man, Despair") as the lady in question is scheduled to wed Ko-Ko that very afternoon. As the populace announce "Behold the Lord High Executioner!," the bridegroom-to-be himself enters to describe in song the social nuisances he should like to get rid of in his new capacity ("I've Got a Little List").

Now it is the turn of the lady in the affair to put in an appearance. Yum-Yum, accompanied by her sisters, Pitti-Sing and Peep-Bo, is returning home from school for her wedding ("Comes a Train of Little Ladies"/"Three Little Maids from School"). She is clearly indifferent to her guardian, but she is full of excitement at seeing Nanki-Poo again. Ko-Ko makes an effort at winning his little lady's esteem by having Pooh-Bah—who is an awful lot of noble Lords rolled into one—pay her and her sisters some exaggerated attentions, but Pooh-Bah finds such *lèse majesté* painful even when salved with large amounts of money ("So Please You, Sir, We Much Regret").

Left alone, Yum-Yum and Nanki-Poo ponder over their plight. He reveals that he is, in fact, no musician but the very son of the Mikado of Japan. He has fled his father's court to escape the marital ambitions of an elderly lady called

Katisha. This unprepossessing female claimed before his royal father that he had flirted with her, and he has been forced to run away and disguise himself as a second trombonist in the Titipu town band to avoid the marriage that would be the legal consequence of such a dalliance. The two young lovers dare not even express their love because of the nation's stringent laws against unconnubial behavior, so they are obliged instead to talk of what they would do and say if they could ("Were You Not to Ko-Ko Plighted"), accompanying their song with what would seem to be the most illegal of illustrations.

Ko-Ko has worse problems to worry about than a meager alienation of affection, for his fine new position seems to be leading him into trouble ("My Brain It Teems"). The Mikado has noticed that, since the installation of the new Lord High Executioner, no executions have taken place in Titipu, and he is threatening to descend in state to reduce the city to the status of a village if no one has been decapitated by the time a month has passed. Ko-Ko, if he is not to accomplish the unlikely task of cutting off his own head, must find a substitute. As he soliloquizes painfully on the subject, Nanki-Poo enters with a rope. Rather than endure life without Yum-Yum, he has decided to hang himself.

Ko-Ko leaps at the chance. Instead of hanging himself, how would the young man like a month of splendidly luxurious existence at the end of which he would be prettily and relatively painlessly decapitated? Nanki-Poo agrees to postpone his death for a month on one condition. He must be married to Yum-Yum right away so as to spend that one last month in connubial bliss. But, as the celebrations and the finale begin, a melodramatic crone appears. It is the dreaded Katisha, come to claim her bridegroom ("Oh Fool, That Fleest My Hallowed Joys"). The people of Titipu laugh her aside ("For He's Going to Marry Yum-Yum"), and Katisha storms off Mikado-wards brandishing her complaint.

Act 2 In Ko-Ko's garden, Yum-Yum is being attended to by a chorus of girlfriends who are preparing her for her wedding ("Braid the Raven Hair"). Yum-Yum is pleased with her appearance and wonders artlessly why it is that she is so much more attractive than anybody else in the world ("The Sun Whose Rays"). The prospective duration of her wedded bliss, however, casts a cloud over her happiness, a cloud which she attempts to dispel in a madrigal ("Brightly Dawns Our Wedding Day"). If Nanki-Poo's future fate brings a tear to her sympathetic eye, that is nothing to the reaction provoked by Ko-Ko's next piece of news. Pooh-Bah has discovered a law decreeing that a condemned man's wife has to be buried alive with his corpse. Now, Yum-Yum is very much in love with Nanki-Poo, but there are limits. On the other hand, if she doesn't marry Nanki-Poo and get buried alive, she must marry Ko-Ko. It's really a toss up as to which is the worse fate ("Here's a How-de-do").

It's a problem all round really. If Nanki-Poo isn't permitted to marry Yum-Yum then he will commit suicide immediately, which puts Ko-Ko to the ghastly and virtually impossible necessity of finding another victim before the Mikado arrives. Nanki-Poo generously offers to be beheaded on the spot, but it then turns out that Ko-Ko suffers from humanity: he can't even kill a bluebottle. But does the deed really have to be done? Couldn't they just pretend that Nanki-Poo has been executed? After all, all the noble lords of the realm as incarnate in Pooh-Bah will swear an affadavit to the execution if suitably bribed. Pooh-Bah, in his capacity as Archbishop, can also marry Yum-Yum and Nanki-Poo and they can run away out of the story.

With so many obliging officials to help out, the thing is soon accomplished and off the newlyweds go, just as the March of the Mikado's troops ("Miya Sama") announces a surprise visit from the supreme potentate. He has come in the company of Katisha ("From Every Kind of Man") with a song detailing his philosophy of letting punishment be suitable to the crime it is rebuking ("A More Humane Mikado") and he is eagerly greeted by Ko-Ko with news of the recent execution, described in luridly colorful detail by the Lord High Executioner and his accomplices ("The Criminal Cried").

Unfortunately, this is not the business on which the Mikado has come to Titipu at all. He has come seeking his missing son and Katisha, seizing the execution certificate, now discovers that the heir apparent has apparently been executed. The punishment for encompassing the death of the heir apparent is something lingering with boiling oil. The Mikado is ever so sorry, but the law is the law and fate does not always deal out a man's just deserts ("See How the Fates Their Gifts Allot"). If the heir apparent is dead then Ko-Ko and his accomplices really will have to join him.

Ko-Ko corners Nanki-Poo and Yum-Yum as they prepare to depart on their honeymoon. Given the circumstances, Nanki-Poo must come back to life. This time Nanki-Poo is less obliging. He is very happy with things the way they are and he has no wish to be revived, for Katisha will certainly insist on marrying him or alternatively executing him and burying Yum-Yum alive in the approved fashion. On the other hand, if Katisha were safely married, it would be a different matter altogether. In that case life would be as welcome as "The Flowers That Bloom in the Spring." Suppose, for example, that Ko-Ko were to marry her?

Alone, Katisha is soliloquizing in melodramatic terms ("Hearts Do Not Break") when Ko-Ko comes to her, steeled to his task. He weakens her resolve with the tragic tale of a little tom-tit who died for love ("Tit Willow"), and soon they are joining in a duet praising the more belligerent aspects of womanhood ("There Is Beauty in the Bellow of the Blast"). The nuptial deed done, Katisha is dragging Ko-Ko before the Mikado to add her weight to his pleas for mercy when Nanki-Poo appears, very much alive! Katisha's fury and Ko-Ko's convoluted explanations are drowned in a joyful finale ("For He's Gone and Married Yum-Yum") as the strange doings in the town of Titipu come to their mostly happy ending.

1890

ROBIN HOOD

A COMIC OPERA IN THREE ACTS by Harry B. Smith. Music by Reginald de Koven.
First produced at the Opera House, Chicago, 9 June 1890. Produced at the Standard Theatre, New York, 28 September 1891, with Henry Clay Barnabee (Sheriff), Tom Karl (Robin), Caroline Hamilton (Marian), Peter Lang (Guy), and Jessie Bartlett Davis (Allan). Played frequently in New York by the Boston Ideal Company thereafter, including seasons at the Garden Theatre in 1893, at the Broadway Theatre, 10 January 1895, and 10 February 1896, with Alice Nielsen as Annabel, at Wallack's Theatre, 4 April 1898, at the Knickerbocker Theatre in 1900, and at the Academy of Music, 8 September 1902. Produced at the New Amsterdam Theatre, 6 May 1912, with a cast including Walter Hyde, Bella Alten, Edwin Stevens, Anne Swinburne, Pauline Hall, and George B. Frothingham; at Jolson's Theatre, 18 November 1929, with William Danforth, Roy Cropper, and Olga Steck; at Erlanger's Theatre, 27 January 1932, with Danforth, Howard Marsh, Charlotte Lansing, John Cherry, and Eleanor La Mance; and at the Adelphi Theatre, 7 November 1944, with George Lipton, Robert Field, and Barbara Scully.

Walter Hyde is the dashing Robin Hood,
with Bella Alten as his Maid Marian,
in a photo from the 1912 revival
of DeKoven and Smith's musical.
White Studios, photographers.
Courtesy Performing Arts Research Center,
New York Public Library, Lincoln Center.

CHARACTERS

Robert, *Earl of Huntingdon, afterward* Robin Hood

Sir Tristram Testy, *Sheriff of Nottingham*

Little John

Friar Tuck

Allan-a-Dale

Will Scarlet

Guy of Gisborne

Marian, *daughter of Lord Fitzwalter, afterwards called* Maid Marian

Dame Durden, *keeper of an inn on the border of Sherwood Forest*

Annabel, *her daughter*

Mark o' the Mill, *a villager*, etc.

Act 1

At Nottingham Fair, the townsfolk are making May-Day merry (" 'Tis the Morning of the Fair") in song and Morris Dance. Friar Tuck, a portly member of a philanthropic outlaw band that inhabits nearby Sherwood Forest, is auctioning off to the poor people of the parish the proceeds of his companions' latest robberies ("Auctioneer's Song"), whilst pretty Annabel, daughter of the gruesome Dame Durden, takes time off from joining in a "Milkmaids' Chorus" to steal a kiss or two from another of the outlaw band, the minstrel Allan-a-Dale.

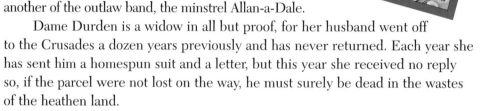

Dame Durden is a widow in all but proof, for her husband went off to the Crusades a dozen years previously and has never returned. Each year she has sent him a homespun suit and a letter, but this year she received no reply so, if the parcel were not lost on the way, he must surely be dead in the wastes of the heathen land.

Part of the entertainment at the fair is an archery contest, and all the best bowmen of the region are to take part ("Come the Bowmen in Lincoln Green"/Madrigal: "All Is Fair in Love and War") including young Robert of Huntingdon, twenty-one years of age that very day and thus due to inherit his father's title and fortune from the hands of its guardian, the Sheriff of Nottingham. He is, unbeknown to him, also due to inherit a bride, for the King has decreed that the Lady Marian Fitzwalter shall wed the new Earl of Huntingdon; a page has been sent to the Sheriff, who is also guardian of Lady Marian's fortune, to tell him the news. Lady Marian, being of a decisive disposition, has decided that she does not wish to be wed sight unseen, and she has, therefore, donned a page's clothing and come to Nottingham herself, carrying the all-important letter ("I Come as a Cavalier").

She meets Robert at the fair and informs him of the King's command, but she is not able to keep up her imposture for long. Robert and she are soon joining happily in duet at the thought of their imminent marriage ("Though It Was Within This Hour We Met"). They are, however, counting without the machinating Sheriff of Nottingham ("I Am the Sheriff of Nottingham") who has altogether more personal plans afoot. He means to marry Marian off to his minion, Sir Guy of Gisborne, whom he intends to declare as the legitimate heir to the earldom of Huntingdon.

Sir Guy is perfectly delighted at the thought of being a peer and wedding a beautiful court lady and is quite willing to give up all claims to the money that goes with both the position and the bride, money that the Sheriff has every intention of keeping for himself. Guy is only worried that he may lack the technique to win Lady Marian's heart, so the Sheriff offers him a lesson in instant wooing, practiced on a passing milkmaid, who just happens to be

Marian, doing a spot of eavesdropping in disguise ("When a Peer Makes Love to a Damsel Fair").

Robert wins the archery contest and returns to general acclaim to come before the Sheriff of Nottingham and demand the handling over of his titles of nobility and his fortune (Finale). The Sheriff refuses and produces his faked documents showing that Guy is the legal heir to Huntingdon. At this evil news, Marian quickly hides the King's decree ordering that she should marry the heir of Huntingdon, and Robert, taking leave of his beloved, sets out for Sherwood Forest to join the band of outlaws.

Act 2 At Dame Durden's inn on the fringe of the forest, the outlaws are taking their ease ("Oh, Cheerily Soundeth the Huntsman's Horn") as Will Scarlet entertains them with the song of "The Tailor and the Crow." Robert, now known as Robin Hood, has become the leader of the jolly band and they have gone from success to success, but he cannot be wholly happy for he is without love. He has heard that Marian is to be wed to Guy of Gisborne and believes that she has forsaken their love. To forget his faithless lady, he flirts with the saucy Annabel and, to the fury of Allan, promises to sing a serenade under her window that night. Little John counsels Allan to drown his *chagrin d'amour* in "Brown October Ale."

The depredations of Robin Hood have caused great annoyance to the Sheriff, and he has spent much time and trouble trying to track down the mysterious outlaw chief. Finally, the Sheriff who prides himself on the efficacy of his "eagle eye," disguises himself as a tinker and, in the company of the quaking Guy, comes to Dame Durden's inn to try to unearth Robin Hood personally ("Tinker's Song"). The outlaws soon penetrate his disguise and, leading him on, get him thoroughly drunk (Pastoral Glee; "O, See the Lambkins Play") before vanishing, leaving the sodden Sheriff to pay the bill.

The reward for his failed impersonation is harder than a mere hangover for, when Dame Durden comes to collect her reckoning, she recognizes the suit that he is wearing. It is the homespun she made for her husband. Here, at last, is her man returned from the wars. Unrecognizable he may be after so many years away, but he is surely her husband. The Sheriff cannot admit to having slyly purchased the garment from one of Friar Tuck's auctions, for he would then be liable to be arrested by himself as a receiver of stolen goods, and he has to submit to being led tipsily away by the delighted Dame.

Lady Marian, in spite of what Robin has heard, has remained faithful to her love and now, at last, disguised in a suit of Lincoln green, she has escaped from Nottingham and is heading toward Sherwood to join the outlaw band (Forest Song: "'Neath the Greenwood Tree"). The first person she meets on arriving at the inn is Annabel, and she is taken back to hear that Robin has been making advances to the girl and proposes to serenade her that night. She decides to take Annabel's place at the casement window to catch her recalcitrant lover at his flirtation.

Alas, the harm has already been done. Allan-a-Dale, driven to excesses by what he sees as Robin's attempts to steal his Annabel, informs on his leader. The Sheriff now knows that Robin Hood and Robert of Huntingdon are the same man, and he sets in motion a plan to trap him as he comes to deliver his serenade. So, as Robin carols out his song to the disguised Marian ("A Troubadour Sang to His Love"), the Sheriff, Guy, and two strong men creep upon them, led by Allan. In the darkness, Allan cannot know that Marian has revealed her identity and that the misunderstanding with Robin has been cleared up. He only hears her promise to wed Robin and, wild with jealousy, he points out his captain to the Sheriff.

He is soon made aware of his mistake and, as Robin struggles in the arms of the Sheriff's men, Allan hurries to bring the outlaws to set him free. The Sheriff is taken prisoner instead, and he will not try to win his escape by confessing that he is Dame Durden's long lost husband. Even death is preferable to that! He prefers to be branded a thief and be led to the village stocks (Finale). But Nottingham has the last laugh, for Guy has stirred himself at last and brought the town archers to the rescue of their Sheriff. As the act ends, Robin is dragged away to prison and Marian is condemned to wed the false Earl of Huntingdon.

Act 3

In the courtyard of the Sheriff's castle in Nottingham, the execution of Robin Hood is being prepared. An armourer is fashioning chains to bind the captive ("Armourer's Song") and, beneath his basso voice, we see that the armourer is none other than a disguised Will Scarlet. His chains will have a special weak link that will allow Robin to break his bonds at the given moment.

Friar Tuck and Little John have their own plan to rescue their captain. Dressed as monks, they will go to Robin's cell on the pretense of hearing his holy penitence and, while there, Tuck will exchange clothes with Robin, allowing him to escape under a monk's cowl. Allan-a-Dale, too, has come in monkish robes to bring comfort to his Annabel who has been carried off to the castle to be forcibly married to the Sheriff in a double ceremony with Guy and Marian (Song of the Bells: "The Bells of Saint Swithins").

The Friar and Robin accomplish their swap, and Robin comes forth free from his jail. His outlaws have captured the bishop who is heading for

Nottingham to celebrate the weddings and Robin proposes to take his place. When the Sheriff orders his men to bring the outlaw out from his cell to witness Marian's wedding, he is furious to find him gone and determines to hurry on with the ceremonies before anything else can happen

After time out for a quintet ("When Life Seems Made of Pains and Pangs") and a Country Dance ("Happy Day! Happy Day!"), the girls are brought forth to be led to the altar (Finale). The doors of the church are thrown open and there stands Robin Hood, revealed in his Lincoln green with all his band at his back. The Sheriff is thrown into confusion and when, to boot, it turns out that King Richard has come back from the Crusade and granted a full pardon to Robert of Huntingdon for the exploits of Robin Hood, the wicked Sheriff has to avow himself beaten and allow a happy ending.

The original score of *Robin Hood* did not include Friar Tuck's "Auctioneer's Song," which, along with Marian's waltz song "Heart, My Heart!" and the show's most important hit, "O, Promise Me" (De Koven/Clement Scott) were added prior to the show's London opening. "O, Promise Me" was sung in London in the third act by the baritone Hayden Coffin as Robin, but it was allocated to the contralto Jessie Bartlett Davis as Allan and repositioned in the second act in the Broadway production. Other songs subsequently added include the duet "A Time Will Come" (Robin/Marian) and the solo "A Maiden's Thought" (Annabel).

1910

NAUGHTY MARIETTA

A MUSICAL COMEDY IN TWO ACTS by Rida Johnson Young. Music by Victor Herbert. Produced at the New York Theatre, 7 November 1910, with Emma Trentini (Marietta), Orville Harrold (Dick), Edward Martindel (Étienne), Marie Duchêne (Adah), Harry Cooper (Simon), and Kate Elinore (Lizette). Played at the Olympic Theatre in 1916. Played at Jolson's Theatre, 21 October 1929, with Ilse Marvenga, Roy Cropper, Lydia van Gilder, Richard Powell, and Eulalie Young. Played at Erlanger's Theatre, 16 November 1931, with Marvenga, Cropper, Ann Carey, Robert Capron, and Young. A film version was produced by MGM in 1935 with Jeanette MacDonald (Marietta) and Nelson Eddy (Dick).

The spurned creole Ada (Mare Duchêne) tries to cajole her unkind master (Edward Martindel). White Studios, photographers. Courtesy Performing Arts Research Center, New York Public Library at Lincoln Center.

CHARACTERS

Captain Richard Warrington, *an American*

Simon O'Hara, *his servant*

Sir Harry Blake, *an Irish adventurer*

Lieutenant Governor Grandet

Étienne Grandet, *his son*

Rudolfo, *an Italian street musician, keeper of the marionette theatre*

Florenze, *the Governor's secretary*

Marietta d'Altena

Adah, *a quadroon, slave of Étienne*

Lizette, *a casket girl*

Manuele, Nanette, Felice, Fanchon, Graziella, Francesca, etc.

Act 1   The scene is the Place d'Armes in the French colony of New Orleans, some time in the eighteenth century. It is early morning and, as the night watchman passes on his way, the square begins to come alive with the vendors of flowers and fruit, tropical birds and sugar cane, street sweepers, fortune tellers, and a group of convent pupils on their way to school (Opening Chorus). Among the early risers this morning is Étienne Grandet, the son of the colony's acting governor and a great favorite with the local girls. Étienne has just returned from a trip to France, and the girls anxiously bring him up to date with the news: the dreadful pirate Bras Priqué has been abroad, terrorizing the merchant ships attempting to serve New Orleans, and now the town fountain is haunted by the ghost of one of his victims. From the depths of the dried-up fountain a mysterious melody has been heard—even the priest has heard it.

Étienne laughs aside the suggestion of a ghost and he also laughs silently at the tales of Bras Priqué for, unknown to all but his father and to his slave and mistress, the quadroon Adah, that frightful buccaneer is none other than Étienne himself. In search of both adventure and personal gain he has led a group of disaffected ruffians in plundering the sea coast whilst using his father's position to protect himself from suspicion.

Local curiosity is truly aroused when a strange group of rugged-looking men march into town ("Tramp, Tramp, Tramp"). A mixture of Canadian woodsmen, Tennessee mountain men, Kentucky farmers, and Indians, dressed in skins and furs and old uniforms, they are led by the stalwart Captain Dick Warrington and his Irish lieutenant, Sir Harry Blake. Captain Dick's infantry, as they call themselves, are, with the consent of the King of France, out to capture Bras Priqué, for the pirate has been attacking the English ships that provide provisions for their settlements. But they do not think to find their prey in New Orleans amongst the fashionable French. They have merely come to present themselves and their credentials to the Governor and to get his signature on the warrant for the pirate's arrest. They have also come for another and more tender reason. A bride ship is due to berth, bringing a group of poor French girls, the casket girls, dowried by the King of France and destined to be wives to the colonists. The men have spied the girls as their ship watered at Mozambique, and they hope that among them they may each find a wife.

The first part of their mission is balked, for the Governor has apparently departed for France and Étienne's father is ruling in his place. The temporary Governor is a bloated, somnolent idiot who has become known to the people as Monsieur By-and-By because of his inability to make a decision. He is also a cowardly party to Étienne's double identity, taking half the proceeds of his depredations as hush money, yet refusing to acknowledge even a sleeping part in the operation. He is perfectly aware that Étienne has the real Governor imprisoned on a Caribbean island as part of his plan eventually to turn Louisiana into a dictatorship under his own control.

Lieutenant Governor Grandet comes to the market place to oversee the arrival of the casket girls ("Taisez-Vous"). The men gather round excitedly as the brides arrive, and hurry to engage them in conversation. One girl, a plain and gawky creature called Lizette, finds herself ignored until Simon O'Hara, Captain Dick's Yiddish low-comic servant, takes a shine to her. Grandet is alarmed at being asked to sign Captain Dick's warrant, but Étienne is amused at the situation and he elaborately offers his hospitality to the Americans.

If they had stayed in the square a moment longer, they would all have heard the ghost. From the urn of the fountain comes a silvery voice with a fragment of song (Song from the Fountain: "Ah, Sweet Mystery of Life") and an instant later a very unghostly head appears. The voice comes from a diminutive Italian girl who describes herself as "Naughty Marietta." Marietta was one of the casket girls, but she ran away from the ship at Mozambique rather than be married off to some uncouth colonist, and made her way alone to New Orleans.

She dallies too long over her song and is discovered but, fortunately, her discoverer is Dick whom she already knows. When he and his men encountered the bride ship at Mozambique they had exchanged words and looks and Marietta counts on him, as a friend, to help her to remain hidden. Dick is reluctant to get involved. Women are not a part of his life, and Marietta's flirtatious ways trouble him ("It Never, Never Can Be Love"), but he arranges for her to pose as the missing son of the Italian singer and puppeteer, Rudolfo, and to work in the marionette theatre as a boy.

Before she leaves with her new "father," Marietta turns to Dick and repeats the melody that she had earlier sung from the fountain. It has been foretold that she shall only lose her heart to the man who can complete this melody that came to her in a dream. Would he care to try? Dick refuses roughly and is irritated to catch himself unconsciously whistling the unfinished tune minutes later.

Lizette has so far drawn a blank with the men of New Orleans, but she doesn't show any signs of accepting Simon, until he stages a fine piratical piece of braggadocio to impress her ("If I Were Anybody Else But Me"). Adah is suffering more deeply for she senses that Étienne is cooling toward her, and she attempts to read the future of her love in the cards ("'Neath a Southern Moon").

Rudolfo brings his little "son" to sing in the square (Italian Street Song: "Zing, Zing") and Marietta carries off her act convincingly in front of Étienne. Then the Lieutenant Governor arrives on the scene with alarming news: a dispatch has come from the King of France offering 10,000 francs reward for the recovery of the Contessa d'Altena who has run away from her family and is known to have exchanged places with a casket girl and sailed for the colonies.

The Contessa has the peculiar habit of singing an unfinished melody. Étienne tries the tune and the populace immediately recognize it—it is the ghost's tune. The ghost and the missing casket girl must be the countess.

Sir Harry Blake happens on the scene and spies Marietta. Before Dick can stop him, he has spilled the beans. Why, surely that is one of the casket girls, dressed as a boy? Étienne immediately seizes Marietta (Finale), but she refuses to admit her identity. She agrees that she is no boy, but insists equally that she is not the missing Contessa. A fight between Dick's followers and Étienne's guards seems to threaten, but Governor Grandet, once again, will not take firm action and, eventually, the girl runs off with Rudolfo.

Act 2   Marietta spends her time learning from Rudolfo how to work the marionettes (Dance of the Marionettes: "Turna Like Dat-a, Pierrette"), but she finds that Étienne will not let her go so easily. He is convinced that she is the Contessa, but he is also attracted to her, and he persuades her that she should come to the quadroon ball, a gay but louche local version of the Saturnalia, where he hopes to make her his own ("You Marry a Marionette"). She is reluctant, for Dick has warned her that these occasions are dangerous and immoral, but when she thinks that Dick has been paying attentions to Adah, she promptly agrees to go. She will not attend as Étienne's partner, but she will be there.

The ball is a vibrant, highly-coloured affair, peopled by the most swaggering members of the creole establishment ("New Orleans, Jeunesse Dorée") all gambling, dicing and drinking, and womanizing ("The Loves of New Orleans"). Lizette is there, still in search of a husband ("The Sweet By-and-By"), since Simon, who has been appointed to the post of whipping boy (with no whipping) to the Governor, has now got the idea that he can do better for himself. He is going to find the end to Marietta's dream song and win himself a genuine Contessa.

When Marietta arrives, she is taken aback by the license of the ball, and when Étienne steps in swiftly to claim her she asks to be taken home. Then she sees Dick arriving. He had said he would not attend, and she is sure that he has come to see Adah. She will not believe that he has come with the idea of protecting her, and she proudly sweeps off to the dance floor on Étienne's arm ("Live for Today").

Lizette makes a play for the Governor in the hope of arousing Simon's jealousy but, although the Governor proves to be quite ready for a flirtation, the ploy fails when Simon refuses to take the bait. Étienne has more serious matters for his father's consideration. Since Marietta is undoubtedly the wealthy and titled Italian contessa, it is imperative that he take her to wife. With the political and financial advantages thus achieved, their plan for a Louisiana republic will be greatly aided and their coffers filled.

When he proposes marriage, Marietta asks him what he intends to do with Adah, and she is appalled to hear Étienne declare that he will sell his slave to the highest bidder. Leaving him, she finds Dick, sad amongst the gaiety of the ball and aware that he is in the clutches of emotions that are new to him ("I'm Falling in Love With Someone"), but she has no time to answer him for Étienne appears and loudly announces to the assembled company that he is going to auction Adah. The broken-hearted quadroon, seeing that she is likely to be sold to an old and ugly Indian, appeals to Dick to help her and, to Marietta's jealous disbelief, Dick tops the auction.

Taken by fury, Marietta leaves Dick and, announcing herself as the Contessa d'Altena, publicly plights herself to Étienne. Realizing that her anger will pass, Étienne determines to make the most of the moment and demands that the marriage take place immediately. The quadroon girls hurry away to deck the bride out in suitable splendor but Adah remains. Dick tells her she is a free woman, and she gratefully returns his gift. She can stop the wedding. If he tears Étienne Grandet's right sleeve he will find his true name tattooed there—Bras Priqué.

After Simon has entertained with an incidental song congratulating himself on his cushy new position ("It's Pretty Soft for Simon"), Dick goes into action. He exposes Étienne as the pirate but, to his amazement, finds himself unable to take the miscreant prisoner. Simon is the Grandet family's whipping boy and, by the law of the land, liable to punishment on behalf of the family for any of their misdeeds. The squalling servant is grabbed by the governmental guards and, with Lizette wailing in his wake, dragged away.

Marietta appears, dressed for her wedding, and hears the truth of the situation from Adah. She refuses to wed Étienne and, in spite of the Governor's threat to enclose her in a convent, defies him. Locked in a room, pounding at the door, she suddenly hears a voice outside. It is her own dream song ("Ah, Sweet Mystery of Life") and the voice is Dick's. He appears at the window, and soon the two are in each other's arms.

Étienne discovers them but, before he can take any action, Captain Dick's infantry appear. They have released Simon from prison and are hot on the trail of Étienne and his pirates. But the ball does not end in a battle. Étienne gives Dick best over Marietta and, as the lovers join in another reprise of their song, the pirates are allowed to escape.

1917

OH, BOY!

A MUSICAL COMEDY IN TWO ACTS by Guy Bolton and P. G. Wodehouse. Music by Jerome Kern.

Produced at the Princess Theatre, New York, 20 February 1917, with Anna Wheaton (Jackie), Tom Powers (George), Marie Carroll (Lou Ellen), Hal Forde (Jim), and Edna May Oliver (Penelope).

A silent film verson was produced in 1919 by Albert Capellani with Creighton Haley, June Caprice, and Joseph Conyers.

A poised, plotful moment from the original production.
While the action takes place prompt side, downstage,
the chorus dutifully look straight out front.
White Studios, photographers.
Courtesy Performing Arts Research Center,
New York Public Library at Lincoln Center.

CHARACTERS

Jane Packard

Polly Andrus

Jim Marvin

George Budd

Lou Ellen Carter

Jackie Sampson

Miss Penelope Budd

Briggs

Constable Simms

Judge Daniel Carter

Mrs. Carter

Waiter, etc.

Act 1

When the telegram boy calls at George Budd's bachelor apartment at Meadowsides, Long Island, there is no one home but Briggs, his faithful butler. Suddenly the window sash flies up on the evening air, and a whole parade of garish young things step daintily off the fire escape and into the living room (Opening Chorus: "Let's Make a Night of It"). This desperately jazzy crew is headed by Jim Marvin, an energetically up-to-date young dude equipped with the latest slang, an unquenchable cheek, and some decidedly loud clothes, who has invited them all to George's home for a loud party to celebrate the fact that his polo team has just won a silver cup.

Boring old George, who won't go out burning up the night spots of Long Island with them, can jolly well host their party and there is no way that he can object because once upon a time, as Jim never ceases to remind him, Jim saved his life. Strangely enough, it seems that, for once, George has gone out for the evening, but Jim is undeterred as he shepherds a handful of self-indulgent flappers into the dining room to plunder his friend's liquor and larder.

The reason George is not at home is that he is eloping. He has been off to a minister with his sweetheart, Lou Ellen Carter, and when they creep quietly into the apartment they are all ready to enjoy their first night as Mr. and Mrs. Budd ("You Never Knew about Me"). They have disappeared into the bedroom before Jim and his entourage emerge and, in spite of Briggs's pained warnings about the noise and the landlord, Jim launches into a paean in praise of the available female ("A Packet of Seeds").

The song-and-dance routine creates enough racket to make George and Lou Ellen peep out to see what is going on, but Briggs has hustled the unwelcome guests back into the dining room so all the newlyweds spy is the telegram that the butler has left perched on a bachelor statue awaiting George's return. It is a telegram that throws a certain coat of consternation over the honeymoon.

George was brought up by his Quaker Aunt Penelope, and she is still his guardian, holding control over his finances and his family estate, both of which it is in her power to withhold if George should in any way misbehave. George had written to her, telling her that he had met a marvellous girl and was hoping to get engaged and, in reply, Aunt Penelope's telegram cautions severe restraint and lengthy consideration. George, of course, has already been unrestrained and inconsiderate. He has skipped the engagement and gone straight to the marriage. What will Aunt Penelope say and, worse, what will she do? Clearly Aunt Penelope must not be allowed to know that the rash deed has been precipitately done and, since the telegram also vouchsafes the information that she is on her way to Meadowsides post haste, that means that Lou Ellen is going to have to, temporarily, go back to her parents. The honeymoon is off.

The dining room is only a door's distance from the living room, and it is inevitable that, before long, Jim Marvin will find out his host is home. George has just time to hide Lou Ellen in the bedroom before the revellers are upon him. He is in no mood to host Jim's childish party, and he is not displeased when the landlord turns out to be of a like mind. Jim, however, is not fazed. He drags George off to charm the landlord into submission and, as soon as he is gone, Lou Ellen tiptoes from the bedroom to make her escape unseen. She is out of luck, for Jim's gaggle of girlies spot her and she has to pretend that she is part of the party. When the girls insist that she join them at their next party-stop at the Cherrywood Inn Cabaret she demurely declines, telling them that she is no flapper but "An Old-Fashioned Wife."

Jim's famous charm does nothing for the landlord, and the girls have to be bundled off to the Cherrywood Inn, while George sadly escorts Lou Ellen to a taxi to deliver her back home. This means that Jim is alone in the apartment when he finds himself confronted by a desperado with a gun. This particular desperado, however, is a pretty girl called Jackie, and she is not attacking but escaping.

She was at the Cherrywood Inn having a nice evening when a rather tiddly old gentleman called Tootles made a pass at her. The old gentleman was so tiddly that he insisted on getting up on a table and reading a particularly magnificent speech that he had prepared for a big function the next day and, when a policeman intervened to quiet him, he kicked the policeman and started a fine ruckus. In the mêlée, Jackie became entangled with the policeman, and she defended herself womanfully, an act that involved a rather hefty attack on the policeman's left eye. Now she is in flight from the law, and she has taken the fire escape and the open window as a route to safety.

The policeman, P. C. Simms, is right behind her but, when he knocks on the door, Jim passes Jackie off as George's wife and, since Simms had taken off his glasses before going into battle, he is not able to recognize his assailant. Unfortunately, Jackie has left behind a clue. She lost her handbag in the scuffle and it may incriminate her. Jim gallantly offers to return to the cabaret and rescue it and also to find Tootles and make him absolve Jackie of any blame in the affair. Jackie is duly grateful ("A Pal Like You") and, since she dare not leave the apartment without blowing her cover to the vigilant Simms, Jim suggests that she spend the night in George's bed. Old George can have Jim's sofa for the night. Jackie is only too pleased to accept and by the time George returns she is decked out in Lou Ellen's baby blue pyjamas, ready for bed.

George is penning a rueful note to Lou Ellen (Letter Song: "I'll Just Dream About You") when a strange woman emerges from his bedroom in his wife's pyjamas. Jackie does her best to explain her ghastly dilemma, and George is sufficiently convinced to continue the charade when Simms puts in another lightning visit, producing his new wedding certificate as evidence that he has just been married. And so Jackie stays at George's place "Till the Clouds Roll By" while George heads out in the rain to spend the night on Jim's uncomfortable sofa.

When he returns home the next morning he finds that he has an early morning visitor. Lou Ellen had started to break the big news gently to her family by telling them that she is engaged to George, and Judge Carter, her father, has come straight around to give George the once over. Unfortunately, Jim has arranged for his bunch of jazz babies to meet at George's place prior to a beano at the Country Club, and the Judge is treated to an unexpected whirl of girlie gaiety, which seems out of place in the apartment of what is supposed to be a serious young man.

George scares him away with a story of unstable explosives but he has to endure an entire song and dance from a spare flapper ("A Little Bit of Ribbon") before Jackie emerges dressed in the best combination of Lou Ellen's trousseau she can find to replace her rather obvious evening gown. Jim, meanwhile, has been on the trail of Tootles, and he comes by bearing the only clue he has been able to dig up. It is a piece of paper with a speech on it, the speech that Tootles was proclaiming the previous night at the Cherrywood Inn.

George's home is now full of women, all of whom have absolutely nothing to do with him, and Aunt Penelope is expected at any minute. Briggs must go to the train and waylay her. But his next visitor is even more disastrous than an aunt. Lou Ellen turns up with her mother who is intent on inspecting George's morals and, when Mama sees George's apartment filled with the noisiest specimens of modern youth and hears tales of rowdy parties and threatened eviction, she becomes thunderously protective of her daughter. When Jackie bursts forth from the bedroom and lets slip that she had stayed there all night, it is Lou Ellen's turn to crumple, but George comes up with a fine answer. This lady is his aunt—Aunt Penelope.

Jackie does her best to give her interpretation of an up-to-date Quaker ("The First Day in May") but it is her turn to be dumbfounded when Judge Carter returns to meet his wife. It is Tootles! Since he is a Judge, he should be able to square her with the police easily but, since he is clearly also a married man who was out on a spree, Jackie still has a bit of persuading to do. When Judge Carter sets off for the Country Club, where he is to make the presentation speech for the Polo Trophy, Jackie determines to follow.

Act 2   We're now at Meadowsides Country Club and Jim and his little friends open the act with a song ("Koo-La-Loo") before a black-eyed Briggs staggers on in search of George. He waylaid Aunt Penelope all right and tried to lock her in the kitchen, but Aunt Penelope defended herself in a most un-Quakerish way, popping him one in the eye before setting off in search of her missing nephew. Briggs can share his pains with P. C. Simms who is sporting a shiner from Jackie's attack of the previous night. Simms is still determined to track down his assailant but he is distracted by the remembrance of Lou Ellen's baby-blue pyjamas. He can't get them off his mind and is wondering how he could get a pair like that for his wife. When George and Jackie arrive at the club, he greets them embarrassingly as Mr. and Mrs. Budd, and immediately gets on to the topic of the wretched pyjamas.

Jim is dashing around the place being the life and soul of everybody's existence and he is only momentarily disappointed when Jackie shows signs of being rather fond of George. She, however, is equally fond of Jim, for she is a girl with eclectic tastes ("Rolled into One"). When the Judge and his wife are around, she resumes her Quaker aunt act, but Mrs. Carter is already suspicious of her daughter's fiancé and is determined to investigate him and his peculiarly young aunt very closely. In the meanwhile she intends Lou Ellen to be kept well away from George, and she bulldozes her husband into forbidding the two young people to speak to each other ("Oh, Daddy, Please").

Jackie, still on the trail of her handbag and her good name, offers Judge Carter a straight swap. She will return the speech he is due to make in a short while if he will get back her handbag from the voracious Simms. The Judge goes off looking for something with which to inebriate the policeman while Jim encourages Jackie into thoughts of future bliss when it's "Nesting Time in Flatbush." Jackie finds it quite exhausting keeping up the different personas of wife, aunt, and flapper with the various men whose paths she has crossed in the past twenty-four hours, and she orders a stiff brace of Bronxes to help her get through it all while Lou Ellen, unable to speak to her George, consoles herself with the thought that "Words Are Not Needed."

Now who should march onto the scene but the real Aunt Penelope who is horrified when Simms points her in the direction of Mr. and Mrs. Budd. George married! Of course: Simms saw him in his apartment last night with his wife dressed in her lovely blue pyjamas. The Quaker lady totters and asks for a glass of water, just as the waiter arrives with the Bronxes ordered by the phoney Miss Budd. Aunt Penelope drinks them down and suddenly her world starts to swim. When she incoherently challenges George about the blue pyjamas, he steers her solicitously toward the ladies' room to lie down.

While Jackie, Jim, and George pop in an irrelevant piece about "Flubby Dub the Caveman," Lou Ellen runs into Aunt Penelope in the ladies' room and hears the story about the blue pyjamas. She immediately recognizes the offending garments as her own, but who was the woman inside them? Lou Ellen heads swiftly toward George for an answer, but she is unable to force him into speech, owing to the promise made to her mother not to communicate with George until Mama's investigation is done. For once, George is thankful for Mrs. Carter's intervention. Lou Ellen gathers her mother to her side and demands that George answer her question and also that he explain who Jackie is, since it is plain that she is not his aunt.

Before the explanations can begin, Aunt Penelope spots Briggs. There is the maniac who attacked her and tried to lock her up. Simms leaps to do his duty and, to free his hands, plumps Jackie's handbag into the arms of Judge Carter. The Judge swiftly exchanges the bag for his speech as Aunt Penelope demands to know whether she has dreamed the whole strange affair. And did she also dream that George was married?

No, she did not. George gently brings forward Lou Ellen to introduce her as his wife, much to the confusion of Simms who is perfectly sure that it was the other girl who was wearing the blue pyjamas. Nonsense, responds George heroically, Jackie is the wife of Jim Marvin. Well, she soon will be, and with any luck nobody will ask any more questions about the previous twenty-four hours' goings on in Meadowsides, Long Island.

Several other songs were played in the show at the early stages of its production including "Be a Little Sunbeam," "The Land Where the Good Songs Go," and "Ain't It a Grand and Glorious Feeling."

THE STUDENT PRINCE

A MUSICAL PLAY IN TWO ACTS by Dorothy Donnelly based on *Old Heidelberg* by Rudolf Bleichman, a version of *Alt Heidelberg* by Wilhelm Meyer-Forster. Lyrics by Dorothy Donnelly. Music by Sigmund Romberg.

        Produced at Jolson's Theatre, New York, 2 December 1924, with Howard Marsh (Karl-Franz), Ilse Marvenga (Kathie), Greek Evans (Engel), Raymond Marlowe (Detlef), Roberta Beatty (Margaret), John Coast (Tarnitz), and George Hassell (Lutz). Played at the Majestic Theatre, 29 January 1931, with Edward Nell, Jr., Eliz Gergely, Hollis Davenny, Hassell, and Adolf Link (Toni), and at the Broadway Theatre, 8 June 1943, with Frank Hornaday and Barbara Scully.

        Film versions were produced by MGM in 1927 with Ramon Novarro and Norma Shearer and in 1954 with Edmund Purdom (sung by Mario Lanza) and Ann Blyth.

"Deep in my heart, dear . . ." Howard Marsh
and Ilse Marvenga as the dutiful Prince and
his royally unsuitable sweetheart.
White Studios, photographers.
Courtesy Performing Arts Research Center,
New York Public Library at Lincoln Center.

CHARACTERS

Prince Karl-Franz *of Karlsberg*

Dr. Engel, *his tutor*

Count von Mark, *Prime Minister*

Lutz

Hubert

Josef Ruder, *proprietor of the Inn
of the Three Golden Apples*

Gretchen, *a serving girl*

Toni, *a waiter*

Detlef, Von Asterberg, Lucas,
students

Kathie, *Ruder's niece*

Princess Margaret

Grand Duchess Anastasia

Captain Tarnitz, etc.

Act 1

The scene is the palace of Karlsberg ("By Our Bearing So Sedate"). The young Prince Karl-Franz, grandson of the present aged King, has completed his education by successfully passing the entrance examination for Heidelberg University, and preparations are being made for him to take up his place there for one year prior to assuming his responsibilities of state. The Prime Minister, von Mark, has arranged that his long-time tutor, Dr. Engel, will go with the boy ostensibly to help him find his way in the city but, in reality, to keep him under surveillance. Engel, after years spent at the palace of Karlsberg, is only too happy to return to the happy scenes of his youth ("Golden Days"), although he does not relish the role of royal spy.

It has been decided that the Prince will live during his stay in Heidelberg at Dr. Engel's old lodgings at Josef Ruder's Inn of the Three Golden Apples, and the royal valet, the self-important Honorable Johann Heinrich Peter Lutz, has been sent on ahead with the page, Hubert, to prepare his rooms. Lutz is not likely to be impressed by an inn, and less so by one that is noisily frequented by beer-drinking, hard-singing students ("To the Inn We're Marching").

The day of his arrival being the first day of term, the students are celebrating particularly cheerfully (Drinking Song) and pouring out their good humour and their admiration for Kathie, the personable waitress of the establishment ("I'm Coming at Your Call"). She is happy to encourage their preference for play over work ("Come Boys, Let's All Be Gay, Boys"), and the boys of the Saxon fraternity vote her the unchallenged German equivalent of Queen of the May.

Lutz is determined that the Prince shall have nothing to do with this tawdry hostelry but, before he can do anything to stop the planned course of events, the Prince's carriage is announced and the welcome flowers and song prepared for him by Kathie ("In Heidelberg Fair") have gone into action. The Prince is delighted by his first view of life outside Karlsberg Castle, of the sounds and sights of student revelry ("Gaudeamus Igitur"), and of the lovely Kathie, so Lutz has little chance of persuading him that the inn is not good enough. As Engel stays to refresh his happy memories ("Golden Days"), Karl-Franz is introduced first to the student leader Detlef who invites him to join the Saxon Corps and then to Kathie who strikes a chord in his heart, which leaves them singing happily together of love ("Deep in My Heart").

As the finale to the act begins, the students crowd round the newcomer to learn whether he has made his choice of fraternity ("Come, Sir, Will You Join Our Noble Saxon Corps"). He will not be a Prince here, just a student and plain Karl-Franz, with all the thirsts that a student has for beer, knowledge, and girls. To the strains of the Drinking Song, the Prince responds with an old Heidelberg serenade ("Overhead the Moon Is Beaming") as the act ends in joyful celebration of the coming of spring ("The Carnival of Springtime").

Act 2   The Prince takes happily to his new life under the very indulgent eye of Dr. Engel and the disapproving but impotent sighs of Lutz. The valet takes it on himself to sit up all night waiting martyr-like for his master's return, but he is not averse to flirting himself with the serving girl, Gretchen, when no one is looking. Karl-Franz's first all-night inn crawl ends happily back at the Three Golden Apples with the students still drinking and still singing ("Student Life") until their energy runs out, but it proves to have been an ill-timed escapade. To the horror of Lutz, the Prince has unexpected visitors: the Grand Duchess Anastasia and her daughter, the Princess Margaret, to whom Karl-Franz is to be betrothed by the order of his dynastically minded grandfather and the government.

Lutz holds the dragonistic Duchess at bay while Karl-Franz effects a swift wash and brush-up before being introduced for the first time to the woman whom he is to marry. Their interview is pleasant but formal, but no sooner has the royal party departed than Karl-Franz is struck with a kind of panic. Princess Margaret represents everything from which he has escaped: the gloomy halls of Karlsberg Castle, and the feeling of compunction and of imprisonment that contrasts so terribly with the wonderful freedom he has experienced in his brief time in Heidelberg.

Impulsively he calls to Kathie. He is in love with her and she with him and they must flee from Heidelberg and the sphere of influence of Karlsberg to a place where they can be happy together. They will go to Paris this very moment. Kathie rushes off to pack, but she is preparing for a journey that will never take place. Prime Minister von Mark is at the door with severe news. The King is dying and Karl-Franz must return to Karlsberg immediately so that he can be officially betrothed to Margaret before the King breathes his last.

Karl-Franz tries to resist. He has only just begun to live as a man. He was promised a year of freedom and already he is being dragged back to the straitjacket of kingship. But even his dear Dr. Engel is on von Mark's side. Karl-Franz has a duty not only as a king, but as a grandson and he must return to the side of the dying King ("Come, Your Time Is Short"). When Kathie returns full of excitement and ready to take the Paris train ("We're Off to Paris"), she is met with sad and serious faces. Karl-Franz promises that as soon as he can he will return, but the girl is wise enough to know better as she bids a fond farewell to the Prince she loves ("Thoughts Will Come to Me").

Two years have passed. Karl-Franz is King of Karlsberg and still unwed for he has found the excuse of court mourning sufficient to delay his official betrothal to Margaret. The Princess, in the meanwhile, has accepted very obviously the attentions of the dashing Captain Tarnitz ("Just We Two"), and the Duchess and the politicians are worried and not a little annoyed at the delay in the cementing of this important marriage. The time eventually comes when it seems the King can no longer avoid this particular responsibility. He has already agreed to an imminent marriage when Toni, the little waiter from the Three Golden Apples, appears at court.

Far from being angry at Toni's holding him to a laughing promise that he should one day be a king's butler, Karl-Franz is delighted to see again someone from those few happy months spent in Heidelberg. In two years no one else has made any contact. But Toni brings sad news. The Three Golden Apples is not what it was. Detlef has married a Professor's daughter, and von Asterberg and Lucas have become instructors themselves—they are joyous students no longer. Ruder and the inn have fallen on hard times and Toni has lost his job. Only Gretchen, who inherited some money from a wealthy relative, is prosperous and she is about to buy the inn from Ruder.

And Kathie? Kathie is still there, but she is no more the blithe Kathie of earlier days. She is still unmarried, but she no longer dances gaily with the students; she merely weeps alone in her room. Toni's description tugs at the King's heart as he thinks back to those happiest days of his life ("What Memories") and suddenly his resolution is made. He will, he must go back just once to Heidelberg.

As before, Lutz goes ahead to announce the King's coming and, not incidentally, to renew his acquaintance with the now wealthy Gretchen. His condescension gets its reward when the forthright Gretchen rejects him roundly and tells him she is to be married to his page, Hubert. Before Karl-Franz can arrive, the inn has another visitor, Princess Margaret. In spite of her overt flirtation with Tarnitz, Margaret is, and has been ever since that first curious meeting, in love with the man whom politics have dictated should be her husband. She understands his unhappiness and she has come to ask Kathie to be noble enough to lift the burden of his wishes and promises from Karl-Franz's heart.

Although there is no doubt that the love between the two of them is as strong as ever, she asks Kathie to go away from Heidelberg and to marry. Then and only then will the King be able to put the possibility of their being together out of his mind forever and make a new beginning in the life he must follow. Kathie realizes that Margaret loves the King and her own heart is eased by the thought that Karl-Franz will have a loving wife. She agrees to go and, as the

Princess hurriedly leaves at the sound of the approaching students, she says a fond farewell to the scene where she too knew, all too briefly, real happiness.

The students who are singing their way to the Three Golden Apples are not, however, the students of today. They are Detlef, von Asterberg, Lucas, and Karl-Franz himself. As the men enter the inn, the two lovers come face to face. Kathie tells the King that she is to go back to her hometown to wed the fiancé of her young days and she bids him not to be lonely, for love, in the shape of Margaret, will walk by his side. As the students serenade the King and his future Queen, Karl-Franz and Kathie bid each other goodbye knowing that "Deep in My Heart" they will always remember each other.

ROSE MARIE

A MUSICAL PLAY IN TWO ACTS by Otto Harbach and Oscar Hammerstein II. Music by Rudolf Friml and Herbert Stothart.

Produced at the Imperial Theatre, New York, 2 September 1924, with Mary Ellis (Rose Marie), Dennis King (Jim), and William Kent (Herman).

Film versions were produced by MGM in 1928 (silent) with Joan Crawford and James Murray; in 1936 with Jeanette MacDonald, Nelson Eddy, Allan Jones, Reginald Owen, and James Stewart; and in 1954 with Ann Blyth, Howard Keel, Fernando Lamas, Bert Lahr, and Marjorie Main.

Rose Marie La Flamme (Mary Ellis) is all set to go through the "Door of My Dreams" with a squadron of bridesmaids . . . and the wrong man. It's all right; she doesn't. White Studios, photographers. Courtesy Performing Arts Research Center, New York Public Library at Lincoln Center.

CHARACTERS

Émile La Flamme

Rose Marie La Flamme, *his sister*

Jim Kenyon

Lady Jane

Blackeagle

Wanda

Sergeant Malone

Hard-Boiled Herman

Edward Hawley

Ethel Brander

Caretaker, etc.

Act 1

High in the Canadian mountains, at Fond du Lac, Saskatchewan, the meeting and drinking place for the trappers, hunters, and travellers of the area is Lady Jane's hotel ("Vive la Canadienne"). It is a rough-and-ready place, full of men who live for the day and whose pleasure comes in drinking and womanizing in the intervals between days spent trying to break a living out of the Rocky mountains. Tonight seems quiet enough, although there is inevitably some undercurrent of potential trouble tugging just beneath the surface. The Mountie Sergeant Malone is trying to chat up the pert hotel owner while the smoothly dapper city man, Edward Hawley, is keeping his eye cocked for the little French Canadian girl, Rose Marie La Flamme. Rose Marie is also being sought by her brother Émile who fears she's off somewhere with the miner, Jim Kenyon. The half-caste Indian, Wanda, is watching Hawley. She purposely dances very closely up to him and provokes a show of jealous violence from her lover, the rough and drunken Indian, Blackeagle.

Into this seething set of relationships stalks a little fellow bundled up in a flurry of furs to protect himself from the mountain cold: It is Herman, self-christened Hard-Boiled from his wish to present a tough appearance. His presence adds yet another twist to the amorous complications in the room for "Hard-Boiled Herman" is the preferred man of Lady Jane.

The bar has emptied by the time Jim Kenyon returns, having secretly returned Rose Marie to her brother's room after a romantic walk under the mountain moon. Sergeant Malone is amazed to see the change in a man known as one of the hardest-drinking, heaviest-gambling, craziest scallywags in the area. Love has certainly tamed Jim Kenyon, the love of "Rose Marie" who, before he came, would entertain none of the many local men who paid her suit. But, in love or not, Jim Kenyon is a man who will stick up for himself and his, and he has a quarrel with Blackeagle. He knows that the Indian is trying to edge in on his claim and make off with gold from the lands belonging to Jim and Herman. This quarrel, he insists, will be settled by producing the correct paperwork and not, in spite of Herman's itchiness, by gunshots. Malone backs Jim up, but threatens the belligerent Herman with the law of "The Mounties" who arrive on cue with their song.

Émile is getting ready to depart for his trapping grounds at the Kootenay Pass. He will be taking Rose Marie with him, with the express intention of removing her from the undesirable presence of Jim. The girl ingenuously expresses her love for Kenyon ("Lak Jeem") to both Émile and to Hawley, whom Émile is keen that she should marry, and this only confirms her brother in his haste to leave Fond du Lac.

Wanda, who has laid the drunken Blackeagle to bed in their cabin, has come back to the hotel to try to revive her old affair with Hawley, and the worried Hawley realizes that, if he is to wed Rose Marie without scandal, he must settle with his old love for all time. He plans to call at the cabin and pay her to keep away from him before he leaves for the hunting grounds with Émile and Rose Marie. But Émile and Hawley are not the only ones to be maturing plans. Jim knows perfectly well that Émile is going to take Rose Marie back to the Kootenay Pass, and he plans to follow them there. He arranges with the girl that they shall meet in an old house, which she calls her castle, high on the rocks by the so-called lovers' stone. The stone is in a valley with a marvellous echo, and it is ancient lore that the Indians of old called down with a special cry to the maidens of their choice to win them in marriage ("Indian Love Call").

In Blackeagle's absence, Hawley visits the Indians' cabin and, repulsing Wanda's eager advances, offers her money. Wanda is not to be denied the man she covets, and she forces Hawley into an embrace, but they are hurried apart by the sound of an approaching footfall. The newcomer is Jim who has come to show the Indian the deed maps that will settle their quarrel. Hawley hides while Wanda gets rid of Jim but, when Hawley also goes to leave, Wanda lures him back for one more embrace. It is once too often, for this time Blackeagle does indeed discover them. The Indian attacks Hawley murderously, but Wanda takes a knife from the table and, as the two men struggle, she stabs Blackeagle in the back. As he falls, dying, Hawley looks on in horror.

Jim has rejoined Herman at the crossroads and they continue on their way, unaware of the drama that has occurred behind them. Soon they reach the Kootenay Pass and Jim installs himself in the little house up the valley from the Totem Pole Hotel where Émile and Rose Marie are based. From there Jim can keep in touch with Rose Marie by means of their Indian love call. But Émile is not fooled and he urges Rose Marie to forget Jim and instead take the love of the well-off Hawley who will buy her all the "Pretty Things" a woman should have.

Unease is in the air when Wanda turns up at Kootenay dressed in showy finery bought with the money given to her by Hawley. She has a wicked tale to tell. When Sergeant Malone and his Mounties came to the cabin to investigate Blackeagle's death, they found Jim Kenyon's map, and Wanda has convinced them that it was Jim who stabbed the Indian. Jim is wanted for murder.

Herman indulges in an incidental piece of "Eccentric Dance" and a comic scene and song ("Why Shouldn't We") with Lady Jane, before the story continues with Rose Marie turning down Hawley's offer of marriage Hawley does not give up. He patiently tries to persuade her to come to Quebec to see how comfortably life can be lived. He enlists the chic Ethel Brander to help him dazzle Rose Marie with the delights of town. Rose Marie is torn between this adventure and staying near Jim but, when the girl is out of the way, Wanda tells

Émile her faked story of murder and announces that Sergeant Malone and the Mounties are on their way to arrest Jim. The worried Émile and Hawley go off to discuss their strategy, and Wanda takes the opportunity to lead an incidental dance routine ("Totem-Tom-Tom").

Meanwhile, other events are in progress. Jim has received an offer to go to Brazil to organize some mining works for the Brazilian government. He must leave for Brazil straight away or lose the contract. Rose Marie will have to decide whether to leave her home and her brother to go with him. It would perhaps be safer for her to go with Hawley to Quebec and wait for his return. But, if she truly wishes to stay with Jim, she must come to him that night at the castle, and they will slip away together across the border to America and be married. If she decides not to, she must sing the "Indian Love Call" to him up the valley one last time and he will leave alone.

Rose Marie tells Jim that she has already made up her mind. She will follow him wherever he goes. He must return now to the castle, and she will follow in twenty minutes so that they are not seen leaving together. Jim departs and, when Hawley and Émile come to get Rose Marie to leave for Quebec, she refuses to go. But then Sergeant Malone arrives, armed with a warrant to arrest Jim for the murder of Blackeagle. Unbelieving, Rose Marie bursts into tears, but she wins from Émile the concession that he will not disclose Jim's hideout to the Mounties if she will go to Quebec and marry Hawley. It is, of course, only a matter of time before he is discovered, but Rose Marie knows a way to help him escape the Mounties. Announcing that she has always promised to sing the love call of the Indians to the man she will wed, she begins to sing, ostensibly to Hawley, the song that signals to Jim, at the other end of the valley, that he must go on alone.

Act 2

In Quebec, Rose Marie becomes gradually more reconciled to Hawley, as Ethel Brander convinces her that Jim murdered Blackeagle not over the mining claim, but in a fight over Wanda. Herman is also in Quebec, for Lady Jane has sold her hotel and bought a fancy goods shop in the town and he has finally married her. He flirts, she seeks consolation from Malone and is caught being kissed ("Only a Kiss"), but their everyday little quarrels are all put aside when Jim turns up. He has brought Wanda with him, and the half-caste girl takes every opportunity to cause trouble. When Rose Marie sees them together and hears what the girl has to say she is left in no doubt that Jim is guilty and, refusing to listen to his protestations, she turns to Hawley for comfort. Jim, who has risked his life to return to Quebec to see her again, has to go away disillusioned ("I Love Him")

The preparations for Rose Marie's wedding to Hawley are in progress ("The Minuet of the Minute") when Wanda tries her hand again. This time she comes to try to threaten Hawley, for her passion for her old lover lingers on and she cannot suffer the thought of his marriage. But her newly acquired clothes and her furtive manner have alerted the suspicions of Malone who is lurking nearby, getting ready to arrest Jim. Herman is also on to Wanda and, by pretending that Hawley is accusing her of the murder of Blackeagle, he gets her to talk. When Jane threatens to interrupt at the wrong moment, he hastily gets rid of her and she thinks that, once again, she is being two-timed ("One Man Woman").

Finally, the wedding begins ("Doorway of My Dreams") but, as Rose Marie walks toward her husband-to-be, Wanda dramatically stops the procession to reveal the truth. She is the murderer. She killed Blackeagle to protect the man she loves—Hawley. Rose Marie knows now that everything that has been said of Jim is false. While Herman, Jane, and Malone hurry to find him at the lodgings where the Mounties have tracked him down, Rose Marie heads back to Kootenay. Jim is sitting alone outside the castle dejectedly singing the "Indian Love Call" when, from down the valley, Rose Marie's voice answers him. As the curtain falls, they are in each other's arms.

1924

LADY, BE GOOD!

A MUSICAL PLAY IN TWO ACTS by Guy Bolton and Fred Thompson. Lyrics by Ira Gershwin. Additional lyrics by Desmond Carter. Music by George Gershwin.

   Produced at the Liberty Theatre, New York, 1 December 1924, with Adele Astaire (Susie), Fred Astaire (Dick), and Walter Catlett (Watty).

CHARACTERS

Dick Trevor

Susie, *his sister*

Shirley Vernon

Josephine Vanderwater, *an heiress*

Jack Robinson

Buck Benson *of Life magazine*

J Watterson (Watty) Watkins, *a lawyer*

Manuel Estrada

Mr. Rufus C. Parke, *trustee of the Seth Robinson estate.*

Jeff

Bertie Bassett

Daisy

Sammy Cooper, Sheriff's Deputy, etc

Fred and Adele Astaire play a couple of down-and-outs (who can still afford evening dress!) who dance and charm their way to a happy ending apiece. White Studios, photographers. Courtesy Performing Arts Research Center, New York Public Library at Lincoln Center.

50

Act 1

Dick and Susie Trevor are orphans who live in Beacon Hills, New England. Dick is an inventor, full of bright ideas, but ones that don't shed much light on the subject of making money, so the pair are eternally broke and behind on every kind of payment, particularly the rent. Although they are penniless orphans, Dick and Susie have some jolly upper-crust friends. Dick is in love with Shirley, who is rich and middle-class enough to go out selling charity buttons with a bunch of like-mindless girls ("Buy a Little Button from Us"). Dick would like to be able to propose to Shirley and she would love to hear him do it ("We're Here Because"), but his awkward finances don't allow him to consider supporting a wife, and he doesn't seem to have thought of taking a job.

The Trevors' landlord finally gives up on them, and the bailiffs are sent to evict them from his house. They end up on the sidewalk, and Susie arranges the furniture under a convenient streetlamp, which they can use to supply both light and (with the globe taken out) electricity for the kettle at the public expense. They can only hope that it doesn't rain. Since Dick is in love with Shirley and Susie isn't in love with anyone, she decides that she will have to sacrifice herself to a marriage with a rich man to get them out of their pickle, but, for the moment, a more pressing problem is supper—they don't have any. They will just have to accept that invitation from execrably rich Jo Vanderwater to her swanky party and hope that there is plenty of food provided.

Susie is sitting under her lamppost feeling sorry for herself when a shabby-looking tramp comes by. He is ever so charming, and whimsical enough to propose marriage to her but, since he has nothing more to offer than a hayloft as a home, Susie has to decline sweetly. The tramp has walked all the way from Mexico and is heading hopefully for his old home in fashionable Eastern Harbour but, alas, it turns out that he is a disinherited chap and home for him is certainly not where the hearth is.

Susie's next visitor is less amusing. Buck Benson is a newspaperman on the lookout for a story, and a pretty girl stranded on the sidewalk looks to him like a photo opportunity. Susie is swift to bargain for a fee for being snapped but she is gypped when Benson promises to send her a check. There is still no ready cash in the Trevor till. It will have to be Jo Vanderwater's place, and Dick will have to grit his teeth when amorous Jo starts clinging to him. But all will be well, they are sure, while the two of them stick to each other ("Hang on to Me").

Jo's party is in fashionable swing ("Oh, What a Lovely Party") and the guests are dancing a lucky-dip kind of a dance designed to give them random partners ("The End of a String") when Dick and Susie arrive, angling themselves ever nearer to the food that is being carried toward the buffet. Josephine's comical lawyer, Watty Watkins, arrives around the same time and, since the heiress is in a confidential mood, he is soon hearing how the Trevors' eviction is all part of a plot.

Jo has persuaded the landlord—who happens to be her uncle—to throw the pair out so that Dick, gnawed by penury, may finally understand the advantages of a wealthy marriage. Tonight she intends to use her charms to convince him totally and utterly. Watty is scornful of her vamping technique and takes it on himself to give her an in-depth lesson, a lesson that ends up with him demonstrating embraces on his client in a manner rather more enthusiastic than professional.

Dick finds his way to the side of his Shirley, and a few new stars come down from the heavens to find a place in their eyes, but when the showy dancing starts it is Susie who partners him in a thorough exploration of "Fascinating Rhythm." While the Trevors are displaying their dancing technique, Shirley encounters an unexpected guest. It is Susie's tramp who, she learns from some conversation with the globe-trotting Buck, is called Jack Robinson and who is the disinherited nephew of the madly rich and recently deceased Seth Robinson. Susie isn't too worried about that. She's happy just to see him again ("So Am I"), although sad that it is only for a goodbye. He's off to Eastern Harbour and solo poverty.

Watty Watkins may have the wealthy Miss Vanderwater as a client, but it soon appears that he is a distinctly shady gentleman. In the shadows of the Chinese lanterns that decorate the Vanderwater lawns, he is cornered by a very ferocious *caballero* with a complaint. Watkins has taken a fee from this gentleman to pursue the case of his sister, a Mexican lady who married an American gentleman who was sadly killed in an accident immediately after the wedding. Watty is supposed to be pushing the lady's claim to the immense estates of her brief husband, but he has had no success, being rather hampered by the lack of any documentary evidence of the marriage or, indeed, the presence of the lady herself.

The Mexican's sister is actually in jail following an episode with a bullet and a gentleman's head, but her gun is now in the hands of her brother and Watty is not inclined to argue about the details of his duty. He promises that he will approach the trustees immediately and establish beyond any molecule of doubt the right of Señorita Juanita Estrada to the fortune of Mr. Jack Robinson. To accomplish this, Watty needs a Spanish lady with some urgency and, since the real one isn't available, he tries to persuade penniless Susie to perform a little impersonation ("Oh, Lady, Be Good"). Susie, alas, will not be party to such a deception, even for almost ready cash.

As the party rises to its height, a triumphant Josephine calls all her guests together to make an announcement. She and Dick Trevor are engaged. He has finally asked her to marry him. Shirley is broken-hearted but sweetly understanding—Dick must have Jo's millions to make his life comfortable—but Susie is simply furious that he should sacrifice love for money (Finale), and she is determined that the wedding will never take place. If it is money he wants, she will make it by playing the role of the Spanish lady for Watty.

Act 2   Polite society is taking its ease ("Linger in the Lobby") in the Palm Court of the Robinson Hotel in Eastern Harbour when Dick arrives in search of his sister. She is busy preparing her foray as a señorita but, when Dick tries to discover what she is up to, she sidetracks him with small talk and dance steps ("I'd Rather Charleston").

While Dick mopes over Shirley ("The Half of It, Dearie, Blues"), daffy Daisy confirms to her sweetheart, the bumbling house detective Bertie Bassett, the outline of the plot, which has been rather trampled on in the course of all the dancing. Her Uncle is the trustee of the Robinson estate which should have been inherited by old Seth's nephew, Jack, who was sadly killed in Mexico leaving his widow as the legal legatee. That widow, a glamorous Mexican, is due any moment at the Robinson Hotel to meet with Rufus C. Parke, the attorney for the estate. Susie turns up to play her part and gives an exaggerated display of stage Spanish acting, which is apparently enough to convince most people ("Señorita Juanita"), but Dick is not fooled and he almost spoils the whole trick by insisting on knowing what his sister is doing.

A much bigger threat to Watty's plan emerges when Buck turns up and hears the tale of inheritance. Jack Robinson dead? What nonsense. Why, he saw him at Jo Vanderwater's party just the other night. With the aid of a disappearing waiter and a bottle of gin, Dick and Watty convince the reporter that his eyes are not to be trusted under the influence of alcohol but, unfortunately for them, as soon as they have left the bemused Buck alone, Jack turns up. He is amused to hear that Parke is entertaining the suit of a gorgeous lady who claims to be his wife and more than curious when he meets Susie and finds out that she is the lady in question.

When Bertie and Daisy bring Parke the news that Jack Robinson is still alive, the ground begins to quiver under Susie's feet and denunciations start to drizzle down. Watty's Mexican death certificate and Susie's impersonation come under sudden scrutiny, and the jubilant Bertie handcuffs himself to Watkins with delighted bravado. At last he has earned his sleuth's stripes. Then, to everyone's amazement, Jack himself appears and, confronted with his "wife," he confounds Bertie and Parke by agreeing with great enthusiasm that Susie-Juanita is indeed his wife. Bertie is made to look extremely silly, particularly when he finds that he has lost the key to the handcuffs and cannot separate himself from Watty.

That evening the Yacht Club Dance is in progress at the Robinson Hotel with the entire cast in attendance. The furious Watty has no ticket, but he is obliged to attend as Bertie wishes to be near his Daisy. It turns out that, in fact, they have just been secretly married and Daisy is aghast to hear that her bridal night is going to have to be shared by a manacled lawyer. Propriety is satisfied when the key turns up and the lock is undone in plenty of time.

The entertainment continues ("Little Jazz Bird"/"Carnival Time") and Dick and Susie somehow get to singing about a "Swiss Miss" before sweet Shirley comes by to recoup her Dick and Susie falls into the arms of Jack, ready to spend her honeymoon in some luxurious environment far from the sidewalks of Beacon Hill.

1925

No, No, NANETTE

A MUSICAL COMEDY IN THREE ACTS by Frank Mandel, Otto Harbach, and Irving Caesar based on *My Lady Friends* by Mandel and "Emile Nyitray" and *Oh James!* by May Edgington. Music by Vincent Youmans.

Produced at the Globe Theatre, New York, 16 September 1925, with Louise Groody (Nanette), Charles Winninger (Jimmy), Wellington Cross (Billy), Josephine Whittell (Lucille), and Eleanor Dawn (Sue). Produced at the Forty-sixth Street Theatre, 17 January 1971, in a revised version with Susan Watson, Jack Gilford, Bobby Van, Helen Gallagher, and Ruby Keeler.

Originally produced at the Garrick Theatre, Detroit, 23 April 1923 and the Harris Theatre, Chicago, 7 May 1923.

A film version was produced by Warner Brothers in 1930 with Alexander Gray, Bernice Claire, and Zasu Pitts. A second film was produced by RKO in 1940 with Anna Neagle, Victor Mature, and Pitts, and a third, under the title *Tea for Two*, using only a little of the original score supplemented by numbers by Youmans and other composers, was produced by Warner Brothers in 1950 with Gene Nelson and Doris Day.

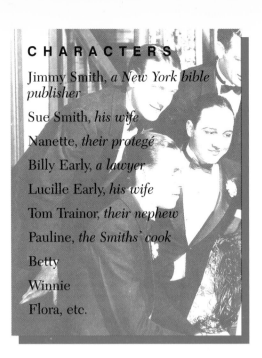

CHARACTERS

Jimmy Smith, *a New York bible publisher*

Sue Smith, *his wife*

Nanette, *their protegé*

Billy Early, *a lawyer*

Lucille Early, *his wife*

Tom Trainor, *their nephew*

Pauline, *the Smiths' cook*

Betty

Winnie

Flora, etc.

Whether it's a case of advising "no, no, Nanette"
or of making "a ring around Rosie,"
the boys of the chorus are always on hand.
White Studios, photographers.
Courtesy Performing Arts Research Center,
New York Public Library at Lincoln Center.

Act 1

Jimmy Smith has done very well out of the bible. From humble beginnings, he has worked up a publishing business worth a great deal of money, principally from his dealings in the good book. He has been helped in his climb to the heights of bankability by the modest and well-regulated spending habits of his loving wife, Sue, who keeps his lovely home immaculate with the help of just one servant. At the moment (but not for much longer) that extremely demanding position is held by a lady called Pauline who is not at all fond of her parsimonious and eagle-eyed mistress. She does, however, like Mr. Smith and, most particularly, Miss Nanette. Nanette is not strictly family. She is the orphaned daughter of friends of Sue's, and Sue has brought her up in the most irreproachable fashion to have all the virtues necessary to be a good wife to a good man.

Sue's strict ideas are, however, a little binding on the girl, and Nanette sometimes yearns to have some of the freedoms her friends have. When the show opens, some of those friends have come to the house ("Flappers Are We"), hoping to persuade Nanette to spend the weekend with them at the seaside where Jimmy has a cottage. Predictably, Sue will not hear of Nanette going away anywhere with girls who rouge and smoke, even when Billy Early, Jimmy's friend and lawyer, goes into raptures about the attractions of "The Call of the Sea."

Billy's wife Lucille is Sue's best friend, but she is as unlike Sue as can be. When she puts in an appearance at the Smith house, she is sporting an extravagant new dress and she is not ashamed to say that she has been shopping again, spending money that Billy hasn't yet earned. It is part of her philosophy of marriage. She has too often seen in the newspapers tales of faithful wives whose husbands spent their money on gaudier women and she has no intention of going that way. She wants the whole attention of her husband and, although the men may gather to appreciate the effect she makes, she returns the compliment and remains totally true to her Billy ("Too Many Rings Around Rosie").

Although Nanette has not been out in the world, she has met one young man. He is Billy's assistant, Tom Trainor. Tom has honourable intentions toward Nanette, but he is a bit of a stick. It takes time and encouragement before he can confess his love to her ("I've Confessed to the Breeze"), and he is horrified when Nanette tells him that she wants to raise a little hell before she settles down.

Jimmy Smith arrives happily home and soon begins a familiar conversation with Sue. He would love her to go out and spend some of the money that he has made over the years on pretty things for herself, but a carefulness with money has become ingrained in Sue and she cannot do it. Lucille points out Jimmy's willing free-handedness as an example to the ever-complaining Billy, but Billy, in return, is quick to support the validity of Sue's soundly reasoned replies. When Sue won't spend his money, Jimmy relieves a little of the frustration by giving twenty dollars to Nanette to go on a shopping spree, and he is delighted at the joy it gives her ("I Want to Be Happy").

It isn't the first time he's done this. The earlier occasions have been a little further from home, and now he needs to talk to his lawyer about it. His generosity and his wish to see pretty little girls happy have led to his opening charge accounts at expensive stores for Betty whom he met on a railway station, Winnie who has literary ambitions, and buxom widowed Flora. It has all gone a bit far, and now he needs to put an end to the extravagant use those girls are making of their opportunities. To that end he offers Billy a fee, which will pay all Lucille's bills, to fix everything up and tactfully remove the girls from his life. Poor Jimmy. Even his latest gift causes trouble when Tom finds Nanette going out to spend her money. When she refuses to tell him where she came by the cash and resents being interrogated by him about her every step ("No, No, Nanette"), they end up quarrelling.

That is only the beginning of a series of suspicions in the Smith house. Flora telephones and Jimmy goes into a spasm of guilt. She is coming to town. He must get out quickly. Overheard snippets of conversation, the unfortunate phone call, and a naturally suspicious mind set Lucille wondering whether Jimmy and Billy are not up to something. She finally leads Sue into sharing her suspicions and, when Jimmy makes bumbling excuses for suddenly going away, Sue decides that Lucille's suggestion of a private detective should, perhaps, be followed.

Billy decides he will make a beginning to his new assignment by setting off to visit the respective homes of Betty, Winnie, and Flora to inform them that their credit has been terminated. Jimmy, in his turn, will head for the seaside cottage where he ought to be safely out of the way, but he can't resist one extra kindness. Nanette has never been to the seaside: very well, she shall come with him. The girl is over the moon, and even turns down a dinner engagement with the repentant Tom ("No, No, Nanette") to rush away for her secret weekend, as Pauline mumbles something about a useful grandmother.

Act 2   Nanette's first day at the seaside is a lot of fun ("A Peach on the Beach"), and Jimmy is enjoying seeing her enjoying it while, equally, doing his best to lie low, waiting out of town until all his little embarrassments have been paid off. What he doesn't know is that Billy's firm has apparently sent out telegrams to the three young ladies with whom he is supposed to be settling, telling them to come to the cottage. Betty is the first to arrive, and she is draping herself all over the embarrassed Jimmy when Winnie turns up and gets highly indignant. Both of them have assumed that the generosity Jimmy has shown must one day require a return, but both are staggered to find that they are not the only one on the list. They go heavily into competition to win back their vanishing Sugar Daddy. Jimmy can only gasp pleasantly: "Fight Over Me."

When Billy turns up, it transpires that he has never sent any telegrams and a dreadful suspicion enters his lawyer's mind. Perhaps Lucille and Sue are on their tracks. He is staggered to find Nanette there, but much less staggered than Tom who has to be appeased by a glib little tale assuring him that his beloved certainly has not spent a night alone with a married man in a seaside cottage but with her grandmother down the coast. Then, and only then, can they indulge in another picturesque little duet imagining the bliss of a private "Tea for Two."

Lucille is the next to arrive and the web of pretense gets thicker and thicker as Billy wildly dreams up corroborative details for the conflicting stories that have already been set in motion. Lucille, unfortunately, has procured undeniable evidence of Jimmy's apparent philanderings for she has met Flora. Flora didn't come to the seaside. She turned up at the Smith home, luckily while Sue was out, and informed Lucille that she was there to marry Jimmy Smith. Lucille's answer was to direct her to the cottage and, at the same time, to join the general exodus to the seaside herself to find out what was going on.

The red-faced Billy goes into some quick talking to exonerate himself from any suspicions of straying, and he gets a sharp warning from his wife as to just how far he may go with his shenanigans ("You Can Dance with Any Girl at All"). Whatever else he is, however, Billy is quick-witted. While Flora and the other two lovely vampires are reminding Jimmy pressingly of his oft-expressed wishes to see them happy, Billy comes up with a grand trick. He tells the girls that Jimmy has turned all his money over to his wife. Either they take the generous severance offer he is making them and depart, or they get nothing.

The girls are busy taking out their disappointment on Billy when who should walk in but Sue. Mistaking the situation, she assumes that the girls are Billy's little indiscretions and that the dreadful tales she has heard of Jimmy's flirtations are, in fact, his friend's faults. Billy has been marauding under Jimmy's name.

The girls, seeing that they must keep up this fiction if they are to get their money, join in the pretense enthusiastically, but what is Sue's horror when the girls tell her that there is a fourth little lady at the cottage . . . Nanette. As misunderstandings and subterfuges rise in a dizzying vortex, Billy finds himself damned as a philanderer before his horrified wife. Jimmy, silencing his friend's qualms with the contents of his wallet, assumes a position as the moral hero of the moment, and it is agreed that everyone shall stay at the cottage until the situation is sorted out.

Act 3   Billy cannot get Lucille to talk to him on the phone to make his peace ("Hello, Hello, Telephone Girlie"), but he has no time to paddle in his puddle of self pity, for Betty, Winnie, and Flora have all decided that things are getting too hot at the seaside, and they are anxious for the lawyer to finalize their settlement and let them go home. Sue, still believing Billy the guilty party, takes the part of the "injured" girls, and keeps stoking the settlements up higher without realizing what she is doing.

Lucille is having a *crise*. She is ranting against Billy on the one hand and, on the other, she is horribly upset that she may be losing him ("Where Has My Hubby Gone Blues"), but when she talks with the girls her eyes are quickly opened: how could her Billy spend money on these girls? He doesn't have any! It is only a quick step from there for her to learn that the real Sugar Daddy is Jimmy, and another for her to bring the horrid news to Sue. But Betty, Flora, and Winnie, who have no qualms about squeezing Billy and Lucille if necessary, have a soft spot for Jimmy and for his suddenly woebegone wife, and they come through with some truth and some advice for Sue. Jimmy has used them to spend the money his wife wouldn't spend, to get them dolled up in the way his wife wouldn't. If she wants him to stay at home, she must let him spend his money at home.

So, after Nanette and Tom have sketched in a little more of their now-I-believe-you-now-I-don't love affair, and Nanette and Billy have managed to twist the scene to allow them to dance a number together ("Take a Little One-Step"), Sue makes an appearance dressed up to the nines. Jimmy hears her on the phone, extravagantly spending thousands on houses, cars, jewellery, and clothes, and is horrified. But Sue tells him that, since she must spend his money—their money—or see it spent by a succession of girls, she will spend it herself.

But Sue loves her Jimmy and she cannot punish him for long, and soon all is put to rights. Before long Betty, Winnie, and Flora are hustled back to whence they came, and Sue and Lucille are back in their husbands' arms. It only remains for Nanette to square herself and her various stories with the stiff-necked Tom. When he asks her if she is able to swear to being a good woman she tells him she cannot. She admits to having taken twenty dollars as a gift from a married man. Until that money is repaid, he insists, it is impossible for them to be honorably united. Jimmy has the answer. He produces twenty dollars, which he lends to Tom and then demands its return as the money taken from him by Nanette. The quickness of the event defeats any reasoning and enables everyone to line up and remind themselves one last time that "I Want To Be Happy."

The original Chicago production of *No, No, Nanette* underwent considerable changes including the cutting and introduction of numerous numbers. Neither "Tea for Two" nor "I Want to Be Happy" were featured in the first night score but were added during the run along with "I'm Waiting for You" (Tom and Nanette). The London version of the show added the songs "I've Confessed to the Breeze" and "Take a Little One-Step," which were used again in later productions. On Broadway, "Who's the Who?" (Lucille), "Pay Day Pauline" (Pauline, Jimmy, Billy), and "My Doctor" (Pauline) were also included in the score although the last song was subsequently cut. The version of the show synopsized above is the one published after the initial Broadway run and generally played since.

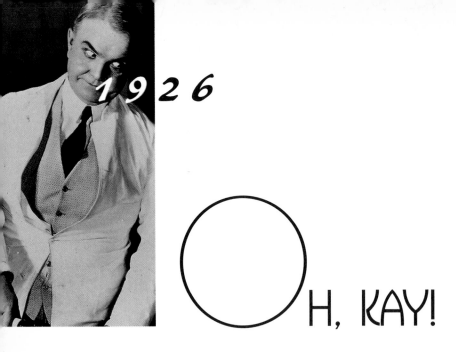

1926

OH, KAY!

A MUSICAL COMEDY IN TWO ACTS by Guy Bolton and P. G. Wodehouse. Lyrics by Ira Gershwin. Additional lyrics by Howard Dietz. Music by George Gershwin.

Produced at the Imperial Theatre, New York, 8 November 1926, with Gertrude Lawrence (Kay), Oscar Shaw (Jimmy), Victor Moore (Shorty), and Harland Dixon (Larry). Produced in a heavily revised version at the Richard Rodgers Theatre, 1 November 1990, with Angela Teek, Brian Mitchell, and Helmar Augustus Cooper.

A silent film version was produced by First National in 1928 with Colleen Moore, Lawrence Gray, Alan Hale, and Ford Sterling.

The butler's a phoney!
Shorty McGee (Victor Moore) is a rum-runner,
but he can still pour a glass of wedding champagne.
White Studios, photographers.
Courtesy Performing Arts Research Center,
New York Public Library at Lincoln Center.

CHARACTERS

The Duke of Durham, *a titled English bootlegger*

Lady Kay, *his sister*

"Shorty" McGee, *another bootlegger*

Larry Potter, *another bootlegger*

Jimmy Winter

Constance Appleton, *his wife*

Judge Appleton, *her father*

Revenue Officer Jansen

Molly Morse

Phil *and* Dolly Ruxton, *twins*

Daisy, Mae, Peggy, Chauffeur, Assistant Revenue Officer, *etc.*

Act 1

A bevy of feather-dusting local lasses is tidying up the living room of Jimmy Winter's handsome Long Island home in preparation for its popular owner's return that evening ("The Woman's Touch"). Perhaps he should not have been quite so free with his latchkey for, while Jimmy has been away, these helpful ladies are not the only ones who have been in and out of his home. It is 1924, the era of prohibition, and the coast of Long Island has become the playground of the rum runners. Their vessels safely anchored outside territorial waters, the suppliers of illegal alcohol use the cover of darkness to ferry their intoxicating merchandise to land, and the members of one group have found this large, empty house an ideal entrepôt.

The uninvited guests are rather an unusual group of smugglers, for their titular head is none other than a genuine duke who, impoverished by the vicious British tax system, has come to the land of opportunity to go into a form of business in which tax has no place. The Duke of Durham's team is made up of his sister, the Lady Kay, and two locals, "Shorty" McGee and Larry Potter. Once he has heard the news of Jimmy's impending arrival, the Duke's first actions are to cancel that night's rum run and start making arrangements for the hurried removal of the hundreds of cases of liquor stashed in the house's cellars. Larry merely takes time out to join a pair of pretty local twins in an incidental song-and-dance routine ("Don't Ask").

The next visitor to this extremely busy empty house is an official one, a revenue officer, but his little examination of the scene of what he is sure is a crime is interrupted by the arrival of the happy householder in the company of his new bride, Constance Appleton. Constance, it must be said, is not a blushing ingénue. She is a surprisingly wary and indeed acidulous young woman who shows every sign of growing up to be a proper dragon. It is not quite clear why the fun-loving Jimmy has seen fit to get tied to her, particularly as his first brush with wedlock, some many years ago, was such an unfortunate affair. A drunken college prank once had him committed to matrimony with a person called May, but it was a ceremony that had no sequel and, after a nice life as a virtually unmarried man, Jimmy applied for an annulment to permit him to marry Constance.

The arrival of the newly-wed Winters is quickly spotted by the Duke and Shorty (there are, after all, just-married suitcases all over the living room), and the presence of Shorty is soon espied by the jack-in-a-box of a revenue officer who suspiciously challenges his presence in the house. Shorty passes himself off as Jimmy's new butler (it's a long story, but Jimmy ordered a butler and a maid and Shorty sent them away, so a butler is expected) and, when Jimmy settles in, a butler he duly becomes both as an alibi and also as a means of keeping an eye on the hoard in the cellar until it can be safely lifted out.

As Shorty, in his new disguise, serves up the wedding-eve champagne, a shocking telegram arrives. The lawyers were unable to get the annulment through in time and Jimmy and Constance have been illegally married. The furious Constance packs her bags and heads for the nearest inn and, when she has gone, the conversation, not unnaturally, turns to women. Jimmy is led into the remembrance of a lovely girl who saved him from drowning the previous summer when he swam a little too far from his Long Island beach, but his reverie is interrupted by the bevy of damsels who made so free with their feather-dusters a few hours previously. They have now come back to welcome Jimmy and to be sung to of how each and every one of them is a "Dear Little Girl." Shorty is delighted at the sight of all this feminine pulchritude but he is thoroughly taken in and confused when the identically dressed identical twins, Dolly and Phil, keep popping up from incomprehensible places.

When all the girls have been bundled off to wherever chorus girls go when there isn't a number requiring their presence on stage, Jimmy begins to make ready for bed. It is a horrid night, thunder and lightning, and activity too, for the guns of the revenue officers' sloops can be heard outside making mincemeat of some poor bootlegger's boat. Then, into the darkness of the Winter living room, creeps a dripping, oilskinned miscreant. Not a terribly hardened miscreant, for a blast of thunder makes her drop her revolver and, when Jimmy politely returns it, he discovers that the watery creature is none other than his long-lost rescuer. She is Lady Kay, the Duke's derring-do sister. Kay has beached her rum-running motorboat, clonked a revenue officer on the head, and hurried for shelter to what she thought was an empty house.

Needless to say it is not long before the ubiquitous revenue officer is banging on the door. Jimmy hides Kay in the bedroom and puts on an innocent air as the officer details Kay's crimes and lingeringly describes the penalties for harboring a criminal. When he is gone, it seems safe for Kay to come out, but the officer does a quick return and catches Kay and Jimmy together. She passes herself off as his newly acquired wife and, with the just-married baggage as witness, manages to be convincing. Given the state of the weather, there is no possibility of Kay venturing out again, so it is decided that she will have to stay the night. Before they go off to their beds at the end of the scene, they sing a duet ("Maybe") with which to bring down the tabs.

In the morning, the Duke sets out to look for his lost sister with Potter in his wake. He stops off at Jimmy's house, finds the bedroom door locked, and this somehow gives Potter—who is an absolute champion at irrelevant numbers—the cue to talk about his red-hot mammy and launch into a song-and-dance routine with the chorus who have poured into Jimmy's early morning living room ("Clap Yo' Hands"). They all have to be cleared out of the house before Kay can chastely emerge from the bedroom. She has to be removed from the house pretty soon, as Constance may very well call by and, given his tricky marital status, it really wouldn't do for another woman to be found in Jimmy's bedroom. A more immediate threat is the revenue officer who doesn't seem to be after revenue anywhere else except in this one particular house. In front of him, Kay and Jimmy have to keep up their newlyweds act ("Do, Do, Do").

Before long the Winter house is filling up once again. Kay has to be hidden when Constance and the Duke both pass through, and then—oh, dear—the Judge, Constance's jowled father, arrives to scowl heavily over his lapsed son-in-law, ordering a repeat marriage ceremony under his own aegis for that very afternoon. The suspicious Constance hears noises from the bedroom and will not be stopped from investigating and, when she opens the door, there stands Kay. But the situation is saved for she is no longer clad in Constance's morning coat but rigged out as an English maid. She has every right to be in the gentleman's bedroom, for she is Jane the maid, the butler's wife. With a bit of connivance from Shorty, the day is saved for the moment, but the future still looks grim. It seems that Jimmy is going to be handed over in wedlock to Constance that very afternoon and, for Kay, who has realized that she is in love with the prospective bridegroom, that is an ending devoutly to be prevented.

Act 2   The wedding arrangements progress as the chorus watch photographs of the "Bride and Groom" being taken. Kay, in her guise of Jane the maid, is determinedly still on the premises doing everything she can to make Jimmy realize that she would make a much better mate than the prissy Constance. She fills in the time by singing the ballad "Someone to Watch Over Me," and Potter puts in another appearance with the chorus to sing about his "Fidgety Feet" when he actually should be doing something about the booze in the basement. Needless to say, the revenue officer turns up too (with a rather nasty sniffle from standing under too many windows in the pouring rain), and he is befuddled to see the same lady who was the previous night introduced to him as the loving wife of Jimmy Winter being paraded this morning in cap and apron as the wife of Shorty the butler.

Kay and Shorty have to go into action in their pretended occupation when the Judge and Constance require lunch. The menu and the service are decidedly erratic, and the meal descends as low as comedy can go until the Appletons stalk out, offended, leaving Jimmy to dance an oddly insouciant number ("Heaven on Earth") with an incidental flapper before the revenue officer comes back for another examination of the situation. He is reasonably surprised to hear that Jimmy is to be wed that afternoon, considering that he saw him in a certain *déshabille* with a new wife just the night before, and staggered when Kay appears dolled up in one of Constance's most glamorous gowns. He has to be convinced once again that she is not Jane the maid but Mrs. Winter; they just look alike in his eyes, and the fortunate arrival of the twins helps to prove the point.

Kay is feeling pretty miserable as the time for the new wedding approaches, but suddenly she has an idea, one that will not only stop the wedding, but also get the liquor away from the house; to make it work, she needs help from Shorty. When Jimmy sees her all dressed up, his last resistance snaps and he ends up kissing her—minutes before he is to be wed to Constance. Finally the dreaded wedding begins, but as the Judge starts to read the marriage service, he is interrupted by a revenue agent who announces that he has come to arrest Jimmy for allowing his house to be used as a depot for smuggled alcohol. The liquor in question is to be transferred to his trucks immediately, and Jimmy taken away to face charges.

The agent is, of course, a disguised Shorty, who is planning to rescue bridegroom and booze in one go, but his plans are sideswiped when the real revenue officer turns up and arrests both the Duke and Kay, and charges Jimmy with harboring a criminal. Then, in front of Constance and her glowering father, he relates how he found Kay in Jimmy's pyjamas, passing herself off as Jimmy's wife, the night before. What should have been a wedding ends with Constance and the Judge having palpitations and everyone else locked in the cellar under arrest. While the revenue officer is supervising the loading of the contraband drink onto the trucks, the contrabandists are plotting to escape. The Duke does his best by getting inside a barrel of beer and being rolled away but, when all is loaded and the trucks roar off, Kay and Jimmy find that the cellar door has been left open and they can just walk out. How very curious.

That evening, everyone gathers at Jimmy's house. Several chorus members get their chance at a bit of a song and/or dance, and they all join together to say nice things about Kay ("Oh, Kay, You're OK with Me"). Somewhat unexpectedly, the revenue officer comes along too and he has a surprise up his sleeve. He isn't a revenue officer at all but a famous hijacker, the Blackbird, and he's simply hijacked their liquor, fifty thousand dollars' worth! But Shorty and Potter have the last laugh. Did he look at his truck drivers? He did not and, if he had, he would have seen that they were not his own men but theirs. The liquor is safely on its way under the Duke of Durham's flag. The Blackbird is furious and swears he will have revenge. Kay has no visa for the United States, he will have her arrested as an illegal immigrant. But he is too late. She is a true U.S. citizen; for the past few hours she has been Mrs. Jimmy Winter. This time, Jimmy is married for keeps.

1926

THE DESERT SONG

A MUSICAL PLAY IN TWO ACTS by Otto Harbach, Oscar Hammerstein II, and Frank Mandel. Music by Sigmund Romberg.

Produced at the Casino Theatre, New York, 30 November 1926, with Robert Halliday (Pierre), Vivienne Segal (Margot), and Eddie Buzzell (Bennie) and subsequently played at the Century and Imperial Theatres. Produced at the Uris Theatre, 5 September 1973, with David Cryer, Chris Callan, and Jerry Dodge.

Film versions were produced by Warner Brothers in 1929 with John Boles and Carlotta King, in 1943 with Dennis Morgan and Irene Manning, and in 1953 with Gordon MacRae and Kathryn Grayson.

General Birabeau (Sheppard Strudwick) cannot know that the terrorist chief he's trying to bring to justice is his own son. Pierre Birabeau (David Cryer) is the Red Shadow. Friedman-Abeles, photographers. Courtesy Performing Arts Research Center, New York Public Library at Lincoln Center.

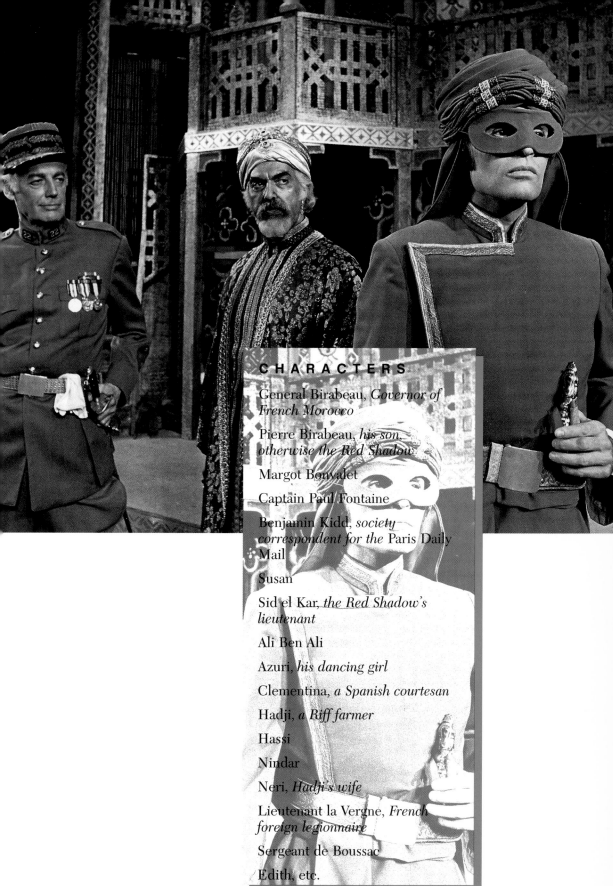

CHARACTERS

General Birabeau, *Governor of French Morocco*

Pierre Birabeau, *his son, otherwise the Red Shadow*

Margot Bonvalet

Captain Paul Fontaine

Benjamin Kidd, *society correspondent for the* Paris Daily Mail

Susan

Sid el Kar, *the Red Shadow's lieutenant*

Ali Ben Ali

Azuri, *his dancing girl*

Clementina, *a Spanish courtesan*

Hadji, *a Riff farmer*

Hassi

Nindar

Neri, *Hadji's wife*

Lieutenant la Vergne, *French foreign legionnaire*

Sergeant de Boussac

Edith, etc.

Act 1

In their Moroccan hideout, deep in the Riff mountains, a group of anti-French Arab guerillas are taking their ease ("Feasting Song"). Their activities over the past years, under the leadership of the mysterious Red Shadow, have been increasingly successful. This very day, they have blown up a strategic French dam, liberating the waters to fertilize once again the Arabs' traditional farming lands; yet there is no complacency in their hearts. Over recent weeks they have found themselves under increased pressure, owing to the redoubled activity of the French military under their new commander, Captain Paul Fontaine, and they have several times come near to discovery and annihilation.

Their skill in the desert and the speed of their horses have saved them (Riff Song), but it is said that Captain Fontaine has promised to bring the head of the Red Shadow as a gift to his fiancée, Margot Bonvalet, on their wedding day. The men would like to make a strike against this woman, but their leader will not permit it. Margot Bonvalet is not their enemy and she must under no circumstances be harmed.

The truth is that, under his Arab disguise, the Red Shadow is himself a Frenchman, Pierre Birabeau. Eight years earlier, he left Paris and joined the army in Morocco in an effort to win sufficient glory to be able to pay court to this very Margot Bonvalet but, in resisting orders to raid Arab villages, he fell foul of the colonial administration and was publicly struck to the ground by the Governor as a traitor. Resigning from the army, he feigned a brain-damaged foolishness in everyday life while creating his position as an Arab Robin Hood in secret. When his enemy, the Governor, died, he was ironically succeeded by none other than Pierre's own father. Pierre now lives in Government House itself, still keeping up his role as a fool before his family while leading the Arabs against his father's men as the Red Shadow. And now his Margot is here, in Morocco, to wed Paul Fontaine, the son of his old enemy.

The Riff hideout receives an unexpected visitor when the Red Shadow's men capture a funny little fellow wandering about in the desert. He is Benjamin Kidd of the *Paris Daily Mail*. Normally a society columnist, he has been sent to Morocco as an emergency war correspondent, and he is decidedly lost in his new job, both metaphorically and in fact. Today he went riding with Pierre Birabeau, the Governor's silly son, got separated from him, and fell into the hands of this bloodthirsty band. Bennie's life is saved by the Red Shadow's intervention and the men decide that, in return, he must agree to act as a spy at the French headquarters.

The Riffs and their leader gallop off to pursue a dangerously approaching division of Fontaine's troops but, no sooner have they departed, than Fontaine leads his men into the encampment. The hideout of the Riffs is discovered. He sets up guards with machine guns to kill all who should return, and triumphantly envisages his victorious return to his Margot. Among the rocks, however, hides one to whom that name is anathema: the Arab dancing girl, Azuri, with whom Fontaine had been involved in his earlier days in Morocco. Not without great anguish will she allow her rival to wed the man she loves.

Back at Government House, Bennie Kidd's secretary, Susan, is worrying and sighing over her adorable little boss ("I'll Be a Buoyant Girl"), and she is relieved when he turns up, not too much the worse for wear, with horse-weary buttocks and a pretty tall line in newspaper copy. The other soldiers' ladies are more bored than worried: their lives in this colony, with their husbands and lovers out chasing Arabs all the time, are dreary ("Why Did We Ever Marry Soldiers?"), and they are delighted when Margot livens things up a bit by purloining some military uniforms for a little charade (French Military Marching Song) to keep them amused.

Margot hasn't found life in Morocco at all to her taste. She imagined it to be a deliciously romantic place where all sorts of splendidly Elinor Glynnish adventures would happen, but she just sits at home and watches her fiancé going through the daily grind of military business and longs for a little "Romance" in her life. At least, today, there is a bit of drama, for the returning Paul announces that he has discovered the Red Shadow's lair and laid an ambush for him. Silly Pierre, who has brought Margot some flowers, cannot resist putting in a question as to what will happen if the Arabs should never return to that camp.

Alone with Margot, Pierre tentatively tries to emerge from his image as a harmless friend with an offer of a gentle kind of love ("Then You Will Know"), but Margot is set on a very different course. She gets Fontaine to show Pierre how a man should woo ("I Want a Kiss") and leaves him, maddened at being unable to step from behind his disguise, to dance off with her fiancé.

Bennie, in spite of his sworn oath, doesn't want to be an Arab spy. He doesn't want to be anything that involves knives and guns and things, and he's determined to catch the very next train back to France. He also doesn't want to have anything to do with the clinging Susan. She's not his type at all—she doesn't have "It."

Azuri comes to Government House in secret to try to win back the love of Paul Fontaine. She promises that she will reveal to him the identity of the Red Shadow if he will forget Margot and leave with her, but she is rejected by the disbelieving Fontaine and thrown out by General Birabeau, and she departs threatening a real vengeance. Worried at her words, Birabeau thinks it might be best for Fontaine to lie low a little while. He should wed Margot immediately and leave on a French ship due to berth that very night.

Margot, overhearing the conversation, is furious. She does not wish to wed anyone yet; she has not lived. The distressed girl is left alone with her longings for adventure until adventure comes surely to her in the shape of the Red Shadow. He appears from nowhere to stand passionately beside her, offering her romance amid desert sands and under moonlit skies ("The Desert Song"), and she replies by striking him across the face with her whip in a manner doubtless culled from a romantic novel. By the time she has recovered sufficiently to cry for help, he has vanished.

When Fontaine hears that his prey is so close, he determines to set out in pursuit immediately, but Margot stops him. If he does so, they will miss their ship. He must choose: either take the Red Shadow or marry her. It seems that Fontaine must relinquish his quarry but, as the wedding preparations begin, the Riff fires are seen on the nearby hills and he cannot resist giving chase. He vows that he will return with the Red Shadow's turban to celebrate their wedding. No sooner has he left, however, than the Riffs invade the house. There is none to resist them, and the Red Shadow takes the fainting Margot off in his arms to the desert.

Act 2 At the palace of Ali Ben Ali, in the Riff Hills, where a group of captive Spanish dancing girls ("My Little Castagnette") are being looked over as potential harem material, the courtesan Clementina entertains with a more graphic description of their profession (Song of the Brass Key). With his own camp put *hors de combat*, the Red Shadow has chosen the home of the helpful Ali as the place to bring his captives. Margot has struggled all the way, in the fashion of the best of romantic heroines, but Susan hasn't struggled at all, though she might as well have for all the good it has done her. In fact, little does she know that as soon as she has been bundled off to the bath, she has a rival; the amorous Clementina, who has a special taste for weak Englishmen, targets Bennie, who quickly looks like being "One Good Man Gone Wrong" before he can have any say in the matter.

Bennie takes the first possible chance to get out of this place. When the Red Shadow proposes to send Susan back to Fez to tell Birabeau that Margot is safe, Bennie changes clothes with her, but he is discovered and faced with a dusty death by exposure in the desert as a punishment for his cowardly attempt at escape.

Meanwhile, there is discontent in the Riff ranks for the men are unhappy that their raids are being used not to further their cause but to aid their leader in his love affair. The Red Shadow challenges any one of them to dispute his leadership and, when there is no reply, he charges them to hold to their oath and follow him in everything as they have sworn. Ali cannot understand why he should go to such pains for a woman: In his Eastern view a woman and the love of a woman are treasured but ephemeral things ("Let Love Go"/"One Flower Grows Alone in Your Garden"). To the Red Shadow, however, there is only this one woman ("One Alone") and for her he will risk all.

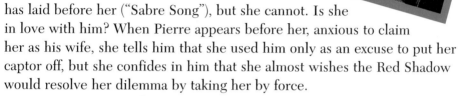

The Red Shadow visits Margot in her room but, when he attempts to woo her in manly style, he is taken aback to hear her say that her heart is given to Pierre Birabeau. She has been cured of her romantic notions. The Red Shadow promises that, if this is so, he will no longer pursue her. She shall leave here as Pierre's bride. When he has gone, Margot agonizes over her feelings. By all rights she should stab this man to the heart with the sabre he has laid before her ("Sabre Song"), but she cannot. Is she in love with him? When Pierre appears before her, anxious to claim her as his wife, she tells him that she used him only as an excuse to put her captor off, but she confides in him that she almost wishes the Red Shadow would resolve her dilemma by taking her by force.

Pierre retires to take on his alter ego, but, when the Red Shadow returns to tell Margot that he is taking her off into the desert, he is brought face to face with General Birabeau whom the treacherous Azuri has led to the palace. The General offers to fight the Red Shadow for Margot's freedom but Pierre is unable to lift his sword against his own father and, before the amazed eyes of his band, he refuses. By this act, he forfeits his rights at the head of the Riff band and is condemned to be left alone in the desert to survive or die.

Birabeau brings Margot back to Fez to great acclaim ("All Hail to the General") but Paul can see in Margot's eyes what has happened. He vows that, in spite of the standing order to capture the Red Shadow alive, he will bring him in dead. Bennie and Susan also arrive back. They have survived an ordeal of two days and nights in the desert and are pale and weak but, it emerges, they have found out one thing. Apparently Susan does have "It." Azuri, too, puts in an appearance. She has come to claim her reward and her revenge and she takes both. With the money in her hand, she drunkenly reveals to Birabeau the true reason why the Red Shadow would not fight him. The rebel leader is his own son and now, under his orders, Fontaine has gone out to hunt him down to the death.

But, like Bennie and Susan, Pierre has survived his desert ordeal and made his way safely back to Government House. Since he can no longer lead the Riffs, he has made a plan that will allow him finally to give up the feeble persona he has worn. He presents himself before his father with the clothes and sword of the Red Shadow and announces that he has beaten Fontaine to the blow: he has fought and killed the Red Shadow. But his father knows the truth. This tale will do for the world at large and, now, with Pierre at his side, he will work for a better understanding with the local people. Margot, distraught at the news of the death of the hero she loved, confronts Pierre furiously, only to come finally to a realization of the truth in his arms.

1927

SHOW BOAT

A MUSICAL PLAY IN TWO ACTS by Oscar Hammerstein II based on the novel by Edna Ferber. Lyrics by Oscar Hammerstein II. Music by Jerome Kern.

Produced at the Ziegfeld Theatre, New York, 27 December 1927, with Norma Terris (Magnolia), Howard Marsh (Ravenal), Helen Morgan (Julie), Jules Bledsoe (Joe), and Charles Winninger (Cap'n Andy). Produced at the Casino Theatre, New York, 19 May 1932, with Miss Terris, Dennis King, Miss Morgan, Paul Robeson, and Winninger, and again at the Ziegfeld Theatre, 5 January 1946, with Jan Clayton, Charles Fredericks, Carol Bruce, Kenneth Spencer, and Ralph Dumcke. Produced at the Uris Theatre, 24 April 1983, with Sheryl Woods, Ron Raines, Lonette McKee, Bruce Hubbard, and Donald O'Connor. Produced at the Gershwin Theatre, 2 October 1994, with Rebecca Luker, Mark Jacoby, McKee, Michel Bell, and John McMartin.

Film versions were produced by Universal in 1929 with Laura La Plante, Joseph Schildkraut, Alma Rubens, Stepin Fetchit, and Otis Harlan; and in 1936 with Irene Dunne, Allan Jones, Helen Morgan, Paul Robeson, and Charles Winninger. A third version was produced by MGM in 1951 with Kathryn Grayson, Howard Keel, Ava Gardner (singing dubbed by Annette Warren), William Warfield, and Joe E. Brown.

Soubrette Ellie May Shipley (Dorothy Stanley)
and her partner Frank (Joel Blum) provide
a sample of what customers can see on board the
"Cotton Blossom" in the 1994 revival of *Show Boat*.
Michael Cooper, photograph.

CHARACTERS

Cap'n Andy Hawks *of the* 'Cotton Blossom'

Parthy Ann Hawks, *his wife*

Magnolia, *their daughter*

Gaylord Ravenal, *a riverboat gambler*

Julie La Verne

Frank Schultz

Ellie May Chipley

Steve Baker

Joe

Queenie

Windy, Rubberface, Pete, Vallon, Backwoodsman, Jeb, Jake, Kim, etc.

Act 1   The scene is the bank of the Mississippi River at the town of Natchez some time in the 1880s. The negro stevedores of the town are working on the wharf, loading bales of cotton, but the show boat *Cotton Blossom* is in town, so the words that mean work to the stevedores mean entertainment to the rest of the townsfolk. The nightly show on Captain Andy Hawks's boat features the lovely Julie La Verne and handsome Steve Baker. It's a mighty popular show and the folks turn out merrily to greet the jolly Captain as he introduces his stars, his soubrette, Ellie May, and the heavy man, Frank Schultz (Parade and Ballyhoo).

But all is not happy in the little family of theatre folk on the *Cotton Blossom*. Pete, an engineer on the boat, has fallen for Julie and, although she is married to Steve, he has sent her a gold pin as a gift. Julie has given it to the black servant, Queenie, and Pete is furious. He tears down her photo from the showboard on the levee and makes veiled threats against Julie, which are put to an end when Steve knocks him down and Andy fires him. Parthy Ann, the Captain's stentorian wife, eternally unhappy at spending her days with show boat riff-raff, insists that her teenage daughter, Magnolia, cease all contact with a woman who causes such problems.

Passing through Natchez—and it can only be passing through as, for some past misdemeanour, a twenty-four hours pass is all the local sheriff will allow him—comes the dashing young riverboat gambler, Gaylord Ravenal. Looking lazily at the river, Ravenal contrasts his happy-go-lucky life with the sometime yearning for something more tangible ("Where's the Mate for Me"). As he lounges on the riverbank, Magnolia Hawks appears on the deck of the show boat and his eye is caught.

She strikes up a conversation and he takes her for an actress, but she longingly tells him that, although she would dearly love to be part of that exciting world of let's pretend, it isn't so. Ravenal is happy to "Make Believe" with her. The scenario he wants to act out is comprised of a little lovemaking, but he is just winning his first kiss when the law arrives and he has to depart in a hurry, leaving Magnolia brimming over with excitement at the new feelings that have entered her life. Old black Joe, Queenie's man, has seen Gaylord Ravenal's kind before, up and down the river. Better ask "Ol' Man River," who knows everything, what the boy really is.

Magnolia and Julie get together secretly in the kitchen, and the young girl pours out her tale of romance. Julie can see that she's got it properly. It's the old story: "Can't Help Lovin' Dat Man." Queenie is taken aback to hear Julie sing that song. Why, it's a negro song, and with Queenie's version of the words it can suit her Joe just as well. It goes to show that things like love are the same all over.

Captain Andy has his actors at rehearsal, preparing for the next evening's performance of *The Parson's Bride*. Magnolia watches longingly as Julie and Steve mark their roles through but, when Ellie arrives and whispers something to Steve, the rehearsal starts to fall apart. Julie is dreadfully upset and she cannot continue the play. The jealous Pete has been at his work again. In this state miscegenation is unlawful, and Pete has found out that Julie is a mulatto and that here her marriage with Steve is a crime. He has taken the photo he tore from the showboard to the sheriff as evidence. Steve whips out his knife and, making a small cut in Julie's finger, sucks the blood from the wound. When the sheriff arrives, he swears before God that he, like Julie, has negro blood in him and the company are all able truthfully to support him.

Their word prevails against that of the unprepossessing Pete, and no action is taken, but Steve and Julie know that they cannot now stay with the *Cotton Blossom*. Everyone agrees they must leave immediately to escape any further trouble, and Captain Andy agrees that tomorrow's show will have to be cancelled. But a replacement pair of actors is swift to appear. Magnolia leaps at the chance to play Julie's role, and Frank has brought back a drinking companion from the town who has all the qualifications for a leading man—the very personable Ravenal. Since he needs to get out of town quickly, and since the play-acting gives him a chance to make love to Magnolia with impunity, he is happy to accept the job. Joe watches the young people as they start to rehearse. This one is going to bring some changes on "Ol' Man River."

Out on the levee, Ellie, downhearted at Frank's dilatoriness over proposing to her, takes the glitter off the imaginations of some local girls with an unflattering picture of "Life on the Wicked Stage," while Queenie helps to fill the cheaper sections of the house with an altogether different kind of ballyhoo to that cried by Captain Andy to the politer patrons (Queenie's Ballyhoo: "C'mon Folks"). When the show starts, the new actors do well until a backwoodsman in the upper reaches takes exception to Frank, in the villain's role, manhandling Magnolia. When he brings out a shotgun, the petrified Frank crawls from the stage, leaving the play in shreds. Captain Andy is obliged to mount the boards and, in a protean display, he acts out the remainder of the play alone.

Later that night, when Magnolia has momentarily escaped Parthy's vigilance, she meets Ravenal on deck. He asks her to come to church with him the next day, while Parthy is out of town, and marry him. She agrees, and under the stars they sing "You Are Love."

"The Wedding" takes place on the levee at Greenville, and a last minute attempt by Parthy, Pete, and the sheriff to blacken Ravenal out of his bride cannot stop them. As the married pair climb into a carriage, the chorus reprises "Can't Help Lovin' Dat Man."

Act 2

The World's Fair of 1893 (At the Fair/Speciality Dances/"In Dahomey," etc.) sees Ravenal and Magnolia prosperous and happy ("Why Do I Love You?"). Parthy and Andy are there too, but they have no idea that their daughter's husband supports her on the proceeds of gambling.

The action moves on a decade, and it can be seen that things have taken a sad turn. As Ravenal's gambling succeeded or failed, Magnolia and her baby daughter have lived life on a saw's edge: one day staying in a fine hotel, another unable to pay the rent on poor rooms. At the moment they are in a particularly bad way, and their landlady is ready to turn them out. Frank and Ellie, now touring on the vaudeville circuits as a double act, come to take rooms in a boarding house where the present occupants are about to be evicted and, to their shock, they discover that the unfortunate concerned is Magnolia.

She tries her best to keep up a pretense before them but, when a note arrives from Ravenal, she breaks down. It encloses his last money to help her through and to keep little Kim at her convent school, and tells her that he cannot burden her with his unfair self any longer. Because he loves her, he must go away. Magnolia cannot believe it. Love for her husband has sustained her through ten impossible years and now he is gone. She cannot bear to return to the show boat and her mother's sneers, and she gratefully snatches at Frank's suggestion that she should try for a job at the Trocadero club where he and Ellie are to work.

At the club, the resident singer is running through a number ("Bill"). It is Julie: an older, badly aged, and overdressed Julie with a bottle all too handy, but still with the charisma she always had. She has left the stage by the time Frank arrives with Magnolia but, standing in the dark, she hears the little girl she loved pouring her heart into "Can't Help Lovin' Dat Man." Julie comes to a decision. She pens a note to the club owner, resigning her place and telling him to take Magnolia instead. While Magnolia is getting herself a job, Ravenal stops off at the convent to take one last look at Kim, and, as he leaves, he leaves her as his only legacy one last verse of "Make Believe."

At the Trocadero New Year's Eve entertainment, the apache dancers dance, Frank and Ellie perform "Goodbye, My Lady Love," and Captain Andy, who has come to town with Parthy Ann, arrives with three chorus girls, having slipped the leash for a night of fun. Frank spots him and hurries over to tell him that Magnolia is to sing tonight for her future. It is vitally important that she be a success. When Magnolia does appear, she begins nervously ("After the Ball") and the audience turns restive, but Andy calls out to her in encouragement and, seeing her father, she gains courage and warms to her task, taking the audience with her. By the time the song ends, she has them singing along happily. Magnolia is at the end of penury and at the start of a new career.

By 1927 that career has taken her through fame on the musical stage to retirement, and daughter Kim has moved up to take her mother's place as the musical comedy star of the day. Frank and Ellie have gone to Hollywood where their adopted son has become the latest child star of the silver screen, while back on "Ol' Man River," Joe still totes his bales and not too much changes.

Then, one day, Andy runs into Ravenal; a slower, gentler Ravenal. Magnolia has never seen him since the day he left her, although he has watched her in the theatre from afar. Now he cannot resist Andy's happy suggestion that they should meet again. As the patrons gather for the show boat performance, much as they did thirty years earlier, Ravenal and Magnolia come face to face and, just as it was all those years ago, it is Magnolia who speaks first, Magnolia who leads Ravenal back to the deck where they sang "You Are Love" together, and it is Magnolia who kisses him. On "Ol' Man River" things just keep rolling along.

Show Boat has been produced with a variety of endings and also with a number of songs by both Kern and other composers used as variants to the layout described here.

1931

Of THEE I SING

A MUSICAL COMEDY IN TWO ACTS by George S. Kaufman and Morrie Ryskind. Lyrics by Ira Gershwin. Music by George Gershwin.

Produced at the Music Box Theatre, New York, 26 December 1931, with William Gaxton (Wintergreen), Victor Moore (Throttlebottom), Grace Brinkley (Diana), and Lois Moran (Mary). Produced at the Ziegfeld Theatre, 5 May 1952, with Jack Carson, Paul Hartman, Lenore Lonergan, and Betty Oakes.

John (William Gaxton) and Mary (Lois Moran) on the election trail, and they're using much more sophisticated vote-grabbing methods than today. Put Love in the White House? Oh, yes! Vandamm Studios, photographers. Courtesy Performing Arts Research Center, New York Public Library at Lincoln Center.

CHARACTERS

John P. Wintergreen

Alexander Throttlebottom

Louis Lippman

Francis X. Gilhooley

Matthew Arnold Fulton

Senator Robert E. Lyons

Senator Carver Jones

Sam Jenkins

Diana Devereaux

Mary Turner

Miss Benson

French Ambassador

The Guide

Chief Justices, Maid, Vladimir Vidovitch, Yussef Yussevitch, Scrubwoman, Senate Clerk, etc.

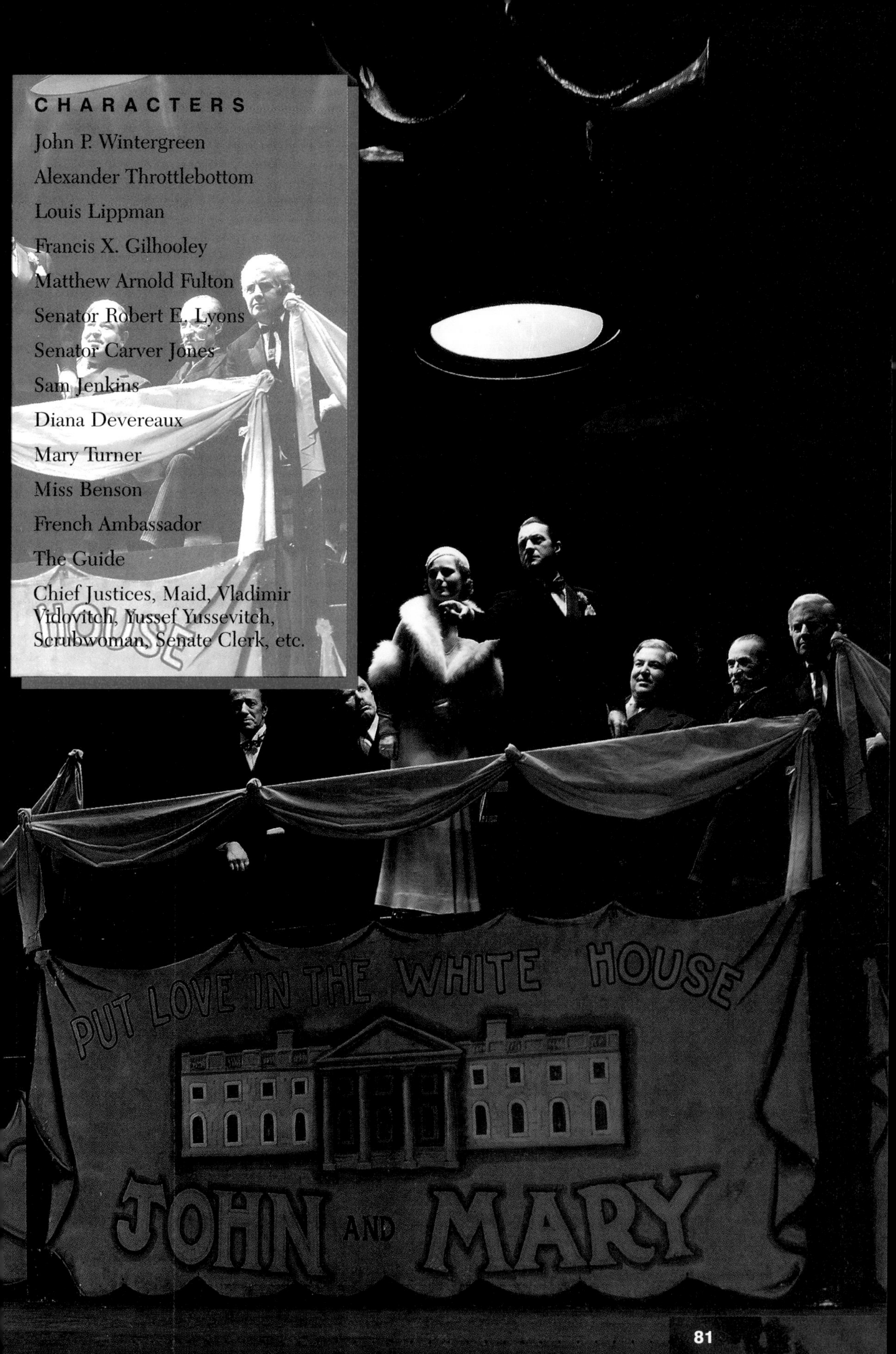
PUT LOVE IN THE WHITE HOUSE
JOHN AND MARY

Act 1   The party convention is over and, after
sixty-three ballots, a candidate has been chosen to
contest the election for President of the United
States of America ("Winstergreen for President").
The National Campaign Committee can put up
their feet with a glass of whisky in their
manipulative hand and pride themselves on their
ticket of John P. Wintergreen for President and
what's-his-name (the one whose name they
pulled out of the hat) for Vice-President.

The influential gentlemen behind the party and the
candidate are relaxing in their hotel room warming up their time-
honored clichés in preparation for the election, when an interloper appears. He
is almost thrown out until they realize that he is what's-his-name, the Vice-
Presidential candidate, otherwise Alexander Throttlebottom. Throttlebottom
isn't at all anxious to be Vice-President, and he is only persuaded of the
significance of his task when it dawns on him that if the real President should
be incapacitated he would get the plum job.

For the moment, John P. Wintergreen is in full possession of all his faculties
and it seems that he is going to need them, for the contest shows every sign of
being a closely fought affair. If he is to make sure of his election, this guy needs
a gimmick, something that will rally every right-sort-of-thinking American to
vote for him: But what? What does the common person prize above anything
else? The august gentlemen of the Committee decide to ask a common person,
and the hotel chambermaid is put to the inquisition. What does she care about
most—apart, of course, from money? She ponders a bit and opts for love.

Love? Of course, that's it! Wintergreen is a bachelor. He must fall in love
with a typical beautiful American girl and conduct his romance with her
diligently right up to polling day. The whole of America will get behind him in
his romance and, when it comes to voting, their hearts will guide their hands to
that little pencil cross. It is a racing cert. There is just one problem.
Wintergreen isn't in love. He doesn't have a girl.

This problem is no problem to a band of men like the National Campaign
Committee. They will hold a contest and find the most gorgeous girl in America,
and Wintergreen will have his beloved. The party machine goes into action to
promote John P. Wintergreen for President on a platform of Love, and soon a
bevy of beauties is lined up on the boardwalk at Atlantic City to audition for the
role of First Lady ("Who Is the Lucky Girl to Be?"/"The Dimple on My
Knee"/"Because, Because").

Wintergreen is dazzled by the display of finalists, of whom the deeply
Southern Miss Diana Devereaux is the most forward, but horribly nervous at
the thought of being married to any of them. After all, he doesn't know them. As

the girls go off to undergo their final judging, Wintergreen confides his fears to the secretary, Mary Turner. These girls may look great in bathing suits, but can they sew, can they make a bed, can they cook? Mary makes comforting noises at him. Everyone can cook; why, she herself makes corn muffins. Wintergreen's mind is distracted from his plight long enough to sample the corn muffin in Mary's lunch-box and suddenly his nervousness turns to determination: Mary Turner is the girl he wants.

Now the Committee return to announce Diana Devereaux as the winner of the contest ("Never Was There a Girl So Fair"), but Wintergreen refuses to wed the Committee's selection. Miss Devereaux cannot bake corn muffins and he is going to marry Mary Turner ("Some Girls Can Bake a Pie"). In spite of the rejected winner's complaints, Wintergreen has his way and John and Mary go on the campaign trail, their bandwagon decorated with banners crying "Woo with Wintergreen" ("Love Is Sweeping the Country"), pledging their troth in front of an audience of thousands at Madison Square Garden ("Of Thee I Sing, Baby") in between the wrestling and the baseball results. If John becomes President of the United States, Mary promises to wed him.

On election night there is no doubt about the success of the campaign. As the most preposterous results pour in, John's victory is quickly assured and we next meet our hero on his Inauguration Day (Entrance of the Supreme Court Justices), delivering his address to the country not on political subjects but on his marriage to Mary ("Here's a Kiss for Cinderella"). But no sooner is that marriage pronounced than a little cloud arrives to rain all over this blissful scene. Miss Diana Devereaux is feeling jilted ("I Was the Most Beautiful Blossom") and she has come to serve the President with a writ alleging breach of promise. The assembled Chief Justices have to decide: which is the more important, justice or corn muffins? There is no contest. Corn muffins win hands down. John and Mary can rest easy on their White House bed.

Act 2   John and Mary are installed in the White House and at the head of the nation and its enormous machinery of government ("Hello, Good Morning"). Throttlebottom is still living in his downtown lodgings and hangs around the White House wondering when someone is going to tell him what to do. When he learns from a White House guide that it is the Vice-President's job to preside over the Senate, he rushes to find a street car that will take him to the Senate House.

Wintergreen is getting along fine looking after the country, and Mrs. Wintergreen is getting on equally fine looking after him, but the little cloud that hung over their Inauguration has not gone away. Miss Diana Devereaux has supporters and her support is growing daily. John and Mary take little heed of the eager questioning of the nation's newspapers on their reaction to Miss Devereaux's action ("Who Cares?"), but they are obliged to take the threat seriously when the French Ambassador calls ("Garçon, s'il vous plaît") to add his demands to those of the insistent "most beautiful blossom." It appears that Miss Devereaux is the illegitimate descendant of an illegitimate descendant of Napoléon ("The Illegitimate Daughter"), and France, therefore, takes her rejection as First Lady as a national insult. This is an international crisis and, when John refuses to have his marriage to Mary annulled and marry Diana, an incident is threatened.

The Committee cannot allow this and decides that expediency rules. The President must do as the French demand or resign. John, however, is adamant. He refuses to have his marriage dissolved and he refuses to resign, so the Committee decides that the only possible way to impose their will is to impeach him. But if the President is removed, who will take his place? Of course, the Vice-President! What's-his-name. Throttlebottom is suddenly thrust into the limelight.

The "Roll Call" of the Senate leads into other business as Throttlebottom tries to bring the impeachment of the President before the representatives of the nation. The French Ambassador is called as a witness, then Diana Devereaux describing in an accent that has veered from deep south to shallow French how she was unjustly "Jilted," and the voting is going one-sidedly against Wintergreen when Mary rushes into the room with shattering news ("Who Could Ask for Anything More?"): She is going to have a baby. Diana's case falls in fragments as the whole Senate celebrates the fact that "Posterity" is just around the corner.

John is pacing the corridors of the White House in traditional style when the French Ambassador comes with a new condition. He consents to the baby being born but, since John's refusal to wed Diana has resulted in France being deprived of a baby, the baby must be given to France to help in the increase of her national birth rate. John stands firm. No child of his will be anything but a freeborn American.

A parade of baby carriages, gifts from the nations of the world, files through the antechambers of the presidential home, and the high functionaries of America gather as the great moment approaches ("Trumpeter, Blow Your Horn"). Finally it is announced: The President is the father of a boy . . . and a girl. The French Ambassador is beside himself. France is deprived of not one child, but two. Diplomatic relations are severed and war threatened until the undeniable logic of the case is sorted out. If the President of the United States is unable to fulfil his obligations, then they must be fulfilled by the Vice-

President. Alexander Throttlebottom must marry Diana Devereaux and, presumably, provide as many contributions to the French birth rate as possible. It's constitutional. Now everything can end happily.

The 1952 revival interpolated the song "Mine" taken from the sequel to *Of Thee I Sing, Let 'em Eat Cake*.

1934

ANYTHING GOES

A MUSICAL COMEDY IN TWO ACTS by Guy Bolton and P. G. Wodehouse. Lyrics and music by Cole Porter.

Produced at the Alvin Theatre, New York, 21 November 1934, in a revised version by Howard Lindsay and Russel Crouse, with William Gaxton (Billy Crocker), Ethel Merman (Reno Sweeney), Victor Moore (Moon), and Bettina Hall (Hope Harcourt). Produced at the Orpheum Theatre, 15 May 1962, in a revised version with Hal Linden, Eileen Rodgers, Mickey Deems, and Barbara Lang. Produced at the Beaumont Theatre, 13 October 1987, in a revised version by Timothy Crouse and Jerome Weidman with Howard McGillin, Patti LuPone, Bill McCutcheon, and Kathleen Mahoney-Bennett.

A film version was produced by Paramount in 1936 with Bing Crosby, Ethel Merman, Charles Ruggles, and Ida Lupino and another, differing largely from the stage show in both script and score, in 1956 with Crosby, Zizi Jeanmaire, Donald O'Connor, and Mitzi Gaynor.

The cast of the 1987 touring production, featuring Leslie Uggams (front center), wave goodbye to their audience from a bit of deck space that's seen its share of action over the past couple of hours. Photograph © Martha Swope.

CHARACTERS

Billy Crocker

Elisha J Whitney, *his employer*

Reno Sweeney

Sir Evelyn Oakleigh, Bart.

Hope Harcourt

Mrs. Wadsworth T. Harcourt, *her mother*

Reverend Dr. Moon *alias* Moon-Face Mooney, *Public Enemy Number 13*

Bonnie Latour

The Purser

Bishop Dobson

Ching *and* Ling, *two Chinese*

William Oakleigh, *Sir Evelyn's uncle*

Mrs. Wentworth, Mrs. Frick, Ship's Captain, Ship's Drunk, Detectives, Cameramen, Reporter, etc.

Act 1   Elisha J. Whitney, business tycoon, is about to sail for Europe but, before departing, he has a painful duty to perform. He has to sack his lovable but inefficient general manager, Billy Crocker. Billy arrives at the pier full of beans with an extra special surprise for his boss: he has persuaded the delicious nightclub singer, Reno Sweeney, to switch her booking and travel on the same ship where, as a personal favor to her old friend Billy, she will ensure that Whitney has one helluva Atlantic crossing. Reno is a great career girl. She started life as a professional evangelist before switching to clubbing with equal success. But she hasn't had any success in getting Billy to think of her as anything other than a pal even though she confesses to him, with unmistakable meaning, "I Get a Kick Out of You."

The reason for Billy's failure to fall is that his heart is already given to a girl with whom he spent nine hours in a taxi a few months back. Unfortunately he then lost track of her, but the feeling has remained. What with that and getting sacked, Billy ought to be really depressed, but he is one of life's bouncers and, in spite of everything, he is soon off down to the docks to bid "Bon Voyage" to Whitney and Reno.

On board, the press are lined up to photograph the departing celebrities. Whitney of Wall Street is worth one quick snap before the photographers turn their attention to juicier stuff in the delectable shape of the business heiress, Hope Harcourt, and her aristocratic English fiancé, Sir Evelyn Oakleigh. And, of course, a bishop, bound for an ecclesiastical conference with two heathen Chinese in tow, is altogether less interesting as media fodder than Reno and her glamorous backing group, the Angels.

A little piquancy is added to the scene by the arrival of two detectives. They are there to make an arrest, for they have discovered that two wanted criminals have booked their passage on the ship and are about to try to escape the inescapable clutches of the U.S. law, disguised as clergymen. The detectives set off in search of the oriental bishop just as "The Reverend" Moon-face Mooney and Miss Bonnie Latour sidle aboard at the last moment. Moon soon knows that he is in trouble: First, there are the detectives, and second, his colleague, Snake-Eyes Johnson, Public Enemy Number One, hasn't showed. With Billy's collusion, he succeeds in hiding himself from the law among Reno's Angels, from where he sees the protesting bishop arrested and hustled off the ship.

The ship is about to leave, and Billy, who has just been rehired by Whitney to complete some important unfinished business in New York, is preparing to go ashore when he comes face to face with Hope Harcourt. Miss Harcourt is none other than the lost girl from the taxi, and Billy's plans suddenly take a somersault.

If he stays on board, he has all the time between New York and London to detach Hope from her fiancé. It's worth a try.

The only trouble is that Billy has no cabin, no ticket, no passport, and no money. But he does have a friend in the person of the grateful Moon who, now that the ship has set sail, is safely away from the clutches of justice. He is also solo, and he has half a cabin, a passport, and Bonnie to spare as a result of the nonappearance of Snake-Eyes. The cabin Billy is pleased to take, but Bonnie and the passport are politely refused. He is, after all, on this trip to win the heart and hand of Hope Harcourt and he has limited time. He goes straight to work and, having persuaded Sir Evelyn into a bout of mental seasickness, he is soon lounging alongside his lady love on the open deck sharing mutual memories of sleepless nights since their last meeting ("All Through the Night").

Alas, Sir Evelyn may be easy to dispose of for the duration of a duet, but disposing of him and his pretensions more permanently is a different matter. The alliance between Hope and Evelyn is a dynastic one with heavy overtones of business, for she is the heiress to the Bailey's Products Corporation and he will one day head the Grayson's Limited empire. Bailey's is secretly in trouble and, to save the family—just like so many a Ruritanian Princess—Hope must make a marriage of convenience. All this, however, she cannot tell Billy. He knows only that she will sing duets with him but that she insists on marrying Evelyn.

Billy gets installed in Moon's cabin without too much difficulty but he is taken aback to find that Whitney has the cabin opposite. Since Billy is supposed to be in New York finishing that million-dollar deal for his boss, he can't be caught on the high seas. Moon solves the problem by stealing the short-sighted Whitney's spectacles, but there are soon plenty more problems to be dealt with.

The Purser gets a cable from New York to say that the person travelling with Moon is, in fact, Public Enemy Number One, and Moon has to come clean with Billy and admit that he, himself, is Public Enemy Number Thirteen (with ambitions to climb in the rankings). Billy is now labelled as a wanted criminal so he will have to be hidden. A disguise is called for and, since the passengers will obviously be carefully looked over, they decide he will have to be crew. Bonnie volunteers to remove a sailor suit from its owner as a quartette of sailors render a shanty ("There'll Always Be a Lady Fair") to cover the scene change.

Up on deck, Bonnie attracts a crowd of sailors ("Where Are the Men?") and dances her prey off into the wings to be despoiled of their clothes. Hope, in the meanwhile, is having a very different kind of time with Evelyn. He doesn't seem to know what the words "passionate" or "jealousy" mean and, business apart, it really doesn't look as if he's any keener to marry her than she is to get hitched to him. But he certainly is in Billy's way and Billy, desperate to make the most of his chance, decides to call up the reserves in the shape of Reno. How would she like to vamp the Englishman away from Hope so that Billy can carry on his romance in peace?

Like a true friend Reno agrees to help, winning Billy's fond thanks ("You're the Top"), but she quickly finds that she rather likes her task and manages to unbend Evelyn enough to win from him an invitation for a drink in his cabin. She plans with Moon—who turns out to be another of her nightclub pals—that he shall burst into the cabin and discover her, clothes awry, in the arms of the fiancé of Hope Harcourt, thus providing perfect evidence for breaking off the engagement. However, when Moon does his bit, he finds a fully-dressed Reno being entertained by Evelyn in just his shorts and singlet. All Moon's imaginative threats go for nothing. Contrary to expectations, Evelyn insists he would be delighted to have a tale broadcast that pictured him as a fervent lover, particularly to Hope. Even the production of Moon's pet machine gun wins him no points: The charade is a failure.

Billy's disguise as a sailor has run its course, and a new one is now needed if he is to keep one step ahead of the pursuing purser and his staff. With the help of Moon and Reno, he steals the trousers off a sleeping passenger, inveigles a drunk into taking off his jacket for a fight, and constructs a beard from hair shaved from the horrified Mrs. Wentworth's prized Pomeranian. The new disguise makes him into Señor Arturo Antonio Moreno and gives him time to rendezvous with Reno, who reports on her progress with Evelyn: In spite of the failed scenario in the cabin, she is doing all right. Believe it or not, he has kissed her! Before she knows it, she'll end up a Lady. In this day and age, after all "Anything Goes." It certainly does, for when Mrs. Wentworth recognizes Billy's beard and pulls it off, revealing him to the world as Snake-Eyes Johnson, he finds that instead of being flung into the brig he is lionized by the passengers as a celebrity.

Act 2 As the adored "Public Enemy Number One" Billy is invited to dine at the Captain's table, and pestered for autographs and souvenirs while his handkerchief is auctioned for charity. When he tries to raise Moon's stock with tales of how the "Reverend" is leading him toward the straight and narrow, Moon is asked to conduct an evangelist meeting in the ship's lounge. He doesn't know how, but he puts up a fair show with a little help from Reno ("Blow, Gabriel, Blow") who has a whole evangelical career to put at his disposal.

Unfortunately, the "confessions" which come forth from the passengers aren't particularly effective, except for Evelyn's admission of a bit of hanky-panky with a Chinese maiden in a paddy field. Finally, it is Billy who comes out with the real goods. Hope has cooled toward him because of his ready assumption of the identity of Snake-Eyes and, to win her regard back, he tells the truth, scorning the passengers and the Captain for making such a fuss over a murderer. As a result, he is frogmarched off to the brig by the furious Captain with Moon,

who has tried to save the situation by admitting his
own Public Enemy status, right behind him.

The last part of the Atlantic crossing is made
in rather less comfortable circumstances than the
first. Billy is truly disconsolate, but the
irrepressible Moon spreads continuous jollity
and advice to "Be Like the Bluebird." They
have for fellow cell mates the Bishop's two
heathen Chinese who, in spite of their
downtrodden looks, are expert card players and
have succeeded in relieving the entire third class of the
contents of their wallets. The passportless Billy and the wanted Moon
are to be re-exported to America, but the Chinese will be put ashore in England,
and this gives Moon an idea. To while away the time, he suggests a game of strip
poker. If the Chinese are sharp, Public Enemy Number Thirteen is sharper, and
he and Billy are, fortuitously, just the same collar sizes as the gullible orientals.

At the Oakleigh family seat, preparations are being made for the wedding
of Hope and Evelyn, a wedding that Evelyn's uncle sees more as a merger than
a marriage. Both the participants are thoroughly miserable. The preparations are
interrupted by the arrival of three voluble Chinese who demand to speak to
Uncle Oakleigh. Needless to say, it is Billy and Moon who have escaped from
the brig disguised in the clothes they won at cards, and somehow they have
fished up a third Chinese garb for Reno. They stage a big scene, pretending to
be the parents of little Plum Blossom who was deflowered by Evelyn in a paddy
field, and demanding that reparation be made. Uncle Oakleigh offers to buy
them off and, to the annoyance of the other two, Moon is only too happy to
accept a cash offer of settlement.

While Moon accompanies Oakleigh to the place where he signs his checks,
the other two make contact with Evelyn and Hope. Evelyn would much rather
marry Reno, and Hope, although she does not want her family to suffer
bankruptcy, admits that "The Gypsy in Me" compels her to long for Billy.
Suddenly Billy spies Whitney in the house. What is he doing there? It turns out
that he is a business connection of the Oakleigh family. Then, and only then,
does Billy find out who everyone is, and hear the story about Bailey's and
Grayson's and the marriage-cum-merger that is being miserably planned.

Billy quickly realizes what is up. Oakleigh is trying to diddle the
Harcourts, Whitney, and everyone else. He is trying to sneak in and marry a
firm, which is not a bankrupt concern at all but, if they only knew it, worth
millions. Billy makes a stand. He marches straight up to Whitney to pour out his
discovery and, before the furious Oakleigh can stop it, Whitney has made and
Hope has accepted a large cash offer for the firm she believed to be on the
rocks. Since she now has nothing to merge, the marriage is promptly called off

and, as the proceedings roll up, Billy gets his Hope, Evelyn makes a lady out of Reno, and a tidy cable arrives from Washington fixing Billy's passport problems and declaring the indignant Moon "harmless." Harmless? He still has Uncle Oakleigh's large cheque in his pocket and it's quite clear that he isn't going to give it back.

The original Broadway score of *Anything Goes* also included the song "Buddie, Beware" which was later deleted. Subsequent productions began the process of filling up revived Porter shows with songs detached from his less-successful musicals. The 1962 Broadway version included in its score the "Heaven Hop" and "Let's Misbehave" from *Paris*, "Take Me Back to Manhattan" from *The New Yorkers*, "Let's Step Out" from *Fifty Million Frenchmen*, and "Friendship" from *Dubarry Was a Lady*. The 1987 revival included "It's D'Lovely" from *Red Hot and Blue* and "Friendship," reinstated "Buddie, Beware," and added "Easy to Love" and "No Cure Like Travel," which had been cut from the show before the original Broadway opening, "I Want to Row on the Crew" from the college show *Paranoia*, and "Goodbye Little Dream, Goodbye" previously performed in *Red, Hot and Blue* and *O Mistress Mine*.

ON YOUR TOES

A MUSICAL COMEDY IN TWO ACTS by Richard Rodgers, Lorenz Hart, and George Abbott. Lyrics by Lorenz Hart. Music by Richard Rodgers.

Produced at the Imperial Theatre, New York, 11 April 1936, with Ray Bolger (Junior), Tamara Geva (Vera), Doris Carson (Frankie), Luella Gear (Peggy), and Monty Woolley (Sergei). Produced at the 46th Street Theatre, 11 October 1954, with Bobby Van, Vera Zorina, Kay Coulter, Elaine Stritch, and Ben Astar. Produced at the Virginia Theatre, 6 March 1983, with Lara Teeter, Natalia Makarova, Christine Andreas, Dina Merrill, and George S. Irving.

A film version, which used the dances but no sung music, was produced by Warner Brothers/First National in 1939 with Vera Zorina and Eddie Albert.

Vera Barnova (Tamara Geva) and
Junior Dolan (Ray Bolger, kneeling)
star in "Slaughter on Tenth Avenue,"
the show-within-a-show of *On Your Toes*.
Vandamm Studios, photographers.
Courtesy Performing Arts Research Center,
New York Public Library at Lincoln Center.

CHARACTERS

Phil Dolan III (Junior)

Phil Dolan, *his father*

Lil Dolan, *his mother*

Frankie Frayne

Sidney Cohn

Vera Barnova

Peggy Porterfield

Sergei Alexandrovitch

Konstantine Morrosine

Hank J Smith, Stage Doorman,
Joe McCall, Oscar, Ivan, Dmitri,
Louie, etc.

Act 1

The curtain rises on a vaudeville stage where The Dolans are working on their number, "Two a Day for Keith." Ma and Pa Dolan have a continuing difference of opinion over the rights and wrongs of their son, Junior, working in the act. Pa can see the makings of a grand vaudevillian in the kid, but Ma is determined that he should have a proper schooling and the chance to follow in the footsteps of her side of the family as a respectable teacher of music. Battle lines are drawn, but when Pa catches Junior dating a girl from a number-two act, he is shocked to the core of his traditional soul. There will be no more vaudeville circuits for Junior; he will go to school.

Fifteen years later, Junior has achieved his mother's dream. There he is, up in front of his music class at the Knickerbocker University, teaching "The Three Bs"—that is Bach, Beethoven, and Brahms. His students show promise. One, Frankie Frayne, has had a song accepted for publication, and another, Sidney Cohn, is writing a jazz ballet which Junior is watching develop with a keen interest. None of the class knows anything of Junior's days as a dancer, so no one is more surprised than Frankie when she finds him dancing in the empty classroom to the music of Sidney's ballet. Junior is sure that with a great choreographer—maybe even someone from the Russian ballet—Sidney's score could be a hit, and Frankie knows how she can help. Peggy Porterfield, who finances the ballet, is a family friend. She is longing to do something new and exciting, and Frankie promises to introduce Junior to her. In exchange, he's got to look over her new song, which happens to start with the words "It's Got to Be Love."

Vera Barnova, star of the Russian ballet, is having a tantrum. The main reason for this is that she suspects her costar and lover Morrosine of infidelity. He has been seen in public with a girl so, even if he isn't unfaithful, everyone thinks he is and that makes Vera utterly furious. When Peggy Porterfield comes to talk to her about a jazz ballet that she wants the company to stage, Vera is delighted to hear that it casts her as a striptease girl, but she is really more interested in the potential of the men involved as lovers.

Sergei Alexandrovitch, the head of the company, will not hear of such a production. He is for tradition and *Swan Lake* ("Too Good for the Average Man"). Morrosine's arrival is greeted with a shower of abuse from Vera and, when Junior is introduced, she makes a dead set at him in front of her partner/lover. When Junior is left alone with the electric ballerina, theoretically to allow him to tell her about the new ballet, she instead tells him the story of the *Princess Zenobia* ballet, illustrating its various phases, with Junior as a surprisingly expert partner, up to its amorous finale. The ballet is clearly not a million miles from vaudeville.

Junior's students haven't been seeing much of him since he got involved with the Russian ballet, and involved is the word. Peggy has him learning a chorus role in *Princess Zenobia* in order to get the atmosphere of the world of which he is about to become a part. When he does show up at school he suddenly gets round to telling Frankie that he's in love with her. She has her doubts about him and Vera, but she's happy to launch with him into a duet dreaming about an Arcadian life somewhere where "There's a Small Hotel."

Backstage at the first night of the season's *Princess Zenobia* performances, Junior is showing Frankie around the set when Peggy arrives with a crisis. They have lost a slave. One of the dancers has been locked up by the police, and that leaves the chorus of slaves one chorine short. Junior is needed. He has more or less learned the piece. He will have to go on for the missing blackamoor. Junior quickly turns himself into a Russian and a black slave and, after a quick brush-up of the steps, he joins the company.

The ballet proceeds in its traditional Russo-Arabian nights combination of poses and gymnastics until the scene with the slaves arrives. Unfortunately, Junior has not only forgotten to black himself up beyond the chin but, since he hasn't performed this number under combat conditions, he gets an attack of stage fright and starts to go embarrassingly wrong. As the scene unfolds, he gets into the most grotesque positions, turning the whole piece into a farrago of low comedy. Sergei is livid, but the audience rather enjoys it. Perhaps the Russian ballet has a sense of humor after all.

Act 2

Whatever the cause, the box office certainly improves. But neither this nor an impressive play-through convinces Sergei that he should stage Sidney Cohn's jazz ballet; *Slaughter on Tenth Avenue* is not for his company. In the meanwhile, Vera is still having screaming matches with Morrosine and tête-à-têtes with Junior who is trying to divide his time judiciously between the ballet and Frankie. Peggy pops in with a bit of fairly irrelevant advice to the effect that "The Heart Is Quicker Than the Eye" before Junior's balancing act comes unstuck when he invites Frankie to lunch and is then commanded to dance attendance on Vera. Since he needs Vera's support over *Slaughter on Tenth Avenue* he has to leave Frankie stranded and wondering at her feelings ("Glad to Be Unhappy").

Junior gets Sergei and Peggy down to the school to look at the talents of his pupils. Hank J. Smith gives his song "Quiet Night" and Frankie's new song "On Your Toes" is sung and danced by the class while, in between times, Peggy finds the occasion to inform Sergei that unless he produces *Slaughter on Tenth Avenue* she will ask for her million dollars worth of support back. The dancing of "On Your Toes" ends up mixing the tap-dancing students with the ballet dancers of the Alexandrovitch company as the scene shifts to the theatre.

Slaughter on Tenth Avenue is in rehearsal and Morrosine is having problems with the syncopated rhythms of the piece. He isn't at all pleased when Junior offers to demonstrate. In fact, he goes berserk and Sergei has to knock him out with a stage brace to stop him wrecking the place. Unfortunately, before taking this decisive action, Sergei has ordered the stage doorman to call a policeman and a representative of the law arrives to find a comatose body on the stage. Junior explains that it is part of the show and, as Sidney strikes up the score, Junior goes into a long dance routine descriptive of a gangland murder. It convinces the policeman but, better, it convinces Sergei that Junior can dance this role in the ballet. Juniorvich Dolanski will star in *Slaughter on Tenth Avenue.*

By opening night, Vera has made up her latest fight with Morrosine and all is again sweetness and light between them, but Junior is dancing the star role in the new ballet and that makes Morrosine very upset. He is so upset that he has paid a hit man to sit in the front row of the audience and pick off his rival in the heat of his performance. The ballet is performed, with Vera playing a striptease girl and Junior dancing the role of the hoofer who gets involved with her in the sleazy Tenth Avenue joint where she works but, as the dance scena rises to its climax, Junior is handed a note by one of the other dancers. It is a warning about the gangster in the front row. The police are apparently on the way, but in the meantime he has to remain a moving target. The last part of the dance is repeated over and over, until an exhausted Junior sees the policemen running down the aisle to arrest the gunman.

Backstage, Frankie is quickly in his arms as congratulations flow from all sides. Ma and Pa are there, and Vera thoroughly reconciled with Morrosine who seems to have rid himself of his homicidal instincts, but the song that rounds it all up, for better or for worse, is that dream of peaceful happiness— "There's a Small Hotel."

The 1954 revival interpolated "You Took Advantage of Me," originally used in *Present Arms.*

1940

PAL JOEY

A MUSICAL IN TWO ACTS by John O'Hara based on his own short stories. Lyrics by Lorenz Hart. Music by Richard Rodgers.

Produced at the Ethel Barrymore Theatre, New York, 25 December 1940, with Gene Kelly (Joey), Vivienne Segal (Vera), and Leila Ernst (Linda). Produced at the Broadhurst Theatre, 3 January 1952, in a revised version with Harold Lang, Miss Segal, and Patricia Northrop.

A film version was produced by Columbia Pictures in 1957 with Frank Sinatra, Rita Hayworth (singing dubbed by Jo Ann Greer), and Kim Novak (singing dubbed by Trudy Ewen).

Mrs. Simpson (Vivienne Segal) entertains her latest toy-boy, Joey (Gene Kelly), in what she likes to think of as a little den of iniquity—until he becomes a liability. Vandamm Studios, photographers. Courtesy Performing Arts Research Center, New York Public Library at Lincoln Center.

CHARACTERS

Joey Evans

Mike Spears

Gladys Bumps

Vera Simpson

Melba Snyder *of the* Herald

Ludlow Lowell

Linda English

Kid, Agnes, Mickey, Diane,
Dottie, Sandra, Adele, Francine,
Dolores, Valerie, Amarilla, Ernest,
Victor, Stage Manager, Louis,
Commissioner O'Brien, etc.

Act 1

At a second-rate nightclub on the south side of Chicago, a song and dance boy is auditioning for an emcee job. A bit of a song ("Chicago"), a bit of dance, plenty of side punctuated by a few cheap lies, and Joey Evans is hired. The song and dance were ok, the side was right for the job, and the lies were transparently harmless enough for club owner, Mike Spears, to know that this is a punk with little head but plenty of tongue. Besides, he knows Joey got kicked out of his last second-rate club for fiddling with an unprofitable female, so he's got him and his level pretty well taped. Gladys Bumps, the singer at the club, is up on Joey's past too, so he cuts none of that sort of cheese with her, even though some of the other girls aren't on the same line. Anyhow, he's the new man in the act, and they rehearse him into the number "You Mustn't Kick It Around."

Linda English is looking at some dogs in a pet shop window when a man alongside her pulls the old line. Old though the line may be, there's always a girl that hasn't heard it, and Linda happens to be that girl. Soon the chat about the little fellers in the window turns to other things as Joey Evans goes into his big fantasy biography. Linda is duly taken in, but the Evans line of chat doesn't have the hoped-for finish, as Linda is staying on her brother's couch, she doesn't have a car, and the meeting ends instead with a song and not with action ("I Could Write a Book").

At the club, the girls open the entertainment with a song ("Chicago") and Joey goes into his spiel. At the end of his act, he sees Linda there with a boyfriend and goes up to talk to her, but he is soon distracted. During his performance, Mrs. Vera Prentiss Simpson has arrived with a party. She has been interested by the look of the new emcee, and Joey is ordered by Mike to attend to the needs of this rich and influential patron. It is quite clear what the lady's intention is, and Joey is cocksure enough to give her no quarter. Vera is an old hand at this game, and she is quick to have her revenge on the boy who thinks he can play with her on his own terms. She walks out of the club and a furious Mike tells Joey he is sacked.

Joey makes him a wager. If Vera doesn't come back in the next couple of nights he'll go, and he'll go without pay. Mike is sceptical, but he's in a no-lose situation, so he agrees to the wager as Gladys leads on the next part of the entertainment ("That Terrific Rainbow"). While all this has been going on, no one has noticed that Linda has gone.

Vera doesn't come back and Joey gets the push. When he calls Linda, she hangs up. When he calls Vera with some brusque remarks about getting him sacked, she doesn't hang up. Maybe she didn't go back to the club, but now she's caught ("What Is a Man"). She turns up at closing time on his last night of work and catches him before he leaves. Without any illusions, and giving better than she gets, she picks Joey up and Joey bids the girls goodbye ("Happy Hunting Horn") for the meanwhile.

Vera sets Joey up with an apartment and clothes from a shop that clearly knows her well. She's "Bewitched," bothered, and bewildered by this cheap young man, but experienced enough to look at herself going through the affair knowing exactly why and what she's doing. She is still able to feel jealousy, however, and when Linda turns up on the staff of the outfitter's shop and Joey talks to her, Vera invents a tale gruesome enough to dispose of the girl for the future. Her biggest gift to Joey is a nightclub of his own. He counts himself really in the big time as he looks forward to the opening ("Pal Joey").

Act 2 All the gang from the old club have migrated to the new one. The tenor, Louis, leads in the opening number ("The Flower Garden of My Heart") of the rehearsal for opening night and the hard-boiled Miss Melba Snyder of the *Herald* comes to interview Joey for her paper. He pulls his fantasy biography on her and she shrugs it into her pad. If he wants that old line, so be it. To her, he's unexceptional; she's been through it all in the line of duty ("Zip"). The next visitor is less accommodating. Ludlow Lowell passes as an agent and he shoves some papers at Joey to sign. Joey isn't keen. He's doing all right without an agent, but some urging words from Gladys on Lowell's fame and influence catch his fancy and, without taking too much care, he signs Lowell's papers as the rehearsal continues with Gladys's number "Plant You Now, Dig You Later."

The morning after his opening, Joey is disconsolate to find that the papers have given little mention to him and spent much more space commenting on Vera's presence and clothes and the names of her party. Vera is now at the stage of needing to make the most of Joey. She knows he won't last and, right now, she needs what he can give her. At least in the tawdry little apartment she has bought him she knows she's got him to herself ("In Our Little Den").

Linda comes one day to bring a COD parcel to the club, and, while she is waiting for Mike, she overhears Lowell and Gladys plotting to blackmail Vera and her husband over Joey. She hurries home and loyally gets straight on the phone with a warning. Vera is a mite suspicious of this girl and her relationship with Joey, but Joey is always all words when he denies anything so why should he be different over her. His natural reaction is defense ("Do It the Hard Way").

But Linda is straight: She turns up at the apartment and spills out what she has overheard, dispelling Vera's suspicions with an open-eyed view of Joey with which Vera can only concur ("Take Him"). With a brisk thanks to Linda, Vera calls her friend the police commissioner. When Lowell and Gladys turn up with their demands, Joey gets indignant and is laid out cold by the phoney agent, but the blackmailers get their comeuppance when Commissioner O'Brien turns up on cue and arrests them.

Now it's time for Vera to call it a day. When things get to this stage it's always time to call it a day. Vera gently asks Joey how he is fixed. Then she calls the bank to close his check facilities and wishes him good luck. She's "Bewitched," bothered, and bewildered no more.

Joey is looking moodily in the pet shop window when Linda appears beside him. She invites him to supper at her sister's place and Joey switches on again. He can't . . . he's off to New York for this musical comedy. Perhaps if he's passing through again. . . . Linda hopes so, and she goes. He stays outside the shop looking after her as the curtain comes down.

1943

OKLAHOMA!

A MUSICAL PLAY IN TWO ACTS by Oscar Hammerstein II based on *Green Grow the Lilacs* by Lynn Riggs. Music by Richard Rodgers.

Produced at the St. James Theatre, New York, 31 March 1943, with Alfred Drake (Curly), Joan Roberts (Laurey), Celeste Holm (Annie), Lee Dixon (Will), and Joseph Buloff (Ali). Played at the Broadway Theatre, 29 May 1951 with Ridge Bond, Patricia Northrop, Jacqueline Sundt, Walter Donahue, and Jerry Mann. Produced at the Palace Theatre, 13 December 1979, with Laurence Guittard, Christine Andreas, Christine Ebersole, Harry Groener, and Bruce Adler.

A film version was issued by Magna in 1955 with Gordon MacRae, Shirley Jones, Gloria Grahame, Gene Nelson, and Eddie Albert with Charlotte Greenwood as Aunt Eller and Rod Steiger as Jud.

CHARACTERS

Aunt Eller Murphy

Curly

Laurey Williams

Will Parker

Jud Fry

Ado Annie Carnes

Ali Hakim

Gertie Cummings

Andrew Carnes

Ike Skidmore, Cord Elam, Fred, Slim, Jess, Mike, Joe, Sam, Ellen, Kate, Sylvie, Armina, Aggie, Chalmers, etc.

Curly (Alfred Drake) and Laurey (Joan Roberts) in the surrey with the fringe on top. This team photo also includes Ado Annie (Celeste Holm) and her pair of beaux, Will Parker (Lee Dixon) and Ali Hakim (Joseph Buloff). Vandamm Studios, photographers. Courtesy Performing Arts Research Center, New York Public Library at Lincoln Center.

On a fine new century's summer morning, somewhere in Indian territory, Aunt Eller Murphy is sitting in the sun, churning her butter, when a happy song ("Oh What a Beautiful Mornin'") heralds the approach of Curly, a handsome young cowhand who has come to ask Eller's niece, Laurey, to partner him to the box social at the Skidmore place that night. Laurey, who is listening anxiously behind the curtains, saunters out and plays hard to get and, when Curly describes "The Surrey with the Fringe on Top" that he'd be taking his date to the dance in, she hides her fascination behind a jibe that he must have hired such a gig. What a pity he'll have no one to ride with him in it. Curly is darned if he's going a-begging for the girl's favor and he laughs back at her that there is no fancy wagon—he just made the whole thing up. Laurey, out of countenance, goes at him with the carpet beater and flounces off.

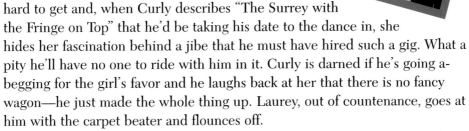

The next bit of action in the neighborhood comes when jolly Will Parker turns up, delighted at having won $50 in a steer roping contest in the big city. His sweetheart's pa promised if he ever had $50 he could have her hand, and Will is off to lay claim to Ado Annie Carnes. He's bought a naughty "little wonder" peep-show toy for Pop Carnes and is full of stories about the modern marvels to be seen in "Kansas City."

Curly is perplexed over women, and over Laurey in particular. She treats him so mean, does it signify she has her eye on someone else? Although Aunt Eller assures him that the girl is all his and just being womanly, Curly is worried, especially when he learns that the hired hand, Jud Fry, has it sweet for Laurey too. Jud is a dark, moody man whose work isn't to be denied, but he cannot be thought of as pleasant company for a young girl. In her pique at Curly over the surrey trick, Laurey impulsively promises Jud to be his partner at the social, and Curly, who really had hired the gig, is left instead to drive Aunt Eller to the dance.

Suddenly Laurey is worried. If her aunt is going to ride with Curly, she will be alone with Jud all the way to the dance. That scares her, but it scares her even more to renege on her promise and tell Jud that she will not go. She has seen the way he looks at her, and she has seen the disreputable pictures pinned up in his room in the smokehouse. Well, she has made her bed and she must lie in it, but it won't be easy.

The next visitor at the ranch house is the peddler Ali Hakim and, along with Ali Hakim, comes Ado Annie Carnes. She's a bit taken aback to hear that Will Parker is home from the city so soon, for she's dated to the peddler for the social. When Laurey tells her she must pick which of the two men she really wants as a husband, Annie just simply can't. They're both so nice and she has low defenses ("I Cain't Say No!"). It is clear that what Ali Hakim has in mind is an arrangement a little less permanent than marriage and, when Will arrives and talks to Annie in permanent-sounding terms, the peddler is mighty relieved. Only trouble is, Will has spent all his $50 prize on presents, so he doesn't have the all-important $50 any more, and it's back to square one as far as Pop Carnes and the wedding are concerned.

All the girls from down the road stop off at Aunt Eller's place to freshen up before the social, and giggling Gertie Cummings makes unabashed eyes at Curly. Laurey pretends not to care and, to her friends, she declares that she'll start all over with a new feller ("Many a New Day"). Annie is busy changing men again, too. Since Will has spent his $50 and isn't eligible, it follows logically that Ali Hakim can have her after all. The peddler tries every way he can think of to wriggle out of such a thing, but Ado Annie's father's shotgun proves a mighty persuader and he finds himself trapped ("It's a Scandal! It's an Outrage").

While the girls are getting their picnic hampers ready for the dance, Laurey and Curly come together alone, and Curly asks her awkwardly if she really intends to partner Jud to the dance when everyone expects her to come with him. Since neither is willing to be the first to give in and admit his or her real feelings, they both pretend it's better that they shouldn't be seen too regularly together. It might cause people in the neighborhood to get the wrong ideas about them ("People Will Say We're in Love"). When they have played their little scene, he goes off and she ends up in foolish tears.

Curly goes to the smokehouse to have matters out with Jud. It's a rough place and Jud Fry is a rough man. He keeps a gun to hand and pictures of naked women on his wall. Keeping his eyes off Jud's sexy postcards, Curly notices a rope and hook and the conversation turns to hanging. Curly pictures Jud hanged and dead and how his funeral would be with all those people he never knew liked him come to mourn ("Pore Jud Is Daid"). Jud is momentarily confused by the thought of being liked, but he is better at hate. Where he last worked, the whole family died in a fire after treating a hired hand badly.

Finally, the two men get to the point of Curly's visit, and each warns the other off Laurey. In an attempt to make an impression, Jud lets off his gun, and Curly returns the favor by putting a bullet clean through a knot hole in the smokehouse wall but, before things can go any further, Aunt Eller and some of the other folk rush up to see what is happening and a fight is averted.

Ali Hakim takes the opportunity to try to interest Jud in some of his more male-oriented items, but Jud shows interest only in knives. What he wants is one of those "little wonder" peep-show things that has a hidden knife in it. When a man turns it to see the girl disrobe, he gets the knife in his throat. That sort of thing is outside Ali's trade. He offers Jud postcards, but Jud is sick of pictures of women—he wants the real thing ("Lonely Room").

Laurey has made a purchase from the peddler. It is a bottle of smelling salts, which he claims are descended from the Ancient Egyptians and have the virtue of making your mind clear. Right now, that's what Laurey needs. She takes a sniff and, under the influence of the crystals, she begins to dream ("Out of My Dreams"). In a ballet, her dream takes shape: a frightening vision of a powerful Jud destroying Curly and carrying her off. When Laurey comes to her senses, the real Jud and Curly are there, in front of her. She heads for Curly but, as she passes, Jud grabs her arm. She dare not resist him and she lets herself be led away, leaving behind a hurt and puzzled Curly.

Act 2 At the Skidmore place, the farming folk and the cowhands are getting together ("The Farmer and the Cowman"). Will Parker meets up with Ali Hakim and gets real mad at the peddler for taking Ado Annie away from him. If he'd only still had the $50 that he spent, the peddler wouldn't have had a look in. Ali Hakim sees a glimmer of hope. He begins, one by one, to buy at exaggerated prices all the gifts Will brought back from Kansas. When he sees the "little wonder" he draws a line. A thing like that he certainly won't buy but, since Jud chances by, he lets Will sell the dangerous toy to Jud. Finally, Will has his $50 again!

Meanwhile the dance's box sale is going on under Aunt Eller's organization. Each man buys a lunch hamper and, in return, gets as his partner the girl who goes with it. There are just two to go. The first is Annie's. Pop Carnes forces Ali to up the bidding, but things go haywire when Will Parker leaps in to bid a whole $50. He's got the hamper but he's lost his bride, because he no longer has the money. Ali Hakim gulps and bids $51. He's saved.

Then it is time for Laurey's hamper. Jud Fry enters the bidding purposefully but, when it seems that he is going to win the auction, Curly sells off his saddle and then his horse and gun to get the cash to beat him. The auction over, Jud heads toward Curly and tries to get him to use the "little wonder," but Aunt Eller intervenes, demanding to dance, and Jud's evil plan is spoiled. Will Parker is intending to spoil a few plans too. He has his $50, he has Pop Carnes's grudging blessing, and he has the date named for the wedding, so now he intends to give Annie a bit of a lecture: She's got to quit playing the field. They're engaged, and with him its "All Er Nuthin'."

Jud has watched and maneuvered all through the dance for an opportunity to get Laurey alone but, when he finally does, his courtship is so aggressive that the girl takes fright. When he gets frustrated and loud at her repulsing him, she turns on the hired hand and, with anger replacing her fright, tells him he is fired. Quietly, he lets her go and, with an awful look, leaves her. When Curly comes to find her, she takes comfort in his arms and pours out to him the tale of Jud's scary behavior. Now, at last, Curly gets around to a few real, sincere words. All the games are forgotten as he asks Laurey to marry him and she, laying aside her foolish, light behavior, says yes.

Meanwhile, Ado Annie is saying goodbye to Ali Hakim with rather more enthusiasm than is natural in a girl who has just got engaged to another man but, when Ali has gone, her mind can't concentrate on him any more, so she goes right back to concentrating on the man who is there. For the moment, Will Parker can rest easy.

A few weeks later Curly and Laurey are married. They are starting a brand new life in a brand new state, for "Oklahoma" has just become part of the United States of America. Ali Hakim comes back on the scene again. His flirtatious ways have finally earned him a shotgun wedding and he's been tied up to the impossible Gertie Cummings. Will Parker takes his revenge with a passionate kiss for the bride and, suddenly, Ado Annie finds out what jealousy is all about.

The farmers come down to Aunt Eller's homestead that night to rouse the newlyweds from their bed, and the two young people join in the good-natured traditional knockabout until, suddenly, Jud Fry turns up. He is there for revenge and he has a knife. In spite of everything the other folk can do, he attacks Curly and, as they fight, Curly throws Jud. The villain falls on his own knife and he is killed.

A black horror falls over the wedding day. Curly does not know what to do. By rights he must give himself up to the law, even on his wedding night. But Aunt Eller has other plans. The marshal and the judge are both here among the crowd. They can have a trial right here on the porch, declare the boy "not guilty," and then the honeymoon can go on just as intended. The officials feel they ought to protest, but Aunt Eller's stern eye wins out and that is exactly what happens. Justice is done in double quick time, and the pair drive off in the surrey on another beautiful morning to start their wedded life.

1944

On The Town

A MUSICAL IN TWO ACTS by Betty Comden and Adolph Green based on the ballet *Fancy Free*. Music and additional lyrics by Leonard Bernstein.

Produced at the Adelphi Theatre, New York, 28 December 1944, with Betty Comden (Claire), Nancy Walker (Brunnhilde), Sono Osato (Ivy), Adolph Green (Ozzie), John Battles (Gabey), and Cris Alexander (Chip). Produced at the Imperial Theatre, 31 October 1971, with Phyllis Newman, Bernadette Peters, Donna McKechnie, Remak Ramsay, Ron Husmann, and Jess Richards.

A film version was produced by MGM in 1949 with Ann Miller, Betty Garrett, Vera-Ellen, Gene Kelly, Frank Sinatra, and Jules Munshin

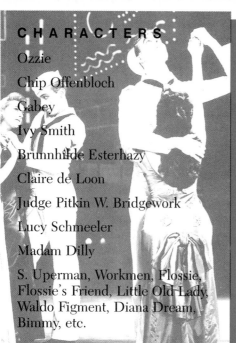

Sailors on twenty-four-hour leave
find themselves twenty-four-hour partners.
Vandamm Studios, photographers.
Courtesy Performing Arts Research Center,
New York Public Library at Lincoln Center.

Act 1

Down at the Brooklyn navy yard at six o'clock on a summery morning ("I Feel Like I'm Not Out of Bed Yet") a ship has just docked and is disgorging its complement of bell-bottomed boys on to the wharfside. Amid the dash and bustle, three wide-eyed lads stop stock still and look around. It is their first time in New York and they have just one day to experience the big city and all the things it has to offer ("New York, New York").

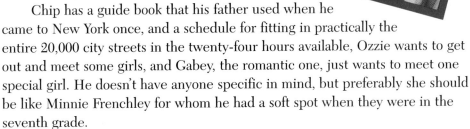

Chip has a guide book that his father used when he came to New York once, and a schedule for fitting in practically the entire 20,000 city streets in the twenty-four hours available, Ozzie wants to get out and meet some girls, and Gabey, the romantic one, just wants to meet one special girl. He doesn't have anyone specific in mind, but preferably she should be like Minnie Frenchley for whom he had a soft spot when they were in the seventh grade.

As the three friends head for the subway, Gabey's mind gets made up for him. A bill-poster is putting up a showcard announcing this month's Miss Turnstiles—a subway travelling cutie selected at random to decorate the train stations for a few weeks. The boys read the caption: Ivy Smith is studying singing and ballet at Carnegie Hall and painting at the Museum of Modern Art, she's a champion sportswoman, she's a home-loving girl who just adores nightclubs—this is one superior girl! Gabey decides there and then that Ivy is the girl he wants to spend his day in New York with. He'll go and find her. Among the 2,500,000 women in New York, he'll find her before the evening. In spite of the screams of a little old lady, Gabey pockets the showcard and the boys set off for their day on the town to howls of "vandals!"

Chip and Ozzie generously offer to give up their sight-seeing and girl-chasing respectively to help Gabey track down Miss Turnstiles. Gabey will head for Carnegie Hall, Ozzie for the Museum, and Chip will try to contact the subway people. So, while Ivy Smith is being crowned as the average New York Miss Turnstiles, and the little old lady is setting a policeman after the thieving sailors, the boys split up to pursue their quest.

Chip doesn't get far before he is taken off course. A female cab driver called Hildy Esterhazy has just been sacked and she has her cab for one more hour and one more jaunt before she has to take it back and hand it in. Hildy has decided that she's going to pick a good 'un for her last fare and Chip just fits the bill. His protests that he has to help find Ivy Smith for his pal are smothered under Hildy's vigorous attentions as she prevails on him to "Come Up to My Place" instead of sight-seeing, particularly as most of the sights in his daddy's guidebook don't exist any more.

Ozzie also goes astray. Instead of going to the Museum of Modern Art, he ends up in the Museum of Natural History in the prehistoric department alongside a complicated reconstruction of a dinosaur and a reproduction of the apeman, *homo pithecanthropus*. His amazing resemblance to this beast provokes the enthusiastic interest of the pretty student anthropologist, Claire de Loon, and soon he has her undivided intellectual attention. Claire has taken up anthropology at the advice of her fiancé, Judge Pitkin W. Bridgework, in order to concentrate her mind on intellectual things and to rid herself of her old habit of getting suddenly and violently carried away by sensuality. With a little help from Ozzie she is soon having a major relapse ("I Get Carried Away") and the two of them are leaping about the museum in a very prehistoric style until they accidentally come in contact with the dinosaur and the whole painstakingly reconstructed skeleton crumbles in a million fragments to the floor. They flee the scene of their crime with the museum staff and another policeman in their wake.

Gabey is still on course, but going slowly. The big city isn't the same as a ship. When you don't know anybody, it can be a "Lonely Town." Finally he makes it to Carnegie Hall. All sorts of activities are going on there, but Ivy Smith is actually on the premises, having a singing lesson from the tippling charlatan Madam Dilly. Ivy has been a little overdescribed in her publicity. She is actually a cooch dancer at Coney Island who longs for finer things and who, to better herself, has been taking classes for which she can ill afford to pay. She is $50 in debt to the dreadful Madam Dilly who is herself in need of the money to replenish her supply of Scotch.

Ivy is standing on her head for the good of her resonators, while Madam Dilly pops out for a fresh bottle, when Gabey walks past and recognizes her. When he asks her for a date she at first plays hoity-toity but she is dying to say "yes," and she quickly drops her act and agrees to meet him that evening in Times Square. The date is no sooner made than Madam Dilly sweeps back in and sweeps the sailor out of her salon. Sex and singing don't mix—her own failure to make stardom is the living proof ("Do-do-re-do")—and Ivy needs success so that she can pay Madam Dilly her $50.

Claire and Ozzie make it safely back to Claire's luxurious apartment and are busy letting themselves go when who should walk in from the kitchen but Pitkin W. Bridgework with champagne for two to celebrate his engagement to Claire. Bridgework is an unflappably nice guy, and he charmingly splits the bubbly three ways and insists that Ozzie remain to look after Claire while he goes off to a meeting. He and his fiancée can go out to Diamond Eddie's later for their celebration.

While this enthusiastic pair carry on letting themselves go, Hildy and Chip have arrived at Hildy's scruffy apartment where Hildy is anxious to show off her best feature to her young man ("I Can Cook Too"). It is almost impossible for her to show off her other features because her flat-mate, drippy Lucy Schmeeler, has a cold and has stayed home from work. A quick private word in the bedroom and Lucy, cold or no cold, announces that she is going to an air-conditioned movie.

Gabey waits for Ivy at the appointed time and place ("Lucky"), but she doesn't arrive. On the way to her date she runs into Madam Dilly who is furious to think Ivy is giving up a night's wages to meet a sailor and who threatens legal action over her $50 if Ivy doesn't get herself over to Coney Island real quick. So Gabey is stood up. His friends try to fool him by dressing their respective girls as Ivy, but they don't know that Gabey has actually found the real Ivy and lost her, and the charade falls flat. So here they are on their big night in the big city, all ready to go on the town, but there are only five of them instead of six (Times Square Ballet). It will have to do, until they can be joined by Lucy Schmeeler who has been elected, *faute de mieux*, as a replacement date for Gabey.

Act 2   The first place the gang hits is Diamond Eddie's ("So Long"), but in spite of strenuous efforts they can't get a happy atmosphere going, particularly when the club singer insists on drowning them all in pitying ballads ("I'm Blue"). Lucy Schmeeler mistakes the meeting place and ends up going to another Diamond Eddie's in Yonkers, but the friends do meet up with Pitkin who has come to the club for his cozy evening with Claire. He arrives just in time to pay the bill as the fivesome are rushing off to try the Congacabana.

The Congacabana isn't much better than Diamond Eddie's. The singer there has the same song and Hildy boots her off the stand to give a more positive sort of number ("You Got Me") to try and get the evening going. But the Congacabana gets the thumbs down too and, as Pitkin has just arrived, he is deputized to pay the bill and wait for Lucy while the others rush off to the Slam-Bang.

At the Slam-Bang, fortune smiles at last on their enterprise. Who should be sitting in a corner wallowing in whisky but Madam Dilly and she is able to tell Gabey where Ivy is. Without thinking of the time he has to be back at the ship, Gabey heads for the subway and Coney Island with his four chums following closely in his tracks. Pitkin has a sweet nature; all his life he's turned the other cheek ("I Understand"), but it's getting distinctly pink now as he and Lucy, who is also rather *de trop* in this adventure, are left behind once again.

On the subway, Gabey dozes off and dreams of what he imagines the rich people's playground of Coney Island is like (Playground of the Rich/Coney Island Ballet), picturing himself as the Great Lover being tamed by the glamorous Ivy. On the train behind, the other four are wide awake and regretting that the twenty-four hours are going so fast ("Oh, Well"). When Gabey arrives at Coney Island, he finds it to be a pleasure palace of a rather more gaudy and commonplace kind than the one in his dreams, and he finds Ivy doing bumps and grinds outside a fair booth. Poor Ivy explains about Madam Dilly and the $50 and how she wanted so much to go out with him but didn't dare.

Then, all of a sudden, the whole day comes together. The friends are no sooner all six together than the little old lady from the morning subway, the museum curator, Hildy's boss, and their several policemen all turn up. They are cornered, and sweet-natured Pitkin, the judge, who has decided at last to give up being the eternal nice guy, won't help them out of their fix. They are all under arrest.

Next morning the three boys are escorted back to their ship by a policeman. It's time to go but, as they get ready to climb the gangplank, their girls rush up for a loving goodbye. It was a helluva day. Now the six o'clock whistle blows and, as our friends part, three young sailors, wide-eyed and fresh to the big city, come on to the wharf. They are ready to spend their day's shore leave in the big city in the best style possible. As Chip, Ozzie, and Gabey proved, anything can happen in "New York, New York."

1945

Carousel

A MUSICAL PLAY IN TWO ACTS by Oscar Hammerstein II based on *Liliom* by
Ferenc Molnár. Music by Richard Rodgers.

Produced at the Majestic Theatre, New York, 19 April 1945, with John Raitt
(Billy) and Jan Clayton (Julie). Produced at the Vivian Beaumont Theatre, 24 March
1994, with Michael Hayden and Sally Murphy.

A film version was produced by Twentieth Century-Fox in 1956 with Gordon MacRae
and Shirley Jones.

CHARACTERS

Julie Jordan

Carrie Pipperidge

Billy Bigelow

Mrs. Mullin

Enoch Snow

Jigger Craigin

Nettie Fowler

Heavenly Friend

Starkeeper

David Bascombe

Louise

Dr. Seldon, Bessie, Policeman, Hannah, Arminy, Jennie, Virginia, Penny, etc.

Billy Bigelow (John Raitt) pays the price for trying cheat on life. Jan Clayton is Julie Jordan. Vandamm Studios, photographers. Courtesy Performing Arts Research Center, New York Public Library at Lincoln Center.

Act 1   The opening scene is an amusement park on the coast of New England around the year 1873. A feature of the park is Mrs. Mullin's carousel with its gaily painted horses and its jack-the-lad barker, Billy Bigelow. Mrs. Mullin likes Billy and she likes the amount of feminine business he brings to the carousel, but she is clearly jealous of the girls whom he picks out for his special attentions. She gets sourly steamed up when he pays a little notice to a mill girl called Julie Jordan and she vehemently warns the surprised Julie away from the carousel.

Her timing is bad, for Billy himself catches the end of the warning. He turns on his employer and tells her that she has no control over what girls he sees and, when the quarrel raises itself a tone, Mrs. Mullin, not for the first time, sacks the barker. Julie and her friend Carrie are aghast at the scene, and even more worried when it turns out that Billy probably doesn't have the price of a beer to his name, but the man shrugs off such worries. He's going to get his things and then one of them can go and have a drink with him. He doesn't mind which.

Carrie is open-mouthed with amazement at Billy, and the girls are quite fazed at the fact that he is paying attention to them. The quiet, introspective Julie has never had a boyfriend ("You're a Queer One, Julie Jordan") and Carrie's experience of men is in a very different field. She's going to marry the respectable and reliable fisherman, "Mister Snow." When Billy returns and asks which one of them is going to spend the evening with him, Julie volunteers without hesitation. She faces dismissal from the mill for doing so, for Mr. Bascombe, the mill owner, insists that his girls are in their dormitory on time. When the two of them are seen together by Bascombe and a policeman, her fate is settled. She is as much out of a job as Billy is.

Although she is warned of Billy's reputation as a layabout, a sponger, and a ladies' man, Julie has no qualms about passing the evening with him. She's a strange one—nothing like any of the women Billy has known before. She says she isn't ever going to marry and then, when he asks her, teasing, if she would marry him, the layabout and sponger, Julie has only one simple response—"If I Loved You." At the end of the evening they kiss, and the kiss is not the usual kiss Billy gets from his women.

When they are married, Julie and Billy move in with Julie's cousin Nettie Fowler who runs a snack bar on the beach. Billy is unable to get a job, and he becomes more and more sombre and difficult as the workless days go by. He takes his frustration out on Julie and, one day, a one-sided row ends with his hitting her. Immediately the tale goes around town that Bigelow beats his wife. But if things are not as happy as they should be with the Bigelows, the rest of the folk are lively enough. "June Is Bustin' Out All Over" and there is to be a big clambake on the beach. As for Carrie, she is still awaiting her wedding day and she and Enoch Snow pass the time in dreaming of their future together in the rosiest way ("When the Children Are Asleep").

Billy has taken to hanging around with a known evildoer called Jigger Craigin, and Jigger is heading him for trouble ("Blow High, Blow Low"). He has a plan to rob the mill owner of the payroll he brings each week to the captain of Jigger's ship—three thousand dollars. Billy would never have to worry about a job again. He is tempted, but when Mrs. Mullin comes to try and woo him back to her employ and the carousel he realizes that his old life is better and safer than crime. Only there's a catch: Mrs. Mullin insists that he leave Julie. What's the use to her of a barker whom all the girls chase and who goes home to his wife? He'd better talk to Julie and see whom she puts first.

When Billy goes to talk to Julie, however, she has something very different to tell him. She's going to have a baby. For Billy, that changes everything. Life has a future (Soliloquy). Now he has to make something of himself, he has to make money. There is no other way he knows of to do it. He will have to take part in Jigger's plan.

Act 2   At the clambake ("A Real Nice Clambake"), Jigger tricks Carrie into close quarters with him and causes trouble between her and Enoch who tightly rejects her after finding her innocently flung over Jigger's shoulder ("Geraniums in the Winder"/"Stonecutters Cut It on Stone"). The girls all moan about the problems they have with their men, but to Julie it is all quite simple—if you love your man, that's really all there is to it ("What's the Use of Wond'rin'"). When it is time for the treasure hunt, Julie tries to stop Billy going off as Jigger's partner and, when she feels the knife hidden in his shirt, she pleads with him desperately, but Billy pushes her aside and goes all the same.

Down on the waterfront, Jigger and Billy play at cards, waiting for Bascombe to turn up. When he does, Billy distracts him by asking for the time while Jigger attacks with a knife, but Bascombe is armed with a gun and he is too strong for Jigger. Jigger gets away, but Bascombe covers Billy with his gun as the police hurry to the scene. The thought of a life in jail is too much for Billy and, before he can be taken, he turns his knife on himself. When Julie rushes to take her dying husband in her arms, he holds her hand tightly and tries to explain about what he had hoped for them.

Only when he is dead, and Mrs. Mullin has passed by to say a wordless farewell to her boy, can Julie say to Billy what she never had the chance to say to him while he was living: She loves him, and now she is quite, quite lost. But she has to keep on living; she has to believe in the old maxims she learned as a child and keep them before her as she lives out the rest of what will be a lonely and loveless life ("You'll Never Walk Alone").

Now it is time for Billy Bigelow to go before his maker ("The Highest Judge of All") or, rather, the Starkeeper of the heavens. Before he can pass through even the back gate of heaven, he's got to add some better deeds to those of his worthless life. He has one chance: The rules of heaven allow him to return to earth for one day to try to right some of his wrongs.

By the quirks of heavenly time, it is now fifteen years later in New England and Julie's child, Louise, is a grown girl. She is not a happy child, for she suffers from the stigma of Billy's deed just as he suffered, in his youth, from the misdeeds of his own father. Even Carrie's son, Enoch Jr. (one of the nine she has borne to Mr. Snow), who has a tenderness for Louise, wounds her with careless references to their respective places in life.

Billy takes up the Starkeeper's offer and goes down to earth to face Louise. He tells her some of the kindlier things about her father—how he made people laugh, how handsome he was—but when he tries to get close to her, and makes her a gift of a star he has brought with him from heaven, the girl becomes suspicious. In frustration at his failure to make her understand him and his gift, Billy hits out at her just as, in life, he hit out at Julie when his frustration couldn't be released any other way. Frightened at his forcefulness, Louise runs to her mother, but Billy does not have the courage to allow himself to be seen by his wife. He can only speak aloud of his love for her knowing that she cannot hear. Julie picks up the star he has left and holds it close to her heart. She does not need to be told.

At Louise's graduation, Billy stands unseen and listening as the kindly, wise speaker of the occasion speaks of fortitude and compassion and right ("You'll Never Walk Alone"). Billy can only will Louise to believe in what the man says . . . and is it a coincidence that the speaker bears a strange resemblance to the Starkeeper?

1946

Annie get your gun

A MUSICAL COMEDY IN TWO ACTS by Herbert and Dorothy Fields. Music by Irving Berlin.

Produced at the Imperial Theatre, New York, 16 May 1946, with Ethel Merman (Annie) and Ray Middleton (Frank). A revised version was produced at the New York State Theatre, 31 May 1966, and played at the Broadway Theatre, 21 December 1966, with Merman and Bruce Yarnell.

A film version was produced by MGM in 1950 with Betty Hutton and Howard Keel.

Who says you can't get a man with a gun?
Annie (Ethel Merman) did.
You just have to know what to do with the gun.
Vandamm Studios, photographers.
Courtesy Performing Arts Research Center,
New York Public Library at Lincoln Center.

CHARACTERS

Annie Oakley

Dolly Tate

Winnie Tate

Frank Butler

Charlie Davenport

Colonel William F. Cody,
"Buffalo Bill"

Chief Sitting Bull

Foster Wilson,
proprietor of the Wilson House

Mac, *the property man*

Major Gordon Lillie,
"Pawnee Bill"

Tommy Keeler

The Wild Horse Ceremonial
Dancer

Little Jake, Nellie, Minnie,
Annie's brother and sisters

Sylvia Potter-Porter, Trainman,
Waiter, Porter,
Mr. and Mrs. Schuyler Adams,
Riding Mistress, etc.

Act 1   Buffalo Bill's Wild West Show is about to hit Cincinnati, Ohio, for a four-day season ("Buffalo Bill"). Charlie Davenport, the show's advance manager, has come along to the Wilson House, a hotel on the outskirts of town, to drum up interest by issuing a challenge to the locals to face the show's sharpshooting Frank Butler, a suave gentleman whose attraction for the girls is evident ("I'm a Bad, Bad Man"). Neither Butler nor the ladies of the show, buxom Dolly Tate and her pretty daughter Winnie, can woo permission from the experienced hotel proprietor to host their contest, and the show people prepare to go on their way to more hospitable places. Dolly has just sat down to catch her breath, before plodding on, when the bird that decorates her hat is severed by a shot and, as she watches, horrified, a young woman strides on to claim her prey.

The markswoman is Annie Oakley, and she has come with her little brother and sisters to sell her game to the hotel. Mr. Wilson can't help being interested. The birds have all been expertly shot with one hole through the head, with no pellets in them for the guests to break their teeth on. Annie has no idea what to charge for her wares. She doesn't have too many ideas about anything except shooting. She can't count up to two dozen or make out a bill—where she comes from, folks are used to "Doin' What Comes Natur'lly," and they haven't the need for all that palaver.

Mr. Wilson is intrigued when he hears Annie's off-hand stories of her prowess with a rifle, and he gets a practical demonstration when she casually slices the head off the cockerel on his hotel sign. Perhaps he has got someone to challenge that fool Wild West feller who wanted to bet him a hundred dollars against bed and lodgings for his whole troupe. Annie is always happy to take up a sharpshooting challenge and she agrees without hesitation to be Wilson's champion.

The next person Annie meets is Frank Butler and, without knowing who he is, she tells him confidently about the challenge she has accepted. She also falls for him mightily. But Frank has dimples and dimity ideas about "The Girl That I Marry," and Annie is left to rue the fact that she apparently has only one talent and "You Can't Get a Man With a Gun." When she gets to the contest, which has drawn a fine crowd, she is startled to see who her opponent is to be but, at the end of a long drawn-out contest full of fancy shooting, it is Frank who first misses the target and Annie who is acclaimed the winner.

Charlie Davenport is quick to see the potential usefulness of this feminine crackshot and he tackles Frank about taking a partner. The act could do with a fillip. Frank won't hear of it but, when Annie begs to come along just as his assistant, he thinks again and, as Charlie, Frank, and Buffalo Bill celebrate the fact that "There's No Business Like Show Business," Annie Oakley becomes a member of the Wild West Show.

With Annie around, the Wild West company has to get used to a lot of crazy behavior, but only Dolly Tate, who has been displaced as Frank's assistant, seems to come out the worse for it. Annie does her little bit in the show successfully, but her most important thoughts are centered on trying to become one of those pink-and-white type girls whom Frank has said he admires. Frank has been keeping an eye on Annie, but from a professional point of view only. He knows that she is good and that she should be allowed to do more in the act and, when it seems that they will have to share an audience with Pawnee Bill's show in Minneapolis, he realizes that the show could use Annie as a novelty attraction to pull business away from the competition. Perhaps she could have just one or two secondary tricks to perform. She's not really a challenge to him, this funny little creature, this gun-toting girl who doesn't act like a proper girl. Has she ever been in love? She hasn't—not mutually—but she's heard about it and she lives in hope ("They Say That Falling in Love Is Wonderful").

Annie is working up a special trick to surprise Frank with and Buffalo Bill asks her to perform it in Minneapolis. Charlie assures her that Frank will be thrilled, so Annie happily agrees. Davenport goes to work to stir up some challenging publicity and, as the train rattles toward Minneapolis, Annie, with no thought in her head of the debut to come, cheerfully puts her little brother and sisters to bed with a "Moonshine Lullaby."

When they get to their destination, Annie's first act has nothing to do with her big performance. She heads off to the pawnshop with Dolly Tate's gold watch, adeptly purloined, to hock it for enough money to buy a ring for Winnie and her boyfriend Tommy. The idea is that the loving young pair should get through the wedding, take back the ring, and retrieve the watch all before the disapproving Mrs. Tate has had time to notice it's missing. Then they can live happily ever after ("I'll Share It All With You"), and no one will be any the wiser.

Meanwhile, Charlie has blazed Annie's name and picture across the outside of the tent, and the novelty seems to be attracting a crowd. This doesn't please Frank and he demands that for the next town the old billing be retained. It does nothing for Pawnee Bill either, and he retaliates by producing Big Chief Sitting Bull, the victor of Little Big Horn, as his guest of honor for the night, thus pulling back half the queue that had been lining up for Buffalo Bill's show. Sitting Bull has come into some money because the wretched oil that has been ruining his farmlands has become saleable, and Charlie Davenport sees in him a possible source of backing, but the Chief has three rules in life: no red meat, no get feet wet, and *no put money in show business*.

Annie is properly taken aback to see her new billing, but she happily agrees to forego it when Frank explains that it isn't right. She makes him promise to watch her perform that afternoon and he gives her a kiss for luck, which leaves her poleaxed and him declaring that, in spite of all his experiences with the ladies, this time he's been caught on one foot ("My Defenses Are

Down"). He's been caught more ways than that. When Annie performs the special new trick she'd been saving, trusting in Charlie's word that Frank will love it, he is livid at being upstaged. Fuelled by Dolly Tate's accusations, he sees the exhibition as a plot by Annie to take his star place in the show, and his feelings for her are swallowed up by anger and jealousy.

Annie is desperate at his reaction but, if Frank doesn't want to know her, Sitting Bull does. The Chief is fascinated by "little sure shot" and he declares he will adopt her into the Sioux tribe as his daughter ("I'm an Indian Too"). Her joyful initiation as an Indian is spoiled when a note comes from Frank. He is leaving Buffalo Bill to take employment with Pawnee Bill, doing his old act with Dolly Tate. Annie may be the best shot in the whole world but it's the same old story, "You Can't Get a Man with a Gun."

Act 2

On a cattle boat heading for New York harbor sit a down-on-their-luck little group comprising Buffalo Bill, Charlie Davenport, Chief Sitting Bull, and Annie Oakley. They are returning from a triumphant European tour during which they were fêted and adored and which has lost them every cent of their capital. Every cent of Sitting Bull's capital, that is, for the charms of Annie Oakley tempted him to break his third big "never" and he has lost all the money eased out of the U.S. Government on this theatrical speculation. They have their press cuttings, and Annie has a chestful of medals pressed upon her by the admiring crowned heads of Europe, and that's it.

Buffalo Bill is even less cheerful when he hears that Pawnee Bill's show, featuring Frank Butler, is playing nightly at no less a venue than the Madison Square Garden, and Annie is no more happy to hear that Frank is the season's darling of the society ladies. But Sitting Bull has an idea. Pawnee Bill may have the cash, but they have the acts. How about a merger? Annie thinks that's a right good idea, as long as she and Frank get to merge as well ("I Got Lost in His Arms").

Pawnee Bill seems disposed to be friendly. In fact he arranges a swell reception at the plush Hotel Brevoort to welcome the famous Buffalo Bill team back to New York. Tommy, who toured with Buffalo Bill, and Winnie, who stayed with her mother and Pawnee Bill, meet up again and renew their vows of love ("Who Do You Love, I Hope"), and Dolly doesn't even interrupt. The reason soon becomes clear. Pawnee Bill's bookkeeping isn't any better than his old rival's. They may be playing to good business at the Garden, but someone has done his sums poorly and Pawnee Bill's show is only surviving on "investments" from the society ladies he and Frank have been courting. They think that Buffalo Bill has money and they, too, are out to effect a tactful merger.

In the meanwhile, Annie is getting an eyeful of New York society and she isn't too keen on what she sees. So this is what Frank has been seen out with. Her prospects of getting back on the same team as her man seem to have taken a knock when Dolly Tate finds out the truth. If both sides are as poor as each other, what's the use of a merger between two dead ducks? The only asset anyone has is the chestful of golden, bejewelled medals Annie has brought back with her. When Annie realizes that only the proceeds from the sale of her trophies will allow the merger with Frank to go ahead, she promises she will sell them. After all, what does she want with jewels? ("Sun in the Morning"). But first she wants Frank to see her wearing them.

Frank and Annie finally meet up again and they are soon in each other's arms happily reprising "They Say That Falling in Love Is Wonderful." Frank offers Annie his three gold medals as a gift but, when she opens her coat to display the gifts of royal Europe, he is crushed all over again. Within no time they are arguing about who is the better shot, the merger is off, and a challenge match is on. All her trophies, representing everything she owns, Annie will gamble against Frank's three medals.

The shoot-out is arranged to take place on Governor's Island the next morning, and Dolly Tate arrives there early, planning to sabotage Annie's guns. She is caught in the act by Sitting Bull and Charlie and stopped, but then Sitting Bull has a thought. If Annie wins the match she will lose Frank, but if she loses the match . . . The two men end up merrily completing the very act of sabotage they had prevented Dolly from committing.

The two competitors face up to each other ("Anything You Can Do"), the shooting begins and, to her amazement and horror, Annie misses the first targets. Frank steams ahead on the score line and, as he heads for a win, all his warmth toward Annie returns. When she changes guns, succeeds in scoring again, and becomes her old cocksure self, his manner changes too. Sitting Bull has to interfere. Annie always said that she couldn't get a man with a gun, but he has news for her: Here is a gun she can get a man with. He hands her the sabotaged rifle.

Finally the message sinks into Annie's brain. She happily carries right on missing the targets until she ends the competition a joyful loser. She hands over her medals but Frank doesn't want to take them and, when she insists, he in turn hands them on to the two Bills. They will be the foundation of the new Wild West Show, starring Mr. and Mrs. Frank Butler—the best sharpshooting team in the world.

The song "An Old-Fashioned Wedding" was written by Berlin for the 1966 revival in which the roles of Winnie Tate and Tommy and their two duets were eliminated.

1947

BRIGADOON

A MUSICAL PLAY IN TWO ACTS by Alan Jay Lerner. Music by Frederick Loewe.

Produced at the Ziegfeld Theatre, New York, 13 March 1947, with David Brooks (Tommy), Marion Bell (Fiona), George Keane (Jeff), and Pamela Britton (Meg). Produced at the Majestic Theatre, 16 October 1980, with Martin Vidnovic, Meg Bussert, Mark Zimmermann, and Elaine Jausman.

A film version was produced by MGM in 1954 with Gene Kelly, Cyd Charisse (singing dubbed by Carole Richards), Elaine Stewart, and Van Johnson.

Jeff Douglass (George Keane) and
Tommy Albright (David Brooks) at
the bridge dividing the vanishing village
of Brigadoon from the real world.
Vandamm Studios, photographers.
Courtesy Performing Arts Research Center,
New York Public Library at Lincoln Center.

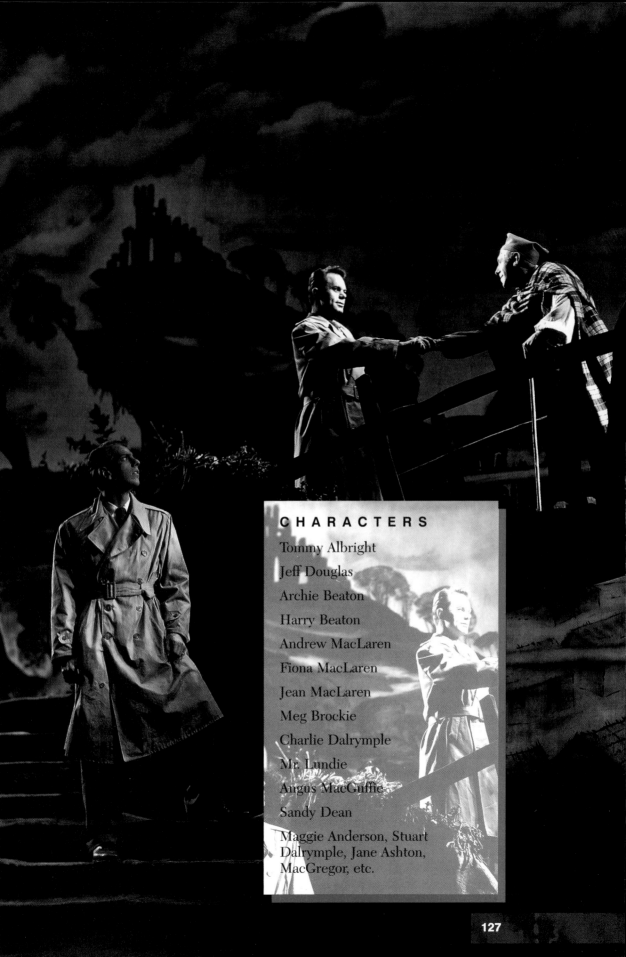

CHARACTERS

Tommy Albright

Jeff Douglas

Archie Beaton

Harry Beaton

Andrew MacLaren

Fiona MacLaren

Jean MacLaren

Meg Brockie

Charlie Dalrymple

Mr. Lundie

Angus MacGuffie

Sandy Dean

Maggie Anderson, Stuart
Dalrymple, Jane Ashton,
MacGregor, etc.

Act 1

In the highlands of Scotland ("Once in the Highlands") two American holidaymakers, out on a hunting trip, have become benighted. Practical, wisecracking Jeff and the more thoughtful and romantic Tommy take rather disparate attitudes to their predicament, but they are both equally taken aback when, to the sound of singing voices ("Brigadoon"), they see in front of them a distant village, shrouded in mist, where there was surely no village before.

In the little village of Brigadoon it is market day "Down in MacConnachy Square" and the townspeople are out in force, to sell—like Archie Beaton who runs the plaid stall with little help from his sullen son Harry, Angus MacGuffie with his farm goods, and lively little Meg Brockie with her cream pails—or to buy, like the MacLaren family, father Andrew and his two daughters, bright and lovely Fiona and pretty, quiet Jean.

Today is Jean's wedding day. She is to be wed to young Charlie Dalrymple this very evening and herein lies the cause of Harry Beaton's clouded brow. He, too, is in love with Jean MacLaren. Meg Brockie, who would marry the first man who asked her, cannot understand that Fiona is content to see her younger sister wed afore her, but Fiona smilingly explains that she is "Waitin' for My Dearie." Until she finds the man of her heart, she is happy to bide her time.

When Tommy and Jeff make their way into Brigadoon, they are surprised to see the quaint native costume sported by the villagers, and flabbergasted to have their money refused at the stalls as unknown coinage, but they are delighted with the attentions paid by the fair villagers. Fiona takes charge of Tommy and Meg Brockie enthusiastically volunteers to look after Jeff. For Charlie Dalrymple, however, today is the end of his keeping company with girls. This evening will be his wedding ("I'll Go Home with Bonnie Jean"), and this afternoon he goes to the MacLaren house to enter his signature in the family bible in the traditional way.

Tommy is bemused by Brigadoon. The people have a strangeness about them and there are odd overheard phrases that he does not understand, particularly references to a "miracle" and "the man who postponed the miracle." But he is entranced by Fiona and, when she goes to gather flowers for the wedding, he accompanies her amongst "The Heather on the Hill."

Jeff, in the meanwhile, has been led off by Meg to a little cottage on the hillside. The cottage is a primitive shack, with little in the way of furniture but a cot and a rocking chair, and Meg has a tale to tell. Her mother was a gypsy who chanced one day on this cottage and found a bonny lad asleep in the cot. So she sat down on the rocking chair and waited, and not long afterwards Meg was born. The weary Jeff is soon relaxing on the cot as Meg entertains him with the tale of "The Love of My Life" in which each verse refers to a different unfortunate affair. When she has finished, Jeff is asleep. With a little smile, Meg sits down in the rocking chair and waits.

At the MacLaren house "Jeannie's Packin' Up" when Harry Beaton comes to deliver Mr. MacLaren's wedding waistcoat and bitterly declares his disillusioned hatred for Brigadoon and everything in it. All the old man's persuasion that Brigadoon is, to the contrary, a blessed town, cannot shake the black-browed boy. Charlie has signed the bible and, although he should not see Jean on their wedding day, he sings to her from under her window begging her to "Come to Me, Bend to Me."

Fiona and Tommy return with their arms full of heather and Jeff reappears in a buoyant mood and sporting a new pair of trousers. The old ones, apparently, suffered from rather rough treatment from the thistles in Meg's cottage. Tommy, too, has a light heart ("It's Almost Like Being in Love"): Brigadoon is almost too good to be true. Then he discovers that, in fact, it is not true. He spies the open bible in which Charlie has just entered his name and notices the date of the wedding: 24 May 1746. Fiona will not give an explanation. All she can do is take Tommy and Jeff to meet Mr. Lundie, the schoolmaster, and the wise man of the village.

Mr. Lundie tells them the tale of Brigadoon. In 1746 the happy little village was direly threatened by a band of marauding devil-worshippers and magicians. The minister, Mr. Forsythe, pondered a way in which Brigadoon could be protected from these forces of evil and, finally, he prayed to God that Brigadoon might simply vanish away out of the path of the sorcerers. His prayer was granted. The village would disappear from the face of the earth, but not forever. One day each hundred years, a hundred years that would pass like a single night in the lives of its people, Brigadoon would reappear in its old place.

So God took Mr. Forsythe to Himself and, in return, granted him his prayer for Brigadoon, but the miracle was delayed for two days to allow Charlie Dalrymple, who was away from home, to return for his wedding. Now, in Brigadoon, it is only two days since the miracle, even though two hundred years have passed in the outside world, and when night falls the village and all in it will go to sleep for another hundred years.

The bells of the kirk begin to ring, announcing the call to Jean and Charlie's wedding, and the village gathers to celebrate their marriage. The ceremony over, the newlyweds begin the wedding dance. Harry Beaton performs a sword dance and then calls Jean to dance with him but, as she does, Harry suddenly stops the dance and kisses her before the amazed company. As Charlie leaps forward to challenge him, Harry draws a dirk. Tommy intervenes to stop the fight, and Harry, full of hatred, takes the ultimate revenge. It is part of Mr. Forsythe's miracle that no one shall ever leave the village. Should they do so, Brigadoon will be condemned to vanish forever. Harry springs away—he is leaving Brigadoon and they are all damned!

Act 2

Among the trees near the edge of Brigadoon, the men of the village are hunting the fugitive ("The Chase") but, as Harry flees towards the borders of Brigadoon, wildly trying to escape the pursuing Jeff, he falls and, plunging from a rocky cliff, he is killed instantly.

Tommy returns to the anxious Fiona and they confess their love for each other ("There But For You Go I") and Tommy wonders if he might be allowed to stay in Brigadoon. But, while the wedding festivities take up where they had left off and Meg Brockie gives out with the story of "My Mother's Wedding Day," Jeff is getting more and more troubled. He blames himself for Harry Beaton's death and is horrified at the thought that Tommy might be bewitched into staying in this unreal dream town. He urges his friend to come away immediately. If once he stays here too long, he will be bound to remain for endless centuries.

When Fiona brings Mr. Lundie to hear Tommy's petition to stay in Brigadoon, she finds that Jeff has shaken not his love but his will. He must, after all, leave before nightfall when the village passes back once more out of the real world. Tommy takes a loving farewell of Fiona ("From This Day On"), and she tells him that she will not be lonely, lost in the mists of time. It is not real loneliness to love in vain, only not to love at all. As the strains of "Brigadoon" announce the end of the day and the mists descend again over the village, Tommy and Jeff take their leave of Brigadoon.

Back in America, Tommy finds it impossible to take up his old life where he had left off. A dozen times a day a word or a phrase catches an echo of Brigadoon and in his mind he sees and hears the place and its people and, above all, Fiona. He calls off his planned wedding to the chic, modern Jane Ashton and, in a rush of realization, books a ticket back to Scotland. Brigadoon may have gone, but he has to return.

Back in the forest where they first blundered into Brigadoon, Tommy and Jeff look at the empty ground where the village stood. Then the music begins again, the song of "Brigadoon." No village appears, but there is Mr. Lundie, a pale figure from beyond the world. The love Tommy bears for Fiona has entered into the miracle and, by its great power, it has awoken Mr. Lundie from his hundred years' sleep. He has come to get Tommy and take him back to Brigadoon and to Fiona. As Jeff watches silently, Tommy falls in alongside Mr. Lundie and the two of them vanish into the highland mist, leaving Jeff alone in the forest.

1947

Kiss me, Kate

A MUSICAL COMEDY IN TWO ACTS by Samuel and Bella Spewack based partly on Shakespeare's *The Taming of the Shrew*. Lyrics and music by Cole Porter.

Produced at the New Century Theatre, New York, 30 December 1947, with Alfred Drake (Fred), Patricia Morison (Lilli), Harold Lang (Bill), and Lisa Kirk (Lois).

A film version was produced by MGM in 1953 with Howard Keel, Kathryn Grayson, Tommy Rall, and Ann Miller.

A helpless Lilli (Patricia Morison) goes boilingly through her role as a singing shrew, with the "encouragement" of a pair of clodhopping hoods (Harry Clark and Jack Diamond).
Courtesy Harry Ransom Research Center, The University of Texas at Austin.

CHARACTERS

Fred Graham (Petruchio)

Harry Trevor (Baptista)

Lois Lane (Bianca)

Lilli Vanessi (Katharine)

Bill Calhoun (Lucentio)

Hattie, *Lilli's maid*

Ralph, *the stage manager*

Harrison Howell

First Gangster

Second Gangster

"Gremio"

"Hortensio"

Paul

Stage Doorman, etc.

Act 1

At Ford's Theatre in Baltimore, a new musical show has just finished its last run through before being presented to the public. The piece is a version of Shakespeare's *The Taming of the Shrew*, improved and musicalized by a half-dozen American writers and composers and starring the popular actor Fred Graham opposite his ex-wife, the movie star Lilli Vanessi. Fred is giving last-minute instructions to the cast, and most particularly to the vivacious Miss Lois Lane, a cabaret performer who is cast in the show as a pert and definitely un-Shakespearian Bianca. He gives rather less attention to his costar, whose seething annoyance at what she sees as a calculated insult bursts out in a round expletive in front of the company. Miss Vanessi stalks off to her dressing room in a huff, leaving her maid Hattie to lead the company in hailing "Another Op'nin', Another Show."

As soon as she is free from the stage, Lois hurries off in search of Bill Calhoun, her old cabaret partner. He has been cast in the show too, as Lucentio, but his behavior up till now has been less than professional. His latest misdeed has been to miss the rehearsal of the curtain calls, and Lois is desperate in case he should mess up their big chance for a career in the legitimate theatre by his offhand attitude ("Why Can't You Behave?"). The free and easy Bill is a gambler in more ways than one. Instead of rehearsing, he has been involved in a card game where, after a bad run, he has ended up signing an IOU for $10,000. Needless to say the penniless dancer was too fly to sign his own name to the chit. He used the name Fred Graham.

It is opening night. In her dressing room, Lilli is on the phone to her fiancé, the wealthy politician Harrison Howell, who has been persuaded for love of her to back the show to the extent of $200,000. From his dressing room next door, Fred harangues her and she answers back with equal force, but recriminations lead to reminiscences and the atmosphere softens as they remember their early days together in third-rate touring operetta companies ("Wunderbar").

As Fred makes his preparations for the show, he is surprised to be interrupted by the intrusion of two rather forceful gentlemen who say that they have called about an IOU. His perplexed denials do him no good, and the gangsters promise meaningfully to return before the night is out. Then they hope to find him in a more remembering frame of mind. While Fred is puzzling over this incident, Lilli has received a lovely bouquet. It is from Fred, a replica of the flowers from her wedding bouquet, and she admits to herself that, beneath the angriness of their relationship and their divorce, she is still in love with him ("So in Love"). She calls through the wall, thanking him happily, but Fred is less than thrilled. The flowers had been intended for Lois.

Now the curtain rises on *The Taming of the Shrew* ("We Open in Venice") and the principal characters begin the play. Lois, as Bianca, is serenaded by her suitors Lucentio, Gremio, and Hortensio ("Tom, Dick or Harry") before Fred, as the virile Petruchio, introduces himself ("I've Come to Wive it Wealthily in Padua") and pledges himself to wed the shrewish heiress, Katharine, as played by Lilli ("I Hate Men"). He woos her rudely ("Were Thine That Special Face"), but suddenly the play takes on a new depth. Between scenes, Lilli has discovered the card attached to the flowers and she is glittering with rage and hurt pride. The scene between Petruchio and Katharine bristles with violence as Lilli takes every opportunity to assault Fred physically, and it ends with the exasperated Fred putting her across his knee, in accordance with the script, and spanking her for all he is worth.

At the interval, the furious Lilli lets all her anger loose on Fred. She calls Harrison to say she is quitting the show on the spot and wants him to marry her that night. Fred threatens that she'll be blacklisted from the stage forever, but he can see in her eyes that old look, so familiar from their married days, and he knows that she means what she says. In the midst of this crisis, the two gangsters turn up to find out how his memory is going. The last thing he needs at this moment is to have to cope with these two goons and their crazy story about a $10,000 debt, but suddenly he realizes that they just might be useful.

Fred decides to own to the debt, but he explains to the two men that he doesn't have the money. It will have to come from the box office at the end of the week. The men are satisfied with that as, in their opinion, the show seems to have everything it takes to succeed, but Fred tells them about his doubts. The leading lady is about to walk out. If she does, they will have to close and that means there'll be no money. As Fred intended, the two men decide to have a friendly little talk with Lilli.

Back on stage the second act is under way ("I Sing of Love"). Finally it leads into the wedding scene of Katharine and Petruchio ("Kiss Me, Kate") during which Fred and the two gangsters, disguised as chorus members, keep the fumingly unwilling Lilli up to the mark. At the end of the scene, as per the script, Fred bodily lifts Lilli up and carries her, struggling, off.

Act 2   In the stage door alley, Fred's dresser, Paul, leads a lazy song and dance complaining of the muggy weather ("Too Darn Hot") while, on stage, *The Taming of the Shrew* continues its lively performance through the deprivation scene ("Where Is the Life That Late I Led?"). By now, in response to his fair lady's frantic phone call, the dignified Harrison Howell has arrived at the stage door with an ambulance. He is embarrassed at meeting Lois, who is quick to recall a pleasant weekend they once spent together in Atlantic City, but equally as quick to assure Bill that she really loves him and is "Always True to You in My Fashion."

Fred's clever setting up of the situation makes Harrison somewhat dubious about Lilli's seemingly gothic tale of being held prisoner in the theatre and he does not react as supportively as Lilli might have wished. He also agrees complacently with every aspect of a satirical portrait of his life (soon to be Lilli's life) as painted by Fred until Lilli, fit to burst, evicts Fred from her room.

While Bill, in the corridor, is serenading his "Bianca" through the procession of messengers bearing gifts from admirers, the gangsters are on the phone, reporting in to the boss. But now it is they who have a problem. It seems that since a few hours ago the boss is no longer the boss. In fact he's no longer anything. This, it would seem, cancels both Fred's debt and their mandate. They thank a despairing Fred and a jubilant Lilli for a delightful evening and prepare to depart. Lilli is free. She does not have to play the last act. She sweeps off to her cab as Fred reprises "So In Love" behind her.

Although the curtain stays stubbornly down, the audience is not without entertainment, for the two gangsters have taken a wrong turning on their way out of the theatre and have ended up on the stage where, with a touch of the old soft shoe, they compound their new theatrical experience in an incidental duo ("Brush Up Your Shakespeare"). The final act of the show opens with the wedding of Bianca and Lucentio but, when the moment comes for Katharine to enter for the famous fountain speech, there is no Lilli. All is lost. Then, suddenly she is there, speech and all ("Women Are so Simple") and, when the kiss comes at the end of the speech, it is Fred and Lilli who kiss and not Petruchio and Katharine.

1949

SOUTH PACIFIC

A MUSICAL PLAY IN TWO ACTS by Oscar Hammerstein II and Joshua Logan adapted from *Tales of the South Pacific* by James Michener. Lyrics by Oscar Hammerstein II. Music by Richard Rodgers.

      Produced at the Majestic Theatre, New York, 7 April 1949, with Ezio Pinza (Émile de Becque), Mary Martin (Nellie Forbush), Juanita Hall (Bloody Mary), William Tabbert (Cable), Betta St. John (Liat), and Myron McCormick (Billis).

      A film version was produced by Twentieth Century-Fox in 1958 with Rossano Brazzi (singing dubbed by Giorgio Tozzi), Mitzi Gaynor, Hall (singing dubbed by Muriel Smith), John Kerr (singing dubbed by Bill Lee), France Nguyen, and Ray Walston.

Luther Billis (Myron McCormick) is into war profiteering, but circumstances and his potential customers don't favor big profits, and anyway he's not very good at it. Photograph by Bob Goldby, Courtesy Harry Ransom Research Center, The University of Texas at Austin.

CHARACTERS

Ensign Nellie Forbush

Émile de Becque

Ngana, Jerome, *his children*

Bloody Mary

Liat, *her daughter*

Luther Billis

Stewpot

Professor

Lieutenant Joseph Cable

Captain George Brackett

Commander William Harbison

Lieutenant Buzz Adams

Henry, Abner, Dinah Murphy,
Janet McGregor,
Yeoman Herbert Quayle, etc.

Act 1   At his island home, the French planter, Émile de Becque, is entertaining Ensign Nellie Forbush of the United States Navy at lunch. Outside the house, his half-caste children play and sing ("Dites-Moi") while, over coffee and brandy, Émile and Nellie are beginning to fall in love. She is from Little Rock, Arkansas, glad to be out of it and busy making the most of the south Pacific while the other American girls are busy hating it ("A Cockeyed Optimist"). He has spent most of his life in the islands after fleeing France at a young age, having killed a man in self-defense.

It is only a fortnight since they met and, although it seems they have nothing in common—the cultured, middle-aged Frenchman and the bright young American nurse—already, privately, in parallel soliloquy, each is imagining what it would be like if the two of them were one. It seems too soon to be thinking like this, but sometimes these things happen with amazing immediacy ("Some Enchanted Evening"). When it is time for Nellie to leave to go on duty, she takes with her an unspoken proposal of marriage.

Back at the navy camp, the men are singing lustily of how "Bloody Mary Is the Girl I Love." Bloody Mary is a tiny, wrinkled Tonkinese who sells grass skirts and shrunken heads to the souvenir hunters from a kiosk on the camp site. She is not the only one to have set up in business for the benefit of the troops. The comical Luther Billis is determined to become a war profiteer and he has invented a self-made laundry system. He has also gone into grass-skirt manufacturing in an effort to edge in on Bloody Mary's market, but he is no match in commerce for the old crone who does him out of his whole stock plus $100 in exchange for a boar's-tooth bracelet. The bracelet comes from an off-shore island, Bali H'ai, which is off-limits to the troops, a restriction which Billis finds particularly galling as, not only are all the best souvenirs to be bought cheaply on the island, but the local women have been evacuated there. The sailors, whose female company is limited to the nursing corps, can only look across the water and agree that "There Is Nothing Like a Dame."

A new arrival on the island arouses a special interest from Billis and sets Bloody Mary drooling. Lieutenant Joe Cable has just got in from the Pacific front line. He is young, good-looking, and, most importantly from Billis's point of view, he is an officer. Officers can take out boats, and a boat is what Billis needs to get across to Bali H'ai. For some reason, Bloody Mary also has an interest in getting Cable across to that mysterious island, and she serenades him winningly with descriptions of the special charms of "Bali H'ai."

The real reason for Cable's visit is unveiled when he meets Captain Brackett and Commander Harbison, the senior officers on the island. It has been decided at top level that an intelligence source is needed on one of the islands at the head of their channel in order to provide advance warnings of Japanese ship and airplane movements. Cable has been chosen to be that source, and he has come to this island to consult with Émile de Becque, whose knowledge of the islands can help him to establish a position where he might be safely and usefully installed.

Before de Becque is brought into the affair, the Americans need to find out how trustworthy he is and, to that end, they call in Nellie Forbush. When she has to answer questions about him, Nellie realizes just how little she does know about Émile. In fact, she knows less than the officers do, for she does not know about Émile's late Polynesian wife and his two children. Letters from her mother in Little Rock make shocked noises about her interest in a middle-aged foreigner and, in fact, everything conspires to make Nellie unsure about committing herself to Émile.

She decides nervously that she must not go on seeing him and, as she scrubs away vigorously under Luther Billis's latest invention, a shower, she declares that "I'm Going to Wash That Man Right Out of My Hair." She has got no further than drying her hair when she comes face-to-face with Émile and her resolution weakens. Remembering her duty, she questions him about his politics and his beliefs and digs for details on his past. She is so relieved when they all come out truly red-white-and-blue that, within minutes, all her good intentions are forgotten and she is happily singing "I'm in Love with a Wonderful Guy."

As a result of Nellie's information, Émile is summoned to a meeting with Brackett, Harbison, and Cable and asked to take part in the mission to put a spy post on his former home island of Marie-Louise. Émile refuses, and willingly admits that he refuses on account of Nellie. He has a chance to make a life with her, which is more important to him than anything else, and he will not risk it on this chancy episode. Without his help, the venture is too dangerous and, for the moment, it has to be called off.

While he is inactive, waiting for the next move from his superiors, Cable decides that he will take the opportunity to go across to Bali H'ai. With the aid of the delighted Billis, the trip is arranged, and once they are there Bloody Mary gleefully takes Cable in hand. While Luther Billis is led off to witness the boar's-tooth ceremony, she takes the young man to a dark little hut in a quiet place and there he meets Liat, a tiny, dark-eyed Tonkinese who seems little more than a child. She is Bloody Mary's daughter. The two young people are deeply struck with each other and, when the time comes for Cable to return to base, he can only with difficulty pull himself away from the arms of this beautiful girl ("Younger than Springtime"). Bloody Mary delivers him to his boat, smiling triumphantly. Lieutenant Cable will be her son-in-law, just as she planned.

Nellie attends a party arranged by Émile for her to meet his local friends. It is a great success and Nellie is in a buoyant mood as the evening comes to an end. When they are left at last alone, Émile chooses this moment to tell her of the part of his life she does not yet know: his Polynesian wife and the fact that Ngana and Jerome are his children. Everything that is Little Rock in Nellie rises up and revolts and, although she tries to fight it, Émile feels her slipping away from him. When they say goodnight, try as she may, it is a very difficult goodnight, and, when Nellie is out of his sight, she cannot prevent herself from breaking into a run.

Act 2   Down at the camp, the troop's Thanksgiving Follies are taking place. Émile turns up with flowers, hoping to see Nellie, but he learns from Billis that she has asked for a transfer to another island. Cable, who has been in hospital with malaria, also puts in an appearance, desperate to get hold of a boat to return to Bali H'ai and visit Liat, but Liat is there, brought by Bloody Mary with a calculated ultimatum. Either Cable marries her, or she will marry the girl to another rich white man, a drunken planter who will beat her. When he does not reply immediately, Mary pleads with Cable: she will work for them, make money, all they will have to do is be happy ("Happy Talk").

Joe Cable is torn, but the small town America in him still has the upper hand. He cannot marry Liat. Furious, Mary dashes to the ground the gold watch he has given Liat, and drags the girl away. As he painfully reprises the final lines of "Younger than Springtime," on the stage of the camp theatre the final act of the Follies is being announced. It is a travesty of what has just been seen: Nellie is a white-suited sailor singing raucously to Luther Billis as a dusky maiden of his being her "Honey Bun."

After the show, Émile succeeds in meeting Nellie. He tries to reason with her but, although she admits her reaction is stupidly emotional, Nellie will not reconsider. She was born like that, and that is all there is to it. The bitter, heartbroken Cable has worked it out otherwise. It isn't born in you, all this hatred, all these prejudices. It is instilled in you by others who want their own prejudices supported ("You've Got to Be Taught"). He has decided that, if he survives his mission, he will not go back to America. He will come back here, to Bali H'ai, where everything he cares about is. For Émile it is different. When all you care about has been taken from you, then where do you go? ("Once Nearly Was Mine") The answer comes quickly when Cable asks him to think again about joining him on the expedition to Marie-Louise. This time, with nothing to lose, de Becque agrees.

In the base radio room, Brackett listens impatiently for the first messages to come from Cable and de Becque. The men have been successfully delivered to Marie-Louise by submarine, an operation facilitated when the attentions of the Japanese (as well as half a million dollars worth of U.S. Navy rescue operations) were diverted to fishing stowaway Luther Billis out of the water after he had fallen out of the baggage hold of the plane accompanying the mission. Finally contact is made, and Joe and Émile come through with first-rate intelligence reports.

Days pass, and the information continues to flow, leading to many otherwise impossible strikes by the American forces against the Japanese. The Americans are winning the upper hand in an area where previously they had little success. Nellie, in the meanwhile, has heard talk among the wounded in her care. She has heard them talk of the Frenchman who is involved in their raids and, finally, she goes to Brackett to ask if they are speaking of Émile. Brackett allows her to wait to hear Émile's voice over the radio but, when it comes, it is with bad news. Joe Cable has been killed in an attack. Then, in the middle of the broadcast, the sound of an approaching airplane is heard and the radio goes dead.

Down on the beach, Nellie walks alone, reflecting bitterly on her stupidity to a refrain of "Some Enchanted Evening." She can only hope and pray that Émile will return. As she walks, Bloody Mary appears with Liat. The old woman is dazed and defeated, because Liat has refused to marry the planter: She will marry no one but Lieutenant Cable. Nellie cannot say anything, but clasps the little girl chokingly to her breast.

The camp is on the move. The whole picture in the South Pacific has changed and the Americans are now moving forward. Amid all the excitement, no one mentions the fate of the Frenchman out on Marie-Louise. His part has been played and, alive or dead, it seems as if he has been forgotten. Up at Émile's home, Nellie is playing with Ngana and Jerome, singing "Dites-Moi" together, when another voice joins in. It is Émile, battered and dirty, but safe. The children rush to meet him, and he moves straight on to meet Nellie. At least their story will have a happy ending.

1950

Guys and Dolls

A MUSICAL FABLE OF BROADWAY IN TWO ACTS based on a story and characters by Damon Runyon. Book by Abe Burrows and Jo Swerling. Lyrics and music by Frank Loesser.

Produced at the 46th Street Theatre, New York, 24 November 1950, with Sam Levene (Nathan), Vivian Blaine (Adelaide), Isobel Bigley (Sarah), and Robert Alda (Sky). Produced at the Broadway Theatre, in a revised version, 21 July 1976. Produced at the Martin Beck Theatre, 14 April 1992, with Nathan Lane, Faith Prince, Josie de Guzman, and Peter Gallagher.

A film version was produced by Samuel Goldwyn in 1955 with Frank Sinatra, Blaine, Jean Simmons, and Marlon Brando.

The Oldest Established Permanent Floating
Crap Game in New York rolls into action.
Photograph by Bob Golby,
Courtesy Harry Ransom Research Center,
The University of Texas at Austin.

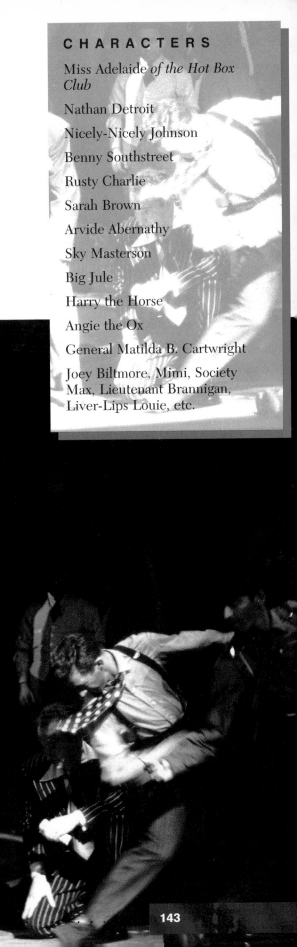

CHARACTERS

Miss Adelaide *of the Hot Box Club*

Nathan Detroit

Nicely-Nicely Johnson

Benny Southstreet

Rusty Charlie

Sarah Brown

Arvide Abernathy

Sky Masterson

Big Jule

Harry the Horse

Angie the Ox

General Matilda B. Cartwright

Joey Biltmore, Mimi, Society Max, Lieutenant Brannigan, Liver-Lips Louie, etc.

Act 1

The scene is Runyonland, that busy, cosmopolitan Broadway world of guys and dolls. Three guys are looking over the day's scratch sheet, trying to pick a winner or two ("Fugue for Tinhorns"), when the mission band, headed by Miss Sarah Brown, passes by spreading its hopeless message of temperance ("Follow the Fold"). The guys can appreciate a doll like Miss Sarah, but they don't have much time for the mission dodge, for they are heavily involved in a much more interesting thing known as the crap game—a little bit of action and some dollars, but a thing to be kept well out of the sight of Lieutenant Brannigan and his fellow cops.

Nathan Detroit runs the crap game when he can find a suitable spot to set up, and right now that is a problem. The usual places seem to have all come under Brannigan's attention, and the only possibility left is Biltmore's garage where the owner wants cash down to let them in. Cash is one thing Nathan doesn't have. Things look sticky for "The Oldest Established Permanent Floating Crap-Game in New York" and for good old reliable Nathan. This is particularly regrettable as Sky Masterson is in town, and Sky Masterson is well known as one big gambling man. He'll bet on anything. What a lovely, lucrative game Nathan could get going with that guy if only he had a place.

There is one particular person who has to be hoodwinked when a crap game is on the boil and that person is Nathan's girl, the Hot Box chanteuse Miss Adelaide. She and Nathan have been engaged for more years than anyone can remember without getting around to a wedding, but Adelaide lives in only slightly battered hope that one day they'll make it together all the way down the aisle. She is not at all keen on her Nathan getting involved with the crapshooters and she has extorted from him a faithful promise to leave the game alone. This means Adelaide has to be sweet-talked out of the way before Nathan can get down to business with Sky Masterson.

Nathan desperately tries to win the money to pay Biltmore from Sky with a set-up bet, but Sky is too smart for that. He'll bet on anything, but he can smell a set-up. What Nathan ends up with is a thousand dollar bet that Sky can't persuade Miss Sarah to go with him on a trip to Havana the next day. It's a serious bet, so Sky goes to work seriously. He goes to the mission and poses as a repentant sinner in an effort to attract the mission lass's attentions, but it isn't long before the truth leaks out and Sky has to use an angle. The mission isn't doing too well. In fact, it's fairly laying an egg. The big meeting next Thursday with General Matilda B. Cartwright in attendance shows every sign of being dismally thin. Sky guarantees Miss Sarah one dozen genuine sinners in attendance in return for a dinner date. Sarah is shocked at his duplicity and makes it clear to him that the man for her will certainly not be a gambler ("I'll Know") but, when Sky kisses her, it takes a long time for her to slap his face.

Adelaide gets through entertaining at the Hot Box ("A Bushel and a Peck"), meets up with Nathan, and the topic turns, as the topic has a habit of doing with Adelaide, to marriage. Adelaide has told her mother long ago that they were already married and, over the years, she has steadily embellished her story, inventing a family and lots of other little details, so couldn't they just get married really? She's had plenty of time to get everything together. All they need now is a license and a blood test. But then a passing chorine blows Nathan's plans for reviving the crap game and Adelaide dissolves in a plaintive wail. He'd promised! Nathan slinks away as Adelaide sombers into the psychosomatic cold she's had for fourteen years waiting for her wedding ring (Adelaide's Lament), and gets ready to wait some more.

The guys have noticed that Sky does not seem to be having much luck with Miss Sarah. It looks like Nathan's bet will be good and the game will be on. It just goes to show that real guys didn't ought to get sidetracked by dolls when there's a man's game to be played ("Guys and Dolls"). Miss Sarah, however, is not having much luck herself. Business really is bad at the mission and the General has come to say that they will have to close down the branch. Sky steps in on cue and Sarah remembers his promise. One dozen genuine sinners for one date; it could save the mission.

The crapshooters have gathered from near and far, even the illustrious Big Jule from Cicero, Illinois, is here, and Nathan still doesn't have his venue booked. The big-spending guys are all standing around on the street when Officer Brannigan passes by. The gathering looks a bit obvious, so the boys cover up by saying it's a stag night for Nathan—he's finally getting married—and who should overhear this bit of news but Miss Adelaide. And she thought the gathering was a crap game! How marvellous of him. They will get married tomorrow night right after she's finished her set at the Hot Box. Under the circumstances, there can be no escape and Nathan can only agree. That disposes of Brannigan and Adelaide; now the guys only need Sky Masterson with the thousand dollars from his losing bet to pay for Biltmore's garage, and the game can start. Suddenly Nathan goes white: The mission group marches by and there is no Sarah with them.

Sarah is in Havana. She is dragging Sky round the sights until he drags her into a café for a milk shake. The milk shakes here have quite a taste—it's called rum—and Sarah shows quite a taste for them, so she is soon tipsily free of inhibitions and dancing closely in Sky's arms ("If I Were a Bell"). He takes her carefully back to New York and it is a soberer Sarah who arrives at the mission at 4 A.M. just in time to see Adelaide returning happily from her wedding shower. It seems a strange time of night for people to be up and about, but to Sky it's "My Time of Day" and this particular 4 A.M. is special because he's in love and so is Sarah ("I've Never Been in Love Before").

Suddenly there are crap players everywhere and whistles blowing: Nathan found a place all right—the guys have been playing their game in the mission. Sarah is filled with remorse. She has been fooled by Sky. He set it up for his friends. The moment between them is gone and she is back to being the old Sarah Brown.

Act 2   Down at the Hot Box Adelaide is doing her set ("Take Back Your Mink") when Nicely-Nicely Johnson comes to deliver a message. Nathan can't come to meet her—he's gone to see a sick aunt. Adelaide knows all about sick aunts. It's the crap game, of course. It's still going on. Adelaide starts sneezing miserably.

Sarah Brown isn't much happier. The big meeting is due any time and it is going to be a fiasco. Of course, that isn't all. She is still thinking of Sky. Arvide, her fellow mission worker, gives her some kindly advice: If she loves Sky and he loves her what does it matter who or what he is? ("More I Cannot Wish You"). What Sarah has forgotten is that she is holding Sky Masterson's marker for an unpaid bet, but Sky hasn't forgotten and he's a good player. He always pays his debts.

Nathan has got the game going down in the sewers. It has gone on for a whole day nonstop and everyone would like to finish, but Big Jule is a big loser and his gun says that the game goes on. He also wishes to bet on credit and to use his own dice. Now this is against all the rules and it does not seem at all like a good idea, especially to Nathan who is forced into losing all the money he has made to Big Jule's imaginary winning throws. Sky arrives at the right moment to stop this cheating and he proposes a strange game. He will play the gamblers not for their money, but for their souls. For each throw he wins, the loser is bound to show up at the mission meeting. He calls for lucky dice ("Luck Be a Lady") and starts to throw.

One by one, the guys emerge from the sewer and head for the mission. Adelaide catches up with Nathan. There's still five minutes left before midnight, they can still go and get married like the license says. When Nathan says he's going to a prayer meeting, it seems like a really crude excuse. Adelaide bursts and, in spite of his protestations of love ("Sue Me"), she storms off in a fury of sniffles.

At the mission, Sarah is about to give up in despair when the room begins to fill with real reprobates. It is Sky's promised contribution to the meeting. One by one the guys get up to give awkward testimony before the General and, when

Nicely-Nicely's turn comes, he launches into a really colorful confession ("Sit Down, You're Rocking the Boat"). No sooner has he finished than Brannigan arrives. He asks Sarah if she will testify that these guys ran a crap game in the mission the previous night. Sarah looks coolly down at the assembled sinners and replies with deep sincerity. Why, she never saw them before in her life.

Adelaide and Sarah end up in the street together contemplating men—their own in particular—sitting on a couple of bundles of newspapers in the wee hours of the morning. That's when Adelaide finds out that Nathan was telling the truth about the prayer meeting and Sarah finds out that she is really in love with Sky. What are they mooning on about? What they need to do is get on and "Marry the Man Today" and fix him up the way they want him subsequently.

Sarah and Sky are married in the mission and Sky takes up a new position in life, carrying the big drum in the mission band. Since Nathan wasn't able to fix a place for his wedding, he and Adelaide make it a double wedding and, if Sky's still talking odds and Nathan seems to have caught Adelaide's cold as the curtain falls, well, that's what happens with "Guys and Dolls."

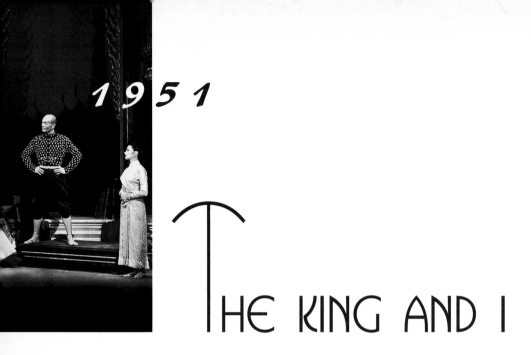

1951

THE KING AND I

A MUSICAL PLAY IN TWO ACTS by Oscar Hammerstein II based on the novel *Anna and the King of Siam* by Margaret Landon. Music by Richard Rodgers.

Produced at the St. James Theatre, New York, 29 March 1951, with Gertrude Lawrence (Anna), Yul Brynner (The King), Dorothy Sarnoff (Thiang), Doretta Morrow (Tuptim), and Larry Douglas (Lun Tha). Produced at the Uris Theatre, 2 May 1977, with Yul Brynner, Constance Towers, Hye-Young Choi, June Angela, and Martin Vidnovic and played at the Broadway Theatre, 7 January 1985, with Brynner and Mary-Beth Peil.

A film version was produced by Twentieth Century-Fox in 1956 with Deborah Kerr (singing dubbed by Marni Nixon), Brynner, Rita Moreno, Terry Saunders, and Carlos Rivas (singing dubbed by Reuben Fuentes).

The King of Siam (Yul Brynner) greets his gaggle of children under the eyes of Anna (Gertrude Lawrence) and Lady Thiang (Dorothy Sarnoff). Friedman-Abeles, photographers. Courtesy Performing Arts Research Center, New York Public Library at Lincoln Center.

CHARACTERS

Anna Leonowens

Louis, *her son*

The King

Prince Chulalongkorn, *his son*

Lady Thiang, *his chief wife*

The Kralahome

Tuptim

Lun Tha

Sir Edward Ramsay

Captain Orton

Phra Alack, Interpreter, Princess Ying Yaowalak, etc.

Act 1

A sailing vessel is making its way up the Gulf of Siam toward Bangkok ("Arrival at Bangkok"), carrying on board Mrs. Anna Leonowens, a widow from Singapore, who has been appointed governess to the children of the King of Siam. Anna brings with her her own son, Louis, and just a little apprehension, which she attempts to dispel by her own particular method ("I Whistle a Happy Tune").

Apprehension returns at the sight of her reception committee, a group of seminaked Siamese, headed by the large and also seminaked Kralahome or Prime Minister, but Anna Leonowens is not a woman to be daunted. She has accepted her job and made her terms—twelve pounds a month and a house of her own—and she will stick to them. She also intends that the King shall stick to them and, when the Kralahome intimates that she will be lodged in the palace, she protests firmly that her contract calls for her own house. She concedes, however, that she will come to the palace for the meanwhile and speak to the King on the subject at a suitable time.

Several weeks later, the King receives an emissary from Burma, the courtier Lun Tha. Lun Tha has brought a gift for the King from the Prince of Burma, a young woman called Tuptim, but it is clear that during the journey from their own country to Siam the two young people have fallen in love. Tuptim is duly handed over to the nonchalantly appreciative King and left to reflect bitterly on her unhappy position ("My Lord and Master").

Now, and only now, the Kralahome judges it time to introduce the wilful school teacher to the King. Anna has had enough of sitting in her rooms and is eager to begin work, but she also wishes to speak to the King to raise the small matter of her accommodation. The King brushes this unimportant request aside with a barrage of his own thoughts. Does she appreciate the plans he has to bring the best of Western culture to Siam? How did she like the fireworks and the acrobats at last week's funeral? Perhaps she can teach the Lady Thiang and his other wives as well as his sixty-seven children? House? What house? She will live in the palace. And he is gone, leaving Anna to the curiosity of his wives who are much amused by her hoop skirt and gloves.

Lady Thiang tries to make Anna aware of the way things are in the palace. The King is all, and that is never and can never be questioned. Tuptim and Lun Tha, for example, will never see each other again, but the girl has the King, and what could she want more? Anna has her own thoughts both on the omnipotence of the King and the misfortune of the young lovers. Alone, without her much loved husband, she appreciates their plight deeply ("Hello, Young Lovers"). However, any reservations that she may have about her position vanish when the King formally introduces the children to her (March of the Siamese Children). She will love them, and they will love her.

Anna's western teaching soon brings new ideas into palace thought ("Children Sing, Priests Chant") and, although he would never admit it publicly or even privately, the King proves not unwilling to learn. He is enlightened enough to know that the King is not omniscient as his ancestors believed, and generous enough of spirit to want to use any available knowledge to do the best for his land and for his family, but he finds it difficult to be sure precisely what is good and what is right ("A Puzzlement").

In the schoolroom, Anna finds much enjoyment in making friends with her young charges ("The Royal Bangkok Academy"/"Getting to Know You"), but she meets some difficulties when she tries to put the simplistic teachings of Lady Thiang into a wider perspective by showing the children a world map, or in explaining such phenomena as snow and ice, which the Siamese children have never seen. The King supports her, even when he has not the knowledge required ("So Big a World"), but they come to disagreement perpetually on the subject of Anna's promised house, and she reacts angrily when he refers to her as a servant. If the King does not carry out his word on her accommodation, she will leave Siam.

Lun Tha and Tuptim have been meeting secretly ("We Kiss in a Shadow") but fearfully. Anna has acted as a chaperone for these meetings and they know that, if she goes, they will never be able to see each other again. In the privacy of her room, Anna gives vent to her anger over the King's stubbornness regarding her house ("Shall I Tell You What I Think of You?"). She cannot stay in a country where a contract is thus disregarded and where she is treated with such a lack of dignity. She will leave, she must leave, before she becomes so attached to the children that she cannot.

The Lady Thiang comes to Anna and begs her to go to the King. He cannot come to her, his position and his pride will not allow it, but he needs her. Her outburst against him, and the discovery of a British letter describing him as a barbarian and suggesting the annexing of Siam as a protectorate, have hurt him deeply. He needs help and he needs advice, but they must not sound like help and advice. He is a man and a King, a wonderful man who wants only to do good and a King who would be wise and strong, but he needs support. As Lady Thiang pours out her own deep love for the man and the King ("Something Wonderful"), Anna realizes that she must do as she is asked.

When she attends on the King, the atmosphere is lighthearted. He plays tricks on her, putting her into ridiculous positions in an effort to keep up the protocol of keeping her head at a lower level than his, and yet allows her transparently to dictate what he should do in answer to the accusations of barbarism. It is decided that when Sir Edward Ramsay, a British diplomat from Singapore, pays a visit, he should be allowed to see the efforts that the King is making toward civilization. There will be a dinner, a ball, and a theatrical presentation, and the women will be dressed in Western clothes. But there is little time to put such a plan into effect for Sir Edward's ship is already announced. The King orders the court on to its knees to pray for help in their efforts to impress the British (Prayer to Buddha), and slips into the prayer a promise to build for Anna the bungalow she has pestered him for since her arrival, before impishly lying down flat on his face so that she must do the same.

Act 2

The Eastern ladies dressed up in hoop skirts are distinctly ill at ease ("Western People Funny") and also worryingly short of underclothes, but the King is unconcerned at their dress and more dubious about the bare shoulders of Anna's evening gown. When Sir Edward Ramsay arrives, the women are thrown into a panic by his monocle and, forgetting all pretense of civilization, fling their hoop skirts over their heads confirming that Anna was right to have worried about their lack of underclothes. Ramsay is an old admirer of Anna's and the sense of intimacy between them irritates the King who insists on taking Anna into dinner himself, leaving his guest to follow.

While the evening's festivities are going on in the palace, Tuptim is planning to meet Lun Tha. Lady Thiang, who sees everything, warns her not to. Lun Tha has been ordered away from Siam that night. Tuptim disregards her warning and the two young people meet to plan her escape ("I Have Dreamed"). Tuptim is to present the entertainment for the King's foreign guests and, after it is over, she will make her way secretly to the ship to join Lun Tha. Anna finds the two together and is told of their plan. In spite of her loyalty to the King, she can only condone their flight as she remembers her own young love.

The entertainment is in the form of a masque representing the story of Uncle Tom's cabin, the flight of the slave Eliza across the snow, and the chase of wicked Simon Legree ("The Small House of Uncle Thomas"), recited by Tuptim with more emotion than is good for her cause. The King is not sure he approves of the moral of the play, but on the whole the evening is a success and Sir Edward can depart secure in the knowledge that, whatever the King of Siam is, he is no barbarian. The King is grateful to Anna for her part in the success and, to the embarrassment of both of them, he gives her an expensive ring from his own hand as a gift, but the happiness of the moment is shadowed when the King is brought the news of Tuptim's flight. Anna pleads with the King not to be hard on the girl. She is, after all, only one woman among so many in his household, and of so little importance. He will not listen to her (Song of the King).

The King is in an expansive mood and the conversation turns on poetry, on romance, and on English ideas. Anna attempts to express the feelings of a young girl making her debut in society, meeting and dancing with a young man for the first time ("Shall We Dance?"). She dances a little, then realizes that the King is looking at her as he might at one of his dancing girls. She stops abruptly but he insists that she continue. She must show him how English people dance together. Anna begins to teach him to polka as a teacher would, but the King wishes to dance as a couple does, and his arm stretches firmly around her waist as they dance around the room.

The scene is broken by the Kralahome's announcement that Tuptim has been taken. The girl rushes in and falls at Anna's feet for protection but, when the King rejects her passionate plea not to hurt Tuptim, Anna turns on him with stinging words. He has never loved, he cannot understand. Furious, the King prepares to whip the girl personally but under Anna's eyes he cannot. Flinging down the whip he storms out and the Kralahome turns bitterly on Anna. This is what she has made of their King with her Western ideas; a King who cannot even take a whip to a traitor. It would have been better if she had never come to Siam. Lun Tha has been killed attempting escape, Tuptim is utterly broken and has no wish to survive him, and Anna has seen in the King the part of him that is his heritage and which she can neither understand nor accept. She gives the Kralahome the ring to return to the King. She will be on the next boat out of Bangkok.

Anna is packed and preparing to embark when Lady Thiang comes to her bringing a letter from the King. He is ill, very ill. It is his heart, the heart she accused him of not having, that is the problem. To Lady Thiang's wise eyes, it is also his strangely vanished will to live. The letter contains all the best of the man: his struggle for excellence, his admission of his own failings, and his gratitude to Anna for her help. She must go to him.

She arrives only just in time. The King is weak and dying. The children are called and they, too, beg Anna not to leave them. Prince Chulalongkorn, who will succeed his father, is there, a young man who will be needing guidance. Anna orders her baggage to be unpacked from the ship. She will stay to help the King's son as she has helped the father. As the new King, prompted by his father, issues his first edict—replacing the Eastern kowtow with Western bowing and courtesies—the old King dies and Anna, kneeling beside him, takes his lifeless hand and kisses it.

FITCH - 36

1955

DAMN YANKEES

A MUSICAL IN TWO ACTS by George Abbott and Douglass Wallop based on Wallop's book *The Year the Yankees Lost the Pennant*. Music and lyrics by Richard Adler and Jerry Ross. Produced at the 46th Street Theatre, New York, 5 May 1955, with Stephen Douglass (Joe Hardy), Gwen Verdon (Lola), and Ray Walston (Applegate). Produced at the Marquis Theatre in a revised version, 3 March 1994, with Jarrod Emeck, Bebe Neuwirth, and Victor Garber.

A film version was produced by Warner Brothers in 1958 with Tab Hunter, Verdon, and Walston.

Lola apparently always gets what she wants. If it's Joe Hardy she's after, she seems to be going the right way about it. Friedman-Abeles, photographers. Courtesy Performing Arts Research Center, New York Public Library at Lincoln Center.

JACOBY - 4   FITCH - 36   ANDERS - 3

CHARACTERS

Joe Boyd,
a real estate salesman, later Joe
Hardy

Meg Boyd, *his wife*

Mr. Applegate

Sister

Doris

Gloria Thorpe,
a newspaperperson

Benny van Buren, *manager of the
Washington Senators*

Sohovik, *a ballplayer with the
Washington Senators*

Smokey, *another one*

Vernon

Henry

Rocky

more ballplayers

Mr. Welch, *owner of the
Washington Senators*

Lola

Lynch, Miss Weston,
Commissioner, Postmaster, etc.

Act 1

On the porch of his home in Washington D.C., real-estate salesman Joe Boyd is watching a televised ball game with the single-minded passion of the total devotee. His wife, Meg, sewing alongside him might as well not be there; it's the ball season and in the ball season nothing exists for Joe but the Washington Senators ("Six Months Out of Every Year"). Unfortunately, his team isn't doing too well. In fact, right now they're losing a game and lying seventh in the league behind the all-conquering Yankees, and Joe is getting ulcers over it. He knows what's wrong. The team needs one decent long-ball hitter. He'd sell his soul for one. And, goodness me, a second or two later, that's just what he's being given the chance to do.

In a discreet whiff of music, a dapper stranger who calls himself Mr. Applegate appears on the porch with a proposition. He will turn Joe into the ballplaying hero who will save the Washington Senators in exchange for that little thing, his soul. Come on, it's not that uncommon. How does he think half the politicians and car-park owners in town got started? Joe hesitates: He will have to leave his wife, his job, and what if he changes his mind? In the real-estate business they have a thing called an escape clause; he wants one of those. Mr. Applegate tetchily agrees. He wants to get the whole plan into operation before those damn Yankees sew up the season. Joe's escape clause can operate up to midnight on September 24, but after that, no go.

Joe leaves a loving note for Meg ("Goodbye Old Girl") and hands himself over to the devil. No sooner has he done so than Applegate makes a magical pass and suddenly a new version of Joe appears. He is twenty years younger and raring to go. So they do.

At the Washington Baseball Park, Benny van Buren, the manager of the Senators, is trying to instill some spirit into his team following their thrashing at the hands of the Yankees. Skill is only part of what is needed, he tells them, you've got to have "Heart." He fobs off a lady newspaperperson, Gloria Thorpe, who comes in search of a nice negative story to drape across her column, and he isn't exactly thrilled when the suave Applegate turns up with Joe, insisting that the boy be given a trial. Another aspiring rookie is the last thing he needs.

He sends Joe off with one of the team for a few practice balls but, when he hears the unexpected results of this exercise, he lets the boy loose in the park. The first thing the barefoot boy does is hit the ball right over the wall in front of the popping eyes of Gloria Thorpe. She is immediately on the trail of a story and when she scents a mystery in the lad's background she fires in with all questions blazing. Joe gulps out that his hometown is Hannibal, Missouri, and Gloria has soon encaptioned that into a nicely flip headline. "Shoeless Joe from Hannibal Mo" is on his way.

Joe shoots quickly to the top with his superhuman efforts on the ball field, but he isn't at all happy with the press he gets and especially Gloria's typical fact-fiction reporting. Washington's team is gradually climbing in the league, and all Miss Thorpe and her colleagues do is snipe at the boy who won't give them lush stories on his private life. The team owner comforts Joe. What do they care? On the twenty-fifth of September, the pennant will be theirs.

The twenty-fifth? That date jogs Joe's memory and he remembers his escape clause. They'd better have the championship sewn up before that last day's game or else he is damned. Applegate has that annoying condition on his mind too. He needs to organize things so that the pennant is still on ice before the last day's games so that Joe can't sneak out of paying his dues. He's under no illusion—Joe would like to. He's clearly got a longing to see Meg again ("A Man Doesn't Know"). A diversion is needed, so a diversion is arranged. She is called Lola and she touts about "A Little Brains, A Little Talent" and a lot of charms. Lola is a practiced homewrecker and Joe is all hers to go get.

Back at home, Meg sadly makes do with the company of her baseball-fan friends, Doris and Sister, who are persuaded that Joe will never return. Then one day a young man turns up wanting to rent Joe's old room. Meg likes him and agrees, but when Doris and Sister come in they recognize the boy as the famous ball player, Joe Hardy. In spite of Applegate's attempts to stop him, Joe moves back in to his own home. So now, as the Senators' winning streak continues, Applegate decides it is the moment to introduce Lola into the game. Joe is stunned by the sexy beauty who is, as she informs him, irresistible ("Whatever Lola Wants"), but he's inherently monogamous and he doesn't succumb as expected. Applegate, irritated, rubbishes Lola's line in seduction and determines instead to start a newspaper scandal about the boy's living with Meg, which will force him to move out.

While the fan clubs celebrate the imminent winning of the pennant in songs and dance ("Heart"), and Lola pops in her own one-woman fan club contribution ("Who's Got the Pain"), further trouble is being brewed for Joe. A handily placed aside from Applegate has Gloria Thorpe heading for her typewriter to declare to the world that the mysterious Joe Hardy is, in fact, a banned player from the Mexican league called Shifty McCoy.

Act 2   It is September 24, the day by which Joe needed to win the pennant, and he isn't playing. He's been suspended and called before the Baseball Commission to defend himself on the charge of being McCoy, and the Senators have to get on without him. They've just got to forget him and keep their minds on winning "The Game." In spite of all they can do, they lose, and the championship is up for grabs.

Joe meets Meg on a park bench. He has made up his mind what he is going to do. He will clear his name before the day is out and then he will exercise his escape clause and go back to being plain Joe Boyd again. He comforts Meg that her Joe will return. If she could only believe it, he is really "Near to You" at this very moment.

Back at Applegate's apartment, the devil is plotting nastily. Tonight he will ensnare Joe into renouncing his escape with the dream of winning the pennant for the Senators and then, tomorrow, in the vital game, he will bewitch Joe into throwing the game. Half of Washington will die of apoplexy. When Joe turns up to tell Applegate that he is exercising his escape clause, Applegate tries one more trick: The escape clause has to be taken at the witching hour. At midnight that night, when Joe's hearing is in session, if he still wishes to get out of his contract he must step with Applegate into the next room and he will be changed back to his old shape. When the boy has departed, the devil muses nostalgically over how much easier it was to accomplish his diabolical works in historical times ("Those Were the Good Old Days").

At the Commissioner's session, Joe is questioned about his alleged origins in Hannibal, Mo. Gloria has negative evidence from the birth registers and has brought an aged postmaster to swear that no one called Joe Hardy ever lived in Hannibal, but Applegate counters with a gentle admission that Joe was illegitimate and Meg, Doris, and Sister (who really *are* from Hannibal) turn up to greet Joe as an old friend, causing the befuddled postmaster suddenly to change his evidence. If Hannibal knows him, then he cannot possibly be Shifty McCoy, and he must be cleared.

Now it is nearly midnight. Joe signals to Applegate to come into the next room but, as he goes toward the door, Meg holds him back as she goes into a long and passionate defense of Joe Hardy. By her heartfelt deed, she condemns him. Midnight strikes and Joe has not escaped.

Later that night, Joe sits disconsolately with his fellow damnee, Lola. She was once the ugliest woman in Providence, Rhode Island, before she gave in to Applegate. Joe is one of them now, so the "Two Lost Souls" go off to a nightclub together. But Lola is not wholly lost. She has slipped a Mickey Finn to Applegate and the devil is drugged. He is so drugged that he doesn't wake up until it is almost too late to get to the game against the Yankees the next day.

It is all but over, and Washington is 4-3 up as Applegate clambers into the stand with Lola, whom he has revengefully changed back into the old hag that she was. Now it will be Joe's turn to suffer the same fate. As the ball flies from Mickey Mantle's bat toward Joe Hardy, the devil makes his magic pass and, before the eyes of the amazed crowd, a fat middle-aged man leaps impossibly for the vital catch—and makes it! The Senators have won the pennant. The crowd stream on to the pitch, leaving just the aged Lola in the stand, happily waving her scarf in triumph.

The team is celebrating, but no one can find Joe Hardy. He has vanished. Of course he has. He is Joe Boyd again, and he has gone straight back to Chevy Chase, to be reunited with his Meg. They won't ever find him again. As man and wife happily join in a reprise of "A Man Doesn't Know," Applegate appears to try one last throw. He tempts Joe with promises of a World Series win, and he flaunts Lola, now beautiful again, in front of him. But Lola will not cooperate. No one will. Applegate is hopping mad. The devil is defeated, and so are the damn Yankees.

1956

My Fair Lady

A MUSICAL IN TWO ACTS by Alan Jay Lerner based on *Pygmalion* by George Bernard Shaw. Music by Frederick Loewe.

Produced at the Mark Hellinger Theatre, New York, 15 March 1956, with Rex Harrison (Higgins), Julie Andrews (Eliza Doolittle), Stanley Holloway (Doolittle), and Robert Coote (Pickering). Produced at the St. James Theatre, 25 March 1976, with Ian Richardson, Christine Andreas, George Rose, and Coote. Produced at the Uris Theatre, 18 August 1981, with Harrison, Nancy Ringham, Milo O'Shea, and Jack Gwillim, with Cathleen Nesbitt as Mrs. Higgins. Produced at the Virginia Theatre, 9 December 1993, with Richard Chamberlain, Melissa Errico, Julian Holloway, and Paxton Whitehead.

A film version was produced by Warner Brothers in 1964 with Harrison, Audrey Hepburn (singing dubbed by Marni Nixon), Holloway, and Wilfred Hyde-White.

Professor Henry Higgins (Rex Harrison)
tries to put a plum into the vowels of
Eliza Doolittle (Julie Andrews) by
filling her mouth with pebbles:
until she swallows one.
Friedman-Abeles, photographers.
Courtesy Performing Arts Research Center,
New York Public Library at Lincoln Center.

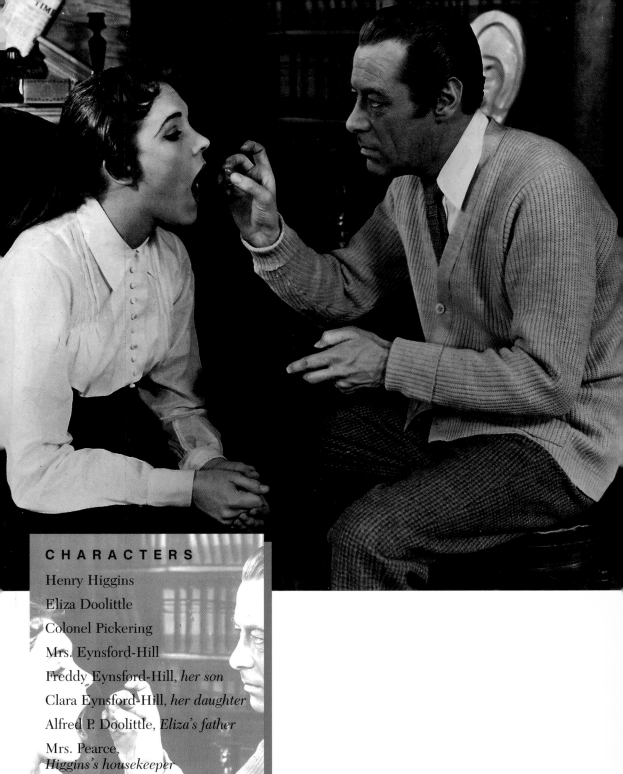

CHARACTERS

Henry Higgins

Eliza Doolittle

Colonel Pickering

Mrs. Eynsford-Hill

Freddy Eynsford-Hill, *her son*

Clara Eynsford-Hill, *her daughter*

Alfred P. Doolittle, *Eliza's father*

Mrs. Pearce,
Higgins's housekeeper

Mrs. Higgins, *Henry's mother*

Zoltan Karpathy

Harry, Jamie, Queen of
Transylvania, etc.

Act 1

Under the columned portico of St. Paul's Church, Covent Garden, a chord of opera-goers are sheltering from the rain while trying to find transport to get them spotlessly to their homes. Among the elegant throng, jostling for a few dry square inches, are the stately Mrs. Eynsford-Hill, her daughter, Clara, and her son Freddy. Freddy's ineffectual efforts to attract a cab ultimately result in his tumbling headlong over a scruffy flower-girl, and sending her bunches of violets scattering into the mud.

The complaining girl gets short shrift and no compensation for her crumpled flowers from Freddy's mother, but she ungraciously accepts a meager three-ha'pence from an amiable Colonel who simply wants to be done with her importuning. A bystander nudges the girl to give the gentleman a flower for his money. There's a copper's nark behind a pillar, writing down what she says.

In the hubbub that follows, it eventuates that the note-taking gentleman is no policeman but Mr. Henry Higgins, a professor of language and an expert on dialects, and he amazes the crowd by placing the origins of some of them within a few streets. It is Henry Higgins's contention that a person is the manner in which he or she speaks ("Why Can't the English?"). It's a contention that means something to the amiable Colonel Pickering who is himself a student of Indian dialects. The two men discover each other's identity and Higgins promptly invites Pickering to be his house guest. The girl, ignored through all this, howls for a bit of attention and, reminded by an opportune volley of church bells of a finer duty, the preoccupied Higgins empties his pocket of change into her basket as he leaves.

Eliza Doolittle has never seen so much money and, as her costermonger friends gather jokingly around, she dreams aloud of how she could spend it ("Wouldn't It Be Lovely").

Up the Tottenham Court Road, Eliza's father, the dustman Alfie Doolittle, is having no luck getting a beer or two on the never-never but, when Eliza passes by and tosses him a half-crown out of her windfall, he launches happily into song praising the virtues of "A Little Bit of Luck."

At Higgins's Wimpole Street home, the next day, the Professor and Pickering are delving into the finer shades of vowel sounds when Eliza turns up. She's come for lessons. She wants to learn to speak well enough to get a job in a flower shop. Higgins is tempted by the sheer awfulness of her speech, and, when Pickering challenges him to a wager, he declares that he will take the girl in hand. He'll teach her to speak well enough to be passed off successfully as a lady of class at the Embassy Ball later that year.

In spite of the qualms of his housekeeper, Mrs. Pearce, Higgins orders Eliza to be taken away, bathed, and dressed. Then he lays out his intentions. The girl will stay in the house, be fed, clothed, and taught, and he will win his bet. After that she can do what she likes. Pickering is a little more respectful of Eliza's feelings and feels he must make sure that no advantage is taken of the girl, but Higgins laughs the suggestion off; he has no intention of letting a woman into his life. She would merely disorder it ("An Ordinary Man").

The exercise is well under way when, one day, Alfred Doolittle turns up at Wimpole Street. Under the pretense of reclaiming his daughter, he is out to get some boozing money from these well-heeled gentlemen. He is stopped short in his little bit of blackmail when Higgins coolly tells him to take the girl away, and he has to backtrack hurriedly. But the dustman's uncomplicatedly amoral reasoning over the selling of his daughter at a reasonable rate appeals to Higgins who ends up giving the rogue five pounds and sends him off happy. Eliza is not so happy. She is having an awful time getting her vowels straight and, when Higgins deprives her of lunch and dinner until she has got them right, she explodes in a private rage of frustration ("Just You Wait").

Time passes and, working day and night, Higgins patiently and sometimes less patiently instills good speech into the girl's mind and mouth. Then, one weary night, it all comes together. Higgins, Pickering, and Eliza caper around the room in delight as all the plans Higgins has made start to blossom ("The Rain in Spain"). Eliza is blissfully unable to think of bed when it is all over and, as she relives her delirious dance of triumph in Higgins's arms, she happily sings to all who will listen "I Could Have Danced All Night."

Eliza's first public trial is at Ascot (Ascot Gavotte) when Higgins brings the girl to join his mother's society friends in her box. If Eliza's vowels are now in order, however, the content of her conversation is apt to lapse from time to time. She stuns Mrs. Higgins's guests with her perfectly pronounced East End expressions, which Higgins hastily passes off as the latest society small-talk but, ultimately, she goes beyond the pale. In the excitement of a horse race, she howls out to her horse to "move your bloomin' arse." Tableau.

Ascot makes Eliza one conquest. Freddy Eynsford-Hill falls in love with the exquisite, unusual girl and he takes to wandering asininely around Wimpole Street just to be "On the Street Where You Live." In the light of the Ascot debacle, Pickering is anxious to call off the wager. Higgins, however, is determined to continue and, with Eliza working hard to erase the mortification of her last foray into society, he is confident of success. Six weeks later, the night of the Embassy Ball arrives. Eliza appears at the ballroom on Higgins's arm, looking radiant, and attracts immediate attention, but some of that attention is unwelcome. Zoltan Karpathy, a language expert who has turned his skills to unsavory uses, moves in on the girl, sensing some sort of a mystery and, as the curtain falls, he animatedly leads Eliza into a dance (The Embassy Waltz).

Act 2

At three o'clock in the morning the tired party arrives home. Higgins's bet has been won, and Pickering jubilates "You Did It" as they retail the evening's events to Mrs. Pearce. Karpathy insisted that Eliza was no English lady, but a Hungarian Princess! In all the celebrating, no one has thought to address one word of congratulation to Eliza herself and, when all the fuss is done and Higgins goes to look for his slippers, they are hurled at him from the other side of the room by the tearful girl. Now that the bet is over, what is to become of her? Higgins is genuinely surprised. He hadn't really thought about it. He supposes she might marry or, as she said at the start of the whole affair, go and work in a flower shop. But he hadn't really realized she'd be leaving.

Eliza bitterly asks him what is hers to take away and what must be returned, and when she pointedly gives him back a ring he had given her as a gift, Higgins, unwilling to have his emotions stirred in such a way, finally gets angry. Flinging the ring in the fireplace, he stalks out. As soon as he is gone, Eliza runs to retrieve the ring, but, after a few vengeful lines of "Just You Wait," dissolve into sobs. She changes and packs and is leaving the house when she sees Freddy, posted in his usual position at the doorstep singing "On the Street Where You Live." He tries to comfort her with words of love, but Eliza has had enough in the way of words from Higgins and she explodes into a demand for action ("Show Me").

The confused Eliza makes her way back to her old haunts in Covent Garden, but no one there recognizes her in her new persona until she meets her father coming out of a pub, all dressed up with a flower in his buttonhole. He's getting married to the woman he's lived with for so many years, and it's all Eliza's fault. Apparently Higgins told a millionaire philanthropist that the most original moralist in Britain was a dustman called Doolittle and the old chap left Alfred £4,000 a year in his will. With that sort of money, there's no way he could continue his old happy-go-lucky life. He's been delivered bound and gagged into the middle class, and that means marriage ("Get Me to the Church on Time").

Meanwhile, back at Wimpole Street, Eliza's flight has been discovered. The two men try to set a search in motion while the uncomprehending Higgins muses on the unpredictability of women ("Hymn to Him").

Eliza, not knowing where to go, unable to fit either into her old life or her new, finally finds her way to Mrs. Higgins's home. Mrs. Higgins is totally sympathetic. The men have behaved abominably and Eliza is quite right to walk out on them. When Henry turns up, expecting help and sympathy, he is staggered to find his mother calmly take Eliza's part.

Face to face, Eliza tries to explain to Higgins the sort of consideration she wants from him. It isn't love—if she wanted that, there's Freddy and loads of others—it is more like friendship. But the interview breaks down through lack of a common understanding and the frustrated Eliza, thrusting for any weak spot in her teacher's composure, swears that she'll marry Freddy and go and teach phonetics with Zoltan Karpathy. This really does rouse Higgins to anger and Eliza, with the upper hand at last, is triumphant as she tells him what she will do "Without You." She is magnificent, and Higgins is all approval: This is the Eliza he likes. Then, with what sounds like a final goodbye, she is gone, and Henry Higgins calls helplessly for his mother.

Higgins cannot get used to the idea that she will not be coming back ("I've Grown Accustomed to Her Face"). Alone in his study, he switches on a recording of Eliza's voice, which he made in the early days of their lessons, and, as he listens, head in hands, Eliza enters. Turning off the machine, she gently mimics her old voice. Higgins looks up. If he would let himself, his face would show everything from relief to pure joy. But he doesn't. He simply asks, as he asked the previous night, for his slippers. Eliza understands that this is all she will ever get. She can take it or leave it and, for the moment, she is apparently going to take it.

1956

CANDIDE

A COMIC OPERETTA IN TWO ACTS by Lillian Hellman based on the satire by Voltaire. Lyrics by Richard Wilbur. Additional lyrics by John Latouche and Dorothy Parker. Music by Leonard Bernstein.

Produced at the Martin Beck Theatre, New York, 1 December 1956, with Max Adrian (Pangloss), Robert Rounseville (Candide), Barbara Cook (Cunegonde), Louis Edmonds (Maximilian), and Irra Petina (Old Lady). Produced in a revised version in one act with a new book by Hugh Wheeler and additional lyrics by Stephen Sondheim at the Chelsea Theatre Centre, Brooklyn, 19 December 1973, and the Broadway Theatre, New York, 8 March 1974, with Lewis J. Stadlen, Mark Baker, Maureen Brennan, Sam Freed, June Gable, and Deborah St. Darr (Paquette).

The incurably optimistic Candide (Robert Rounseville) and his mentor Pangloss (Max Adrian) go through many excruciating trials on their way to the final curtain. This one is the Spanish Inquisition. Friedman-Abeles, photographers. Courtesy Performing Arts Research Center, New York Public Library at Lincoln Center.

CHARACTERS

Voltaire/Dr. Pangloss/The Governor of Buenos Aires/Host/Sage

Candide

Cunegonde

Paquette

Maximilian

Old Lady

Baron, Grand Inquisitor, Baroness etc.

Act 1

Voltaire, the eighteenth century author of *Candide*, is himself the commentator for this version of his picaresque and picturesque tale of philosophical devotion. More, throughout the evening, he joins the story to play various crucial characters in the lives of the wandering Candide and his beloved Cunegonde. To begin the evening, he introduces us to the principals of the story.

The setting is Westphalia and the castle of the Baron Thunder-Ten-Tronck, where the happy inhabitants include, apart from the aforesaid Baron and his Baroness, their lovely and innocent virgin daughter, Cunegonde, their spotlessly beautiful son, Maximilian, their pretty bastard nephew, Candide, and the Baroness's buxom and willing serving maid, Paquette. To each of these "Life Is Happiness Indeed." What is the reason for their supreme happiness, for their joyful consciousness of their own perfections and that of their situation? Why, it is the philosophy that has been inculcated in them by a great and glorious teacher: their tutor, Dr. Pangloss, who reasons with a satisfied passivity that all is for the best in "The Best of All Possible Worlds." This philosophy extends from things minimal and physical to things great and metaphysical, and Pangloss has a syllogism to fit every question, proving without doubt that everything in the world is incapable of improvement and that all events are happy events.

Today, at the dismissal of class, Paquette is ordered to stay behind for her additional lesson in advanced physics. Cunegonde, in an endless quest for knowledge, makes an excuse to return to the schoolroom and there she finds the good Dr. Pangloss astride the compliant maidservant. She innocently asks for an academic explanation and is treated to a lecture on specific gravity of which the relative positions of the Doctor and Paquette are allegedly an example. Although this lesson is somewhat ahead of the curriculum, Cunegonde hurries out to find Candide and put to the test her new knowledge, and the pair find that it is indeed a most pleasant piece of philosophy ("Oh, Happy We").

Unfortunately, they have chosen a somewhat open piece of terrain for their experiment and brother Maximilian, happening to glance out a baronial window, spies the two in carnal action and squeals. The family Thunder-Ten-Tronck abandons its dinner to descend upon the bastard in the garden and, as Cunegonde explodes into wails of tears, Candide finds himself banished from his homely castle and from Westphalia, ghastly imprecations ringing in his ears against ever returning.

In the middle of a desolate heath on the way out of Westphalia, the young man pauses to sing of how he is sustained by Dr. Pangloss's philosophy ("It Must Be So"). Even if it is not immediately obvious, there is undoubtedly some good reason behind this seeming tragedy. But right now Bulgaria is invading Westphalia by the same route that Candide has chosen to leave it, and a chance encounter with some Bulgarians ends with our hero tied up in a sack, pressed for the Bulgarian army. That very army has, meanwhile, arrived at the gates of Schloss Thunder-Ten-Tronck and all the reigning family are slaughtered pitilessly. All, that is, except Cunegonde who is captured by a soldier with a facility for business: There are 97 men in his regiment and, at 20 ducats a go, Cunegonde is going to make his fortune.

Later, as a thoroughly ravished Cunegonde crawls wearily off a pile of abandoned corpses, a turn in the fortunes of the battle results in the captors of Candide being mown down, leaving the boy abandoned in his sack. At a distance from each other, the young people recall plaintively the happy innocent days they once knew together, but fate has decreed that the two of them shall, for now, follow very different paths. Candide, saved from his sack by a passing troupe of players, joins them as a bad touring actor, while Cunegonde, after her rapid-fire expansion of experience, becomes an ever-improving prostitute. She improves to such an extent that she ends up in Lisbon as the much bejewelled mistress of both a rich Jew and the Grand Inquisitor under a convenient time-sharing arrangement ("Glitter and Be Gay").

Candide is also destined to turn up in Lisbon. Swept ashore in an earthquake, he meets among the corpses none other than Dr. Pangloss who has, it appears, escaped the sack of Schloss Thunder-Ten-Tronck but has lost his nose as a result of syphilis. He is not depressed, for syphilis is a product of the New World and had the New World not been discovered he could never have experienced potatoes, tobacco, and chocolate. It is still the best of all possible worlds. However, when the good doctor expounds his impeccably optimistic philosophy before an apparently dying man, he is in for an unpleasant surprise. The false corpse is a spy of the Inquisition and he is arrested for heresy.

Pangloss and Candide are dragged captive to Lisbon where the daily entertainment of the "Auto Da Fé" is in inexorable progress. Pangloss is sentenced by the Inquisitor and hanged. Candide is stripped and whipped before the very eyes of a fainting Cunegonde. When the flagellation is over and the lords of the Inquisition have departed, an old lady comes to cut Candide down and, in the days that follow, she restores the lad to health and vigour with the aid of magic ointments known only to the old ladies of "This World."

When he is at last whole again, the old lady secretly leads him into the presence of the beloved he thought dead ("You Were Dead, You Know"). As the two duet happily in Cunegonde's apartment, the old lady returns to warn that the Jew is on his way to visit his mistress. Cunegonde tries to explain the Jew and his position in her life to Candide, but her efforts are cut short when her furious demiprotector bursts in, draws his sword, and chases the young man jealously around the room. But, in his pursuit, he slips and drops his sword and, when Candide helpfully retrieves it and offers it back to him, the Jew, rushing ever onward, accidentally and fatally impales himself on the proffered blade.

At midnight, as the time-sharing arrangement allows, the Inquisitor arrives to take his share of pleasure and, egged on by Cunegonde's descriptions of repeated ravishment, Candide skewers him too. This most innocent lad has the blood of two of the most superb citizens of Lisbon on his weapon. He and his lady love must flee the city.

With horses supplied by the old lady, they head for Cadiz where, to their horror, Cunegonde's jewels are pilfered by a friar picked up for a night's entertainment by the old lady. In an effort to atone, the good dame attempts to sell what remains of her unobvious charms ("I Am Easily Assimilated") but without success. It is Candide's physical attributes that come to their aid. He accepts an offer to lead a muscled relief party to the Jesuits of Montevideo, and the little party board a vessel for the New World.

In Cartagena, Colombia, another group of Europeans is arriving under less comfortable circumstances. The Governor of the area, having gone through the entire female population in his pursuit of pleasure, is looking among the newly imported slaves for potential amusement, and who should be among them but Paquette. It is not she who takes his fancy, however, but another Caucasian who turns out to be Maximilian ("My Love") dressed up in feminine attire to fulfill the unusual sexual tastes of the captain of the slave ship. The Governor is not at all pleased when he finds that his new love is male, and he sells Maximilian off to the Jesuits, who apparently go in for such things.

Close behind, the ship bearing Candide, Cunegonde, and the old lady is in sight of land. Their trip has been enlivened by the telling of the old lady's life story, a gory tale of frequent sexual defilement, which is reaching its climax with a particularly nasty incident involving Barbary pirates and the lady's buttocks when they are attacked. It is pirates again, so Cunegonde and the old lady are carried off for another round of ravishment, leaving Candide to reach the Jesuits of Montevideo alone.

What is his surprise to find there, among the gentlemen of the order, both Maximilian and Paquette ("Alleluia"). He gives them the happy news that Cunegonde is also living and promises that, though she is once again temporarily lost, he will find her, rescue her, and wed her. But in spite of all his debasements, Maximilian is still a Thunder-Ten-Tronck, and he is murderously livid at the idea that his sister should marry a bastard. As he chases Candide angrily around the church, the young man hides behind a statue. Alas, in his flight, he accidentally knocks the stone figure forward and it falls to the ground, crushing the vengeful Maximilian to death.

That night, two young Jesuits slip off into the jungle, fleeing from the monastery and the deed. But Paquette and Candide, for it is they, are not long lost. Deep in the rain forests of South America they stumble on the wondrous and perfect land of El Dorado, where the streets are made of diamonds and the animals can talk and even sing (Sheep's Song).

The old lady, meanwhile, has been rejected by the pirates as unravishworthy and abandoned on a rocky coast. There she is laid low by the anaesthetic dart of a local pygmy looking for food but, deemed inedible, she is swapped off to a German botanist for three machetes and then exchanged for unmentioned favors to the madame of a brothel. But she is destined before long to meet up again with Candide and Paquette.

Tiring, at last, of the perfection of El Dorado and anxious to find Cunegonde, the pair finally return to Cartagena accompanied by two sheep loaded with gold and jewels. They learn that the pirates have taken Cunegonde to Constantinople, and Candide anxiously accepts the Governor's offer of a boat. Alas, the wily Governor is only after their sheep and the gold, and the boat he gives them is full of holes ("Bon Voyage"). The travellers founder on a desert island, but the sheep struggle ashore with them and, when they are rescued, the five head richly for Constantinople. There they find Cunegonde, an odalisque in a wealthy man's household. Candide offers nearly all their gold and jewels for her release and then hands over the last of their money to buy the freedom of Maximilian who has somehow, uncrushed, fallen into the same Turkish hands.

All the little band are back together again at last. But they are in Turkestan, without a penny and without an idea. At the suggestion of the old lady, they visit a nearby cave to consult the Wisest Man in the World, but who should they find there but a rather hazy Dr. Pangloss in the midst of a panorama of books full of varied philosophic wisdom. After their many perilous years following the Pangloss creed, they find now that their master seems to have abandoned it himself in favor of a new philosophy: the work ethic. Candide, ever obedient, vows to buy a little farm. There, the years of tribulation and wandering over, they will work from dawn to dusk and "Make Our Garden Grow." At last they can exist in rustic simplicity far from the evils of the world, tend their fields, and milk their cow. As their paean to their new life ends, the cow falls dead. It is the pox.

The first version of *Candide* included a number of musical pieces that were not retained in the revised version, including Candide's Lament, the Venice Gavotte (both of which were partially used in rewritten numbers), "The Simple Life," "Paris Waltz," "Quiet," "El Dorado," "It Must Be Me," "What's the Use?" and "No More than This." "Life Is Happiness Indeed," "This World," and The Sheep's Song were introduced in the 1973 production described here, and the Auto Da Fé scene extended.

1957

THE MUSIC MAN

A MUSICAL COMEDY IN TWO ACTS by Meredith Willson based on a story by Meredith Willson and Franklin Lacey.

Produced at the Majestic Theatre, New York, 19 December 1957, with Robert Preston (Harold Hill), Barbara Cook (Marian), Iggie Wolfington (Marcellus), and David Burns (Mayor).

A film version was produced by Warner Brothers in 1962 with Robert Preston, Shirley Jones, Buddy Hackett, and Paul Ford, with Hermione Gingold as Eulalie.

The "think system" of music teaching can bear fruit—
it all depends on what you want to hear. Harold (Robert
Preston), Marian (Barbara Cook), and a happy ending.
Friedman-Abeles, photographers.
Courtesy Performing Arts Research Center,
New York Public Library at Lincoln Center.

CHARACTERS

Harold Hill, *a travelling salesman*

Charlie Cowell

Mayor Shinn

Eulalie MacKechnie Shinn, *his wife*

Zaneeta Shinn, *their daughter*

Ewart Dunlop

Oliver

Hix

Jacey Squires

Olin Britt

Marcellus Washburn

Tommy Djilas

Marian Paroo

Mrs. Paroo, *her mother*

Winthrop Paroo, *Marian's brother*

Amaryllis

Alma Hix

Maud Dunlop

Ethel Toffelmeier

Mrs. Squires

Constable Locke, Gracie Shinn, Conductor, etc.

Act 1

It's the fourth of July in the year of 1912, and a train is making its rhythmical way through the depths of the state of Iowa. One compartment is occupied by a number of travelling salesmen, passing the time as they rattle on to their next pitch in playing cards and discussing the details of their mighty profession ("Rock Island"). Each of the men has his say on the reasons for success or failure, but Charlie Cowell has just one dictum—you've got to know the territory.

The conversation turns to a fellow name of Hill, Professor Harold Hill. This fellow, it seems, has laws all his own. He is a music man. He sells band instruments to the hopeful parents of the country towns, and he sells fine. But Charlie Cowell has had the bad experience of following this Hill into town and he knows the second part of the story. Hill sells the instruments all right, but he doesn't know a note of music so no one ever gets taught how to play. He's a blight on the good name of the travelling salesman and anyone who follows on behind him is likely to get tarred and feathered by the angry townsfolk. Still, they're all pretty safe in Iowa: Even Hill wouldn't have the gall to try his tricks on good old stiff-necked Iowa. The conductor calls out River City and a quiet gentleman who has been cleaning up in the card game gets up to leave the train. He has heard a challenge. On his suitcase we can read the name Professor Harold Hill.

The "Iowa Stubborn" folk of River City are going about their daily business when Harold Hill arrives in town and, to his surprise, he meets up as quick as blinking with an old comrade-in-charms, Marcellus Washburn. Marcellus has reformed and given up the spiel for the stable, but salesmanship dies hard and he swiftly gives Harold the lowdown on River City. If it's musical instruments he's selling this year then he'd best beware of the town music teacher who is also the librarian. But when Harold hears that this teacher is female, he worries no more.

Next he looks for a wedge. What's new in town? A pool table has just been installed in the local billiard hall. That'll do fine. Harold moves to work, evangelizing with rich-voiced facility on the evils of pool ("Trouble") and the problems it could bring to the parents of River City whose children get caught in its vicious sway. His message catches on and soon the folk of River City are worriedly discussing this new evil in their midst.

Harold, meanwhile, has had Marian Paroo, the music teacher, pointed out to him and he sets off to charm her into believing in him. Marian is not to be easily won over. She gives him a swift brush off and hurries on home to give a "Piano Lesson" to little Amaryllis. The lesson is punctuated by Mrs. Paroo's oft-repeated bewailing of her daughter's unmarried state.

Before she has finished, Marian's ten-year-old brother Winthrop arrives home. Winthrop is a sullen and monosyllabic child, mortified by a bad lisp into tearful quietness. He will not even say "yes" to Amaryllis when she invites him to her birthday party, and the little girl, who is very fond of Winthrop, also ends up in tears. Winthrop just has to be her sweetheart or else she has no one to say goodnight to when the evening star comes out. Marian assures her that it doesn't matter if you don't have someone special, you just have to leave a gap for the name until the right man comes along. As a mollified Amaryllis goes back to the piano, Marian looks out the window at the evening star and herself sings "Goodnight, My Someone."

At the High School Hall, Mayor Shinn is chairing an entertainment in which his wife, Eulalie, holds a leading part. The whole affair falls apart when Tommy Djilas, a lad from the wrong side of the tracks, sets off a firecracker in the middle of Mrs. Shinn's genuine Indian recitation and, when the Mayor attempts to continue with his parish announcements, he is hamstrung by the constant bickering of the four leading lights of the School Board. Order is only restored when Harold rises from the body of the hall to bring up the subject of the malignant pool table. He quickly gets the townsfolk behind him before he slickly shifts the topic from pool to the beneficial influence to the town of a boys' band described in all its flashing brass and color ("Seventy Six Trombones"). Mayor Shinn is not dazzled by this spellbinder, however, and, as the people gather behind Harold, he orders the School Board to inquire into the credentials of this music man.

Harold is by now in full swing. He corrals Tommy Djilas as his lieutenant and, pairing him off with a pretty girl, wins his first allegiance. So far he has made only two mistakes: Mayor Shinn owns the billiard house and the pool table, and the pretty girl is Zaneeta Shinn, eldest daughter of the self-same Mayor. In accordance with Shinn's instructions, he is cornered by the School Board who demand to see his certificates and qualifications for his musical position, but Harold quickly sidetracks them by finding in them the perfect voices for a barbershop quartet. Men who have done nothing but fight among themselves for fifteen years are suddenly in harmony and deeply "Sincere."

Marcellus is amazed when he hears that Harold means to stay in town for four weeks. Four weeks is far too long. By that time, the kids will have had long enough to find out he can't teach them music. But Harold has two systems: One is the Think System for learning music. You don't actually learn to play notes, you just think them and eventually out they'll come. The other is uniforms. Once he's skinned the folk of the cash for the instruments, he waits a little while and then skins them again for the kids' uniforms. When they see those dizzy uniforms, they don't even think about not being able to play. In the meantime, he's out to chat himself up a girl who will see him comfortably through his stay: a nice "Sadder-but-Wiser Girl" who knows her way around.

What he gets is Eulalie Shinn and her group of ladies, all eager to come under his spell. It's too easy. Harold charms Eulalie into the leadership of an instantly formed Ladies Auxiliary for the Classical Dance but, when he happens to mention Marian's name, the ladies go into a twittering gasp ("Pickalittle"). Marian is beyond the pale. She houses dirty books like Chaucer, Balzac, and Rabelais in her library, and everyone knows that she took up with the elderly man who owned the place so that he left her all the books when he died, even though he left the library building to the town. Harold is still ensnared by the pickalittling ladies when the School Board turns up to, once again, demand his credentials. Harold sets them singing "Goodnight Ladies" and makes his escape.

Harold corners Marian in her library and makes a pass at her ("Marian the Librarian") before setting off around the town to sweet talk the parents of River City into buying instruments for their children. Mrs. Paroo signs up for a cornet for Winthrop, who is bug-eyed at the thought of the instrument and the uniform, and she catches some stern disapproval from her daughter who tells her that Harold is nothing but a charlatan. She will prove it. Mrs. Paroo sighs that if she takes that attitude to every man she'll never find one to wed, but Marian has her own ideas about "My White Knight."

The librarian knows her books, and the Indiana State Register on her shelves soon disproves Harold's invented background. She marches off to find the mayor, bearing the evidence that the School Board have been too busy quartetting to unearth but, just as she reaches Shinn, the town erupts. The "Wells Fargo Wagon" is coming in. The people gather round excitedly for their mail and there, among the parcels, are the children's instruments. Before Marian's amazed eyes, little Winthrop bursts out of his mutism with sheer excitement as he takes the shiny cornet in his hands. When the Mayor takes the Register from the librarian to read her evidence against Harold, she secretly tears out the relevant page as she gazes wonderingly at the miracle-making music man.

Act 2

There is plenty of musical action in River City now. Down at the gymnasium Mrs. Shinn's dancing ladies and the harmonies of the School Board ("It's You") are succeeded by the young people with a very different kind of dancing ("Shipoopi"). Mayor Shinn hasn't given up, however. He admits the instruments are here but next thing he wants to hear them played and, in the meanwhile, where are those credentials?

Marian, by now totally under the spell cast by Harold, is a little worried about the lack of conventional tuition. She has to force her practical self to have any faith in the Think System. But, at least, she has now become totally accepted and even admired by the townswomen who, under the influence of the

Professor, have all read Chaucer, Rabelais, and Balzac and voted them delightful ("Pickalittle").

The School Board are still on the trail of Harold and his darned credentials but each time they get too near he succeeds in sidetracking them with the fortunate mention of an old favorite tune which sets them singing ("Lida Rose"). Marian, sitting alone, admits to herself that she is falling in love ("Will I Ever Tell You?"). As for Winthrop, he is a changed lad. Far from being mute, nowadays he just bubbles over with chatter as he describes all the wonderful things he has learned from Harold ("Gary Indiana") even though none of them seems to have anything much to do with the cornet and the famous Minuet in G that the band is supposed to be studying.

Now Nemesis arrives in River City, in the person of Charlie Cowell. Charlie is still smarting from the treatment he has got travelling in behind Harold Hill in other towns, and he has made up his mind that he is going to expose Hill before he can pull the same trick again. This week's train has stopped at River City for a few minutes and Charlie has got off specially to find the Mayor and tell him all about the music man. Hurrying through the town, he asks Marian for directions but, when she discovers why he is there, she occupies his time by flirting with him until he has to run back to the station or miss his train. She is well and truly Harold's accomplice now and, when he asks her to walk with him to the footbridge—the lovers' lane of River City— that night, she agrees to go.

When they take their walk, it is not quite what Harold expected. Marian is under no illusions about him. She knows that his background is phoney and that he is a travelling salesman in every sense, but she admits that he's opened her eyes and her heart in a way she would never have thought possible ("Till There Was You"). As a gage of her feelings, she gives him the torn-out page from the Register, but it isn't until they've kissed and he is strutting back to town that Harold realizes he is in love. He's also in trouble. Charlie Cowell has missed his train and he is heading back to the town square boiling with fury and vengeance. He is going to find the Mayor and denounce Harold before the whole of River City. Marcellus urges Harold to get safely out of town and, as the word spreads, Marian also hurries to warn him to escape, but he refuses. He is staying in River City.

Then he runs into Winthrop, and the little boy, broken-hearted at the exposure of his hero as just another charlatan, sadly and bitterly reproaches Harold with his lies. He wishes he'd never come to River City. But Marian cannot agree. Since Harold came to town things have been different. Look at happy Mrs. Shinn and her ladies. Look at the harmonious School Board. Look at all the kids walking around with their heads held high. Look at Winthrop himself . . . and look at Marian the librarian, the disliked spinster who has finally come out from behind her books and started to live. Harold is still there when the constable comes to put the handcuffs on him.

The Mayor is giving a self-congratulatory speech reeking of tar and feathers when Marian challenges him with the good Harold has done to the town. Sure of his ground, Shinn challenges anyone in the town who supports Hill to stand up and, one by one, they do just that: Mrs. Paroo first, then Zaneeta, then the School Board and the Ladies, and even Eulalie, his wife. Then, to cap it all, Tommy Djilas marches in at the head of the famous boys' band. They're all dressed in the uniforms and carrying the instruments that cost River City's parents their hard-earned money. Marian hands Harold the blackboard pointer as a baton and, with a fervent prayer to the efficacity of the Think System, he begins to conduct. The result is barely recognizable as music, but the good folk of River City see only their children in their uniforms playing music on their instruments and they are delighted. Harold Hill has done what he promised. Even the Mayor has to give in and, as Marian and Harold fall into each other's arms, it seems a fair bet that the boys' band is not the only thing that is just beginning in River City.

1957

WEST SIDE STORY

A MUSICAL IN TWO ACTS by Arthur Laurents. Lyrics by Stephen Sondheim. Music by Leonard Bernstein.

Produced at the Winter Garden Theatre, New York, 26 September 1957, with Larry Kert (Tony), Carol Lawrence (Maria), Chita Rivera (Anita), Mickey Calin (Riff), and Ken LeRoy (Bernardo), and revived there, 27 April 1960, with Kert, Lawrence, Allyn Ann McLerie, Thomas Hasson, and George Marcy. Produced at the Minskoff Theatre, 14 February 1980, with Ken Marshall, Josie de Guzman, Debbie Allen, James J. Mellon, and Hector Jaime Mercado.

A film version was produced by Mirisch/United Artists in 1961 with Richard Beymer, Natalie Wood (singing dubbed by Marni Nixon), Rita Moreno (singing dubbed by Betty Wand), Russ Tamblyn, and George Chakiris.

Children's games turn dramatically dangerous
as a fist-fight gives way to a skirmish with knives.
Ken LeRoy as Bernardo and Micky Calin as Riff.
Friedman-Abeles, photographers.
Courtesy Performing Arts Research Center,
New York Public Library at Lincoln Center.

CHARACTERS

Riff, *leader of the Jets*

Tony, *his friend*

Bernardo, *leader of the Sharks*

Maria, *his sister*

Anita, *his girl*

Chino, *his friend*

Doc

Officer Krupke

Action, A-rab, Baby John,
Snowboy, Big Deal, Diesel, Gee-
Tar, Mouthpiece, Tiger, *the Jets*

Graziella, Velma, Minnie,
Clarice, Pauline, Anybodys,
the Jets girls

Pepe, Indio, Luis, Anxious,
Nibbles, Juano, Toro, Moose,
the Sharks

Rosalia, Consuelo, Teresita,
Francisca, Estella, Margarita,
the Sharks girls

Lieutenant Schrank,
Glad Hand, etc.

Act 1

In a New York street, two rival gangs of young teenagers are playing an elaborate cat-and-mouse game (Prologue). The Jets, a heterogeneous group of what, for lack of a better term, are called Americans, regard the stretch of street as their preserve. Their opponents are the Sharks, a Puerto Rican gang who, to the Jets, are invaders against whom they will protect their property with their fists and, if necessary, with more dangerous weapons. These warring adolescents will, however, close ranks against the adult world, especially when that adult world is represented by the enforcers of the law. No one will break faith with the cockeyed code of their little world, nor let the law take revenge for a bloodied ear or a blackened eye.

Riff, the leader of the Jets, is worried about the threatening presence of the Sharks. He lines up his "troops" (Jet Song) and promises them an all-out fight against the Puerto Ricans to confirm their territory. At the dance at the gym that night, he will challenge Bernardo and his Sharks to a "rumble." As his lieutenant on this important mission, Riff wants to take Tony, a former gang member now grown into a young adult and working in Doc's drugstore, but Tony doesn't want to have anything to do with these sort of games. He's grown out of all that sort of thing and he's looking forward to the next part of his life ("Something's Coming"). But when he finds out that his old buddy has promised to bring him to the challenge, he weakens and agrees to come to save Riff's face with the gang.

At the bridal shop where she works, Bernardo's young sister Maria is having her communion dress made over to wear to the dance. Maria has been brought from Puerto Rico by her brother to be married to his friend, the quiet and shy Chino, and tonight she feels that she is becoming an American. She is disappointed that she must wear white, and such a proper dress, but she is delighted to be going to her very first American dance.

At the dance, the tensions between the two gangs and their girls are bubbling explosively under the surface as they release their energy in some wild dancing. Bernardo arrives with his girl, Anita, and with Chino and Maria, and they join the dancing but, in the middle of the frenetic activity, something happens. Maria and Tony meet and time goes into a delicate slow-motion. They are in a world of their own and instantly in love but, when Tony gently kisses the young girl, he finds Bernardo furiously upon him with orders to keep away from his sister. The angry Bernardo is taking Maria away when Riff intervenes. He wants to issue his challenge. Bernardo icily agrees to meet for a council of war at the drugstore in a half-hour.

Left alone, Tony can think only of the girl he has just met ("Maria"), and soon he is in the back alley behind Bernardo's home trying to see her again. Maria climbs secretly out on to the fire escape to meet him. The world is theirs "Tonight."

Anita attempts to take Maria's part against Bernardo's strictures. They are Americans now, this is not Puerto Rico. In America a girl has some freedom. Tony is American too, even if his family is Polish. What is the difference between him and them? Why should Maria not like him? But Bernardo is not interested in listening to Anita's reasoning. He cannot see beyond the game he plays and the rivalry between the Jets and the Sharks. He must go to his big, important war council at the drugstore. When the boys are gone, Anita leads the girls in song and dance in praise of the wonderful modern conveniences of "America."

At Doc's drugstore, the Jets wait nervously. The PRs are challenged, therefore they have the choice of weapons. They might pick knives or something else dangerous. Doc shakes his head. Why are they fighting over a dumb bit of street? The nervy Action explodes at his implied belittling of the gangs and their rivalry and he has to be calmed by Riff. They must save their aggression for the rumble; right now it's time to stay "Cool." Bernardo and his friends turn up and the talk turns to weapons, but just when it looks as if the fight may turn very nasty, Tony arrives. He scorns them as cowardly for resorting to bricks and bottles, and shames them into agreeing to a fair fist-fight between the best man from each gang. Eyeing Tony, Bernardo quickly agrees, but he is disappointed when Diesel is elected to represent the Jets.

The next day, Tony comes to visit Maria at the bridal shop. She is upset about the fighting and makes him promise that he will stop the rumble, but she is also childishly happy as they innocently act out the wedding they will one day have and sincerely sing their pledge to each other of "One Hand, One Heart."

Evening comes on and the time appointed for the rumble gets nearer (Quintet/"Tonight"). As Bernardo and Diesel prepare to fight, Tony arrives to try to keep his promise to Maria to stop the combat. Bernardo attempts to goad him into a fight himself, but it is Riff who leaps forward in answer to the taunts and attacks the foul-mouthed Puerto Rican. Bernardo, all thought of a fair fight ignored, draws a knife, and Riff is forced to respond in kind. The fight is hard but Riff finally gains the upper hand and seems to have his opponent at his mercy when Tony calls out to him to hold his blow. Riff hesitates and, in that moment of hesitation, Bernardo takes his chance and knifes him dead.

Bernardo stands triumphant, as a free-for-all breaks out all around him, until Tony snatches up his dead friend's knife and, blind with grief and anger, cuts the murderer down. As the police sirens sing in the surrounding streets, he stands there dazed at what he has done, thinking only of Maria, until little Anybodys drags him to safety.

Act 2 Back at home, Maria is in high spirits ("I Feel Pretty") but her happiness is shattered when Chino arrives with news of the rumble and of Bernardo's death.

Maria's only thought is for Tony. Chino, outraged at such treachery, tells her that Tony is her brother's killer and, taking a gun, he coldly leaves the house to go in search of revenge. When Tony climbs up by the fire escape to find her, Maria's distress for her brother is soon overwhelmed by her love, and, as they clasp each other tightly, they sing together of a world where they might be away from all this hatred ("Somewhere").

The boys live in another kind of dream world. They can distance the evening's tragedy from their thoughts enough to lark around and take the mickey out of the police ("Gee, Officer Krupke") but, when Anybodys brings news that Chino is out stalking Tony with a gun, the Jets are forced back into action.

Anita comes to Maria's room and finds it locked. As she knocks, Maria hastily helps Tony out the window. She arranges to meet him later at Doc's, kisses him hastily goodbye, and only then does she open the door and let Anita in. The open window tells its story, and Anita turns bitterly on the girl, full of accusations. Now she has picked up Bernardo's attitudes—Tony is one of them, how can she help "A Boy Like That" who has killed her brother? Maria's answer is simple, she loves him ("I Have a Love"). It is an answer that Anita, whose own lover is lying dead under the highway, can understand. There is nothing more to be said.

The police arrive to question Maria and she sees that her rendezvous with Tony is threatened. In veiled language, she begs Anita to go to the drugstore to warn him and Anita, in spite of everything, agrees. When she gets there, however, she is roughly treated by the gathered Jets in spite of her urgent assertions that she is there to help. Doc comes in in time to stop her from being too badly manhandled, but her will to help these people and their leader is gone. Bernardo was right. They are animals. In revenge, she shouts out that Tony will never see Maria again. Chino has found out about them, and shot her.

Tony is in the basement, hiding till Doc can help him get out of town. Doc brings him the awful news and the anguished Tony rushes into the street, calling madly for Chino to come and kill him too. But, instead of Chino, he sees Maria. They are running joyfully toward each other as a shot rings out. Chino has found his man.

As Tony dies, Maria takes up the gun. Now she hates. Now she, too, can kill. But when it comes to the moment she cannot take her revenge. She can only turn to them all—Jets and Sharks—to come and mourn with her, and so, when Tony's body is lifted from the ground, it is lifted by the Jets and the Sharks together. Together they carry him away, with Maria bravely following behind, as the adults who have gathered at the scene look on, helpless to take part in this wasteful, foolish melodrama of youth.

1959

THE SOUND OF MUSIC

A MUSICAL IN TWO ACTS by Howard Lindsay and Russel Crouse. Lyrics by Oscar Hammerstein II. Music by Richard Rodgers.

Produced at the Lunt-Fontanne Theatre, New York, 16 November 1959, with Mary Martin (Maria), Theodore Bikel (Captain von Trapp), and Patricia Neway (Mother Abbess).

A film version was produced by Twentieth Century-Fox in 1965 with Julie Andrews, Christopher Plummer (sung by Bill Lee), and Peggy Wood (sung by Margery McKay).

Maria Rainer (Mary Martin) wins the von Trapp children with her music; she wins their father, too. Friedman-Abeles, photographers. Courtesy Performing Arts Research Center, New York Public Library at Lincoln Center.

CHARACTERS

Mother Abbess *of Nonnberg Abbey*

Sister Berthe, *Mistress of the Novices*

Sister Margaretta, *Mistress of Postulants*

Sister Sophia

Maria Rainer, *a postulant at the Abbey*

Captain Georg von Trapp

Frau Schmidt, *his housekeeper*

Franz, *his butler*

Liesl, Friedrich, Louisa, Kurt, Marta, Gretl, Brigitta, *his children*

Rolf Gruber

Elsa Schräder

Max Detweiler

Herr Zeller

Admiral von Schreiber, Baron Elberfeld, Baroness Elberfeld, Ursula, etc.

Act 1

As the curtain rises, the bells of Nonnberg Abbey are ringing the Angelus and the voices of the nuns can be heard chanting the "Dixit Dominus." But as Sister Berthe, the Abbey's Mistress of the Novices, summons together the nuns and postulants, the whispered word goes around: Where is the postulant Maria?

Maria is out on the hills. She has been given permission by the Mother Abbess to spend the day among her native mountains, and there she has been pouring out her joy in the song that the hills inspire in her ("The Sound of Music"), oblivious of the fact that she has outstayed her time away from the Abbey.

The next morning, the Mistress of the Novices and the Mistress of Postulants come to the office of the Mother Abbess to discuss the prospects of the postulants. Most are ready to take orders, but Sister Berthe has considerable reservations about Maria. They are reservations that are not shared by the more kindly Sister Margaretta ("Maria"). The Mother Abbess calls the young woman before her and finds her full of sincere apologies for her late return the previous night. She has a further confession as well: she was singing in the hills. The kindly Abbess tells her that the rule against music applies only in the confines of the abbey, and even prompts her to sing again a pretty song that she has overheard her singing in the gardens ("My Favourite Things").

The Abbess knows that Maria is a good and devout woman, but she also knows that she is not temperamentally suited to life under holy orders. The will is there, but the girl's natural exuberance is uppermost. Gently she tells Maria that, for the time being, she must leave the abbey. Maria is distraught but obedient and no little taken aback when she hears that she is to be sent as governess to the family of a widowed naval Captain with seven children. Bolstering her confidence with a reprise of "My Favourite Things," Maria prepares to leave Nonnberg for her new life.

At the home of Captain von Trapp everything is run in a precise military fashion and, when Maria arrives, she finds that the uniformed children and the staff are summoned by a bosun's whistle. She firmly but sweetly declines to respond to or make use of such a fashion of communication and instead puts herself to winning the trust of the children who will be in her care. The von Trapp children have been through many governesses and have set them all to flight, and now they have one who has never had such a job before, in fact one who does not know where to start. It looks as if Maria will have little chance of doing the job she has come to do. But when Maria discovers that the children know nothing of music, her first dilemma is solved. Here is something she can give them, something over which they can become friends. Taking her guitar from its case, she starts to initiate them into the joys of singing ("Do Re Mi").

The eldest daughter, Liesl, is sixteen. It is an age when a girl has no need of a governess and where such an authority is bound to be resented. She also has a boyfriend in Rolf Gruber, the telegraph boy, and they meet in the grounds of the house to sing together with all the enthusiasm of their years about being in love and "Sixteen Going on Seventeen."

While Liesl is at her rendezvous, Maria is getting settled into her room under the gables of the house. The housekeeper presents her with a bolt of material with which to make herself a dress suitable to her new position but, when she asks for further material to make play clothes for the children, she is simply told that the von Trapp children do not play—they march for their exercise. There is nothing she can do to change it. Since the Captain's wife died, all the joyful things of life have been shut out of both his own existence and the children's.

As she kneels to say her evening prayers, Maria spies Liesl climbing secretly through her window. She has been locked out of the house in the rain while meeting with Rolf and she is too scared to try to get in any other way. This way up the trellis she knows, for it is the way by which the children always crept into the governess's room to play tricks on her. Now she is caught, but to her surprise, she finds Maria has no intention of telling her father. She and Liesl will be friends and allies. A flash of lightning and a burst of thunder bring the younger children rushing to Maria's room for comfort, and soon the whole family is perched on the governess's bed while she entertains them with the jolly tale of "The Lonely Goatherd."

There is much talk in the house of a remarriage for the Captain. The lovely and wealthy socialite Baroness Elsa von Schräder has been keeping company with von Trapp, and she has been invited to the house to stay. Another friend, the impecunious impresario Max Detweiler, a mercurial fellow who lives on his wit and charm, is a kind of chaperon for the occasion. While von Trapp and Elsa look at the mountains and edge toward commitment, Max makes use of von Trapp's telephone to make international calls chasing attractions for the forthcoming Kaltzberg Festival. Poverty may have its advantages, but so have riches and, even though he languishes in the former himself, Max prefers the latter in his friends. Poverty is only prized by lovers, and he jokes with Elsa that there will undoubtedly be a problem in any marriage between her and Georg von Trapp. With so many millions between them "How Can Love Survive?"

The occasion of Elsa's visit is the first time that von Trapp has been home since the children were entrusted to Maria's care, and he is horrified when he finds them playing, dressed in the clothes Maria has made them from old curtains. He whistles them back into their formal line and sends them off to change into their uniforms. When Maria protests, and tells him that he is making his children into unhappy little marching machines when what they need is love, he dismisses her harshly.

Suddenly the children's voices are heard. They are singing "The Sound of Music," which Maria has taught them as a welcome to the Baroness. Von Trapp's heart opens again at the song and, in minutes, he is happily surrounded by his children. The sound of music has come back into his life. Elsa watches with mixed feelings. Somehow, she cannot help but be pleased that Maria will, eventually, be returning to the abbey.

Von Trapp gives a party to introduce Elsa to the people of the region, but it turns out to be an awkward affair. The faction in the area that supports the German pretensions in Austria and those who remain solidly nationalistic come up against each other, and political debate takes the place of party chatter. Elsa keeps to her room, unsure of her welcome, and only the children seem truly to enjoy themselves. Maria is trying to teach little Kurt the Ländler when von Trapp intervenes and, taking her in his arms, begins to dance. By the time Maria blushingly breaks off the dance, it is obvious that something has happened between them. Little Brigitta, who misses nothing, tells Maria that her father cannot possibly marry Elsa. He is in love with Maria. The confused governess is plunged into panic.

When Max arrives unexpectedly, it is decided that, to even up the table, Maria must be invited to sit at dinner and she is sent off to change, while the children sing goodnight to the guests in a roundelay that she has taught them ("So Long, Farewell"). Max is delighted at what he hears—the children are a perfect act for the Kaltzberg Festival. While he is arguing with von Trapp over the suitability of such a performance, Maria creeps down the stairs, dressed in her old frock and carrying her case. She cannot stay. She is returning to the abbey.

Back at Nonnberg, it is a long time before Maria can find the courage to emerge from her room and come before the Abbess. When she does, the Abbess tells her that she cannot use the convent as an escape from the world. Love is holy, love between man and woman as much as love of God, and the one does not exclude the other. She must return to the von Trapp family and face life and Captain von Trapp ("Climb Every Mountain").

Act 2   With their Fräulein Maria gone, the joy has vanished from the singing of the von Trapp children and neither their father nor the eager Max can revive the spirit of their performance at the party. Von Trapp will not allow them to talk of Maria. The children will have no more governesses; they will have a mother instead. He is going to marry Elsa. Then, without warning, Maria is back among them; the children come alive again, and Brigitta is quick to convey the news about Elsa. Maria is stopped short, and she tells the welcoming von Trapp that she has returned only until he can make other arrangements.

Given the charged political atmosphere of the times, the number of phone calls for Detweiler from Berlin arouses the annoyance of the fervently nationalist von Trapp. Max easily admits that he practices political expediency. He has no politics of his own and, if the Germans should invade, he would prefer to have some friends among them. Elsa agrees, but von Trapp will not compromise in spite of their advice ("There's No Way to Stop It"), and it is clear that his position is one that Elsa cannot accept.

She will not give up Vienna and her home and her possessions there to be a potential outlaw's bride and, finally, she decides that she must break off their engagement. She knows that von Trapp will quickly find a more suitable wife and, indeed, it is not long before Maria is in his arms and they are singing together of being "An Ordinary Couple." Maria Rainer and Georg von Trapp are wed in Nonnberg Abbey to the strains of a choral version of "Maria."

Max takes advantage of their honeymoon absence to prepare the children for the Kaltzberg Festival, but his preparations are interrupted by some new local officials who demand that the von Trapp house shall, in the wake of the Anschluss, fly the German flag. Fortunately, Max's well-practiced expediency has given him a good government post under the new regime and he is able to face out the situation without committing anyone to anything.

When Georg and Maria return, the Captain firmly refuses to allow the children to sing in public. He also refuses to make any compromises in the face of the German occupation. It is soon clear what this will mean, for, when young Rolf arrives to deliver a telegram, Liesl sees with distress that even he is using the Nazi salute. Few are resisting the invader and many, through conviction or fear, are joining with the Germans.

The telegram is an invitation to the Captain to take up a commission in the German navy, and it is clear that if he does not accept he has little choice but to flee the country. The telegram is already several days old and, on the heels of its reception, the German Admiral von Schreiber himself arrives to put pressure on von Trapp and to order him to report immediately for duty. Maria wins breathing-time for them by showing the Admiral the Festival program. In two days time, the von Trapp Family Singers must appear at the Kaltzberg Festival.

The respite is granted and, at the Concert Hall in Kaltzberg, closely watched by German soldiers, the von Trapp family compete in the Festival with a rendition of "Do Re Mi." Georg follows this with a performance of the deliberately patriotic "Edelweiss," and, when he falters with emotion part way through, Maria and the children pick up the melody and support him to the end.

Max comes on stage and announces that the judges are in deliberation and, to alert von Trapp to the fact that they are under surveillance, dramatically tells the audience that an escort is waiting to take the Captain to his great new commission as soon as the concert is over. He calls on the von Trapps for another song and they give the children's "So Long, Farewell" with its progressively vanishing personnel. When the prizes are announced, and the von Trapp Family Singers are awarded first place, they have indeed vanished. The soldiers leap on to the stage in pursuit, but they are too late.

The family make their way to Nonnberg Abbey for refuge and, when the soldiers come, the Mother Abbess hides them in the gardens. The soldiers search the grounds and suddenly one of them stumbles upon the children huddled in a corner. He goes to shout for his superior, but he sees Liesl and he cannot. The soldier is Rolf. Telling his officer that there is no one there, he leaves the garden and lets the von Trapp family go free.

When all is clear, the Mother Abbess lets Maria, Georg, and the children out of the back gates of the abbey. They must climb through the hills Maria loves and find their way to safety in Switzerland. As the Abbess's voice is heard encouraging them to "Climb Every Mountain," the family sets out through the trees toward a new life.

GYPSY

A MUSICAL IN TWO ACTS by Arthur Laurents suggested by the memoirs of Gypsy Rose Lee. Lyrics by Stephen Sondheim. Music by Jule Styne.

Produced at the Broadway Theatre, New York, 21 May 1959, with Ethel Merman (Rose), Sandra Church (Louise), Lane Bradbury (June), and Jack Klugman (Herbie). Produced at the Winter Garden Theatre, 23 September 1974, with Angela Lansbury, Zan Charisse, Maureen Moore, and Rex Robbins. Produced at the St. James Theatre 16 November 1989, with Tyne Daly, Crista Moore, Tracy Venner, and Jonathan Hadary, and played there again from 28 April 1991.

A film version was produced by Warner Brothers in 1962 with Rosalind Russell (singing dubbed by Lisa Kirk), Natalie Wood, Ann Jillian, and Karl Malden.

CHARACTERS

Rose

Baby Louise, *later* Louise

Baby June, *later* June

Herbie

Tulsa

Yonkers

LA

Agnes

Tessie Tura

Mazeppa

Electra

Uncle Jocko

Mr. Goldstone, George,
Arnold, Pop, Weber, Kringelein,
Miss Cratchitt, Pastey, Cigar,
The Hollywood Blondes,
The Newsboys, etc.

Mama knows best; Mama will show you h
Mama knows how Mama would have don
Ethel Merman as Rose, mot
to stars though she was no
Fred Fehl, photograp
Courtesy Performing Arts Research Cen
New York Public Library at Lincoln Cen

Act 1

Somewhere in Seattle, sometime in the 1920s, there is a children's talent show in progress under the aegis of one of the Uncle Jockos of this world. One of the acts in the contest is Baby June and Company, a blonde tot dressed as a Dutch girl and supported by a less obvious child disguised as a Dutch boy. They have a number called "Let Me Entertain You," and they have a mother. Mother, in spite of an interdiction on all mothers at the run-through, gives stentorian directions to her embryonic little stars from the auditorium and thoroughly disabuses Uncle Jocko of the idea of fixing the contest on behalf of some other and more generous parent. Rose, the mother of Baby June and the Dutch boy (otherwise Louise), has started on a campaign to make a star of her blonde baby, and it would take more than a squad of Uncle Jockos to undermine her determination.

After the kiddie shows come the professional circuits. Rose has had a dream, which has revealed to her a new act that she will call Baby June and her Newsboys. Louise can be one of the boys and somewhere they'll pick up a few more youngsters who will work for the experience, since Rose certainly hasn't the money to pay them. Nothing can stop her in her vicarious drive to stardom. "Some People" may be content to sit at home and live a quiet life, but not Rose.

From Seattle, she talks and hornswoggles her way to Los Angeles, building the act and chasing bookings. At Weber's hall in LA she gets a dull "no interest" until Herbie, the theatre's candy supplier and an ex-variety agent, gives the act a recommendation. Herbie's recommendation isn't wholly disinterested, and his interest is patently more in Rose than in Baby June with or without her newsboys. In fact, Rose and he are mutually attracted, but he wants marriage and she doesn't. She wants show business and he's through with it ("Small World").

The act, in spite of the addition of four newsboys, is pretty much the same as it was in Uncle Jocko's days. June still sings "Let Me Entertain You," though now it's in a ragtime rhythm, and she still dances a breathless combination of every step ever learnt from a brain- and act-picking mother.

Life on the road is not easy: Rose, Herbie (travelling with them as agent), June, Louise, and the three lads of the act, Tulsa, LA, and Yonkers, all share a pair of fourth-rate hotel rooms and live off reheated Chinese food. Rose gets the landlord into a compromising position to keep him from throwing them out when it becomes necessary. When Louise's birthday comes along, the boys bring her gifts pilfered from the five and dime, Rose gives her a lamb, which is to be part of the new act that she has dreamed up—Baby June and her Farmboys—and Herbie turns up with a Mr. Goldstone, whom he has talked into booking the act on the Orpheum circuit. Rose falls all over the man ("Mr.

Goldstone, I Love You"), and Louise, her birthday now forgotten in the excitement, sits quietly in the corner and sings to her "Little Lamb."

Next, it's New York. Time has passed, quite a long time since that single break on the Orpheum that had no tomorrow, but Rose still dresses the girls up in the same childish costumes, they still perform the same juvenile act, and her confidence has not lessened one smidgin. Neither has Herbie's devotion, though Rose has reneged on her promise to marry him if he could get the act onto the Orpheum circuit. Now she wants Broadway. If she can have June's name up in lights just once, then she will marry him. Tomorrow they have an audition for T. T. Grantzinger's Palace. Maybe that'll be it. Herbie won't wait forever, but Rose smilingly tells him "You'll Never Get Away from Me."

Mr. Grantzinger watches Dainty June and her Farmboys and their version of "Let Me Entertain You" unseen, from his suite. The act features a pantomime cow, but is otherwise recognizable as a close relative of the newsboy act and its predecessor. Mr. Grantzinger, amazingly, offers them a contract, but it is for one week and at his downtown variety theatre, and he only makes the offer at all because he fancies he sees in June the makings of an actress. Rose rejects it furiously. No one is going to take her baby away from her. She is going to make her a star, all by herself. So June's chance is blown away. June is no fool; she knows that Dainty June and her boys is a ghastly act and that she is ghastly in it. She is dying to escape, and she and Louise dream what life would be like if Rose had someone else to lavish her energies on; what it would be like "If Momma Was Married."

In Buffalo, Louise sees Tulsa practicing fancy footwork in the alley. She knows what he's up to; he's inventing a dance team act. He's got it all worked out but, as he explains, there's one thing missing. He hasn't got a partner ("All I Need Is the Girl"). By Omaha, he has found one. Tulsa and June run off together and the other boys follow them for, without them, there is no act. Rose is only daunted for a minute. In that minute, Herbie asks her to marry him and settle down, but Rose still has her ambition and it is not to Herbie that she turns but to the previously unconsidered Louise. She has had another dream. It is Louise who will be a star. Her optimism is as high as ever as she starts all over again ("Everything's Coming up Roses").

Act 2   The new act is called Madame Rose's Toreadorables. The farmboys have gone Spanish and Louise is decked out in a blonde wig in a sad attempt to duplicate June's performance. Louise rebels both against the wig and the act— she is not and cannot be June—but she cannot resist the enthusiasm of Rose, supported by Herbie ("Together, Wherever We Go"), and she settles for the rest of the girls being blondes while she stays brunette. The act becomes Rose Louise and her Hollywood Blondes as it heads steadily for the bottom.

In Wichita, they get to play a real theatre. There is only one problem. It is a burlesque theatre, and burlesque is the bare buttocks of the business. They have been booked there only to give the place a thin wash of respectability behind which the strip acts and low comics can play. Rose is livid and ready to march out, but Louise faces her with the reality of their situation. They are penniless. They have to play the date.

Louise shares a dressing room with the stripper Tessie Tura who, with her colleagues Mazeppa and Electra, demonstrates to the girl the essential element of individuality that goes with success on the burlesque stage ("You Gotta Get a Gimmick"). However, the burlesque stage also has its hierarchy, and neither Tessie nor her pals will lower themselves to act as a feed for the comic when there is a dropout. Louise takes the job and the extra ten dollars.

The engagement at Wichita is ended, and at last Herbie has got Rose to say "yes" to him. They are to be married. But, as they prepare to set off, show business gets in the way one more time. The night's guest stripper has managed to get herself arrested for soliciting and the theatre has no one to perform the star spot. The word "star" acts on Rose like a match to brushwood. Her daughter can do it. In the past weeks she has seen that there is nothing to it.

The wedding flies out of Rose's head as she begins to direct a performance for Gypsy Rose Louise. There will be nothing tacky, it will be ladylike and elegant and young, and the old number, "Let Me Entertain You" will do fine. As Louise goes on, Herbie goes off. He has played second fiddle to Rose's dreams once too often. Momma shouts directions from the wings, just as if it were Uncle Jocko's show all over again, as Louise makes her way rather unsteadily through the opening part of the spot. But before she is finished, she is much steadier, and even rather roguish, and she is without doubt a success.

Now it is success all the way: the Alhambra, Detroit; the Philadelphia Diamond Burlesque; and then Minsky's itself as Gypsy Rose Lee becomes an assured and stylish star of burlesque and the Queen of Striptease. Louise loves her new life, the fame and the riches, but Rose still wants to manage her daughter's life and finds it impossible to accept that the successful young star makes her own arrangements both in and out of the theatre. She cannot even run Louise's bath—there is a maid to do that—and she never gets invited to go to any of those grand parties with Gypsy Rose Lee. Louise is ashamed of her. She is banned from backstage.

All that Louise needs, in truth, is to be let go. She offers to set her mother up in a stage school or anything else that she likes, but Rose insists on being needed. All that work, all those years, what did she do it for? Louise answers her quietly, "I thought you did it for me, Momma."

Rose knows she didn't. She did it for herself—Rose. She did it so that she could act out through June and through Louise the performances she was never able to give. And now, on the bare stage of the empty theatre, she gives that performance (Rose's Turn). From the wings, unseen, Louise is watching the almost grotesque display, and she understands. Maybe her mother could have been quite something, given the chance. But she didn't have the chance, and all she really ever wanted was to be noticed. Louise knows all about that sort of feeling. She remembers the days of Baby June when all she, too, wanted was to be noticed. She puts her mink around her mother's shoulders. They are going to a party, the two of them together.

1960

BYE BYE BIRDIE

A MUSICAL IN TWO ACTS by Michael Stewart. Lyrics by Lee Adams. Music by Charles Strouse.

Produced at the Martin Beck Theatre, New York, 14 April 1960, with Dick van Dyke (Albert), Chita Rivera (Rose), Dick Gautier (Birdie), Kay Medford (Mae), and Susan Watson (Kim).

A film version was produced by Columbia in 1963 with Dick van Dyke, Janet Leigh, Jesse Pearson, Maureen Stapleton, and Ann-Margret.

CHARACTERS

Albert Peterson

Rosie Grant, *his secretary*

Ursula Merkle

Kim MacAfee

Mr. MacAfee

Mrs. MacAfee

Mae Peterson, *Albert's mother*

Conrad Birdie

Hugo Peabody

Mrs. Merkle

Gloria Rasputin

Helen, Nancy, Alice, Margie Ann, Penelope Ann, Deborah Sue, Suzie, Linda, Carol, Martha Louise, Harold, Karl, Harvey, Henry, Arthur, Freddie, Peyton, *teenagers*

Mayor, Mayor's wife, Mr. Henkel, Charles F. Maude, etc.

It's telephone time in Sweet Apple, Pa., and the teenagers of the town tie up the lines with their adolescent chatter. Friedman-Abeles, photographers. Courtesy Performing Arts Research Center, New York Public Library at Lincoln Center.

Act 1

Albert Peterson, the company President of the Almaelou Music Corporation, New York, has a problem. The corporation's one and only asset is about to be drafted.

Albert was at college when he gave up his academic ambitions to run the career of Conrad Birdie, budding pop star. He formed a Corporation named after himself, his mother Mae, and their dog Lou and, with the faithful and sometimes loving help of secretary Rosie, he has succeeded in raising Conrad to the status of teenage idol and also in getting $50,000 into debt. Conrad's new-found success should be just about to start paying off this embarrassing total now, but the boy has gone and got drafted and, just to make Albert's day even better, Rosie is resigning. Rosie has gone through eight years of Albert's indecision, eight years of Albert's mother, eight years of double hours and one $5 raise, eight years of waiting for Albert to give up this pop music lark and do the decent thing he has always promised he would do—become "An English Teacher." Enough is enough.

Faced with this rebellion, Albert recants. He promises he will dissolve the company and go back to English just as soon as he has the cash to pay off Conrad's guarantee. Rosie gives in and, now that she has a promise, she takes practical means to hasten her arrival at her goal. From the pack of Birdie fan club cards she takes a card, any card. It says "Kim MacAfee of Sweet Apple, Ohio . . . age 15." Miss MacAfee, declares Rosie, is a lucky girl. She will get a kiss from Conrad Birdie. That kiss will be the hook for Conrad's greatest hit, "One Last Kiss," his goodbye to the girls of America as he goes off to serve President, country, and the draft board. While Albert gets down to writing the song, Rosie gets on the phone to Sweet Apple, Ohio.

It's difficult to get on to Sweet Apple, Ohio, because most of the telephone lines are taken up by teenagers chattering ("The Telephone Hour"). Today's Sweet Apple teen-topic is Kim MacAfee. Kim has resigned as president of the Conrad Birdie fan club because Hugo Peabody has given her his pin and they're going steady. She's practically an adult ("How Lovely to Be a Woman"), which means she can be modern and call her parents by their christian names and smoke cigarettes. However, when the news comes through that Conrad Birdie is coming to Sweet Apple to kiss her, Kim's new found maturity disappears abruptly and she howls for her mommy.

At Pennsylvania Station, Albert is orchestrating Conrad's departure for Ohio with the help of some swooning teenage harmonizers ("We Love You, Conrad"), and encouraging a distraught child facing a Conrad-less life to "Put on a Happy Face." Then mother Mae turns up on a cloud of martyrising reproaches, and Albert promises Rose he will tell his mother about dissolving the company that bears part of her name just as soon as a suitable moment arises. However, when Mae has finished her regular tirade against Rose (an eight-year danger who is clearly trying to get her hooks into Mae's sonny boy) and staging a simulated heart attack, she swans off again without giving Albert the space of a breath to tell her of his plans. A sheepish Albert and a frustrated Rosie are left behind to deal with Conrad and the press.

In front of the newspapermen, Conrad isn't allowed to utter a word. Albert and Rosie know what these fellows want and they trot out every available cliché about his being a "Normal American Boy" until it is time for the teen hero to get on the train. Conrad is simply going from one identical set of fans to another, and his arrival at Sweet Apple is greeted by Kim and her pals with the same Birdie anthem and the same Birdie pledge of loyalty heard through the entire United States of America.

Hugo Peabody is not at all sure that he is happy about Kim being kissed by Conrad. In fact, the very thought is enough to give him a nosebleed, but Kim assures him that a steady is forever ("One Boy"), while a pop star is only an internationally famous celebrity. Rosie has the same sort of idea about Albert, but Albert (and Albert's mother) have other priorities.

The Mayor welcomes Conrad to Sweet Apple with a speech on the courthouse steps, but the speech is cut short by a barrage of screams led by loyal fan Ursula Merkel who squeals for Conrad to talk to them, to tell them the secret of his success. Conrad opens his mouth for the first time in the show and delivers his creed: You just have to be "Honestly Sincere!" One by one, the entire female population of Sweet Apple faints dead away.

Conrad is lodged at the MacAfee household in preparation for the nationwide telecast of The Kiss and the unveiling of The Song. This arrangement has dispossessed Mr. MacAfee of his bedroom and his breakfast, and he is furiously fed up until he discovers that he and the family are going to be seen with Conrad on the Ed Sullivan show. This pays for all. The MacAfee family have been blessed by the greatest blessing God and CBS can grant ("Hymn for a Sunday Evening").

The preparations for the big day continue, and Albert takes his courage in his hands and writes to mother Mae to tell her about dissolving the company. When three days have passed and he hasn't heard anything he even gets momentarily hopeful that she has taken his action lying down but, of course, she hasn't. She has been travelling three days by cheap transport to get to Ohio to play her dying mother routine. She has also brought with her a brassy bit called Gloria Rasputin, who types and tap dances, to be Albert's secretary since she has decided Rosie is getting a bit old for it. Albert is well enough trained to be appreciative and Rosie is, for the umpteenth time, furious. In a ballet scena she illustrates a series of ways "How to Kill a Man" who lets his mother. . . . She is getting her breath back when a determined Hugo comes by. He has decided that he will not permit Kim to be kissed on national television by Conrad Birdie, and the revengeful Rosie agrees with him. She will see what she can do.

The Ed Sullivan show is live on the air as Conrad launches into the premiere of "One Last Kiss." The song finished, he gathers Kim in his arms and, as he does so, Hugo runs forward and punches him. Conrad is knocked out cold in front of seventy-five million viewers. Albert goes mad. Who let that kid in? Rosie did. It was a sort of farewell present. Their altercation over the prone Conrad makes fine prime time viewing until Albert remembers where he is and frantically attempts to get the hymn to the "Normal American Boy" going in a last ditch effort to rescue his promotion.

Act 2   As news of the fiasco flies around the country, Rosie sits back on her heels at the MacAfee house bewailing her wasted years and wondering "What Did I See in Him?" The mortified Kim is having much the same thoughts about Hugo, and she determines to follow Rosie out into the world to live the high life. Albert needs Rosie back, but for the moment he has other more pressing problems. He has managed to reschedule The Kiss for the railway station on the morrow, and now Conrad is insisting on going out to find a night spot in Sweet Apple. He's sick of sitting at home, and he's about to go into the army, so right now, he declares, "I've Got a Lot of Livin' to Do." Out on the streets of Sweet Apple, the boy runs into Kim, who is also looking for some living, so they decide to find the action together. While Mr. MacAfee goes to look for a gun, the elders of Sweet Apple bewail the frightful behavior of "Kids."

The dejected Hugo has ended up at Maude's Roadside Retreat where he tries to order a consolatory drink and is thrown out for being under age. Rosie finds the same bar and, after vampishly ordering a dangerous sounding cocktail, she also gets her marching orders from the wary barman. Before she can be ejected, however, she gets a telephone call from Albert pleading "Baby, Talk to Me." Plumping down the phone, she heads not for the door but, to the bartender's agitation, for an inner room full of men. She invades a Shriners' meeting and before long she has them involved in a wild dance. She finally limps out to be confronted by Hugo, still looking for the wherewithal to drown his sorrow.

Revolution is going on all around town. Albert finally pulls himself together enough to face up to his mother and unshrinkingly tell her to go home; Kim does her best to vamp Conrad, only to freeze him off when she tries to use big words like "jailbait." Then Ursula and the rest of teen-Sweet Apple arrive on the scene to propose whatever an orgy is, and Conrad is glad when the police turn up and bundle him off to prison for depravity. While the newly confident Albert marches off to arrange Conrad's release, Rosie squares up to Mrs. Peterson and faces her out. "Spanish Rose," as Mae insists on calling her so sneeringly, is Rosie Grant from Allentown, Pa., and she's taken enough schtick from Mae in these last eight years. This is the end.

At the railway station next morning, Albert smuggles Conrad out of Sweet Apple disguised as a fur-enveloped woman. The grateful star is willing to forget every cent of the guarantee Albert owes him and give him a managerial contract for life. The new, no-nonsense Albert gets his mother on the train and fends off the MacAfees who are still pursuing Conrad, before Rosie turns up at the station.

She is taken aback when she finds the train has gone, but Albert has news for her. They aren't catching the train for New York, they're heading for Pumpkin Falls, Iowa. As he tears up Conrad's contract, he tells her he has an interview for a post there as an English teacher. He hopes her papers are in order, because they prefer married applicants. As Albert Peterson, English teacher, sings sweetly to his "Rosie," the curtain comes happily down.

A sequel, *Bring Back Birdie*, was produced at the Martin Beck Theatre, New York, 5 March 1981.

1960

CAMELOT

A MUSICAL IN TWO ACTS by Alan Jay Lerner based on *The Once and Future King* by T. H. White. Music by Frederick Loewe.

Produced at the Majestic Theatre, New York, 3 December 1960, with Richard Burton (Arthur), Julie Andrews (Guenevere), and Robert Goulet (Lancelot). Produced at the New York State Theatre, 8 July 1980, with Richard Burton, Christine Ebersole, and Richard Muenz, and played at the Winter Garden Theatre, 15 November 1981, with Richard Harris, Meg Bussert, and Muenz.

A film version was produced by Warner Brothers in 1967 with Richard Harris, Vanessa Redgrave, and Franco Nero (singing dubbed by Gene Merlino).

CHARACTERS

Arthur

Guenevere

Merlyn

Lancelot

Mordred

King Pellinore

Sir Dinadan

Sir Lionel

Sir Sagramore

Morgan le Fey

Nimuë

Squire Dap, Clarius, Lady Anne,
Lady Sybil, Tom, etc.

Arthur (Richard Burton), Guenevere (Julie Andrews),
and Lancelot (Robert Goulet) will make up a happy
Arthurian mé à trois, until the snaky Mordred comes
along and spoils everything.
Friedman-Abeles, photographers.
Courtesy Performing Arts Research Center,
New York Public Library at Lincoln Center.

Act 1

On a hilltop near the castle of Camelot, the court is gathered to celebrate the arrival of their new queen. King Arthur's destined bride, Guenevere, is on her way to Camelot. However, the young king himself is not at his castle to receive her. Instead, he is up in a tree, trying to catch a private glimpse of the lady who will be his wife before having to meet her publicly. For his pains, he gets himself thoroughly chided by his old tutor, Merlyn.

The wise Merlyn has the advantage of having lived backwards. He has been old, and knows everything of time immemorial, and he is getting daily younger. Over the years, he has bestowed on Arthur the benefit of his distilled wisdom, but the boy's youthful head has not knowingly taken in everything offered and soon, Merlyn knows, the future king will have to face the world without his protector. For, since his life is lived in reverse, Merlyn knows what his own fate will be. He will be bewitched by the nymph Nimuë and kept locked for centuries in her enchanted cave and, when that happens, Arthur will be alone for the first time in his life, with only the memories of Merlyn's teachings to guide him in the conduct of his life as a king and a man.

Merlyn will not turn the eager boy into a hawk to let him peek at his beautiful Guenevere, and he orders him back to the castle, wondering what the King's subjects would think if they could see him swinging like a monkey from a tree. Arthur knows precisely what his subjects are thinking. They are thinking "I Wonder What the King Is Doing Tonight?" If only they knew how nervous he is at the thought of marriage. But as he sings his fears to the forest, he hears someone approaching, and he climbs quickly back into his tree. The newcomer is a young woman, and she is praying forcefully to her particular saint, rebelling against an arranged marriage before she's had time to enjoy "The Simple Joys of Maidenhood," which are the rights of every medieval girl.

Curiosity pushes Arthur a little too near the end of his branch and, at an inopportune moment, it cracks, depositing him inelegantly on the ground alongside the girl. She is practically insulted when he doesn't show any eagerness to assault her, but she puts it down to the fact that he has realized she is Guenevere, the King's bride. Or, rather, his intended bride, for she has run away from her attendants with the express purpose of escaping her forced marriage. Arthur, enchanted by her, is anxious to change her mind and sings attractively of the charms of his home ("Camelot") until the court appears and, to her amazement, Guenevere sees the young man honored as king.

An explanation is clearly in order, and, shyly, Arthur tells Guenevere the tale of the sword in the stone and how he became King. By the time he has finished they are sufficiently in love for all the terror to have gone from the thought of marriage. Merlyn, amazed and delighted, sees the boy become a king. How foolish he has been. Arthur didn't need a lecture to make him ambitious; he needed a queen.

Merlyn, however, will never get to know Queen Guenevere for, as he returns to the castle, his fate comes upon him. Nimuë's voice draws him away from Camelot ("Follow Me"), draining from him all the knowledge and wisdom of the centuries. Desperately he tries to remember: Has he told Arthur everything he should know? About Lancelot? About Guenevere and Lancelot? About Mordred? Alas, he never told him about Mordred. . . .

In five years on the throne, Arthur swells into a man, his life's course leading him constantly on to discover the true meanings of things Merlyn had shown him as a child. His discontent with the haphazard warring of his knights breeds the longing in him for a more civilized and civilizing court at Camelot and, from this longing, is born the idea of the order of the Knights of the Round Table.

One first of May, there arrives from France a postulant for the order: the unsmiling, self-serious Lancelot du Lac ("C'est Moi"), and his coming brings back to the King the words of Merlyn who had prophesied that one called Lancelot would be the greatest at Arthur's table.

The Queen and court are out celebrating the May festival ("It's May!") when an old man in a curious garb appears. He is the wandering King Pellinore, condemned to chase the Questing Beast through the ages. He is fed up with the constant routine and longs for a bed and a pillow just for one night, and he is delighted when Guenevere offers him kindly hospitality. The Queen is less amused by the innocently self-satisfied Lancelot, whom she finds insufferably big-headed, and she is pleased to give her favors to three knights who pledge to cause the Frenchman's downfall in the lists ("Take Me to the Fair"). Arthur, who is besotted by the perfection of Lancelot, is angry that Guenevere should show her antipathy so publicly, and he asks her to withdraw her favors. She replies that she will do so only if he commands her as king, and this he cannot bring himself to do. Alone, he wonders at her vehement reaction and muses on "How to Handle a Woman."

When the jousting takes place, Lancelot not only defeats all three knights, but demonstrates practically his belief that his purity allows him to do miraculous things by raising the apparently dead Sir Lionel after his fall. As he passes the Queen, their eyes meet and they gaze at each other transfixed. The King can only look on with troubled understanding. Guenevere knows what has happened and tries to put it away from her ("Before I Gaze at You Again") but inevitably her emotion finds its way into words. Lancelot and the Queen are in love. They know it and Arthur knows it. He faces his dilemma and resolves that, above all, he will be civilized. He loves them, they love him: There can be no joy in destroying them because they love each other. He will be a king first and a man second, and God have mercy on them all.

Act 2

Love grows in Lancelot with a fierceness only to be found in one who has never loved before ("If Ever I Would Leave You"). He and Guenevere are convinced that Arthur cannot know of the bond between them, but the King is not the only one to see his way clearly to the truth. One day there comes to the court of Camelot an evil young man called Mordred. He is said to be the son of the witch, Queen Morgause, and of King Lot, but he knows and Arthur knows that he is, in fact, the son of Arthur himself born of a night when Morgause bewitched the King into her bed. Arthur feels bound to welcome his son to the Round Table and to attempt to make of him a knight, but Mordred has no intention of following the ways of virtue ("The Seven Deadly Virtues"). He is out to make trouble and to win for himself his father's crown and all the lands of England.

The cares and plans of the king's wise and reforming rule weigh heavily enough on Arthur without the extra worry caused by his family, and he longs sometimes to be rid of the cares of state ("What Do the Simple Folk Do?"). Mordred is eager to help him to that end and, to this purpose, he visits the invisible castle of his aunt, the fairy Morgan Le Fey, deep in the woods of Camelot. The sprite is lured to Mordred's side from her unseen life of debauchery and gluttony by the promise of chocolates, and she agrees to entrap Arthur long enough to keep him one whole night away from his castle (The Persuasion). Mordred's plan matures and, as he had foreseen, while the King is away, Lancelot is unable to resist the temptation to visit Guenevere in her room.

She is distraught. She wishes they had never spoken their love, but had rather just let it exist in their hearts, where it could harm only themselves ("I Loved You Once in Silence"). To his pleas to return with him to his home in France, she replies that she will never leave Arthur.

Mordred has other ideas. With a troop of soldiers at his back, he invades the Queen's rooms and exposes Guenevere and Lancelot as lovers. In the scuffle that follows, Lancelot escapes, but the Queen is taken and arraigned for treason. She is condemned to be burned ("Guenevere") but, before Arthur can bring himself to give the order to light the pyre, Lancelot invades the castle with an army. The Knights of the Round Table fall under the French attack and everywhere there is death and destruction. Arthur's dream of a civilized Camelot shatters under the kind of primitive brutality he thought he had replaced.

Lancelot and Guenevere escape to his bastion in France, and the army of Camelot, pursuing them, prepares to join battle with the French outside Joyous Gard. Arthur comes secretly to see his wife and his friend, rejoicing in his heart that they have escaped safely. If they could, all three would much rather return to England to try to right the situation without resorting to the pagan rite of battle, but it is too late. Mordred has taken command of an army and is already plotting war against Arthur as, all around, the world falls back into its old animal ways. Camelot, the Round Table, was it all for nothing?

As Arthur goes to return to his own battle lines, he meets a young boy. He has come, he says, to join the Round Table; to be a Knight and fight for justice and right, as he has heard in the stories people tell. Arthur realizes now that his effort was not for nothing: People will tell stories of Camelot and the Round Table forever. It will continue in tale if not in reality and give hope and ideals to people who hear tell of what Arthur and Lancelot and their fellow knights did in that one brief, shining moment that was "Camelot." As the curtain falls, Arthur sends the lad scurrying back through the battle lines toward a safety where he may carry that shining tale.

1961

How to
Succeed in Business
Without Really Trying

A MUSICAL IN TWO ACTS by Abe Burrows, Jack Weinstock, and Willie Gilbert based on the book by Shepherd Mead. Music and lyrics by Frank Loesser.

Produced at the 46th Street Theatre, New York, 14 October 1961, with Robert Morse (Finch), Rudy Vallée (Biggley), Bonnie Scott (Rosemary), Charles Nelson Reilly (Frump), and Virginia Martin (Hedy). Produced at the Richard Rodgers Theatre, New York, 23 March 1995, with Matthew Broderick, Ron Carroll, Megan Mullaley, Jeff Blumenkranz, and Luba Mason.

A film version was produced by United Artists in 1967 with Morse, Vallée, Michelle Lee, Anthony Teague, and Maureen Arthur.

CHARACTERS

J. Pierrepont Finch

Mr. Gatch

Mr. Jenkins

Mr. Tackaberry

Mr. Peterson

J. B. Biggley

Rosemary Pilkington

Mr. Bratt

Smitty

Miss Jones, *Biggley's secretary*

Bud Frump, *Biggley's nephew (by marriage)*

Mr. Twimble

Hedy la Rue

Miss Krumholz

Wally Womper

Mr. Ovington

Toynbee, Scrubwomen, Policeman, etc.

Ponty Finch (Robert Morse) waves the old school flag of "Grand Old Ivy" under the delighted nose of big boss Biggley (Rudy Vallée). Friedman-Abeles, photographers. Courtesy Performing Arts Research Center, New York Public Library at Lincoln Center.

Act 1 High above ground level, on the outside of the World Wide Wicket Company building, a window cleaner is plying his trade. But this particular window cleaner has much more than spotless panes on his mind. While he squeezes, shines and mops with one hand, his other hand holds a book entitled *How to Succeed in Business Without Really Trying*, which he is devouring as if it were a particularly precious piece of pornography. Ponty Finch wants to be going up in the world that is inside this building, not on a window-washing cradle outside, so, following the book's instructions, he presents himself at the World Wide Wicket Company to ask for a job. He marches right in to the building and straight into a middle-aged gentleman whom he sends tumbling to the ground. He has made a good start, for the gentleman is J. B. Biggley, the president of the company.

Undeterred, Finch tells him that he has come for a job, only to be greeted with a roar. Mr Biggley doesn't know about jobs; he has a whole personnel department to look after that. So Finch heads off toward personnel. He has already won himself one admiring ally in his determined drive toward the first step on the great staircase to success. A pretty secretary, Rosemary Pilkington, has taken a fancy to him, and she promises him that she will talk to her friend Smitty who is secretary to the personnel manager.

Before she can do so, Mr. Bratt, the personnel manager, arrives in a cloud of negative vibes. But Finch has only to mention carefully that he has been sent by Mr. Biggley to see that cloud vaporize under the sun of Mr. Bratt's regard, and, by the time Smitty gets back, Finch has already been given a job in the mailroom and a cigar. Rosemary is delighted. He has made his first step toward success, and she has found someone of whom she can say that she'd be "Happy to Keep His Dinner Warm" in a little house in New Rochelle as he works his way up toward executive status.

Executive status is a huge hike upward from the mailroom, but Finch starts as he means to go on: as a bright, polite, hardworking lad in an office where most people's day revolves around the "Coffee Break." Of course, the first thing to do when you work in the mail room is to get out of the mail room, but Finch quickly finds that there is an obstacle to this elementary part of his progress. Bud Frump, his fellow worker, is the nephew of J. B. Biggley's wife and, like Finch, he too is eager for promotion. He is so eager for promotion that whenever he feels distressed or ignored he rings up his mother, his mother rings her sister, and her sister gets on to Mr. Biggley.

Frump has his eye and his finger on the eager Finch, but our hero is undeterred. He works with an angelic devotion to the internal mail system of the building, he is charming to Mr. Biggley's aging secretary who introduces him to the head of Plans and Systems, and, when it gets around that the job of head of the mailroom is to become vacant, Bud Frump has to get on the phone to his mother very quickly to forestall the obvious challenge of the boy wonder. In this situation, however, the influence of Mr. Biggley and his relatives is nil, for it is tradition that the retiring head of the mailroom should pick his own successor.

Mr. Twimble has been twenty-five years in the mailroom, living his life in "The Company Way" without question or quibble, and his devotion to his work leads him to pick as his heir the best man in the department: Finch. To general surprise, Finch declines modestly. The more experienced Frump must have the job. Such self-abnegation does not go unnoticed, particularly by Mr. Biggley who is very relieved not to have to listen to a tirade on family loyalty from his wife, and before long the astute Finch finds himself given a junior executive post in Plans and Systems instead.

He is out of the mailroom and on his way up. His single-minded pursuit of success means that he has little time or mind for anything else, and the persistent attempts of Rosemary Pilkington to get him to notice her, date her, and/or help her on to the second step of her particular preoccupation, go unnoticed.

Mr. Biggley may be a regular family man but he has all the usual urges of the middle-aged executive, and at the moment those urges are turned in the direction of a cigarette girl from the Copacabana. The luscious Miss Hedy la Rue has been given a crash course in office skills and she is now the latest recruit to the secretarial staff at World Wide Wickets with a large label of do-not-touch pasted warningly across her prow ("A Secretary Is Not a Toy"). The boss is allowed his little weaknesses. Mr. Biggley's other weakness is the traditional middle-aged devotion to his old alma mater: He is a passionate Groundhog from Old Ivy, where he was once voted the least likely to succeed.

On Friday night the personnel of World Wide Wickets dribble out of their offices ("It's Been a Long Day"). Mr. Biggley is not planning on going home. He has a rendezvous with the pneumatic Hedy, and he gets nervous when Frump makes a point of hanging around uttering hints that reek of blackmail. That boy will have to be watched. It is much more agreeable watching young Finch. Why, the next morning when Biggley comes by the office to pick up his golf clubs prior to a match with Mr. Womper, the chairman, there is the devoted young fellow asleep across his desk, his adding machine still in his hand. And what is this? He is humming the Groundhogs' song! Surely he can't be an Old Ivy boy ("Grand Old Ivy")? And he knits. No one, just no one except Mr. Biggley's incorruptible Miss Jones, knows that the head of World Wide Wickets finds his relaxation in knitting, and here is this young, kindred spirit clacketing out a bird-cage cover. What a fellow. Surely he must have ambitions?

Finch owns shyly that one day he would like to be Head of Advertising. That takes Biggley aback. Advertising is the pits. No one wants Advertising.

Why, no Head of Advertising has ever lasted more than a month. In the meanwhile this hardworking lad must have his own office. And a secretary. And lo, the secretary allotted to Mr. Biggley's new protégé is Hedy. Fortunately, Finch's faithful manual has advice on this point. When a secretary is too attractive it may be that Someone Important in the Company has a special interest in her. *Sequitur*: Test her skills. The worse she is at shorthand and typing, the more important her protector is. Hedy is hopeless.

Finch is wide open to being compromised and shot right down to the bottom again, but our lad has a way to turn this potential peril to his own advantage. Hedy is dispatched with a personal message to the private office of his superior, Mr. Gatch, and, as Finch had foreseen, the lecherous Gatch is unable to resist taking a handful of her. The next day, Gatch has gone from the office and Finch has been promoted to Head of Plans and Systems.

Benjamin Burton Ovington is the latest to have been appointed to the post of Head of Advertising and, to mark the occasion, there is to be a reception for him in the World Wide Wicket building. Finch, in his new position, is invited to attend and so, too, is Rosemary who has been allotted to the new executive as his secretary. She buys an expensive new dress in which to stun Finch ("Paris Original"), but she is shattered when Smitty, Miss Jones, Miss Krumholz, and, worst of all, Hedy turn up in identical models. Hedy fills hers out the best, but she is not intended to fill it for long for Mr. Biggley is planning an evening in. Hedy, however, doesn't want to go to bed yet. She is enjoying the party. She just wants a quick freshen-up in Mr. Biggley's office shower and she'll be ready to dance on into the night.

The villainous Frump latches on to this bit of information and sees how he can use it to kill a whole flock of birds with one stone. As soon as Hedy is safely under the water, he tells Finch that Biggley wants to see him in his office. The young man arrives there to find an undressed and oncoming Hedy who threatens to tell Biggley that Finch made advances to her if she doesn't get her way with him.

He kisses her and manhood enters him. Now, at last, he knows what he wants from "Rosemary" and, when she comes to find him, he proposes and she accepts. When Biggley, alerted by Frump, storms in he finds Finch making a meal not of Hedy but of Rosemary. Frump has failed again. But Finch's own business of the evening is still to be done. At the psychological moment, he exposes Ovington as a Northern State man. He is a Chipmunk, a mortal rival of the Groundhogs! Needless to say, this sin earns him immediate dismissal and Finch finds himself promoted to fill the gap created by this sudden departure— he is Vice President in charge of Advertising (Finale).

Act 2 The new Vice President is allotted Rosemary as his secretary, but it proves to be a very unsatisfactory state of affairs for her, as he continues to treat her as a typing machine and not as a fiancée. In the end she makes up her mind to resign, but the other girls in the office will not hear of it. One of them has finally succeeded in realizing every secretary's dream by getting an offer of marriage from her boss: Never let it be said that she let him get away ("Cinderella, Darling"). Shamed out of her resignation, Rosemary sticks to her post and bides her time until that day when she may finally get to keep her man's dinner warm.

Biggley has problems too. Hedy is disenchanted with life in an office and she wants to return to the bright lights of the Copacabana. He has to pour out plenty of "Love from a Heart of Gold" to persuade her to stay.

Frump, meanwhile, has not been idle. Finch has been ordered to come up with a bright idea for a campaign and Frump has an idea for him: a television treasure hunt with a cash bond prize. He does not tell Finch that he has already put this idea up to his uncle himself and been contemptuously rejected. What he does not count on is that the confident Finch ("I Believe in You") will dress up his idea in a different guise and make something out of it. He allots Hedy a leading role in the presentation as the World Wide Treasure Girl, smilingly giving out television clues as to the hiding place of bundles of World Wide Wickets shares, and the project is given the go-ahead. Biggley and Finch decide secretly that the prizes shall be hidden in the buildings of World Wide's ten major American branches.

The big day comes and the all-singing, all-dancing World Wide Wicket show is beamed live across the country ("The Yo-Ho-Ho"). Hedy appears to give out the first clue and finds herself confronted with a man bearing a bible. It is Finch's little last minute touch, a bit of religion to mix with the sex. Hedy must swear on the bible that she doesn't know the hiding place of the treasure. Of course she doesn't know. All the office knows that only Finch and Biggley are in on the secret. But Hedy isn't anxious to commit perjury and somehow she does know, and soon the nation knows that she knows. As the embarrassed Biggley collapses in a purple heap, the whole program falls in ruins.

Finch has come to his worst crisis yet and the only advice his book gives him is to go back to page one and start all over again. The chairman, Mr. Womper, is coming to the office that very day and heads are going to roll or, more specifically, by popular agreement, Finch's head is going to roll. Only Rosemary stands by him ("I Believe in You"): Executive or window cleaner, she loves him and will marry him.

Summoned to face the terrible Mr. Womper, Finch confesses sole culpability for the disaster of the television program. He will take his dismissal like a man and go back to window cleaning. But what is this? Mr. Womper started life as a window cleaner as well, a much better basis for life than all this college nonsense. But how, he demands, could a fellow window cleaner have pulled a bone-headed trick like the treasure hunt? Finch delicately admits that it was actually not his own idea, but that of the President's nephew, and Womper's rage is turned on Biggley. He is a practicing nepotist!

Biggley protests that the details were Finch's, but he gets into a bottomless hole when Womper demands to know who chose the idiotic Hedy as a front girl. When all seems darkest, Finch steps forward to save his boss from the chop, counselling humanity and magnanimity ("Brotherhood of Man") for all. All, that is, except Frump. As the whining Frump is frogmarched away, the rest of the executives of World Wide can breathe again. They have only to face a little reshuffle.

Mr. Biggley keeps his job, but somehow Mr. Womper has ended up marrying Hedy and he is heading off on a long, long ocean-going honeymoon. Naturally, his new responsibilities mean that he has no further time to fulfil his position as chairman of World Wide Wickets and so he has retired. There is no need to ask who will be taking his place. And what does Mrs. Finch think? Rosemary just loves her man whether he's in the mailroom, or chairman, or even President of the United States. Biggley instructs Miss Jones to send a wire to the White House telling the President to look out for his job, as life prepares to go on in "The Company Way."

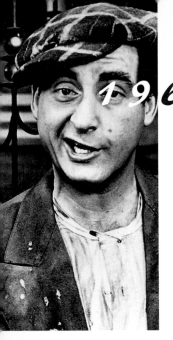

1962

LITTLE ME

A MUSICAL COMEDY IN TWO ACTS by Neil Simon based on the book by Patrick Dennis. Lyrics by Carolyn Leigh. Music by Cy Coleman.

Produced at the Lunt-Fontanne Theatre, New York, 17 November 1962, with Sid Caesar (Noble, etc.), Virginia Martin (Belle), Nancy Andrews (Old Belle), and Swen Swenson (George). Produced at the Eugene O'Neill Theatre in a revised version 21 January 1982 with James Coco, Victor Garber, Mary Gordon Murray, and Jessica James.

Two faces of Sid Caesar, who played all
the men in the life of Belle Poitrine.
Courtesy UPI/Bettmann Newsphotos.

CHARACTERS

Noble Eggleston/Mr. Pinchley/Val du Val/Fred Poitrine/Otto Schnitzler/Prince Cherny

Miss Poitrine

Belle

George Musgrove

Pinchley Jr./Defense Lawyer/German Soldier/General Schreiber/Assistant Director/Yulnick

Momma

Mrs. Eggleston

Patrick Dennis

Bernie Buchsbaum

Bennie Buchsbaum

Ramona VanderVeld

Colette, Ship's Captain, etc.

Act 1

Our story begins in the present, in the opulent Southampton, Long Island, home of Miss Belle Poitrine where the lady in question (the "Miss" is purely honorary and the "lady" wholly misleading) is greeting the young man who is to ghost her autobiography. In it, she promises, she will tell "The Truth." From the very beginning.

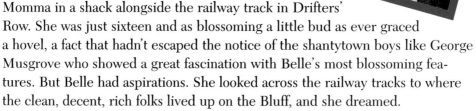

The very beginning was in Venezuela, Illinois, at the dawn of the new century. There Belle Schlumpfert lived with her professional Momma in a shack alongside the railway track in Drifters' Row. She was just sixteen and as blossoming a little bud as ever graced a hovel, a fact that hadn't escaped the notice of the shantytown boys like George Musgrove who showed a great fascination with Belle's most blossoming features. But Belle had aspirations. She looked across the railway tracks to where the clean, decent, rich folks lived up on the Bluff, and she dreamed.

One day, by accident, some teenagers from the Bluff strayed through Belle's backyard on their way to a picnic. The smell of poverty frightened most of them away, but one, an exceptionally perfect youth called Noble Eggleston, was moved by fate to present the contents of his picnic pail to a poor person. Fate also decreed that the door he should choose was that of the Schlumpfert house, but probably had nothing to do with the fact that Belle Schlumpfert happened to be throwing out the garbage at the moment he stuck his head in. Except that, in touching Noble's shoulder to brush away the day-before-yesterday's slops, Belle started something.

It was electric and it played a tune ("I Love You"). Each time they touched each other there was this shock and this tune. Then Noble, deeply moved by this and by Belle's most blossoming features, made a momentous step. He invited Belle to his sixteenth birthday party at the big house up on the Bluff. At last little Miss Schlumpfert was on her way to "The Other Side of the Tracks."

The big house on the Bluff was very rich and overpowering, the guests at Noble's party were very rich ("Rich Kids Rag"), and his mother was very overpowering. She was severely displeased at Belle's presence and, in spite of the fact that Belle and Noble managed to turn their tune into a full-scale duet ("I Love You"), she treated Noble to a lecture on the facts of rich life and ordered Belle from the house. She could never be his, for she had neither wealth nor culture nor social position. But Belle Schlumpfert had determination as well as a blossoming bosom. She vowed that she would go out into the big wide world on "The Other Side of the Tracks" and she would get herself those three sine qua nons of modern life and, when she had them, she would come back and show Mrs. Eggleston.

It wasn't long before Belle found herself a way out of Drifters' Row. The folks down there were having a mite of trouble keeping up with the rental payments to their unsympathetic landlord, the immobile eighty-eight-year-old Mr. Amos

Pinchley, so they went to his offices to grovel in front of him and ask for a little more time to pay. But Pinchley just played with them and then told them gleefully that they would all be evicted. Then, from the crowd of dejected poor people, one stood out in front and told Amos Pinchley plainly what she thought of him.

It was Belle. She didn't shrink from the truth. She just upped and told the nasty old man what no one had ever dared to tell him: He was a hated man. Pinchley didn't like that. He wanted to be loved. So Belle started right in to try and find that little bit of good "Deep Down Inside" him and, my goodness, she found it. Pinchley was soon a changed man and, in gratitude to Belle, he gave her her heart's desire: a little apartment in Peoria where she could study the important things in life like diction, manners, and French cooking.

Mr. Pinchley came from time to time to check up on his protégée and, such was the change in him, that he was soon able to get out of his wheelchair and propose marriage. Belle was there already. Such a marriage would give her wealth, culture, and social position all in one throw and, given the seventy years difference in their age, she would not have long to wait for Noble. Belle threw her arms around her fiancé and something went bang. Amos Pinchley kept a gun in his inside pocket and Belle's generous proportions had been just too much for its trigger. The bullet went right through his heart.

Wealth, culture, and social position were just as far away as ever. It meant starting all over again. Belle's performance at her trial, where Noble's all-American character reference won her a spotless acquittal, attracted the attention of the Buchsbaum Brothers, vaudeville bookers, and with a little persuasion ("Be a Performer") and a lot of publicity, Belle headed out to get herself some culture on the stage ("Oh! Dem Doggone Dimples"). She was quite a hit, until some juicier murderess came along and pushed her off the bill, leaving her to take up a job as a camera girl in the Skylight Roof nightclub.

Now who should turn up one night at the Skylight Roof but Noble Eggleston, fresh from his double first in law and medicine at Yale and Harvard, and about to announce his engagement to Ramona VanderVeld, the girl of his mother's dreams. Belle was distraught. He had promised he'd wait for her. But Noble, try as he might, could not stand up against his mother. And so, while the evening's entertainer, the famous Frenchman, Val du Val, was going through his celebrated love song, "Boom Boom," Belle climbed on to the window ledge, thousands of floors above the ground, and prepared to end it all.

Val du Val could not endure the thought of such a well-endowed girl being wasted on the pavements of Chicago, and, with some well-chosen words in fractured English, he persuaded her to climb down. Before their acquaintance could ripen, however, World War I was declared and everyone decided to go home. Left alone in the nightclub, Belle encountered its owner. She wasn't the only one to have made it out of Drifters' Row. The club belonged to George Musgrove and he still had the hots for her ("I've Got Your Number").

Six months later, a heavily pregnant Belle was doing her bit for the war effort at a doughboy party when all the boys got the call to the front. Someone came up with the bright idea that they should all get married before they went and Belle got paired up with the sweet, dumb, and very short-sighted Fred Poitrine. It was destiny: Someone up there intended all along that she should end up as Belle Poitrine. So Fred got his first kiss ("Real Live Girl") and headed off to the war where, having done his bit by giving Belle his name, he soon succumbed to a wound contracted by catching his little finger in a typewriter key.

Meanwhile, Colonel Noble Eggleston, nine times winner of the Victoria Cross, was fighting glorious battles with the entire German airforce. But, one fateful day, he was shot down behind the enemy lines. At this stage Belle decided that, baby or no baby, it was time to get over there to Europe and do something about finding the man of her heart. So, equipped with a team of like-minded ladies, off she set to bring much-needed song, dance, letter-writing, and advanced medical assistance to the men at the front ("Real Live Girl").

One day, there was brought to the American camp a poor, wandering French officer suffering from amnesia. Who should it be but that great French entertainer, Val du Val and, from a letter in his possession, it appeared that he had suffered a psychological shock at being abandoned by his girlfriend, leading to a total loss of memory. Belle, anxious to return a favor to the man who had saved her life, worked hard with the assistance of the enemy cannons to recall the famous boom-boom song to him and, voilà!, suddenly Val was restored to normal. It was fate. Belle must be his! She must never leave him.

No sooner had Val rushed off to find his helmet, his gun, and his orchestrations than Noble, who had escaped from captivity by the brilliant use of a bribe, turned up. Since it was war time, the old qualifications of wealth, culture, and social position were no longer necessary prerequisites to him and Belle getting together: They could be married that very night. Once more Belle was on the brink of realizing her dreams but alas! the moment Val du Val heard the news he suffered a relapse. A second jilting flung him deeper than ever into amnesia and Belle, unable to bear the responsibility of condemning the man who had saved her life to such a fate, tearfully waved farewell to Noble. It was time to become Madame du Val.

Act 2

Miss Poitrine takes up her story where she left off to allow for the interval. Married for five years and as happy as two people could be who were each in love with someone else, Val and Belle took a trip on that magnificent ocean liner, the SS *Gigantic*, and who should our heroine meet travelling on that very same crossing but Noble Eggleston, now a successful surgeon and judge and married to Ramona. It seemed a lifetime since their childhood vows to each other but, when they touched, the old electricity and that old tune were still there. Unfortunately, so was an iceberg. As Noble organized the entire evacuation of the sinking ship and taught everyone who couldn't swim to do so in one easy lesson, he and Belle carolled out their love song to the waves ("I Love You").

Every single passenger was saved with the exception of Val du Val who, having overheard Belle and Noble's reunion, had lost his memory again and forgotten how to swim. Belle sued the steamship company for the loss of her husband and her luggage and won two million dollars. She had achieved wealth and she was single again. The only difficulty was, Noble wasn't. Not until Ramona's father went bankrupt and Mrs. Eggleston marched her daughter-in-law straight downtown for an annulment. By then Belle was already on the road to culture. Her old friends the Buchsbaum Brothers had gone into films, and anyone with two million dollars was welcome to star in one, nay all, of their movies ("Poor Little Hollywood Star").

One by one the world's greatest titles became grist to Belle's mill in her relentless pursuit of culture until she reached the ultimate in *Moses Takes a Wife* under the direction of the once-great Otto Schnitzler. Unfortunately, Schnitzler got himself killed demonstrating a trick dagger that turned out not to be a trick dagger, and Belle decided to finish directing the picture herself. And what do you know, she won an award: the Golden Turkey. That was culture. Since oil had just been discovered on her back lot she was now also one of the richest women in America, but if she were going to win Noble there was still social position to go ("Little Me").

The best place to find that all-important ingredient was undoubtedly Europe, so Belle packed her luggage-wagons and set off for Monte Carlo to find herself a piece of class as a husband. One night, at the Casino, Prince Cherny of Rosenzweig came to risk the whole of his bankrupt country's exchequer on one throw and gallantly asked Belle to choose the number on which his fate and the fate of his country rested. Belle chose wrong and the Prince collapsed under the weight of a terrible heart attack.

Filled with remorse, Belle locked herself away with the ailing monarch in his bedroom and worked on him day and night for two whole exhausting weeks until she could do no more and the people of Rosenzweig were summoned to bid a last farewell to their Prince ("Goodbye"). When all was nearly over, the last ounce of Belle's bounteousness was poured out. She would pay the national debt of Rosenzweig for the poor dead Prince. She'd what? Suddenly the eye of the Prince quickened and, to the joy of his people, he began to make a remarkable recovery.

Because of Belle, Rosenzweig was saved and her monarch, to express his gratitude, was pleased to dub her the Countess Zoftic. Well, that was enough social position even for Mrs. Eggleston. Belle had only one regret. Since it had looked so certain the Prince would die and, since she had grown rather fond of him over their two weeks together, to spare him any final pain, she had poisoned his wine. So the people of Rosenzweig had to sing their "Goodbye" all over again.

Back at home, Noble had been elected Governor and now, with every obstacle overcome, he was free to ask Belle to be his wife. As they celebrated their future together, Belle persuaded Noble to break the habit of a lifetime and take just one sip of alcohol. It was the end. The wedding never took place. Three weeks later Noble was a hopeless drunk, impeached and sluiced out of office and out of Belle's life.

Alone, Belle settled into a vast mansion on the Bluff, and there she waited, year after year, for Noble to return to her. Infinitesimally, she grew older ("Here's to Us") and still he did not come. There was only George Musgrove who had been faithfully and hopefully following her around the world every step since that night at the Skylight Roof. The Egglestons were a fallen and forgotten family, Noble a drunken bum sailing as a sawbones on a tramp steamer, and his once proud mother reduced to selling apples in the street. Ah, fate.

Then, one day, Belle's little daughter—now grown into a teenager every bit as shapely as her mother had been—came home with a friend: Noble Eggleston, Jr., the spitting image of his father. It was clear that they liked each other, but Belle needed a test. Under Mother's supervision, the two kids touched and, sure enough, the old tune blared forth. Everything would be all right for them, at least. As for Belle, well, she finally gave in and married George Musgrove. When they touch there isn't any music but you can't have everything. Young Belle married Noble jr. and lived happily ever after and there ends the tale of Belle Poitrine.

Well, not quite. For although the dictation is done, there is another chapter to come in the chronicle of the little lass from Venezuela, Illinois. Mrs. Eggleston has nurtured revenge in her bosom since the day the girl from the other side of the tracks brought her and her son to ruin and now she has come, with pistol in hand, to wreak her vengeance. She aims and she fires, just as a sailor walks through the door. It is Noble, dried out, reformed, and once again the hero we knew him as for so long. He falls to the ground clutching his stomach—all those years of effort for nothing.

But wait! There is no blood. If he isn't shot, who is? It is George, of course. If he'd been paying attention to the rest of Belle's story he might have known something like this would happen. At last the tale of Belle Poitrine can have the ending it was always meant to have as, accompanied by the soaring strains of their song ("I Love You"), Belle and Noble walk off together into the sunset.

The revised version altered the framework of the show and omitted the songs "The Truth," "Be a Performer," "Dimples," and "Poor Little Hollywood Star" but incorporated two new numbers "Don't Ask a Lady What a Lady Used to Do" and "I Wanna Be Yours."

A FUNNY THING HAPPENED ON THE WAY TO THE FORUM

A MUSICAL COMEDY IN TWO ACTS by Burt Shevelove and Larry Gelbart based on the works of Plautus. Music and lyrics by Stephen Sondheim.

Produced at the Alvin Theatre, New York, 8 May 1962, with Zero Mostel (Pseudolus), Jack Gilford (Hysterium), David Burns (Senex), John Carradine (Lycus), Preshy Marker (Philia), and Brian Davies (Hero). Produced at the Lunt-Fontanne Theatre, 30 March 1972, with Phil Silvers, Larry Blyden, Jack Collins, Carl Ballantine, Pamela Hall, and John Hansen.

A film version was produced by United Artists in 1966 with Mostel, Gilford, Michael Hordern, Silvers, Annette André, and Michael Crawford.

Hysterium (Jack Gilford) is distinctly un-calm, and with good reason. Many of the funny things that happen on the way to the forum are the making of the finagling Pseudolus (Zero Mostel). Friedman-Abeles, photographers. Courtesy Performing Arts Research Center, New York Public Library at Lincoln Center.

CHARACTERS

Senex, *an old man*

Domina, *his wife*

Hero, *his son*

Hysterium, *slave to Senex and Domina*

Pseudolus, *slave to Hero*

Erronius, *an old man*

Miles Gloriosus, *a warrior*

Marcus Lycus, *a buyer and seller of courtesans*

Philia, *a virgin*

Tintinabula, Panacea, The Geminae, Vibrata, Gymnasia, *courtesans*

The Proteans

Act 1   It is two hundred years before the beginning of the Christian era, and it is springtime.

The evening's entertainment is set under way, in the fashion of the period, by the prologue, a fellow in a toga who introduces the members of the company and informs the audience that, whereas it may be melodrama and tragedy on the other evenings of the week, it is "Comedy Tonight."

The setting of the entertainment is made up of three buildings: To the one side is the *domus* of the elderly Erronius whose children were stolen in infancy by pirates. He has spent a lot of time abroad since then, trying to find them. To the other side is the mansion of Lycus, a vendor of female slaves. And in the middle is the home of Senex, his well-named wife Domina, their exuberantly innocent son, Hero, and their servants one of whom, the curiously named Pseudolus, the prologue lauds at length. Pseudolus, it eventuates, is his own role. There are lots of other roles, but these will be played by a useful trio of proteans, if they can make the costume changes in time.

The action of the play begins with Senex and Domina setting off to visit her mother in the country with a little gift, a marble bust of Domina. The mistress of the house charges her devotedly grovelling slave, Hysterium, to watch over her pubescent son, his well-being and his morals, while she is away, little realizing that Hero, with all the enthusiasm of his teenage years, is already prey to passion ("Love, I Hear").

The boy confides to the rascally Pseudolus that he has fallen for a beautiful girl in the next door house. The next door house! Horror! She is a courtesan! What would his parents say? Hero does not care. He would give everything he has to possess this girl. However, since he owns only a collection of sea shells, twenty minae, and Pseudolus, this is not a likely bargain. Not to anyone except Pseudolus. He would like to own himself, for he has a manic wish to be "Free" and he will devote himself wholeheartedly to bringing the young people together in order to claim this reward.

The flesh-dealer Lycus emerges from his house and pulls up short at the sound of a jingling purse. It is Hero's purse and Pseudolus is jingling it. Pretending he has come into a legacy, Pseudolus demands to see Lycus's stock and, one by one, the choice exhibits of the house are paraded before the slave and the boy ("The House of Marcus Lycus"). But, glorious as they are, none is the beloved of Hero's heart. Lycus denies that he has any other merchandise in stock but, when all seems despair, Hero spots his girl at a high window. That one? Oh, she is a virgin from Crete and already sold to the great captain, Miles Gloriosus, who specified a virgin and was willing to pay 500 minae for the privilege.

Pseudolus sympathizes ostentatiously with Lycus. What a shame about the awful plague in Crete, he does hope the captain's girl will last till his arrival. Lycus goes into a panic at the talk of plague: why, the girl could infect the entire stock. Pseudolus gallantly offers to take her in at his house (it's all right, he has already had the plague) and look after her until she is called for, and Lycus is only too happy to get pretty little Philia out of his house as quickly as possible. And so Hero achieves his heart's desire and a meeting with the girl he adores. It is quickly obvious that the girl is not very bright. In fact, as she admits readily, Philia has only one talent—she is "Lovely." As far as Hero is concerned, that will do.

When Hysterium sees his mistress's son with a courtesan he is fit to dissolve in jitters, and he is only stopped from heading Domina-wards by a timely bit of blackmail by the resourceful Pseudolus who threatens to tell the *materfamilias* about her pet slave's private collection of erotic pottery. Pseudolus has not been idle in other ways either. He has used the time that the young lovers have spent on the last number to fix up an escape route for them. There is a boat waiting around the corner on the Tiber. Off they can sail and he will be free. What a "Pretty Little Picture." There is only one snag. The virgin has a simple morality. The captain has paid for her and so she must wait for the captain.

Given this unexpected hitch, Pseudolus needs a bit more plot. He hurries the young people into the house and filches Hysterium's famous book of potions. He will mix a sleeping draught, knock the virgin out with it, tell Lycus she has died of plague, and send the unprotesting body off with Hero on the boat. Unfortunately, he lacks one vital ingredient for the potion—a cup of mare's sweat—so off he trots to find it.

No sooner has he gone than Senex returns. He has dropped the beastly bust and chipped its nose, so he has had to come back to have the thing repointed. When he kicks his own door, to his delighted surprise, a lovely maiden emerges and cries "Take me!" Philia has got muddled again, and thinks the *paterfamilias* is her captain. Senex does not question his good luck but, before he can move into action, Pseudolus returns with his sweat and Philia has to be explained. She is, he ventures, the new maid. Senex is all approval. He likes maids. In fact, "Everybody Ought to Have a Maid" and he will personally instruct this one in the niceties of housework. Unfortunately his son is in the house, so he will have to educate the new maid in the house of his absent friend Erronius. Pseudolus is ordered to bring her across.

This further unexpected turn of events requires a little more imaginative action from Pseudolus. To forestall the spoiling of Lycus's virgin merchandise before his young master can take possession, Pseudolus sacrifices his hard-won mare's sweat. He drenches Senex's gown with the evil-smelling liquid and the "education" has to be postponed long enough to allow the old man time to have a bath. Senex marches into Erronius's house to prepare himself, and the eternally blackmailed Hysterium is detailed to keep him inside.

In spite of his best efforts to convince himself that "I'm Calm," the chief slave is in all kinds of a state, and, just when he's feeling quite limp with nerves, he finds that he has a situation to deal with. For who should appear on the scene but Erronius himself, back at last from his unsuccessful search for his children (one boy and one girl, stolen in infancy by pirates, and recognizable by a ring showing a gaggle of geese).

Needless to say he is anxious to return to his home and Hysterium has, at all costs, to stop him. Borrowing a little of Pseudolus's inventiveness, Hysterium takes advantage of Erronius's feeble faculties and convinces him that his house is haunted before Pseudolus, coming to the support of the deception with an opportune impersonation of a soothsayer, persuades the old man that he must walk seven times around the seven hills of Rome in exorcism before entering his house. That should give enough time for whatever is going to happen to happen.

When Erronius has gone on his way, Senex emerges and encounters Hero. Then both of them see Philia and see each other seeing Philia, and are puzzled at each other's reaction at seeing each other seeing Philia, and together they indulge in a duet of unworthy thoughts ("Impossible"). Under the orders of Pseudolus, Hysterium has been preparing the sleeping potion and the plan is nearing its fruition when a frustrating flight of trumpets rings out. The Miles Gloriosus is approaching.

Lycus is in a paroxysm of panic. What will happen? Pseudolus once again comes up with an answer. He will impersonate Lycus for the occasion and save the day. He decorates the stage with the most scrumptious of courtesans and, when the great man arrives to demand "Bring Me My Bride," he attempts to interest him in alternative arrangements. But the Miles is not in the mood for second choices. He wants only his bought-and-paid-for bride. Pseudolus is in a mighty fix which only one word can cure. That word is Intermission.

Act 2

The Intermission can hold things up but it can't change them. When the second act begins, it begins with a brief recap from Pseudolus of the position where we left off, and it carries on with the wily slave promising to deliver the Miles Gloriosus his bride as soon as possible. Thus, what seemed like an inevitable evisceration is, at least, postponed. The captain is persuaded to go into Senex's house (which he thinks is Lycus's house) to rest, be entertained, and wait. Senex, in his turn, is bathed and ready in the next door house and awaits his maid. But now Pseudolus and his ever-changing plan meet yet another problem. When he proffers the goblet of wine laced with sleeping potion to Philia it turns out that the wretched maiden is teetotal, and nothing he can do can persuade her to partake of the mixture. Since Pseudolus needs a body to carry out the newest version of his plan, he sets off to find one elsewhere.

Now, to complicate matters further, Domina returns, certain that "That Dirty Old Man of Mine" is up to something lewd. Hysterium is shattered. She is sure to discover at least one of the many deceptions that are in progress and any one of them will be lethal insofar as he and his position of trust are concerned. In the meanwhile Philia, still dutifully awaiting her captain (and still thinking Senex is he), is singing lovingly but irritatingly to Hero about how every bit of lovemaking with her enforced husband will be an expression of her affection for Hero ("That'll Show Him").

Finally, Pseudolus has thought of a way in which to put his plan into action. He needs a dead girl to show the captain his virgin bride perished of plague, and, since he couldn't get a real corpse from the bodysnatcher, he is using a decidedly nervous Hysterium dressed up to look dead and "Lovely." Pseudolus brings on the Miles Gloriosus and shows him his defunct and heavily veiled bride and the soldier is heroically distraught. He must depart unwed and with a broken heart, but before he does so he will give the girl a proper funeral (Funeral Sequence). Light the pyre! The what?! Pseudolus has to deliver a healthy backhander to the corpse, which shows every sign of reviving inopportunely. He tries using the story of the Cretan plague to scare everyone away, but the captain has just come from Crete and knows there is no plague and . . . wait a minute, that corpse is alive!

Soon there are people revengefully running in all directions. Confusingly, there seem to be three Philias—the real one, Hysterium in disguise, and Domina who has dressed up as a virgin to spy on her husband. Old Erronius, on the third time around the seven hills of Rome, also gets mixed up in the mêlée and pounces gleefully on Hysterium, believing him to be his daughter. The Miles Gloriosus and Senex claim Hysterium as their bride and maid, respectively, and controversy reigns until the petrified slave tears off his blonde curls and brings everything to a confused halt.

With everyone together on the stage, the network of fibs fabricated by Pseudolus gradually starts to get dismantled. Since he is clearly to blame, he has nothing left to do but to die by his own hand. Very well, he will take hemlock. Pseudolus grandly orders Hysterium to fetch the potion prepared earlier to make Philia feign death, but Hysterium gives him instead a passion potion brewed to fit Senex for entertaining the maid. The results are alarming but fortunately short-lived.

Finally, Philia is brought forward to be delivered to her captain. At last the merchandise is delivered, but only the Miles Gloriosus is really happy about it. Everyone else looks pretty miserable and poor old Erronius is still there, mumbling on about his children and the ring with the gaggle of geese. The Miles Gloriosus double takes: geese? Why, he has a ring like that. He is the long lost son! Then Philia timidly inquires how many geese are in a gaggle. She, too, has a ring like that. She is the long-lost daughter! So she and the captain are . . . how very fortunate for Hero. So the story ends, with everything that was lost having been found—including Pseudolus' promised freedom—and a reaffirmation that it has indeed been "Comedy Tonight."

The 1972 revival introduced the song "Farewell" and reinstated The Echo Song, which had been cut in try-out during the original production.

1963

SHE LOVES ME

A MUSICAL IN TWO ACTS by Joe Masteroff based on the play *Illatszertár* by Miklós László. Lyrics by Sheldon Harnick. Music by Jerry Bock.

Produced at the Eugene O'Neill Theatre, New York, 23 April 1963, with Daniel Massey (Georg), Barbara Cook (Amalia), Jack Cassidy (Steve), and Barbara Baxley (Ilona). Produced at the Brooks Atkinson Theatre, 7 October 1993, with Boyd Gaines, Howard McGillin, Judy Kuhn, and Sally Mayes.

In spite of all the "romantic atmosphere"
provided at the Café Impériale,
Amalia Balash (Barbara Cook) and
Georg Nowack (Daniel Massey)
share a distinctly unromantic evening.
Friedman-Abeles, photographers.
Courtesy Performing Arts Research Center,
New York Public Library at Lincoln Center.

Act 1

We are in a European city, a slightly curious European city that we would be quite certain was the Budapest of the play on which the musical is based, were it not for the fact that they use pounds, shillings, and pence there. But even in spite of that, it has to be Budapest. The time is the 1930s, the season is summer, and the focus of our attention is a charmingly old- and superior-looking shop that sells beauty products: soaps, skin-creams and perfumes, lipsticks, makeup, and so forth. Opening time is nigh now, and the people who work at Maraczek's Parfumerie are starting to arrive.

First come Ladislav Sipos, an aging—if not already aged—shopman of forty-five, and the lively and enthusiastic delivery boy, Arpád ("Good Morning, Good Day"). They are followed by Ilona Ritter, a slightly tarty good-time shopgirl who's already cheerfully said goodbye to thirty, and then by the slick and dapper Steve Kodály. According to Arpád, who seems to know about these things, Ilona didn't go home last night. She spent the night—again—with her colleague-in-cosmetics, Kodály. But the pair always arranges to arrive at work separately in the mornings. One who has no need of such dissembling is shop manager Georg Nowack. Georg is quite the antithesis of Kodály. He's quiet and soft-spoken, capable, modest, well-liked, and desperately single. He'd no more think of seducing a girl than he would of stealing from his employer. Mr. Maraczek's employees would much rather not be glued to a counter on a hot summer's day, but business is not so good these days—after all, didn't their biggest competitor just close down—and no one wants to find himself out of work. So once the boss arrives, and the shop doors are opened, everyone goes to work with a warm will (Sounds While Selling/"Thank You, Madam").

Georg may be staunchly unattached, but he does actually have a little romance in his life. Once upon a time, he advertised in a magazine for a penfriend, a lady penfriend. It worked. From that shy start has grown up an eagerly enjoyed correspondence with a young woman who addresses him simply as "dear friend." They have never exchanged names or photographs, much less ever met, and Georg—much as he prizes his long-distance affair—shows no signs of trying to get closer to his mysterious correspondent. Mr. Maraczek, who treats Georg rather like a wayward son, is keen that he should find himself the right girl, give up his bachelor ways, and settle down. Just like he did. For, believe it or not, Mr. Maraczek had his moments on the floors of the city dance-halls ("Days Gone By") before he met Mrs. Maraczek and became a loyal and loving husband.

But back to business. Today, Mr. Maraczek has brought in a new novelty line for the store: genuine leather musical cigarette boxes. Georg isn't enthusiastic, but his boss bets him that—even though his own first attempts meet with a cold shoulder—they can sell one of them within an hour.

The shop has not long been open when Mr. Maraczek has a visitor who is not a customer. Amalia Balash is twenty-five, attractive, warm, wonderful, and she wants a job. She used to work for his competitor, so now she's twenty-five, attractive, warm, wonderful, and unemployed. The only trouble is, Mr. Maraczek doesn't want to hire anyone. At least he thinks he doesn't. But when Amalia manages to sell one of the wretched musical boxes to a customer who had no intention of buying such a thing ("No More Candy"), he is completely won over. Amalia gets her job, and Georg loses his bet.

The Hungarian seasons pass, and—as Georg continues his happy love-affair-by-letter ("Three Letters")—things gradually become less happy around Maraczek's Parfumerie. Ilona quarrels with Kodály, the more irritated than wonderful Georg and the more irritating than wonderful Amalia carry on a permanent bickering match, which only the nervous Sipos translates as mutual attraction, and Mr. Maraczek is a different man, tetchy and positively aggressive toward his staff and in particular toward Georg, for whom he had always shown such fondness. In fact, just before Christmas, when he summons Georg to his office over an affair of a burst tube of face-cream, it almost seems that he is trying to get the boy to lose his temper and resign.

Through all these trials, though, Georg has his life line: the letters and the girl of the letters. And now the big day has come. He and she have finally decided that it is time that they met. They have arranged a romantic rendezvous at the Café Impériale and he is as nervous as can be in case he does not live up to expectations ("Tonight at Eight"). Amalia, too, has a date today, and like Georg she has turned up at work all dressed up in her best. But when Ilona quizzes her girl-talkishly about her beau, she has to admit "I Don't Know His Name." No, it's not a blind date. She knows her dear friend as well as can be from his letters. She just doesn't know his name.

Of course, tonight of all nights has to be the night that Mr. Maraczek decides the staff must stay behind and put up the Christmas decorations. Georg offers to come any other night instead, but quickly the tone of the conversation heats up and Sipos is obliged to cause a diversion by knocking down a pile of music-boxes before the inevitable resignation or sacking happens. You have to keep things in "Perspective" and, for the unprepossessing Sipos perspective comes down to just one thing—Don't lose your job, because you may not get another. Amalia is upset too. She can't stay. She won't stay. And she's quite sure that Georg arranged this after-hours working especially because he knew she had this extra-special date tonight. Did he really think she was dressed up like this in order to stay behind and decorate a Christmas tree? If Sipos thought he had deflected danger for tonight, however, he is wrong. The very next time that Georg exchanges words with Mr. Maraczek, only a few sentences have passed before the pair are using dangerous words again, and this time the fatal ones get said. Georg is out. He packs his bags and, as his colleagues bid him "Good Bye, Georg," he leaves Maraczek's Parfumerie for good.

Amalia is sitting at the Café Impériale, with the agreed rose and copy of *Anna Karenina* in front of her, waiting for the man of her letters and wondering ("Will He Like Me?"). And at the same time, back at the store, Kodály is transparently and witlessly re-chatting up Ilona over the Christmas decorations ("Ilona"). Ilona weakens, but when Mr. Maraczek decides instead to send everyone home, the big-mouthed beau backs out of their date for the night, leaving the furious woman to swear that she'll never let herself get taken like that again ("I Resolve"). Then, when everyone is gone, Mr. Maraczek gets a strange visitor, a private investigator called Keller. Mr. Keller has fulfilled his mission and he has answers. The anonymous letter that Mr. Maraczek got was correct: His wife is having an affair with one of his employees. No, its not Georg Nowack, it's Steve Kodály. When the investigator is gone, the phone rings. Its Mrs. Maraczek, explaining to her husband that she has to go out. Maraczek nods tiredly. And when the call is ended, he walks purposefully through the empty shop toward his office. Little, forgotten Arpád sees him put the gun to his head, and he yells. . . .

If Kodály is overconfident in his feminine dealings, Georg is underconfident. Now the time has come, he has decided that he can't go through with the meeting, and he wants Sipos to take a letter to his "Dear Friend" saying that he is forced to cancel. The two men arrive at the Café, where the personnel are doing their best to instill "A Romantic Atmosphere," and the situation soon becomes evident. Georg's letters have come from . . . Miss Balash! But he can't be in love with that awful Miss Balash! Sipos's advice is to find out.

So Georg goes up to Amalia's table. She isn't at all pleased to see him. He is going to mess up her wonderful meeting. And he's not very good company either. Especially when he starts to sing her a story about a girl who went on a blind date and was never seen again ("Tango Tragique"). Finally, he gets so impossible that she screams. This is the last straw for the waiter who's been trying to stop them spoiling his carefully fabricated romantic atmosphere, and he orders them out. Georg shocks him to silence by pretending there was a fly in the wine, but the upset girl has had enough. She reels off a catalogue of Georg's failings and disadvantages, and he can only get up and go. Amalia is left alone to wonder whatever happened to her "Dear Friend."

Act 2   Mr. Maraczek is in the hospital with a hole in his shoulder and Arpád is organizing things. This is the boy's chance to show what he can do in front of his boss, because Arpád has ambitions to rise to be a sales clerk ("Try Me"). Georg comes to visit, too, and now that the misunderstanding over the identity of Mrs. Maraczek's paramour is cleared up, he is reinstated in his job. When he gets to the shop, he finds Amalia isn't there. She's called in sick. So Georg goes to her home to find her. She is terrified she is going to be sacked and determines to get up and come to work ("Where's My Shoe?") but he calms her, gives her some ice cream he has bought for her, and makes up a story about having met her friend as he rushed to catch a train out of town. They talk enough and to good enough effect that by the time he leaves and she sits down to write to her "Dear Friend," she finds her mind running back to Georg ("Ice Cream"). As he heads back to work, he has come altogether more quickly and clearly to the conclusion "She Loves Me." And, for heaven's sake, he's delighted about it.

Ilona's luck has turned, too. After her spat with Kodály the previous night, she walked and walked and walked and, without quite knowing how or why, ended up in the public library. There she ran into this dear, sweet, clearly respectable, thickly bespectacled man called Paul ("A Trip to the Library"). And since it's time for confessions, Sipos has one too. He sent the anonymous letter, on the principle that, in these times of cutbacks, better that Kodály, who deserved to be sacked, should get sacked, than someone else. Like him. As for Kodály, one of Georg's first jobs as temporary boss is, of course, to send him packing. He goes without a hair out of place ("Grand Knowing You") and with grand plans in his mouth.

Maraczek's Parfumerie gets through the Christmas rush ("Twelve Days to Christmas") with triumphant results, and Ilona has a vast till roll of takings to show to Mr. Maraczek when he returns to the shop on Christmas Eve. The boss had planned a festive occasion, but Ilona is off for the evening with Paul whom she is going to make propose to her, Sipos has not only his own family but his family's family to take care of, and Georg has promised to spend the evening with Amalia and her family. Tonight, after all, dear friend is going to put in an appearance and Amalia feels she needs Georg's support. Mr. Maraczek will just have to take the over-the-moon Arpád—newly promoted to full-blown clerkship—to dinner.

Georg and Amalia are about to leave when one of her parcels tumbles to the floor, and as it hits the ground it plays a tune. It's one of those leather boxes that got Amalia her job in the beginning and she thought dear friend might like it. Reminiscences quickly lead to confessions and finally Georg pulls out a letter from his pocket. It is one of Amalia's ones to "Dear Friend." All is now out in the open, and the evening can end on a Christmas-colored clinch.

1964

FUNNY GIRL

A MUSICAL IN TWO ACTS by Isobel Lennart based on incidents in the life of Fanny Brice. Lyrics by Bob Merrill. Music by Jule Styne.

Produced at the Winter Garden, New York, 26 March 1964, with Barbra Streisand (Fanny Brice) and Sydney Chaplin (Nick Arnstein).

A film version was produced by Columbia in 1968 with Streisand and Omar Sharif.

Barbra Streisand as Fanny Brice
parades down a Broadway staircase as a
"beautiful bride" . . . with a bun in the oven.
Friedman-Abeles, photographers.
Courtesy Performing Arts Research Center,
New York Public Library at Lincoln Center.

CHARACTERS

Fanny Brice

Mrs. Brice, *her mother*

Mrs. Strakosh

Tom Keeney

Eddie Ryan

Nick Arnstein

Florenz Ziegfeld, jr.

Emma

Jenny

Mrs. Meeker, Mrs. O'Malley,
Heckie, John, Bubbles, Polly,
Maude, Mimsey, Ziegfeld tenor,
Jody, Adolf, Mrs Nadler, Paul,
Cathy, Vera, Ben, Mr. Renaldi, etc.

Act 1

Backstage at a Broadway theatre, the comedienne Fanny Brice, star of the *Ziegfeld Follies*, is in her dressing room preparing for the evening's performance. It is just another performance, but tonight she is nervous because she is going to see Nick Arnstein again. As she sits in front of her mirror, she goes back in time to the days before she became a success on Broadway—to the year when she was nineteen years old. There is her mother with Mrs. Strakosh and her other cronies sitting around the inevitable card table playing three-cent poker, and here comes Fanny—plain, funny Fanny—off to an audition for Tom Keeney's Music Hall. Mrs. Strakosh shakes her head. Even if Fanny has some talent, what's the use "If a Girl Isn't Pretty"?

Down at Keeney's, the dance director, Eddie Ryan, echoes the same sentiment, and Fanny quickly gets the boot from the chorus audition. Even the cab driver who brought her there, and a couple of workmen at the stage door, spin the same sorry line, but Fanny is irrepressible. She corners Eddie as he leaves the theatre and makes her point—she may stand out in a chorus line, but that's because she's too good. So make her a soloist ("I'm the Greatest Star"). Eddie is convinced enough to stay up all night teaching her a solo routine from the show and the next thing we see is Fanny strutting her stuff in front of the chorus at Keeney's Music Hall in a trial run with "Cornet Man."

After the show, a madly attractive stranger turns up backstage. He is Nick Arnstein, playboy and gambler, and he has come to settle a debt with Keeney. He runs into Fanny, just as she's down on her hands and knees making a dog out of herself, and she's knocked out, especially when it turns out he has seen the show and reckons that she's headed for stardom. When Keeney comes around to say he'll take her on permanently at $40 a week, Arnstein, on behalf of a mythical competitor, offers more and, before she knows it, she's booked at a salary of $110. What would have happened if Keeney had dropped out of the auction? She would have lost her job, of course. Fanny is aghast. Nick has played with her life for the first but not the last time, but right now, as she looks delightedly after him, she supposes that she won't ever see him again.

Months pass, and Fanny makes herself a great reputation at Keeney's. Then, one day, she receives a telegram summoning her to Broadway's New York Theatre to meet the great Florenz Ziegfeld. As her mother and Eddie get her ready to go to the all important meeting, they congratulate themselves on her success ("Who Taught Her Everything She Knows?"). They always knew she would do it.

Fanny Brice becomes part of the *Ziegfeld Follies*; a slightly uncomfortable part to start with for, while she gets to do her "Cornet Man" song, Mr. Ziegfeld also casts her in a production number glorifying the American bride in which she is supposed to be pretty. Now forthright Fanny knows her qualities and, like her mother and Mrs. Strakosh always said, pretty isn't one of them, but Mr. Ziegfeld is master in his theatre and pretty she's going to be. As the Ziegfeld tenor gives forth with "His Love Makes Me Beautiful," a parade of lovely girls illustrate the number, but when Fanny comes on for her portion of the song, she walks down to a barrage of laughter. She has padded out her wedding gown to make it look as if she is a well-gone shotgun bride. At the end of the show, she expects a rocket, but Ziegfeld holds his fire. Her judgment was right this time, but from now on he makes the decisions.

An even better surprise follows: Nick Arnstein turns up out of nowhere, and the electricity between them starts crackling again. He suggests a night on the town for the newest Ziegfeld star ("I Want to Be Seen with You"), but he settles instead for a party in Mrs. Brice's saloon in "Henry Street" where he ends up playing poker with the card harpies. When Nick and Fanny get a little time together away from the crowd, their mutual affinity opens up ("People"), but Nick is a man of the world and Fanny hasn't been anywhere except up on a stage in front of thousands of people she doesn't know, and he knows he isn't going to stop his wanderings and stay around her. Before long he has to go, as suddenly as he came back, leaving Fanny wondering regretfully whether she will ever see him again.

Ten months later, on tour in Baltimore, she does. He turns up from nowhere once more, and takes her to dinner in style, but it's the same old story. He is in town for only a week before he goes to Europe. She is upset and angry, but she covers it with clowning. Since she can't understand what he says when he orders from the French menu, how will she know when he makes a pass at her? He assures her that she'll know ("You Are Woman, I Am Man") and, at the end of the number, they meet in a genuine kiss. Somehow Europe gets forgotten for a while and Nick stays in Baltimore, but when it comes time for the show to move to Chicago he picks up his old plan. It's Chicago for her and Monte Carlo for him. But Fanny has other ideas. Ziegfeld has many stars; she has only one man. Although Eddie begs her not to, her mind is made up and, full of optimism, she quits the show and prepares to follow Nick to Monaco ("Don't Rain on My Parade").

Act 2 Fanny and Nick return from Europe to Nick's Long Island mansion as Mr. and Mrs. Arnstein, and it is quite clear who proposed to whom. Half of Henry Street and the Ziegfeld company are there to greet them, and Fanny happily parades herself as just an ordinary married lady, like Mrs. Strakosh's ever-mentioned Sadie ("Sadie, Sadie").

Soon baby Frances comes along, and then the ever-gambling Nick gets wiped out in a speculation on an oil well. Down at Henry Street there are questions in the air. Is everything all right between the two of them? Mrs. Brice shrugs it off. She doesn't have to worry about her daughter anymore. Let's face it, she doesn't have to worry about anyone anymore. Or, more correctly, she doesn't have anyone to worry about. Eddie and Mrs. Strakosh make a suggestion—"Find Yourself a Man."

Fanny returns to the theatre sooner, much sooner, than she had originally said she would and Nick returns to his grand financial designs. This time it's a casino. He tries to interest Ziegfeld who ducks out of it, but Fanny asks if she can invest and almost forces her money on him. When Eddie worries about it, she brushes him off and returns to a rehearsal for the new show. The rehearsal ("Rat-tat-tat-tat") segues into the opening-night performance in a full-scale *Follies* production number with Fanny clowning away at its center. Once again the evening is a triumph, but for Fanny it is soured by the fact that Nick has not turned up.

When he finally arrives, she blazes out her disappointment at him, but he has his reasons sadly to hand: The casino venture has gone up in the air and all their money is lost. Fanny is cheerful about it—he's lost his shirt before and made it back again in his next venture—but Nick sees it with a different eye. He sees himself as the rich star's adored husband, playing games with her money—money she indulgently lets him lose, for she can make plenty more. Fanny sincerely denies this and Nick knows that she believes what she says, but he knows equally well that what he says is the truth. As he goes to depart, her fearful cry to him not to go brings him back just in time ("Who Are You Now?").

An agent called Renaldi visits Arnstein with an offer of a partnership. It is too good to be true: No investment is needed, just the use of Nick's enormously presentable self and manner. He is ready to accept happily when it becomes evident to him that Fanny has already paid money into Renaldi's firm to buy him a safe job. He turns the offer down and stakes everything on a ballooning venture concerning some bonds.

Fanny is on stage rehearsing when the news comes that her husband has been arrested. He has admitted fraud and embezzlement in the bond affair. Fanny is incredulous. She cannot believe that he would not have come to her to help him out of any difficulty. Mrs. Brice understands only too well why he did not, and she tells Fanny in clear words that with too much love and too little understanding she, Fanny, has been the downfall of Nick Arnstein. The faithful Eddie, as always, takes the view that it is Nick who has let Fanny down, but

Fanny tiredly wonders at his incomprehension: He can never understand what Nick did for her. He made her pretty ("Music That Makes Me Dance").

The time returns to the present when Fanny is waiting longingly for Nick's return. Today he is to be released from prison and he will be coming to the theatre. When he comes, however, it is to tell her that their life together is over. Neither of them will ever change, and he cannot go on as before. A shattered Fanny plays along. Of course he is right. She was going to say the same thing. And so, with love on both sides as bright as it was in Baltimore all those years ago, they part, and this time she knows for certain she'll never see him again. Holding a little memento of their love to her cheek, she begins to sing "Don't Rain on My Parade" as, putting on her make-up through her tears, she builds herself up to face her audience. Her world can end later; right now she has a show to do.

1964

Hello, Dolly!

A MUSICAL COMEDY IN TWO ACTS by Michael Stewart based on *The Matchmaker* by Thornton Wilder. Music and lyrics by Jerry Herman.

Produced at the St. James Theatre, New York, 16 January 1964, with Carol Channing (Dolly), David Burns (Horace), Charles Nelson Reilly (Cornelius), Jerry Dodge (Barnaby), Eileen Brennan (Irene), and Sondra Lee (Minnie Fay). Produced at the Minskoff Theatre, 6 November 1975, with Pearl Bailey, Billy Daniels, Terrence Emanuel, Grenoldo Frazier, Mary Louise, and Chip Fields. Produced at the Lunt-Fontanne Theatre, 5 March 1978, with Channing, Eddie Bracken, Lee Roy Reams, Robert Lydiard, Florence Lacey, and Alexandra Korey.

A film version was produced by Twentieth Century-Fox in 1969 with Barbra Streisand, Walter Matthau, Michael Crawford, Danny Lockin, Marianne McAndrew, and E. J. Peaker.

Carol Channing, as Dolly Levi, acknowledges her
all-singing, all-dancing welcome in the show's 1977 revival.
Courtesy Performing Arts Research Center,
New York Public Library at Lincoln Center.

CHARACTERS

Mrs. Dolly Gallagher Levi

Ernestina Money

Ambrose Kemper

Horace Vandergelder

Ermengarde

Cornelius Hackl

Barnaby Tucker

Irene Molloy

Minnie Fay

Mrs. Rose, Rudolph, Judge, Court Clerk, etc.

Act 1

In the streets of *fin de siècle* New York, the populace is letting rip with a number vaunting the merits of the matchmaker, Dolly Gallagher Levi ("Call on Dolly"). Mrs. Levi is a woman who arranges things ("I Put My Hand In"), but today she is unable to attend to the marital and eclectic other problems of the metropolis for she is bound for the village of Yonkers where she is engaged in supplying a new wife to the widowed and wealthy half-millionaire Horace Vandergelder, and, coincidentally, the winning of that gentleman's approval (on commission) to the marriage of his heiress niece, Ermengarde, to the poor artist Ambrose Kemper.

It is the opinion of the chorus-singing city that Mr. Vandergelder will, in the end, marry Dolly's client, the pretty widow, Irene Molloy, but Dolly Levi has recently had other thoughts. Before she boards the Yonkers train, she looks up and confides in her late husband that—if he doesn't mind—she has a mind to marry again herself, and Horace Vandergelder's fortune seems to her like the perfect mate.

Horace Vandergelder has no idea what fate and Dolly Levi have planned for him. Today, he intends to spend in the city. He will march in a parade and propose to Mrs. Molloy. His house has not had a woman about it for years and it could do with a clean ("It Takes a Woman"). When Dolly arrives in Yonkers, her first care is to sow distrust of Mrs. Molloy in Vandergelder's mind, after which she sets out to tempt him to forget his intentions toward the widow with the prospect of a marital merger with the fabulously wealthy (if ineffably plain) Ernestina Money. Her strategy works. Vandergelder expresses interest in meeting this unknown but eligible sounding lady. As he sets off for town, Dolly gives a quick glance around the room. She is choosing the new shade of wallpaper for the day she moves in. Blue, perhaps? Yes, a very particular shade of blue.

Horace Vandergelder is not the only inhabitant of Yonkers heading for the bright lights of the city today. Down in the bowels of his Hay and Feed Store, his overworked and underpaid employees, Cornelius and Barnaby, have come to momentous decision. While the boss is away, they will close down the store and sidle off for their first-ever glance at the big city, and they won't come home until they've done everything—even kissed a girl ("Put on Your Sunday Clothes").

In Irene Molloy's hat shop in Water Street, New York City, the widow and her assistant, Minnie Fay, are awaiting the arrival of Horace Vandergelder and his proposal. Minnie Fay seems more excited than her employer, who is quite willing to admit that she is about to accept Mr. Vandergelder as a husband solely to escape from her hated position in the millinery business. The sprightly Irene feels much more like a little bit of an adventure, maybe even in one of her own hats ("I'll Be Wearing Ribbons Down My Back"), than marriage with a middle-aged half-millionaire.

This is the moment that Cornelius and Barnaby choose to make a hurried entrance into the shop. It is not that they have an interest in hats, but they have spotted Vandergelder coming down the street and they urgently need a place to hide. They couldn't have chosen less happily, for Horace is coming there to rendezvous with Dolly, prior to meeting Mrs. Molloy, and he seats himself down on a bench right outside the shop to wait.

Cornelius and Barnaby are trapped, but they couldn't be trapped in a nicer place. Cornelius is swiftly smitten by the pretty Irene but, before the acquaintance can be developed, Vandergelder enters and the boys are forced to scramble for a hiding place. It becomes more and more difficult for Irene and the newly arrived Dolly to keep the boys under cover. Dolly finally breaks into a confusingly patriotic song and march ("Motherhood") to hinder and bewilder Vandergelder, and to her delight, Horace is soon convinced that his intended fiancée is hiding a roomful of strange men. He storms indignantly out of the shop to look into the possibilities of the rich Ernestina.

Dolly suggests that the boys should take Irene and Minnie Fay to dinner to make amends and, having picked up from Dolly's imaginative chatter that Cornelius is rich, Irene plumps for a table at the fashionable Harmonia Gardens. Needless to say, this is well beyond Cornelius's pocket but, worse, it is well known that the Harmonia Gardens hosts dancing contests for its guests and Cornelius and Barnaby can't dance. Such a consideration has no fears for Mrs. Levi for dance training is one of her sidelines. Before long she will have them "Dancing."

Off the happy young people go, leaving Dolly alone with her thoughts and intentions. It is time she started living again herself instead of just organizing life for other people. She wants her own fun again before it's too late ("Before the Parade Passes By") but, please, will her dear late Ephraim give her a sign to let her know that it's all right? Horace Vandergelder is getting to be a positive possibility. Mrs. Molloy has been scuttled and the man is, whatever the appearances, all hers just as soon as she knows Ephraim doesn't mind.

In the meanwhile, Vandergelder's pursuit of a wife is not proving very successful. The lovely lady Dolly pointed out to him in the parade as being the available heiress was nothing of the sort. When Horace attempted to pursue an introduction it turned out that she was nothing but a tailor's dummy. Unabashed, Dolly promises that at 8 P.M. that night he can meet the real Ernestina at the Harmonia Gardens. Vandergelder isn't sure that he wants any more of Dolly Levi's introductions but, after all, he's paid for this one so he might as well have it. But after that, that's it. He's had enough of his marriage broker. Dolly is sacked and she is thrilled. The man is as good as hers.

Act 2

Cornelius and Barnaby have been showing their ladies the lights of the town while avoiding any situation that might require the spending of their non-existent money. They invoke "Elegance" as the reason for walking instead of taking a cab, but they end up at the ritzy Harmonia Gardens all the same and they have to go in. Ambrose and his Ermengarde are there too, ordered into the dance contest by Dolly as a part of their courtship and as a challenge to her Uncle Horace Vandergelder who is also there to meet the real, vast, and over-rouged Ernestina.

In one private dining room Ernestina orders her way through the menu at the expense of the glum Vandergelder while, in another, Cornelius throws common sense to the wind and calls for champagne. But when both Horace and Barnaby emerge to tip the bandleader to play their preferred music, they get caught up in the mêlée of dancing waiters ("The Waiters' Galop") and drop their purses. The wrong one is returned to each and Barnaby suddenly finds he is rich. The boys can order the best of everything.

Suddenly everything stops. The waiters are in ferment. An old and loved customer is about to put in an appearance. It is our Mrs. Levi, dolled up like nobody's business, and greeted by the whole staff of the establishment with a ringing "Hello, Dolly!" Vandergelder starts out to give Dolly a piece of his mind about the unsuitable Ernestina, but he somehow ends up dining with her at a table for two alongside the dance-floor with turkey and all the most lavish trimmings served up. Before he knows where he is, the conversation is firmly twisted on to marriage and compatibility and somehow the tenor of the discussion is always against him.

Horace is not that stupid. He recognizes the drift and he has just one thing to say: Under no circumstances will he marry Dolly Levi. He determines to escape from this unwanted *dîner à deux*, but, when he goes to pay his bill, he finds to his horror that his purse contains only a few cents. He is stuck. As Horace stands staggered by his awful plight, the dance contest starts and the couples make their way on to the floor. Good heavens! It's Ermengarde! And Cornelius! And Barnaby! What are they doing here? They are all sacked!

Mayhem ensues and, by the time the confusion is over, everybody is in court for causing an affray. When the case gets under way, Dolly plumps the whole blame for anything and everything, with a special reference to the misery of her clients Ambrose and Ermengarde, on to the unfortunate Vandergelder. When Cornelius steps forward to sum up for the defense, he pours out instead his newly found love for Irene ("It Only Takes a Moment"). This is sufficient cause for the judge to acquit all the defendants except Horace, but Horace is made of stern stuff. He will absolutely not under any circumstances marry Dolly Levi, not even to get out of this mess. Then Dolly plays her trump card. She has no intention of marrying him. She merely wishes to say "Goodbye, Dearie," and the wedding will be at eleven o'clock tomorrow.

Back in Yonkers, Cornelius (with Irene), Barnaby (with Minnie Fay), and Ermengarde (with Ambrose) are all lining up to get their money out of Vandergelder's safe. Cornelius is going to set up his own shop dealing in the same kind of goods right opposite to the Vandergelder store. It is a bad day for Horace but the worst part of it is that he has realized what he really wants: He proposes to Dolly.

Of course, he will take Cornelius back and make him a partner, won't he . . . ? and he'll dance at Ermengarde's wedding to Ambrose . . . ? One at a time, Dolly wins her points. She's nearly there, but where is the sign from Ephraim? It turns up in the shape of some rolls of blue wallpaper. Horace has inexplicably ordered them to repaper the room, and they are precisely the color that Dolly had decided on. And then comes something that no one ever expected to hear. Ephraim's favorite (and very un-Vandergelder) aphorism falls from Horace's lips: "Money is like manure. It's not worth a thing unless you spread it around." It is surely going to be spread around when Dolly gets her hands on it, but Vandergelder is going to have a much more adventurous life with what is clearly a wonderful woman. He can say "Hello, Dolly!" with a real enthusiasm.

The songs "World, Take Me Back" and "Love, Look in My Window" were added to the score for Ethel Merman when she succeeded to the role of Dolly in the original production.

1964

FIDDLER ON THE ROOF

A MUSICAL IN TWO ACTS by Joseph Stein based on the stories of Sholom Aleichem. Lyrics by Sheldon Harnick. Music by Jerry Bock.

Produced at the Imperial Theatre, New York, 22 September 1964, with Zero Mostel (Tevye), Maria Karnilova (Golde), Beatrice Arthur (Yente), Joanna Merlin (Tzeitel), Austin Pendleton (Motel), and Julia Migenes (Hodel). Produced at the Winter Garden Theatre, 28 December 1976, with Mostel and Thelma Lee. Produced at the Gershwin Theatre, 18 November 1990, with Topol and Marcia Lewis.

A film version was produced by United Artists in 1971 with Topol, Norma Crane, Molly Picon, Rosalind Harris, Leonard Frey, and Michele Marsh.

A little aid from the Good Lord wouldn't go amiss.
Zero Mostel as Tevye.
Friedman-Abeles, photographers.
Courtesy Performing Arts Research Center,
New York Public Library at Lincoln Center.

CHARACTERS

Tevye, *a dairyman*

Golde, *his wife*

Tzeitel

Hodel

Chava

Shprintze

Bielke

their daughters

Yente, *a matchmaker*

Motel Kamzoil, *a tailor*

Shandel, *his mother*

Perchik, *a student*

Lazar Wolf, *a butcher*

Mendel, *the rabbi's son*

Grandma Tzeitel, *Golde's grandmother*

Fruma-Sarah, *Lazar Wolf's first wife*

Fyedka

Avram

Mordcha, Rabbi, Nahum, Yussel, Sasha, The Fiddler, etc.

Act 1

The scene is the little Russian village of Anatevka and the time 1905, the beginning of the end of Tsarist Russia. On the roof of the house of Tevye, the milkman, a violinist is seated, scraping away at his fiddle. He is the epitome of the Jewish people of Anatevka who each scratch out a living, as the fiddler scratches out his tune, while perilously perched on the edge of existence as represented by the unsafe roof. They are sustained in this struggle with life by one great asset, "Tradition." Where the traditions came from and why they exist is not given to them to know, but they live by the rules and manners prescribed, and they give obedience to God and his law as interpreted by the rabbi rather than to the laws of the even more distant and nebulous Tsar.

Tevye is a case in point. He works hard to keep his wife, Golde, and their five daughters, and they survive. It will be good when the girls are married. Tzeitel, the eldest, must have her marriage arranged first and Tevye would like it to be to a scholarly man with whom he could indulge his fondness for scriptural debate, but Yente the matchmaker has a surprise to unveil. She has a magnificent match for Tevye's eldest. The well-off and widowed butcher, Lazar Wolf, has taken a fancy to Tzeitel and is willing to offer for her hand.

Given what a poor girl with no dowry might have to accept just to get a husband at all, the sisters are not at all anxious to be found a match ("Matchmaker, Matchmaker"), but Tzeitel has a particular reason for dreading Yente and her interference. She is in love with her childhood friend, the penniless tailor Motel, and they have pledged their troth to each other in secret. Soon the time will have to come for Motel to take his courage in his hands and go to Tevye to ask formally for her hand.

Tevye returns from a day's work in which his carthorse has gone lame. God is getting at him again. He realizes that God has a lot to think about, but would it be such a very difficult thing for Him to lighten Tevye's load a little ("If I Were a Rich Man")? That consideration seems much more important to Tevye than the news of distant evictions of Jews from their villages. It is not more important, however, to a young university student called Perchik who tries to stir the villagers from their regular life with simplistic revolutionary talk. No one will listen to his strange words, but Tevye is enough of a kindly fool to take in this penniless stump orator for the Sabbath meal (Sabbath Prayer).

Golde does not break the news of Lazar Wolf's intentions openly to her husband but tells him only that the butcher wishes to meet with him. Tevye is concerned that Wolf is after his new milk cow, and, when he goes the next evening to meet him, he is momentarily taken aback at his offer. He does not like the butcher and he does not care to have him as a son-in-law, but he realizes that it is a fine social and financial prospect for his daughter and therefore he accepts. The two men drink on the agreement and merrily sing "To Life." As they wander drunkenly into the street at the end of the evening, Tevye is stopped by the local constable with a warning. He has been sent orders to make sure there are some anti-Jewish demonstrations in the area. Since they are friends, he will make sure that these demonstrations are insignificant and Tevye must understand that it will be just for the form. So, on a day you find a rich husband for your daughter, you have to have news like that. What is it with God?

There are problems at home, too. Although Tevye does not know it, he has introduced a disturbing influence into his home in Perchik. When, in return for his food, he teaches the girls from the bible, he perverts the sacred texts to make political points, and in conversations with the bright Hodel he denigrates the solid family traditions by which she lives, teaching her the dance steps of the town instead of the contents of the good book. There is further trouble when Tzeitel takes very much against the marriage arranged for her, and Tevye has to listen to Motel the tailor ask for her hand. They gave each other a pledge? Tevye is stunned. It is the father's position to arrange his daughter's marriage and he has done so. A pledge? This is wholly against "Tradition." But he can see the love in his daughter's eyes and he cannot gainsay her. She shall marry her wretched tailor ("Miracle of Miracles"), but what on earth will he tell Golde?

He tells her by means of a dream. In the middle of the night Golde wakes to find her husband shouting in his sleep and he awakes with a dreadful tale. He dreamed that, in the middle of a feast, Golde's grandmother came to him from beyond the grave and told him that Tzeitel should marry Motel the tailor and not Lazar Wolf. The characters from his dream crowd around the bed as he continues to recount the story. In support of the grandmother's proclamation, there came the dreadful apparition of Fruma-Sarah, the first wife of the butcher. Like a banshee she descended, threatening to be revenged on Tzeitel should she take her place in Lazar Wolf's bed. Golde is thoroughly frightened and agrees that under such circumstances a wedding between Tzeitel and Lazar Wolf is impossible. As she goes back to sleep, Tevye mouths a silent "thank you" to God.

At the wedding of Tzeitel and Motel, Tevye watches sentimentally ("Sunrise, Sunset") as the celebration moves on to the giving of the gifts and the general singing and dancing. Lazar Wolf has brought a gift, but he has only harsh words for Tevye who he considers has made him ridiculous in the village by going back on his bond. There is a further sensation when Perchik takes Hodel to the dance floor—it is not done for a man to dance in public with a woman—but Tevye covers for him as best he can by following up with Golde and the newly married couple. Tradition is broken again, and Lazar Wolf and Yente, the pillars of old Anatevka, leave angrily.

The happy wedding feast is winding to a height of merriment and dancing when the festivities are invaded by a band of Russians. The anti-Jewish demonstration has been scheduled for tonight. The constable is sorry, but it has to be. The wedding party ends in a shower of broken furniture and gifts and Perchik is clubbed down trying to resist.

Act 2

Tevye is still talking to God, but God doesn't seem willing to alleviate the troubles of his life. They just keep on getting heavier and more numerous.

Perchik tells Hodel that he must leave Anatevka and return to the city to be where things political are happening but, before he leaves, he comes out with a stilted profession of love. Hodel says she will consider herself engaged to him and he is content ("Now I Have Everything"), but Tevye refuses his permission. If Perchik is going away, Hodel must find a local bridegroom.

But Perchik is not asking his permission, only his blessing. So now it is only "love" that matters—not tradition, not the father and the mother—and he can't use a dream for an excuse to Golde this time. All this love. Did they have love, he and Golde, when they got married? Do they have it now? Suddenly Tevye wants to know ("Do You Love Me?"). They've battled against life together, side by side, for twenty-five years. If that's not love, what is?

In Anatevka rumor is flowing, and getting more confused as it runs from mouth to mouth ("I Just Heard"). The truth of it is that Perchik has been arrested in Kiev for his political activities and condemned to serve his sentence in Siberia. Hodel knows that, no matter what, she must leave her family and go to him ("Far from the Home I Love"). Bidding farewell to her father, she promises him that she will be married properly, under a canopy, as soon as Perchik is freed.

Soon there is another bit of gossip—a new arrival at the home of Motel and Tzeitel. The town rushes to see, and the rabbi to bless. Motel has, at last, got the sewing machine he has worked and saved for for so many years.

Trouble will not leave Tevye alone for long. Now his third daughter, Chava, wants to get married. She wishes to marry Fyedka, and Fyedka is a Russian. This time Tevye is firm. Whatever else he may permit, whatever else he may suffer, no daughter of his will marry outside the faith. His interdiction goes for nothing. Chava, knowing the risk she runs, goes ahead and weds her Russian. But this time Tevye will not forgive. He will not and cannot be persuaded to accept the marriage. His "Chavaleh" is from this day dead to him.

The outside world and its agents have been breaking down Anatevka and Tevye's family for a long time but the last blow, when it comes, is no less hard. What has been happening elsewhere is now happening to them. The Jews must leave the village: the pogroms are upon them. "Anatevka" is a thing of the past for them. Tevye and what remains of his family, Yente, Lazar Wolf, and the rest of the community bind closely together in the face of fate, but they must go. Tevye and Golde and the two youngest girls will go to relatives in America, Motel and Tzeitel and the baby will join them later, and Chava and Fyedka, who cannot live in a country where such injustice prevails, will head for Cracow. The village of Anatevka and its people will be spread far and wide. As they leave, Tevye beckons to the fiddler on the roof to follow. Wherever they go, and however the world may change, the fiddler and all that he stands for will be with them.

MAN OF LA MANCHA

A MUSICAL PLAY IN ONE ACT by Dale Wasserman based on his television play *I, Don Quixote* and *Don Quixote* by Manuel de Cervantes y Saavedra. Lyrics by Joe Darion. Music by Mitch Leigh.

Produced at the Anta Washington Square Theatre, New York, 22 November 1965, with Richard Kiley (Don Quixote), Joan Diener (Aldonza), and Irving Jacobson (Sancho). Transferred to the Martin Beck Theatre, 19 March 1968. Produced at the Marquis Theatre, 24 April 1992, with Raul Julia, Sheena Easton, and Tony Martinez. First produced at the Goodspeed Opera House, Connecticut, 28 June 1965.

A film version was produced by United Artists in 1972 with Peter O'Toole (singing dubbed by Simon Gilbert), Sophia Loren, and James Coco.

"I am I, Don Quixote,
the Lord of La Mancha."
Richard Kiley as Don Quixote and
Irving Jacobsen as his
faithful Sancho Panza.
Photograph by Fred Fehl.
Courtesy the Theatre Arts Collection,
Harry Ransom Humanities Research Center,
The University of Texas at Asutin.

To the common room of a sixteenth century Spanish prison, a Captain of the Inquisition's Guard brings two prisoners: a tall, lank gentleman of evident courtliness and childlike charm, and his servant, a rotund and straight-forward little fellow, the pragmatic half of what is clearly a long and devoted relationship. Their crime, it seems, is that in the master's egalitarian zeal as a tax-collector (a temporary employment, meant only to furnish the wherewithal to live) he foreclosed on a defaulting monastery dear to the heart of the Inquisitor. For such a crime, Cervantes is to be thrown into this dark and unpleasant prison, among thieves and murderers, to await trial. Their fellow inmates are soon upon the newcomers, despoiling them of their possessions, as they are dragged before the prisoners' top dog, The Governor, to justify themselves in an underworld trial.

Their possessions turn out to be nothing but a trunk of theatrical costumes and properties and a bundle of manuscript, but Cervantes will use these in his trial on the charges proposed by the malicious prisoner known as the Duke. Cervantes pleads guilty to the charges of being "an idealist, a bad poet, and an honest man," but he claims the right to present his case before the jury so that his sentence may be mitigated.

His case will take the form of an entertainment: the tale of a country squire called Alonso Quijana who, from too much reading, formed a passionate rebellion in his heart against the evil ways of man toward man. Leaving aside what men call sanity, he set out into the world as a knight errant, calling himself Don Quixote of La Mancha, dedicated to righting all wrongs. With the assistance of some items from the chest, Cervantes becomes Don Quixote and his servant, at his side, becomes his faithful Sancho Panza ("Man of La Mancha").

Don Quixote and Sancho set out along a great highway to glory (which to Sancho looks remarkably like the road to El Toboso where the chickens are cheap). Quixote revels in expectations of giants, knights, and wizards in his path and, above all, the Great Enchanter who is the most dangerous enemy of all good men. When a structure is espied on the horizon, Quixote calls it a giant and gallops his horse straight at it, but he is foiled by the magic of the Great Enchanter, which changes his foe, at the last moment, into a windmill that brings him tumbling to the ground. Quixote blames his defeat on the fact that he has not been truly dubbed a knight, and he vows to seek out another knight to administer the necessary dubbing. When he spies a great castle on the road, he determines to enter. Sancho, who sees only an inn, loyally follows him.

Cervantes breaks his story to cast the other prisoners in the roles of the inhabitants of the inn: the kindly innkeeper, his less kindly wife, a band of rough muleteers, and several easy-virtued women, in particular a popular wildcat known as Aldonza. Aldonza is pawed by the muleteers, but she holds her own against them as she contemptuously spits forth that she cares not with which of them she passes her night ("It's All the Same"). She takes the money pressed on her by Pedro and leaves him to wonder if he will get what he's paid for.

Into this rough scene arrive the gentle, bedraggled Don Quixote and his curious servant with their high sounding words and their claims of nobility. The innkeeper humors what he sees as a harmless madman who treats the foul company in the inn as gentlefolk, but there is spiteful mirth among the customers when the Don hails Aldonza as a sweet lady and a fair virgin, and worships her as his "Dulcinea."

The Duke intervenes to protest that Cervantes is not offering a conventional defense, but the Governor is intrigued by the tale of Don Quixote and orders it to be continued.

Cervantes now returns to the folk at the home that Alonso Quijana left to take up his quest: his niece, Antonia, his heir-in-law and engaged to be married to the self-important Dr. Carrasco; and his housekeeper, hopeful through many years of an eventual marriage. Hurrying to church, they kneel before the padre to wonder what they can do with their mad provider, insisting of course that "I'm Only Thinking of Him." Carrasco, who begins by declaring that he could not marry into a family where there is madness, soon suffers a change of heart at the thought of inheriting Quijana's fortune through his niece, and he vows sanctimoniously to bring the poor man back to home and sanity.

Back at the inn, Quixote sends Sancho to his Dulcinea with a missive asking for a token to carry into battle. Aldonza is gloweringly uncomprehending of the chivalrous poetry addressed to her by her knight, and she angrily throws a dish rag to Sancho to be the sought-after token. But she is intrigued. She asks Sancho why he sticks with a madman, and Sancho can only reply simply "I Really Like Him." The muleteers mock Aldonza over her knight ("Little Bird") and her missive, and she snaps back that he is just a man and she supposes he wants what every other man wants.

Dr. Carrasco and the padre arrive at the inn in search of Quijana and they find Quixote who, to their surprise, addresses them by name but still persists in his new persona. A barber passes by (Barber's Song), and Quixote attacks him and forces him to render up his helmet—the shaving basin he wears on his head to keep out the sun—and, when Aldonza's token is pinned on top of the helmet as its crest, he has the padre crown him with the "Golden Helmet of Mambrino." The next morning, after he has kept vigil, the innkeeper shall dub him a knight.

He refuses consistently to return home with Carrasco and the padre, but the former, now cognizant of the nature of Quijana's madness, sets out scientifically to force the old man from his folly. The padre is not so sure: Perhaps he is happier in his delusion ("To Each His Dulcinea").

As Quixote prepares to keep his vigil in the inn yard overnight, Aldonza passes by on her way to Pedro and stops to hear his words. She is shaken by his courtliness, his gentleness, and his otherworldly idealism in the face of her unimaginative view of reality, and she is curious enough to listen when he explains to her what his quest is (The Quest/"The Impossible Dream"). When he has finished, she begs him to see her as she really is, but he sees only beauty and purity, and she turns away from him in despair to be manhandled by the angry Pedro who has come seeking her.

Quixote is roused to fury at seeing his lady thus treated, and, armed with his lance, he moves to the attack. With Sancho at one shoulder and Aldonza wielding his sword at the other, he succeeds in laying out the whole band of muleteers and, his valor proven, he has the accommodating innkeeper dub him the Knight of the Woeful Countenance (The Dubbing). But now, when it is time to triumph over evil fallen, Quixote preaches only forgiveness, and he sends the surprised Aldonza to tend to their enemies' wounds. While her knight is busy reaffirming his creed, Aldonza is beaten and raped into unconsciousness by the vengeful muleteers.

The tale of Don Quixote is broken off as the Inquisition's guards descend into the room to carry off a prisoner to be judged and burned. The Duke sneers at Cervantes's fear—this is reality. But Cervantes knows reality: He has lived through battle, hunger, misery, and death. He has seen men wonder why they have lived and wonder whether life itself is a dream, or even the edge of madness. Who, indeed, is to say that wisdom is not madness and madness blessed?

When he takes to the road again, Quixote meets with a whore and her pander and is robbed of all his possessions. He returns to the inn and there he finds the battered Aldonza who throws his fine sentiments at his head and describes in every detail the degrading circumstances of her birth and her life ("Aldonza"). When he replies that still he sees only beauty, she cannot bear it.

Suddenly a challenge is issued. It is the Great Enchanter come to do battle with Quixote. They stand up to each other and the enemy reveals his weapon: a bright, shining mirrored shield in which Quixote sees reflected only his old, foolish self. Everywhere he turns, the evil knight's attendants hold up further mirrors as the Enchanter's voice taunts him with the truth of his pretensions. Weeping and defeated, Quixote sinks fainting into reality, as the knight removes his casque to disclose his identity. It is Carrasco.

Cervantes is warned that his case will be the next to be judged. Scarcely will he have finished justifying himself before one court than he must be summoned before another. He must spin out his tale here until it is time to go. And so the tale of Don Quixote, dragged from blessed fantasy to cruel reality, has its epilogue.

Back at his home, Quijana lies insensible in his bed and none can rouse him until his servant comes by for "A Little Gossip." Into his song creep words of imagination and suddenly Quijana is awake and sane. But he has an awareness of death and, to the satisfaction of Carrasco, he begins to make out his will in favor of Antonia.

Suddenly Aldonza forces her way into the room and falls to her knees beside him, addressing him as "my lord" and urging him to remember Don Quixote and Dulcinea. He has altered her life with his knight errantry, brought her words and thoughts of which she could never have dreamed; he cannot renounce "The Impossible Dream." Then, gradually, Quijana remembers Quixote. Life flows back into him as he calls triumphantly for his sword and rises up magnificently, supported by Sancho and Aldonza, until, with a cry, he is gone. As the padre intones a *De profundis*, the stunned Sancho turns to Aldonza. But she tells him that Don Quixote is not dead. And her name is not Aldonza; it is Dulcinea.

Now the Captain of the Inquisition Guard comes to take Cervantes to court. The Governor returns his manuscript to him and wishes him an optimistic good courage where he is going, for he feels that Don Quixote and Don Miguel are two close kindred. As Cervantes mounts the stairs, the girl prisoner who played Aldonza begins to sing "The Impossible Dream," and the company gradually join in the hymn as the play ends.

1966

SWEET CHARITY

A MUSICAL COMEDY IN TWO ACTS by Neil Simon based on the film *Nights of Cabiria* by Federico Fellini, Tullio Pinelli, and Ennio Flaiano. Lyrics by Dorothy Fields. Music by Cy Coleman.

Produced at the Palace Theatre, New York, 29 January 1966, with Gwen Verdon (Charity), John McMartin (Oscar), Helen Gallagher (Nickie), Thelma Oliver (Helene), James Luisi (Vidal), and Arnold Soboloff (Daddy). Produced at the Minskoff Theatre, 27 April 1986, with Debbie Allen, Michael Rupert, Bebe Neuwirth, Alison Williams, Mark Jacoby, and Irving Allen Lee.

A film version was produced by Universal in 1969 with Shirley Maclaine, McMartin, Chita Rivera, Paula Kelly, Ricardo Montalban, and Sammy Davis, Jr.

Some things are easier to say when
you're not looking eye-to-eye.
Oscar (John McMartin)
and Charity (Gwen Verdon)
at Barney's Chili Hacienda.
Friedman-Abeles, photographers.
Courtesy Performing Arts Research Center,
New York Public Library at Lincoln Center.

CHARACTERS

Charity Hope Valentine

Helene

Nickie

Carmen

Vittorio Vidal

Ursala

Herman

Oscar Lindquist

Daddy Johann Sebastian Brubeck

Manfred, Marvin, Dark Glasses, Brother Harold, Brother Eddie, etc.

Act 1

Charity Hope Valentine carries her heart on her sleeve. More correctly, she carries it on her arm—tattooed there—but it's the same thing. She is a girl who just wants to be loved. At the moment she is wanting to be loved by her fiancé (well, almost her fiancé when he gets his divorce), a young man with dark glasses and a lot of wavy black hair. She has come to meet him in the park, her head full of all those lovely things he is going to say to her. When she meets him and he doesn't, she just says them all herself for him, and then she starts in with her appreciation of him ("You Should See Yourself").

She's been out today looking at furniture and she's brought her savings to pay the down payment on the suite that will decorate their home. Looking down into the lake, she suggests they should throw something in for luck. He does. He throws her in, grabbing her handbag as he runs off into the never-to-be-found. A crowd gathers to watch her struggle drowningly in the water until someone hauls her out to tell her story first to the police and then to the girls at work.

Charity is a dance hostess in the Fan-Dango ballroom. Her friends there are sympathetic but they've heard it all before, and, dress up her tale as Charity will, they know and she has finally to admit that she's been suckered one more time. Poor Charity.

Under the authoritarian eyes of Herman, the dance hall owner, the girls get ready for their nightly grope and glide around the floor of the Fan-Dango ("Big Spender"). As she waits to be asked to dance, Charity thinks back to the beginning of the affair and, as she dances with a sticky-fingered customer, her thoughts follow through the stages of her unfortunate "romance" (Charity's Soliloquy) until, pushing her partner off, she swears never to be taken for a romantic ride again and rushes out of the dance hall.

As she makes her way down the street, Charity passes by the grand Pompeii Club, and, at that precise moment, a man rushes out of the club and bowls into her, sending her flying. Charity is flabbergasted: It is the famous film star Vittorio Vidal and he is having an argument with a lady. As she watches enthusiastically, the argument grows until, as a stroke of bravado against his mistress, Vidal seizes the first girl he sees and whisks her into the glitzy Pompeii Club as his partner. It's Charity.

The patrons of the club are dancing the "Rich Man's Frug" as they enter, and all eyes turn to the unknown girl on Vidal's arm. Vittorio talks mainly about his Ursala, but Charity doesn't care. She gets a telephone brought to the table so she can ring the dance hall and get Vittorio to say something to the girls to prove that she really is where she says she is. Then she faints. Vittorio carries her up to his apartment and she recovers instantly. Then they chat. Mostly she chats as she asks for an autographed picture and some sort of memento to prove that she was actually here ("If My Friends Could See Me Now"), and she has just got around to offering him her body when Ursala attacks the door with her fists.

Charity valiantly climbs into a cupboard while Vittorio goes to get rid of Ursala, but things don't go quite as planned. Soon Vittorio is serenading his mistress with reborn passion ("Too Many Tomorrows") while Charity attempts to smoke a cigarette in the cupboard with disastrous results. Then the pair head for the bed to finish their making-up, and Charity abandons the cigarette for the keyhole. Ursala is still lounging exotically in bed when Vittorio lets Charity out the next morning.

The dance hall girls are aghast that Charity has let such an opportunity slip. She's come away with a lousy photograph and a top hat and a cane when she could have got enough cash to have taken her out of the Fan-Dango for good ("There's Gotta Be Something Better Than This"). One thing Charity's adventure has done, though, is give her the taste for meeting new people in new places, and that night she tries out the local YMCA. The Y doesn't turn out to be quite as gregarious as she expected, because she gets stuck in the lift with a claustrophobic tax accountant called Oscar. She cheers him up with a song ("I'm the Bravest Individual") as they settle in to wait to be freed.

Act 2   When they are finally rescued, Oscar invites Charity to come to church, and, being Charity, she goes. Oscar's church is a strange sort of place. It is in a basement and called the Rhythm of Life Church in honor of its development from a jazz group. The church's chief apostle is one Daddy Johann Sebastian Brubeck ("The Rhythm of Life"), and its creed seems to be made up of welfare and drug resolutions. Before Oscar and Charity can get settled in, the police arrive and they are soon out in the street again, and getting to know each other a little more than they did in the lift. He thinks she's a bank clerk, so she doesn't disillusion him, and he calls her Sweet Charity and doesn't try to lay her. He's different. Her friends make fun of the homey little life Charity is soon dreaming up for herself with her new friend ("Baby, Dream Your Dream"), and Charity promises herself that she will tell Oscar the truth about her job soon.

Oscar and Charity go to Coney Island together and ride the parachute jump together and get stuck again together way up above the ground. This time it's Charity who is scared and Oscar who can assert his budding manhood in protection of his "Sweet Charity," his lovely virginal, innocent Charity. She does try to tell him about the bank, but he kisses her and it's easier and safer just to go back to being a teller for the moment.

Then Charity makes a big decision: She is going to get out. She is going to quit the Fan-Dango. As she wanders alone through Times Square she wonders what will happen to her next ("Where Am I Going?"). She sends a telegram to Oscar. He must meet her in Barney's Chili Hacienda at 1 A.M. and state his intentions—she has to know. When he turns up, she puts him in one booth while she sits in the next so that she doesn't have to look at him while she tells him the truth. She doesn't work in a bank, she's a dance hall hostess. But he already knows. He saw her go in to the Fan-Dango one night and he slipped in and watched. He knows, too, what else some of the girls there do and he doesn't care. He can forget her old career; he wants to marry her. Charity explodes with joy ("I'm a Brass Band"). At last she's almost married! Back at the Fan-Dango, the girls throw a party for their friend and even horrible Herman proves to be human as he admits "I Love to Cry at Weddings." A happy ending is in sight.

But Oscar chickens out. The other men keep trampling about in his mind. All those other men Charity slept with. He thought he could fight it, he thought he could make it not matter, but he can't. Charity fights for her man in her usual way—she's had practice—but Oscar is too strong. It is for her own good that he cannot marry her. Unfortunately, he chooses to make his point rather vigorously just as they walk past the lake in the park. As Charity climbs dripping from the lake once again she sees a Good Fairy, a fairy with wings and things and all covered in tinsel-dust. "Tonight," says the fairy, "It will all happen tonight." So Charity lives to hope and love some more and the Good Fairy turns and goes off. On her back is a sign: "THE GOOD FAIRY—tonight at 8 P.M. on CBS."

The 1986 revival used a different title song, a rewritten version of "I'm the Bravest Individual," and omitted Charity's Soliloquy.

1966

CABARET

A MUSICAL IN TWO ACTS by Joe Masteroff based on the play *I Am a Camera* by John van Druten and the stories of Christopher Isherwood. Lyrics by Fred Ebb. Music by John Kander.

Produced at the Broadhurst Theatre, New York, 20 November 1966, with Joel Grey (Emcee), Jill Haworth (Sally Bowles), Bert Convy (Clifford), Jack Gilford (Herr Schultz), and Lotte Lenya (Fräulein Schneider), and played from 7 March 1967 at the Imperial Theatre. Produced at the Imperial Theatre, 22 October 1987, with Grey, Alyson Reed, Gregg Edelmann, Werner Klemperer, and Regina Resnik.

A film version was produced by Allied Artists in 1972 with Grey, Liza Minnelli, Michael York, Helmut Griem (Max), and Marisa Berenson (Natalia).

The emcee of the Kit-Kat Club
(Joel Grey) welcomes everyone
to an evening of desperately
decadent entertainment.
Friedman-Abeles, photographers.
Courtesy Performing Arts Research Center,
New York Public Library at Lincoln Center.

Act 1

On to the empty stage comes the evening's Master of Ceremonies, a bizarre, androgynous creature who bids the audience an introductory "Willkommen." Here in the cabaret you can leave your troubles behind and believe that life is beautiful.

In a compartment in a railway train heading for Berlin, a young American writer, Clifford Bradshaw, is joined by a nervous German, Ernst Ludwig, who strikes up a brief conversation. Within minutes of his arrival, customs officers enter the carriage preparatory to passing the German border. Cliff's passport is checked and his baggage passed perfunctorily, but Ludwig's case is opened and searched. What is not touched, however, is the briefcase that the German has slyly mixed in with Cliff's luggage. When the officers have departed, Ludwig makes a modest excuse for his imposition. He has bought a little too much perfume and a few too many stockings in Paris. In the baggage of an American they can pass unnoticed. In return for his unwitting help, Ernst offers Cliff friendship and help in the strange city of Berlin. What could be more useful than the name of a cheap, clean rooming house and the offer of his first English pupil: Ludwig, himself? Willkommen to Berlin!

The house of Fräulein Schneider is plain and old but it is also cheap. The chatelaine is willing to take fifty marks a week for a room priced at a hundred on the grounds that otherwise it stays empty and she gets nothing. Fräulein Schneider is a pragmatic woman ("So Who Cares?"). Cliff soon meets his nearest neighbors, Fräulein Kost, a large cheerful whore who passes off a juvenile sailor found in her room as a nephew from Hamburg for the benefit of the moralistic Fräulein Schneider, and the gentle, graying fruiterer, Herr Schultz, whose sweet attentions to Fräulein Schneider are gratefully received. Installed in his new home, Cliff knows he should sit down to his typewriter and begin to work, but Berlin calls him away from writing just as every other town he has gone through has done, and, before long, he quits his room for the sleazy Kit Kat Club and some easy entertainment. The Emcee of this dowdy establishment introduces his line of girls, a determinedly decadent group fronted by an English girl of a strangely child-like would-be sophistication, in a routine called "Don't Tell Mama."

The girl, Sally Bowles, catches sight of Cliff and recognizes an English-speaking face. As soon as the performance is over, she calls him on one of the table telephones and gratefully listens to an English voice. She is younger than her age and determined above all to be shocking and modern, but she is totally likeable and Cliff is happy to answer her babbling questions. Soon, however, her protector arrives at her table and communication is cut. As the hour of midnight approaches, all around the Club contacts are being made ("Telephone Song"), but, for his first night in town, Cliff sits alone and just watches Sally.

Cliff's pupil, Ernst Ludwig, provides him with a little income on which to live. He hints that, if his tutor is in need, a lot more can be made by undertaking some simple trips to Paris on his behalf. One day, their morning lesson is broken in on by an unexpected arrival: Sally. The upshot of her contact with Cliff in the club is that her protector has kicked her out. As he is also a partner in the Club, she is not only without protection but without a job and penniless, so she thought, since Cliff had a room of his own, she might move in with him for a little while. Fräulein Schneider's qualms are settled by the thought of the extra rent, and any doubts Cliff might have had are drowned in the waves of chatter and possibilities that flow from Sally. It's all going to be "Perfectly Marvelous." No one will take any notice; after all, in Berlin everyone has a roommate. Some, so the Emcee assures us, have more than one, a proposition illustrated in song and dance by himself and "Two Ladies."

Keeping at least an ostensibly honest house is a trial for Fräulein Schneider. When she catches Fräulein Kost smuggling in another sailor, she indignantly throws him out, but, when Fräulein Kost threatens to leave at the end of the week, Fräulein Schneider is forced to retreat back behind the status quo. If Kost wishes to stay it must be understood that she does not let herself be seen bringing the sailors in. Herr Schultz is Fräulein Schneider's consolation. Always he brings her something from his fruit shop and today he has outdone himself. Today he has brought her a pineapple! She is overcome at the extravagance of the gift—"It Couldn't Please Me More."

At the club, a group of waiters join the Emcee in a new kind of song. They are exaggeratedly Aryan, scrubbed and ideal, and they sing with a heart-warming sincerity "Tomorrow Belongs to Me."

Cliff writes a little but not enough and Sally stays. They get by and they fall in love. It is very unreal, but Cliff does not wish to get back to responsible reality ("Why Should I Wake Up?") and Sally becomes pregnant. It fits ill with the image she spends her whole life creating for herself, but she would like to keep the baby. Cliff positively wants it, which means he has all the more reason to accept when Ernst Ludwig proposes one of his little Paris trips at a fee of 75 marks. Now money is going to be necessary. The theme of money is taken up by the personnel of the Kit Kat, and the Emcee presents "The Money Song" while displaying a parade of national currencies in scantily dressed female form.

Fräulein Kost is a little surprised when caught letting a sailor or three out of her room to meet with no condemnation from Fräulein Schneider, but she feels she may have found the reason when she sees Herr Schultz emerging from her landlady's room. A saucy remark, however, wins a warm response from Herr Schultz: Fräulein Schneider has just done him the honor of agreeing to be his wife. When Fräulein Kost has raised her eyebrows and departed, the two aging people are left alone. Now what shall they do? Neither can truly believe that the other would wish the opportunistic lie to be the truth and, of course, they both wish it very deeply. Herr Schultz tentatively makes a formal proposal and Fräulein Schneider almost coyly signifies that he has reason to be optimistic. At their age, they will be "Married."

Sally insists delightedly there must be an engagement party, and promises that she herself will ensure a super turnout. When the occasion arrives, all the performers from the Kit Kat turn up at Schultz's fruit shop and the evening is indeed a lively affair. Ernst comes too, to pick up the briefcase that Cliff has brought into the country for him from Paris. Amid the gaiety, Schultz takes a glass or two of schnapps and entertains the company with the touching little Jewish song "Meeskite," but his rendition goes down poorly with some of the guests. Ernst, who is fond of Fräulein Schneider, warns her against the marriage. Her intended husband is not German. Having made his point, he goes to leave the party, but Fräulein Kost calls him back to join in a very different kind of song. As the engaged couple and Sally and Cliff look on with varying emotions, the guests join forcefully in the Nazi song "Tomorrow Belongs to Me."

Act 2 The following morning, Fräulein Schneider comes to the shop where Schultz is tidying up. The party has opened her eyes. She must look to her own situation. It has been a hard struggle to get the little she has in life, and if a marriage to a Jew can imperil that, then she cannot marry him. She has lived fifty years without love and it seems now that she must live the rest of what is left to her in the same way.

Schultz tries to persuade her that she may be unnecessarily frightened. Even if these dreadful people should one day come to power, governments come and go sometimes very quickly. Should they give up their chance of happiness for this one possibility? Suddenly a brick smashes through the shop window. As much as they wish to believe that it is the work of mischievous children, they know the truth. At the Kit Kat Club the Emcee sings and dances with a gorilla. "If You Could See Her Through My Eyes," he insists "she wouldn't look Jewish at all."

Cliff has refused to go again to Paris for Ernst, since he has realized that what he has carried through customs in the briefcases were funds for the Nazi party. To make up the money lost by this refusal, he is trying to find a job. Sally already has one. Max at the Kit Kat has fallen in love with a Communist virgin and so it is all right for Sally to go back to her old job, but Cliff will not hear of it. Fräulein Schneider comes to see them to return their engagement gift and, in response to their amazement, she chides them "What Would You Do?" in her situation. She cannot, like them, take flight to Paris or England or America. Her life and everything she has are here.

Cliff knows that his life and Sally's can no longer be in Berlin the way things are going. The party that was Berlin in the twenties is over. He decides to sell his typewriter to get money to pay their passage out of Germany, but Sally will not hear of leaving. She is not going to abandon her career as a singer, the Kit Kat Club needs her, and Berlin is where she belongs. Here she can be herself in a way she could never be in England. Cliff firmly tells her to wait in the room and, taking his typewriter, he goes out but, no sooner has he left than Sally snatches up her fur coat, her one valuable possession, and rushes out behind him.

Cliff finds her, later that evening, at the Kit Kat Club. She still will not listen to his warnings and she returns defiantly to the stage to deliver her song ("Cabaret"). The song encapsulates Sally's philosophy, or what she would like to think is her philosophy. Drink deep of each hour, get out and take life by the throat, use it for each hour of the short trip from cradle to grave. While she sings, Ernst continues to urge Cliff to make another trip for him and, when the angry boy finally punches the Nazi in the face, he finds himself set upon and beaten up by a gang of thugs. As the punches drive him to the ground, Sally keeps on singing about what she calls Life.

Cliff is packing the next morning when Sally returns. She is pale and drawn, and she answers mechanically to his attempts at cheerfulness. She is not going with him, and she has had their child aborted. When he slaps her, she is almost pleased at the drama of the situation, but the blow does not open her eyes. She still chatters on about what a strange and extraordinary person she is—this poor little girl who cannot bear the thought that she is not in the least strange or extraordinary. Cliff is barely listening. He takes one of the two train tickets from his wallet and puts it on the sideboard. Sally can follow him to Paris or she can stay here in Berlin; it is up to her. Sally puffs her cigarette with a last attempt at style. She's always rather hated Paris, so it has to be goodbye. When Cliff has gone and she has no one to play to, poor, silly Sally deflates.

Cliff boards the train to leave Berlin. There will be no more "Willkommen" here. The Emcee and his girls are seen again with their welcome routine, only this time it is different. It is harder and forcibly bright. There are German uniforms and swastikas in evidence as a singing, dancing Sally brightly reaffirms that life is a "Cabaret." Then it is dark.

The 1987 Broadway revival omitted "Meeskite" and "Why Should I Wake Up," and included two new songs, "Don't Go" and "I Don't Care Much."

Hair

AN AMERICAN TRIBAL LOVE-ROCK MUSICAL IN TWO ACTS by Gerome Ragni and James Rado. Music by Galt MacDermot.

Produced at the Biltmore Theatre, 29 April 1968, with Rado (Claude), Ragni (Berger), Lynn Kellogg (Sheila), and Lamont Washington (Hud). Revived there, 5 October 1977, with Randall Easterbrook, Michael Holt, Ellen Foley, and Cleavant Derricks.

Originally produced at the Public Theatre, New York, 17 October 1967, and subsequently played at the Cheetah Club from 22 December 1967.

A film version was produced by United Artists in 1979 with John Savage, Treat Williams, Beverly D'Angelo, and Melba Moore.

The cutting off of his determinedly long locks
marks a return to the real world
—and to the army—for Claude (James Rado).
Photograph © Martha Swope.

CHARACTERS

Claude

Berger

Woof

Hud

Jeanie

Crissie

Dionne

Angela

Mom

Dad, etc.

Act 1

Hair is not a story, it is a presentation: a presentation of a way of life that the tribe of young people who perform the show are putting forward as their alternative to the established American way of life, its ethical and moral codes, its aims, its satisfactions, and its disappointments. They don't claim that their way is the only way, but they are offering it up for the audience's consideration. It is a way that embraces lots of "freedoms." Freedom in love and in sex, freedom from the rules of standard society, freedom to reject the state, freedom to seek freedom under the influence of drugs. It is a way that seeks pleasure, disguised under all kinds of mystic and ritual names and performances, without responsibility. They all want and hope for a world where they can do and have what they want—preferably for nothing— and be loved for it ("Aquarius"). Others might call it selfish hedonism.

The principal members of the tribe are Berger, a "Manhattan" high-school kick-out who sports the rash of long hair which is the membership badge of the group; Claude, his best friend and a tribal leader, who is threatened with the draft and who would like to have been born in "Manchester, England"; Sheila who lives with them both and who loves Berger, is loved by Claude, and makes posters; Woof who has a longing for Mick Jagger ("Sodomy"); Jeanie who digs deep into drugs, and "Coloured Spade" Hud.

The boys list all the things they haven't got ("Ain't Got No") and the last and greatest of these is "mind." Claude can be positive over only one thing. He still has the bits that make up his body ("I Got Life"). He won't even have that if he gets drafted and sent off by the big boys to fight their war when all he wants to do is stay home, copulate, and go gassy on drugs.

Jeanie sings to the polluted "Air" of Manhattan and the tribe chant mindlessly and rebelliously of the drugs that have made them all what they think is unscrewed-up ("Initials"). Berger celebrates his expulsion from high school ("Going Down") with a handful of pills while Claude takes to marijuana and rambles on narcissistically about the body that the draft doctors have had under their hands. But the most celebratory part of their bodies is still their emblem of belonging to each other, their "Hair," even if the older generation attempts to explain their luxuriant locks away as a simple anthropological urge for finery ("My Conviction").

Sheila is a professional protester, except she doesn't get paid. She makes posters and says things like "groovy" and lusts with gifts after Berger who isn't interested, so all in all the whole experience is a bit lacking for Sheila ("Dead End"). Woof and Berger get involved incoherently with the American flag ("Don't Put It Down"), and decide to follow the fashion by burning it at a kind of rally that they call a be-in. There they can show their colors and be heroically busted for drugs, arrested for being freaks and just noticed. Crissy doesn't go to the rally. She has different preoccupations, maybe. She met a boy called "Frank Mills" who is embarrassingly un-hip, and she wants to see him again.

At the be-in, the tribe chant their preoccupations ("Hare Krishna"), drugs and sex and "love." They respond to warnings and threats from the outraged representatives of the other society only with more chanting, until the frustrated people howl that this unresponsive, irresponsible rabble should be exported immediately as fodder to the Vietnamese guns. The tribe, delighted at having won a response to their inactive action, jubilantly increase their fire. Berger starts removing his clothes and, as the boys begin to ceremoniously burn their draft cards, the others follow suit. When it is Claude's turn, however, he fakes the destruction of his card. He's going to follow where his destiny, that is to say his body, leads him ("Where Do I Go?").

Act 2   The band play "The Electric Blues," whirling themselves into a whole lot of cosmic imagery until they blow a fuse.

Claude has been drafted and Berger wants Sheila to have sex with his friend as a farewell gift. Sheila is irked and won't, not even for the price of having Berger the following night ("Easy to Be Hard"). She says she despises Claude for lacking the courage not to go. The others might be disappointed too, but they know Claude is a friend. Tomorrow he will have his hair cut to become a soldier, but for tonight he looks gorgeous in a long white sari as he shares out his personal belongings indifferently among his friends ("White Boys"/"Black Boys").

But there's the evening to be got through, so it's time for enough drug to carry on ("Walking in Space"), and into the mind-warp that follows rush a series of pictures of war people and war events ("Prisoners in Niggertown"). Claude and Berger almost grow coherent together on what they want from life, but it is more important to get paired off. Who sleeps with whom? "Good Morning, Starshine."

In "The Bed" they are as hung up as they are in the real world, maybe more so, but things are manipulated until Claude and Sheila are left together. Berger goes and Jeanie is sent away. Claude starts telling Sheila about this planet called "Exanaplanetooch" where he comes from and where he's going back to the next day. Not into the army. Will she come too? The lights go out before Sheila finally gives in and Claude gets his "Sentimental Ending." In the morning he goes. His long, severed hair is a gift to Berger, tied up in a paper bag. Sheila is already wearing the white sari.

The score of *Hair* underwent considerable changes between its productions. For the Broadway production several songs used in the original Public Theatre version, including "Exanaplanetooch" and "Dead End," were eliminated, and a considerable body of new material introduced. The musical breakdown given here is based on the printed script of 1969.

1970

Company

A MUSICAL IN TWO ACTS by George Furth. Music and lyrics by Stephen Sondheim. Produced at the Alvin Theatre, New York, 26 April 1970, with a cast including Dean Jones (Robert), Elaine Stritch (Joanne), Susan Browning (April), Pamela Myers (Marta), and Donna McKechnie (Kathy).

When you see what his married friends are like, you don't wonder that Bobby (Dean Jones) has stayed single. Here he suffers the sodden stridency of Joanne (Elaine Stritch). Photograph © Martha Swope.

CHARACTERS

Robert

Sarah

Harry

Susan

Peter

Jenny

David

Amy

Paul

Joanne

Larry

Marta

Kathy

April

Act 1

In a slickly middle-class Manhattan apartment, a group of Robert's lovely, married friends have gathered to give him a surprise birthday party. They haven't paused to consider that maybe Robert doesn't really want to be reminded he is thirty-five, and they are self-centeredly unaware that he probably doesn't want to see all of them at once. They are his lovely friends and they know better than he does what he needs and what he wants.

These friends are not a close-knit bunch. They all know Robert but they don't know each other and, from the dialogue they share while they are waiting for him to turn up and be surprised, it is clear they were better off not knowing each other. They are here only because they all love Robert, and they all want to wish him fortune and his first wife.

He doesn't necessarily want either of those things, and it's a bit hard to work out why he wants Sarah, Harry, Susan, Peter, Jenny, David, Amy, Paul, Joanne, and Larry as friends. Is it just that, among the mad impersonal rush of New York life, they provide him, as he provides them, with "Company"? Today they are giving him that company en masse along with birthday presents and a cake with candles, which he is expected to blow out and make a wish. They could give him the wish, too, and they'd all give him the same one: that he should be like them—married.

Robert goes to Sarah and Harry's place. They fuss over him a lot. Well, actually, they fuss at each other a lot and he's a very useful middle man. Harry's quit drinking for eighteen months (he says) or nearly a year (she says) since getting arrested for drunk driving. They talk about it a lot. Sarah's losing weight so she isn't eating things, but she talks about food a lot. So does Harry. Sarah's been going to karate classes and Harry insists she demonstrate for Robert. So she does and, as she pins an irritated Harry to the floor, a voice from outside reminds us that it's "The Little Things You Do Together" that make a marriage. When the karate looks like it's getting heavy, Robert leaves, and Sarah, with her mouth full of sneaked cake, and Harry, loitering with intent very near the bar, jockey for position to be the last one to leave the room and put out the lights.

Robert poses a question to his married men friends: Are they sorry they got married? It's a sort of yes-and-no situation ("Sorry-Grateful"). There is no answer really.

Peter and Susan are an idyllic pair. He's Ivy League, she's southern belle, and it's safe for Robert to flirt with Susan because it's good form. Peter and Susan also have news. They're getting divorced.

Jenny is very conservative and David is ever so modern. They are puffing at marijuana and feeling very proud of themselves. Decidedly square Jenny says it doesn't affect her and talks a lot, and David boastfully declares himself undoubtedly potted. They all talk a lot and a lot of their talk is about marriage. Robert insists he isn't against it. He's really thinking about it. Right now he's dating an air hostess called April, kooky Marta, and out-of-town Kathy. Robert talks about marriage but he doesn't do anything about it. In fact, as the three girls declare in harmony "You Could Drive a Person Crazy" not doing anything about it. As the evening comes to an end, David assures Robert that dear square Jenny didn't really like the marijuana. She only tried it to please thoroughly modern him. That's the way it's got to be in that family and clever Jenny knows it.

Robert's friends always seem to be trying to pair him off with some nice girl ("Have I Got a Girl for You?"), but he's happy to put off any decision. "Someone Is Waiting," somewhere, who has all the bits that he likes best in all the women he knows. He'll wait for her, this composite girl, and in the meanwhile it doesn't worry him. There are plenty of girls around like April, Kathy, and Marta, and new ones come to New York every day ("Another Hundred People").

Paul and Amy have lived together for years and now they're getting married. Paul is looking forward to it a lot, Amy is really scared. Now that the appointed day is actually here, she knows she can't go through with it. As a choirgirl sings ritualistically, Paul's happy crooning mixes with Amy's frantic patter in debate as to whether or not they are "Getting Married Today." Amy thinks of every reason she can as to why they should cancel or even postpone, and, when she can't think of any more, she simply declares unilaterally that she won't do it. A stunned Paul goes out of the house in the pouring rain, and minutes later Robert is asking the distraught Amy to marry him instead. Well, he knows her. She looks at him. Isn't it funny, she's afraid to get married and he's afraid not to. Still, at least this unlooked-for proposal focuses her mind and a minute later she is chasing off down the street after Paul with his raincoat and her wedding bouquet.

Act 2

Back at the opening birthday party, Robert blows out his candles, prior to some more illustrations of how good he and his friends are at going through life together "Side by Side by Side" equipped with sentiments as original as "What Would We Do Without You?" to brighten their relationship. They all worry about Robert so much, these friends. The "Poor Baby" is all on his own; he has nothing and no one but them.

They are not quite right about that. Robert entertains April the air hostess, talking her into bed with practiced words. In the morning, she has to fly off to "Barcelona" and he pleads with her not to go. He gets a shock when he pleads too well and she says she will stay.

He takes Marta with him when he visits Susan and Peter. They have got their divorce. Peter flew to Mexico for it, and it was so nice down there that he phoned Susan to come on down. They are still living together, of course. It would be irresponsible to actually split up, what with the kids and all.

When he goes to see Larry and Joanne, they all go out for the evening. In a nightclub, while Larry dances, Joanne gets drunk and embarrassing and spits out a stinging serenade to "The Ladies Who Lunch." She propositions Robert and turns him off, and then it's time to pay the bill and go home. Thoughts and talk of marriage seem to have pervaded the whole evening. Do. Don't. Don't. Do. And why? It's enough to drive Robert to a soliloquy of want. What's it all about "Being Alive" without someone to share it with?

It's that birthday party again, back at the beginning of the show. The friends are waiting for Robert to come as they were when the curtain first rose, but he doesn't show. Gradually the message sinks in, and they blow out the candles on the cake themselves, say Happy Birthday, and leave. Thirty-five year-old unmarried Robert stands in the middle of the stage and smiles. He's still his own man. But with friends like this, how long can it last?

GODSPELL

A MUSICAL IN TWO ACTS by John-Michael Tebelak based on the Gospel According to St. Matthew. Music and lyrics by Stephen Schwartz.

Produced at the Broadhurst Theatre from 22 June 1976, at the Plymouth Theatre from 15 September 1976, and at the Ambassador Theatre from 12 January 1977.

Originally produced at the Cherry Lane Theatre, 17 May 1971, with a cast including David Haskell, Joanne Jonas, Robin Lamont, Gilmer McCormick, and Stephen Nathan, and played subsequently at the Promenade Theatre from 10 August 1971.

A film version was produced by Columbia Pictures in 1973 with Victor Garber, Haskell, Jonas, Lamont, McCormick, Katie Hanley, and Lynne Thigpen.

Stories and maxims of the Christian religion, dipped in teeny talk and 1960s styles— the mixture made Godspell a long-lasting hit. Photograph © Martha Swope.

Act 1   A group of young people, of high school age or thereabouts, gather in what seems to be a school playground, backed by a high cyclone fence and sharply lit by powerful, overhead lights. They bring with them a theatre skip, filled with odd costumes in which they dress themselves haphazardly, so that some of them take on the appearance of circus clowns, others of casually dressed teenagers, and others a bizarre combination of the two. Most of them put on clown makeup.

The leader of the group starts the ball rolling with a religious quotation that encourages the rest of his companions to follow his example, quoting statements or paraphrases of statements taken from various philosophers throughout the ages. One quotes Socrates (Prologue/"Wherefore, O Men of Athens?"), then another Thomas Aquinas, Martin Luther, Jean-Paul Sartre, Buckminster Fuller, and John the Baptist ("Prepare Ye the Way of the Lord").

Taking his cue from the words of the Baptist, the leader makes a declaration of the purposes of Christ's mission on earth ("Save the People"), and, using contemporary language, the youngsters give their versions of elements of Christ's teachings, retelling in their own words many of the familiar parables: the tale of the importunate widow (Luke 18.3), the story of the good Samaritan (Luke 10.30), that of "the rich man whose land yielded heavy crops" (Luke 12.16), and the sermon in the mount (Matthew 5). One of the best-known of Christ's saying is told in a minstrel routine (Q: "How can you look at the speck of sawdust in your brother's eye . . . ?" A: "I don't know. How can you" . . . etc.) (Matthew 7.3 and Luke 6.41).

The dialogue is broken from time to time by songs with religious themes and contemporary sounds that range from rock to country and western ("Day By Day," "Learn Your Lesson Well," "Oh, Bless the Lord, My Soul," "All for the Best").

A girl starts to tell the parable of the sower and the seed (Matthew 13.3, Mark 4.3, and Luke 8.5) and this leads into the familiar hymn "We Plow the Fields and Scatter," with the words written by the eighteenth-century German poet, Matthias Claudius, sung to a twentieth-century American tune. Two boys act out the tale of the prodigal son (Luke 15.11), which ends in a celebratory finale as the cast pile cups and flagons on to a trestle table and invite the audience to join them on the stage for a cup of wine during the interval.

Act 2   A reprise of "Learn Your Lesson Well," warning the audience to "pay attention, build your comprehension, there's going to be a quiz at your ascension," signals the start of the second half of the entertainment. After a gospel song urging everyone to "Turn Back, O Man," the leader of the group takes command of the action. One of the players asks him, "By whose authority are you acting like this?," and it becomes evident that the leader is acting out the role of Christ in what has now become a retelling of the events of the last days of his life.

Some of the cast assume the characters of Pharisees. They try to trick Jesus by asking him whether the Jews have an obligation to pay taxes to Rome (Matthew 22.21, Mark 21.17, and Luke 20.25), but Jesus evades their trap ("Alas for You"). When he is asked about the woman taken in adultery, he replies, "The one who is faultless shall throw the first stone" (John 8.3) and the woman is allowed to go free ("By My Side").

The cast sing to Jesus, "We Beseech Thee," and then take their places as the disciples at the last supper. Jesus holds a mirror up to each of them in turn, showing them the absurdity of their worldly, made-up faces. With cream and tissues they wipe away their clownish makeup, for now it is the time for truth.

Swiftly, the events of the betrayal are portrayed before Jesus bids each player farewell ("On the Willows"). He climbs on to the cyclone fence where he hangs, with outstretched arms, as though on the cross, as the company join in the finale ("Long Live God"/"Prepare Ye the Way of the Lord").

Although the piece is described by its author as being "based on the gospel according to Saint Matthew," it in fact makes equally frequent reference to the gospel according to Saint Luke and to other books of the Old and New Testaments.

Jesus Christ Superstar

A MUSICAL IN TWO ACTS with lyrics by Tim Rice and music by Andrew Lloyd Webber.
Produced at the Mark Hellinger Theatre, New York, 12 October 1971, with Ben Vereen (Judas), Jeff Fenholt (Jesus), Yvonne Elliman (Mary), Barry Dennen (Pilate), and Paul Ainsley (Herod). Produced at the Longacre Theatre, 23 November 1977, with Patrick Jude, William Daniel Grey, Barbara Niles, Randy Wilson, and Mark Syers.
A film version was produced by Universal Pictures in 1973 with Carl Andersen, Ted Neely, Elliman, Dennen, and Joshua Mostel.

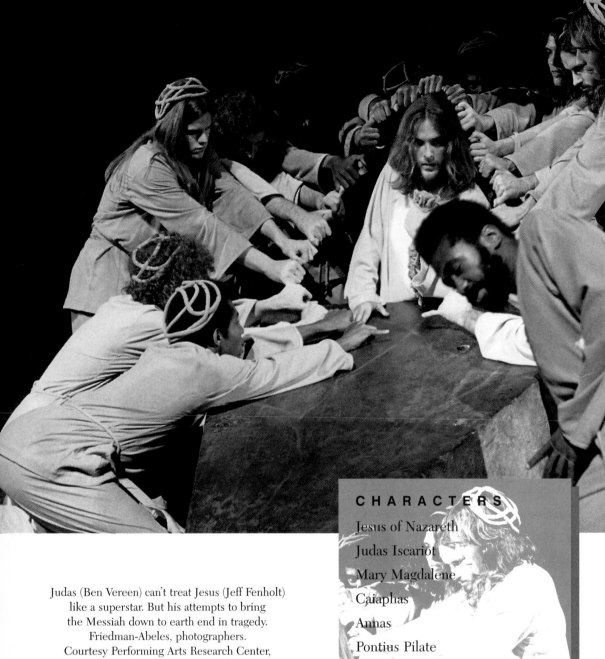

Judas (Ben Vereen) can't treat Jesus (Jeff Fenholt)
like a superstar. But his attempts to bring
the Messiah down to earth end in tragedy.
Friedman-Abeles, photographers.
Courtesy Performing Arts Research Center,
New York Public Library at Lincoln Center.

CHARACTERS

Jesus of Nazareth

Judas Iscariot

Mary Magdalene

Caiaphas

Annas

Pontius Pilate

King Herod

Simon Zealotes

Peter

Three Priests, Maid by the Fire,
etc.

Act 1

This is the story of the last seven days of the life of Jesus of Nazareth, known as Christ. The story is seen through the eyes of his disciple, Judas Iscariot, whose name has descended to posterity as that of the archetypal betrayer because of his delivery of Jesus into the hands of the Roman rulers of Judaea.

At the opening of the piece, Judas, alone, agonizes over the way in which the humanitarian crusade, of which he is a part and of which Jesus is the prime mover and the figurehead, is going. The movement has grown beyond all belief and has taken on characteristics that he finds more than troubling. Jesus is hailed as a Messiah, as a god, and his sayings are repeated, twisted, and repeated again as monstrous prophecies and bywords, while his followers have become fanatical and unrealistic with too much "Heaven on Their Minds."

His fears seem justified. At Bethany on the Friday night, the apostles of Christ gather, eager for words of wisdom about their future, for golden news of the days to come ("What's the Buzz"). Only the whore, Mary Magdalene, attempts to calm the overheated atmosphere. She cools Jesus's brow with a sponge and prompts Judas to accusations of inconsistency in Jesus's attitudes ("Strange Thing Mystifying"). Jesus reacts petulantly in defense of the woman who, in her turn, tries to defuse his anger ("Everything's All Right"), but Judas attacks her for using precious ointments on her master, wasting money, which could have bought food for many poor. Mary's soothing words can only partly allay the prevalent air of dissension.

In Jerusalem, on Sunday, the Priests of the city discuss the danger that Jesus represents to them. His followers are becoming loud and persistent and soon their noise will reach the ears of the province's Roman rulers. If the Romans move in to crush a potential king in Judaea, they will probably also wipe out the religious sector in which that king could have flourished. With a strong feeling for self-preservation, Caiaphas, the chief priest, decides "Jesus Must Die." In the streets the crowds call for Jesus ("Hosanna") and, in spite of Caiaphas's commands, he cannot or will not quiet them. Simon Zealotes urges him to proclaim himself as all the things he is and all the things the people want him to be (Simon Zealotes), but Jesus will not. He offers Simon and the crowd no present rewards but only the promise of a glorious afterlife for the faithful ("Poor Jerusalem").

That night, Pontius Pilate, the Roman Governor of Judaea, has a dream (Pilate's Dream). He dreams of a strange Galilean with whose life his own is seemingly linked. The people of the world weep into eternity for this man, and Pilate himself is despised because of him.

On Monday, Jesus visits the temple (The Temple) and finds that the moneylenders and merchants have set up their stalls in its holy precincts. He ejects them loudly, but it is an effort. He has done so much and, whatever his disciples may say, he is a man, a tired man. When a crowd of cripples surround him, begging to be healed, he cries at them in exasperation to leave him alone. Once more Mary has to soothe him into rest.

She herself has a mind in turmoil, but a very different kind of turmoil. She is in love with Jesus, but with a kind of love that she cannot understand ("I Don't Know How to Love Him") and even less express. In the meanwhile, she shows her love by being a calming influence in his life when everything else conspires to stir him to excesses.

On the Tuesday, Judas, with many misgivings, finally comes to a decision. Since it seems that Jesus cannot control the mob and mass violence seems imminent, he goes to the priests ("Damned for All Time"). From him the eager priests draw the information they need as to where they can catch Jesus alone, for they need to take him prisoner without risking violence by the crowd. Spurning their "Blood Money" Judas gives them the information they want.

At the apostles' supper on Thursday night, the followers of Jesus drown their weariness in wine ("Look at All My Trials and Tribulations"/The Last Supper). Jesus foresees his end and, before the event, bitterly accuses his followers of faithlessness to his memory. Judas cuts short his martyrizing speech on betrayal with counteraccusations. Their ideals are suffering and perishing because Jesus has turned them into part of a cult centered on himself. It has all gone wrong. Someone has to stop him before he makes things even worse.

In the garden of Gethsemane, Jesus prays alone ("I Only Want to Say"). His prayer is one not of inspiration and trust, but one that begs for deliverance from an exhausted evangelical life, which has become a continual trial of his mental and physical strength. What Judas has accused him of is true: He wants to be betrayed, he wants to die.

Act 2

When Judas brings the soldiers to Gethsemane (The Arrest) Jesus offers no resistance. The disciples flee and Peter, as Jesus had predicted at the Last Supper, denies his acquaintance (Peter's Denial).

On Friday, Jesus is brought before Pilate, but Pilate refuses jurisdiction (Pilate and Christ) and sends the prisoner on to King Herod in Galilee. Herod greets Jesus cynically (Herod's Song) with orders for instant miracles, and also refuses to take responsibility for judging him. Faced with the possibility of a capital case, Mary and Peter regret that things have been allowed to go so far ("Could We Start Again"), and Judas, realizing he has been forced by fate and the will of God into being the instrument of Jesus' martyrdom, curses God and hangs himself (Judas' Death).

Jesus is brought back to Pilate (Trial Before Pilate) who is still unwilling to condemn him but, in the face of vociferous demands from the populace and the priests, he orders him to be flogged (Thirty Nine Lashes) instead. But no matter what he does or says, he can get no response from Jesus. The man whom so many hailed as King of the Jews insists that his fate is not in the hands of either of them and finally, in exasperation, Pilate gives up trying to save this enigmatically passive man.

The voice of Judas is heard, wondering why what seemed as if it could have been a great popular movement was allowed by Jesus, and through his mortal failings, to go so soon and so badly wrong. Or was it intended? Was Jesus's short but dramatic career and death all part of the plan to have him become and be remembered as a "Superstar"?

The final scene pictures the crucifixion of Jesus of Nazareth known as Christ (John Nineteen Forty One).

1972

GREASE

A NEW 50S ROCK 'N' ROLL MUSICAL by Jim Jacobs and Warren Casey.

Produced at the Broadhurst Theatre, 7 June 1972, with Barry Bostwick (Danny), Carole Demas (Sandy), and Adrienne Barbeau (Rizzo). Produced at the Eugene O'Neill Theatre, 11 May 1994, with Ricky Paull Goldin, Susan Wood, and Rosie O'Donnell. Originally produced at the Eden Theatre, 14 February 1972.

A film version was produced by Paramount in 1978 with John Travolta, Olivia Newton-John, and Stockard Channing.

An old banger, a cig, a can, and a budding broad with a beehive, and a 1950s schoolboy's happiness was complete. Remember?
Grease. Friedman-Abeles, photographers. Courtesy Performing Arts Research Center, New York Public Library at Lincoln Center.

CHARACTERS

Miss Lynch

Patty Simcox

Eugene Florczyk

Jan

Marty

Betty Rizzo

Doody

Roger

Kenickie

Sonny

Frenchy

Sandy Dumbrowski

Danny Zuko

Vince Fontaine

Johnny Casino

Cha-Cha di Gregorio

Teen Angel

Act 1

At the reunion of Rydell High School's class of 1959, the now successful Patty Honeywell (ex-Simcox) and Eugene Florczyk lead the singing of the "Alma Mater" and Eugene addresses the assembly, bringing back memories of school days in just the way such reunions are supposed to: the best days of your life.

Time rolls back to let us see a bunch of lazy, bored, defiant teenage 1950s boys singing childishly rude words to the same school tune. It's back to school time. At the high-school cafeteria, pretty, babyish Marty and loud and chubby Jan, two members of the Pink Ladies gang, have joined with gang leader Betty Rizzo. Down on the school steps the Burger Palace Boys are saving their dimes for better things than lunch; tough and tattooed Kenickie, jolly Roger, enthusiastic little Doody, and Sonny who talks big and dirty but doesn't live up to it.

The girls soon have something new to dish about. Frenchy, another Pink Lady, brings in a new girl, her neighbor Sandy Dumbrowski, and it soon comes out that Sandy met a boy on the beach over summer. Oooooh! The boys get a similar awakener when it turns out that their leader, the smooth Danny Zuko, has met a girl and spent the summer with her. Of course it was Sandy and Danny who spent the innocent little seaside idyll together, though the two versions that get simultaneously told on back-to-school day don't sound too much like the same story ("Summer Nights"). When the summertime sweethearts meet in company, Danny saves his image as a high-school tough Romeo with an offhand approach that leaves sweet Sandy bemused and upset.

Doody has a guitar, and, in class change, he goes into a fantasy of rock 'n' roll stardom ("Those Magic Changes"), before the scene shifts to a Pink Ladies pyjama party at Marty's place. Sandy has been admitted to the gang, but she still has a lot to learn. She wears a quilted robe while the other girls flaunt themselves in baby-doll pyjamas. She has a tough time living up to the Pink Ladies style, choking on her first cigarette, gagging on dessert wine from the bottle, and finally being sick over the bathroom sink when Frenchy tries to pierce her ears with a pin. Marty has a kimono, a gift from a chap called Freddy she met at a dance who got posted with the marines. This is the cue for a parody girl-group number, "Freddy, My Love."

The boys have been having a really grown-up evening out, stealing hubcaps. Unfortunately the ones they've taken today turn out to belong to a jalopy that Kenickie has bought from money earned working during the vacation. He calls it "Greased Lightnin'" and reckons it will look great once he's done it up. Right now he's putting it to use taking Rizzo out.

When Danny and Sandy meet alone, his greeting is more like it was on the beach. He asks her to a party, but Sandy isn't sure. She thinks she has made herself unpopular with the girls and she's working hard at earning a spot on the cheerleader squad. Her tutor in this all-important art is all-American Patty Simcox. Patty has an eye for Danny herself, and she spreads a little intentional jealousy Sandy's way. Sandy's hurt retorts to Danny's belated attempt to be boyfriendly end with his finding a need to impress the girl. If she's set her eyes and heart on an athlete, he'll try out for the track team.

Down in the park, the kids drink beer, smoke cigarettes, pet, and read fan mags as the voice of disc jockey Vince Fontaine gurgles out of the radio. We find out why Roger is called Rump by the other boys. His hobby is "Mooning," which is to say showing off his bare backside in unlikely places. When Sandy puts in an appearance, collecting leaves for biology class, big-talk Sonny makes as if to rush her off. Rizzo, leaning roughly on Danny, makes fun of Sandy's Gidget style in "Look at Me, I'm Sandra Dee." Sandy catches the end of the parody and she attacks first Rizzo and then Danny whom she accuses of spreading awful things about her. The result of this scene of teenage melodrama is that Danny asks Rizzo rather than Sandy to be his partner at the school dance the next night ("We Go Together").

Act 2

The kids are getting ready to go "Shakin' at the High School Hop," but Sandy is not going. Alone, she sings with her radio of how, for her, "It's Raining on Prom Night." The dance is under the management of the radio's Vince Fontaine and schoolboy would-be rocker Johnny Casino, and it proves the occasion for advances by Patty on Danny, of Vince Fontaine on jailbait Marty, of Eugene on Rizzo, and so on. Kenickie turns up with a blind date—a large, loud piece called Cha-cha—but when Rizzo claims him back, Danny is stranded with Cha-cha for the evening's highlight, the hand jive contest ("Born to Hand Jive"). Cha-cha lives up to her nickname. She's the best dancer in the room, and she and Danny win the contest. But at the end of the dancing he walks off, leaving her on her own.

Frenchy has left school. She has gone to Beauty School instead. At least she had. She's dropped out and she can't face telling her friends. She can't even take a job at the Burger Palace, because then they'd all know. She wishes she had a Guardian Angel, like Debbie Reynolds does in the movies ("Beauty School Dropout"), who'd make everything come all right.

Meanwhile, the Burger Palace Boys have a challenge on their hands. It turns out that the unprepossessing Cha-cha is the steady girl of the chief of a rival gang, and the offended gang is coming that evening for a rumble. Danny isn't there—he's got into the track team and he's training. In the end, the rumble turns out to be a nonevent and the boys have another empty evening, but not so Danny. He's off at the drive-in movie theatre with Kenickie's car and Sandy. She's thrilled when he offers her his ring and talks of going steady but, when he tries to get a bit too intimate, she gives back the ring and runs away leaving him "Alone at a Drive-In Movie."

Jan has a party in the basement of her place ("Rock 'n' Roll Party Queen"), and Rizzo confides in Marty that her period is late. She reckons she might be pregnant. No, it's not Kenickie, it's a guy none of them knows. Marty goes straight to Kenickie with the story but, when he goes to find Rizzo with his responsibilities roused, she shrugs him off and he leaves in hurt. The party breaks up under the strains, but Sandy has seen the truth in Kenickie's face and she quietly wishes Rizzo good luck. Rizzo turns on her angrily, asserting that she'd rather be unpretentious her than all the Sandra Dees in the world ("There Are Worse Things I Could Do"). Sandy ends up back in her room in tears as she hopelessly reprises "Look at Me, I'm Sandra Dee." Then she picks up the phone and calls Frenchy. It's time she made a new start.

Down at the Burger Palace, the boys are getting ready to go watch the Mickey Mouse Club and catch up on the development of Annette's tits. Danny is one of them again. He gave the finger to the track coach and quit the team, and Patty is furious. The Pink Ladies turn up, dolled up in their gear, and with them is a busting, brand-new Pink Lady complete with leather jacket, hoop earrings, gum, and expert cigarette. It's Sandy! Patty is lividly rude until Sandy pokes her one in the eye. Danny is "All Choked Up" at such a breath-taking sight and before too long the ring is back on Sandy's finger. Rizzo's period is coming on, so Kenickie drives her off to the drugstore and all the other kids join in "We Go Together" as they get down to playing out a halcyon days happy ending together.

A LITTLE NIGHT MUSIC

A MUSICAL COMEDY IN TWO ACTS by Hugh Wheeler suggested by the film *Smiles of a Summer Night* by Ingmar Bergman. Music and lyrics by Stephen Sondheim.

Produced at the Shubert Theatre, New York, 25 February 1973, with Glynis Johns (Desirée), Len Cariou (Fredrik), Hermione Gingold (Madame Armfeldt), Victoria Mallory (Anne), and Laurence Guittard (Carl-Magnus).

A film version was produced by New World/Sascha-Wien Films in 1978 with Elizabeth Taylor (singing partly dubbed by Elaine Tomkinson), Cariou, Gingold, Lesley-Anne Down (singing dubbed by Tomkinson), and Guittard.

Fredrik Egerman (Len Cariou) and
Desirée Armfeldt (Glynis Johns)
share some comfortable middle-aged moments,
away from their exhaustingly young partners.
Photograph © Martha Swope.

CHARACTERS

Madame Armfeldt

Desirée Armfeldt, *her daughter*

Fredrika Armfeldt, *her daughter*

Fredrik Egerman

Anne Egerman, *his wife*

Henrik Egerman, *his son*

Count Carl-Magnus Malcolm

Countess Charlotte Malcolm

Petra

Mr. Lindquist, Mrs. Nordstrom,
Mrs. Anderssen, Mr. Erlansson,
Mrs. Segstrom, *the quintet*

Osa, Malla, Bertrand, Frid

Before the action of the play begins, the quintet of singers vocalizes through a few snatches of the musical action of its story ("Night Waltz"). Then they waltz their way into a surreal pattern of changing partnerships among the principal characters and their scenery.

Old Madame Armfeldt, a professional veteran of liaisons with the crowned and the belted, is found playing cards. To her thirteen-year-old granddaughter, Fredrika, she enumerates the three smiles that the summer night bestows on human beings: the first to the very young like Fredrika who know nothing; the second to the fools like her mother, Desirée, the generation between, who know too little; the third to the very old, such as herself, who know too much.

Act 1   At the Egerman house, we meet Anne, the teenage, second wife of middle-aged Fredrik Egerman. She is passing her time in teasing her serious stepson, Henrik, a boy a year older than herself and a seminary student, as he attempts to study. When her husband returns from his lawyer's office, however, she has something new to occupy her butterfly mind. He has tickets for the theatre. They are going to see the actress Desirée Armfeldt in a delicious French play. Anne is thrilled and she can think only of what she will wear and of how wonderful the actress must be. She chatters on childishly to Fredrik as, together in their bedroom, she prepares herself to dress.

Fredrik tries to kiss her, but to no avail. They have been married eleven months and she is still a wife in name only. Aware of the disparity in their ages, he does not wish to press matters sexual until she is ready but, by now, he is more than a little grayed at the edges with polite patience. Her chatter mixes with his thoughts as he wonders, for the hundredth time since their marriage, how he might best open the season for sexual relations "Now."

Downstairs, Henrik is also experiencing frustration. His father doesn't take him seriously, Anne doesn't take him seriously, and even the maid Petra, who pats him away when he tries to kiss and fumble her, doesn't take him seriously. He is always pushed aside and told to wait till "Later."

Anne is not totally unaware of Fredrik's problem but she doesn't recognize its importance. What significance is there, after all, in sex? Still, she promises, "Soon" she will not shy away from his advances. But as he dozes in frustrated snoozing she is certain that she hears him whisper her name.

Another song scene introduces Desirée Armfeldt. She is every inch the successful actress leading what looks to outsiders like "The Glamorous Life."

From time to time she descends from her thespian travels to visit her daughter, Fredrika—who leads a more conventional life in the home of old Madame Armfeldt—in a blaze of unreal glamor, and vanishes again, just as suddenly, to rejoin a trail of shabby hotel rooms on whistle-stop tours.

At the theatre, Anne is uneasy, Fredrik nonchalant. The play is a comedy of *déshabille*, and Desirée Armfeldt takes the role of a woman to whom other people's husbands are an easy and even approved prey ("Remember?"). Anne is convinced that the actress is taking special notice of Fredrik and her, and she finally works herself into a torrent of tears over Desirée's beauty and obvious *savoir faire* and demands to be taken home.

At home, Henrik has had a go at sinning with Petra and suffered a humiliating failure to rise to the occasion. Fredrik and Anne arrive back inopportunely, and the young wife is even more upset by yet another reminder of sex. To her, Fredrik is still the dear, kind Uncle Fredrik who visited her father's home when she was a child. The thought of making love with him horrifies her. But, although she cannot want him herself, she is tearingly jealous at the thought that he may admire Desirée Armfeldt. He puts her gently to bed and, as the strains of old memories ricochet around his head ("Remember?"), he leaves the house and makes his way to Desirée's lodgings.

It is fourteen years since their affair, and, although he is pleased to see her for old times' sake, the main reason for his visit is clear. They catch up on the intervening years until Fredrik ventures ruefully onto the subject of Anne ("You Must Meet My Wife") and, eventually, the delicate subject of her enduring virginity. Desirée, who has cheerfully admitted to a well-proportioned dragoon presently in her life, is horrified at the thought of the celibacy Fredrik has endured and is only too pleased to remedy his situation. They vanish toward the bedroom and the spotlight turns to old Madame Armfeldt singing regretfully of the times when "Liaisons" were things of style and scope, of distinction, not of common desire and emotion.

When the focus returns to Fredrik and Desirée, they have accomplished their reunion and they are about to have a visitor. Desirée's dragoon, the insanely jealous Count Carl-Magnus Malcolm, is at the door. The atmosphere between him and Fredrik is, to say the least, arctic, and all the pair's attempts to explain Fredrik's presence and obviously dishevelled appearance fall sadly flat. The Count has firm convictions about the nature of fidelity ("In Praise of Women"): It is what women practice, and what he practices toward Desirée and toward his wife, Charlotte. Therefore he finds it logical to assume that, in spite of appearances, nothing untoward has happened.

When Malcolm baldly relates the evening's events to his wife the next morning, the name Egerman strikes a chord. Anne Egerman is a schoolfriend of Charlotte's little sister. And so, while the Count sleeps away his leave, his wife—who had hoped for a rather more vigorous homecoming—goes out to tip off Anne about her husband's activities. Like a good wife, she will ensure for Carl-Magnus the fidelity of his mistress.

When Charlotte Malcolm meets Anne, her worldly, wisecracking façade falls to pieces in the face of the young woman's innocence, and she ends up cursing this Desirée Armfeldt who has enslaved both her husband and Anne's. For Charlotte, who knows too much about it, love is a dirty business ("Every Day a Little Death"); for Anne, who knows nothing about it, it looks equally distressing.

When Charlotte has gone, it is Henrik who finds the girl in tears and tries wholeheartedly to comfort her. The tears are quickly gone and Charlotte's anguish, which ought to be Anne's too if she could only understand it, is soon replaced by her customary girlish spirits.

Desirée makes the next move. She has some weeks out from her tour and she returns to her mother's estate. She will invite Fredrik and his family to come for "A Weekend in the Country." The formal invitations go out. Anne is thrilled at an invitation but aghast when she recognizes the name. Fredrik would like to accept, but he will refuse if she insists. Anne tells Charlotte who advises her to go, preferably looking as young as possible so as to shame Desirée back behind her wrinkles. Then Charlotte passes the news to Carl-Magnus who announces that he, that is to say they, will go too, invited or not.

Out in the country, wise young Fredrika is quick to guess what the plan is when her mother asks her if she would care for a new father. There is a snag, of course: Anne. But who knows what a weekend in the country may bring about?

Act 2   It is twilight ("The Sun Won't Set") and the weekend is about to begin. The principals of the piece arrive at the Armfeldt estate and tensions start to build. Desirée is dreadfully flustered at the unexpected appearance of Carl-Magnus, drilled through by the glares of Charlotte and Anne, and finds herself forced into whispers at every turn. And everywhere, everywhere sex raises its head. Charlotte develops a plan, which she confides to Anne, of making love to Fredrik in order to arouse Carl-Magnus's jealousy and make him return to her, while Henrik, obsessed, pours out to Fredrika the admission that, although he is intended for the church, he has fallen madly in love with his stepmother. And still the sun hasn't set. Such a lot of things can happen while one Nordic sun is setting.

On the terrace, Fredrik (at one end) and Carl-Magnus (at the other) are alone with their thoughts, which are largely of Desirée. Fredrik is wishing none of this had happened. If only she had fattened and frowsied in fourteen years, if only he had not found her so attractive all over again, "It Would Have Been Wonderful." Carl-Magnus is grimly replaying the scene of discovery and measuring Desirée's reactions: He has no certitude, nothing to exult in and nothing to forgive. It is unbearable. Desirée attempts tactfully to rendezvous with Fredrik, but Carl-Magnus announces his intention to visit her bedroom that night in spite of the presence in the house of his wife, and the quintet sing nonchalantly of "Perpetual Anticipation."

Dinner is rife with barely concealed determinations and accusations. The Count and Countess Malcolm pursue their purposeful paths, their repartee sparred away without too much gentleness by their targets until, finally, it is all too much for Henrik. Smashing his glass on the table, he shouts to them all to hold their stupid libertine chatter. How can they speak so before a girl like Anne? He rushes angrily from the scene and Anne moves to follow him, but she is recalled by Fredrik. What is left of dinner is pursued in silence, save for an occasional hiccup from the tipsy Charlotte.

The tumultuous Henrik heads for the lake, pausing only to perform a mea culpa for his life and his feelings to Fredrika. When Anne comes looking for him, she too finds Fredrika. The child opens the young wife's eyes to her stepson's feelings for her and the two girls go off together to find the boy before he can do himself harm. Elsewhere in the woods, far from such scenes of sensibility, Petra is getting herself uncomplicatedly laid by Madame Armfeldt's butler.

Fled from the foolishness of the evening to Desirée's bedroom, Fredrik and Desirée take in the sense of Henrik's young words. What is she doing running about in second-rate tours and sleeping with a pea-brained married man? What is he doing trying to bring back his youth with a child bride? She would like to be rescued from all this. Perhaps he would too, but he is not sure. The vision of Anne is still there. He had better go to her or, at least, he had better leave Desirée's room. He should not flirt with rescue if he does not mean to be saved ("Send in the Clowns").

Down by the lake, Anne finds Henrik trying to work out how to hang himself. She takes the rope from him and kisses him, and Henrik finds the virility to say he loves her and to return her kisses. On the ground among the trees, Anne finally finds out about love. As she does, Petra, her healthy sex session over, sings jauntily of how one day she'll marry "The Miller's Son." Until that time, this sort of life will suit her just fine.

Charlotte, sobered and embarrassed by her earlier outburst, apologizes to Fredrik. As he comforts her with kind and understanding words, two figures flit past heading for the stables. They are Henrik and Anne and it is quite obvious what is happening. Quietly, almost tiredly, Fredrik makes no move to follow them or stop them. At the same moment, ignoring Desirée's protests, Carl-Magnus is removing his trousers in her bedroom. In doing so, he glances out the window and sees Charlotte and Fredrik in what looks like a compromising position. Calling for his dueling pistols and hoisting his trousers, he rushes out to challenge Fredrik to Russian roulette. The game ends, like the tale, with a wounded Fredrik in the arms of Desirée.

Fredrika asks her grandmother whether the night has smiled during the evening's events, and old Madame Armfeldt answers that indeed it has: for the young ones and for the fools, very much for the fools. Now it will smile for the old. As she dies, the Night Waltz is heard and the people of the play waltz once more about the stage, paired now as the evening's action has destined them to be.

1975

CHICAGO

A MUSICAL VAUDEVILLE IN TWO ACTS by Fred Ebb and Bob Fosse based on the play by Maurine Dallas Watkins. Lyrics by Fred Ebb. Music by John Kander.

Produced at the 46th Street Theatre, New York, 3 June 1975, with Gwen Verdon (Roxie), Chita Rivera (Velma), and Jerry Orbach (Billy).

"The name on everybody's lips is gonna be . . . Roxie!"
But the murdering Mrs. Hart (Gwen Verdon)
has no idea how short that moment of ill fame will be.
Photograph © Martha Swope.

CHARACTERS

Roxie Hart

Amos, *her husband*

Fred Casely, *her lover*

Velma Kelly

Billy Flynn

Mary Sunshine, *a journalist*

Liz, Annie, June, Hunyak, Mona, *murderesses*

Matron Morton

Go-to-Hell Kitty, Sergeant Fogarty, Martin Harrison, Harry, Aaron, Judge, Court Clerk, etc.

Act 1

It is Chicago, Illinois, some time in the late 1920s. The Master of Ceremonies welcomes the audience to "a story of murder, greed, corruption, violence, exploitation, adultery, and treachery—all those things we all hold near and dear to our hearts," as Velma Kelly sings about "All That Jazz," and a drunken Roxie Hart is seen letting her lover, Fred Casely, into her apartment. Sex is quickly and mechanically over, and we see that all is not well in the little love nest. Fred is calling the affair off and Roxie is not pleased. In fact, she's so displeased that she puts a bullet through his stomach.

Three hours later, the police are there arresting Roxie's husband, Amos Hart, who has confessed to shooting a burglar. Roxie thinks it's real sweet of her "Funny Honey" to take the blame like she suggested but, when he sees who the corpse is, Amos knows this isn't a burglar. It's the man who sold them their furniture. Even poor, dumb Amos can see what's been going on. Out it all comes and Roxie is so annoyed she just puts her hands on her hips and says so what, she shot the fink.

At the Cook County Jail, the six resident murderesses recite the history of their crimes ("Cell Block Tango"). These ladies are under the wing of Matron Mama Morton who runs a fine prison to a fine profit ("When You're Good to Mama"). Velma Kelly has been getting big newspaper coverage, thanks to Mama, and Mama has arranged that she shall be represented at her trial by none other than top lawyer Billy Flynn. She's even fixed the trial date and, after the trial, she'll get Velma on the vaudeville circuits at a wage commensurate with her public notoriety. As long, that is, as Velma is good to Mama.

Roxie makes it seven murderesses under Mama's care. She's been feeling a bit scared since the policeman told her that hers was a hanging offense, and she is looking for a little help. Velma isn't going to oblige but the kindly Mama will, at a price. The price is $5,000 for Billy Flynn. It may sound a lot, but he's never lost a case for a female client yet. So Roxie sets to work on her Amos to wheedle him into getting her the cash.

Billy Flynn is pure showbiz: a man with an electroplated tongue, a great line in sterling sincerity ("All I Care About") and a wallet like a Venus flytrap. He doesn't ask if the client is guilty, just if she has $5,000. Amos can only raise $2,000 but Billy has ways and means. Get the girl on page one and announce that her effects are to be sold to finance her defense. They'll go wild to buy them in the hope that she'll be executed and the stuff will triple in value. He'll even offer to give Amos 20 percent of the takings above $5,000.

The exercise begins with Roxie being introduced to the *Evening Star* sob sister, Mary Sunshine ("A Little Bit of Good"). For the occasion, Billy has supplied Roxie with a suitably heartrending background starting with a convent education and going on from a runaway marriage to a fine slice of poor little lost girl, and finally arriving at the fatal night when "We Both Reached for the Gun" and she killed a man in self-defense. As Billy works her like a puppet, Roxie does her stuff, and, lo and behold, she makes those front pages. She is thrilled. She's always wanted to have her name in the papers—now "Roxie" is the name everyone is going to have on their lips.

Roxie is news and this means that Velma Kelly isn't. There's only room for one murderess on the front page at a time. Suddenly Velma's long-planned vaudeville tour is under heavy threat. Velma is too smart to let jealousy get in the way of business; she simply turns her solo act into a duo and starts trying to persuade Roxie into going partners ("I Can't Do It Alone").

Meanwhile, somewhere in the city, an upper-class lady called Kitty is putting a bullet through a faithless lover. The next morning it is she who has the attention of Billy Flynn; Roxie is out of fashion even before he has her trial date set. Velma wants to talk to him about her trial too but they're both out of luck. Kitty has all the front pages and all the attention, and the girls can see that they've only got themselves to depend on ("My Own Best Friend").

Act 2 Roxie's the smart one, though. She lets out that she's pregnant. So now she's the only pregnant murderess, and the press is back at her side. As Roxie sells her hearts-and-flowers for all their worth ("Me and My Baby"), Velma regrets ragingly that she didn't think of that angle first ("I Know a Girl"). Mary Sunshine spreads moral indignation over the imprisoned, unborn child through pages of newsprint and, before you can say "gallows," Billy Flynn is back on Roxie's case, full of plans.

Amos is jubilant at the thought of being a father, but no one takes any notice of him ("Mr. Cellophane") except for Billy who points out purposefully that he couldn't be the child's father and that therefore he'd better divorce Roxie. This, of course, will make his client even more the persecuted heroine of the *Evening Star* than ever. Roxie's trial date is fixed, and Velma is devastated when she learns that it's her spot that has been rescheduled to make a place for her rival. Just when she'd got her whole trial strategy worked out ("When Velma Takes the Stand"). But Roxie is getting really grand now. Having done one bright thing on her own, she thinks she can do it all and she dismisses Flynn. What does she need him for? She can conduct her own defense.

Katalina Hunyak, one of Mama's murderesses, who doesn't speak American, comes to trial. She has endlessly repeated the only two words of English she knows over the months she has passed in jail—"not guilty." But forty-seven years after the last hanging of a woman, Hunyak is sentenced to death by Cook County and sent to the gallows. It is a very frightened and repentant Roxie who makes her peace with Billy Flynn and allows herself once again to be tutored in trial technique. As the big day approaches, he encourages her with words of showbiz. It's all just a big circus and she is the star. She must get out there and give them the old "Razzle Dazzle."

At the trial, Roxie follows her instructions with the expertise of a seasoned campaigner, turning out a Flynn-ized version of her story, calculated to dampen many a handkerchief and fill many a well-turned column, until she reaches the climax. She fired not only in self-defense, but to save her husband's poor, innocent, unborn child!

As Mama and Velma listen to Mary Sunshine's breathless radio reportage of the trial, Velma gets really hot under the collar. Roxie has nabbed all her little bits of business, her dramatic details worked on over the months and honed for her own trial. She's even pinched Velma's trial shoes with the rhinestone buckles. What a low broad! Together the two women ruminate on whatever happened to "Class."

It is the day of decision. Mary Sunshine trills down her microphone as Billy Flynn sums up, in flawlessly printable rhetoric, his own Roxie Hart tale. Then, just as the verdict is about to be announced, a sensation occurs in a nearby divorce court. This girl has just shot her husband and his mother *and* the defense attorney! The newsmen vanish en masse.

Roxie is devastated. It is almost incidental that she has been found not guilty. As Billy waves goodbye, she stands there with nothing. Amos asks her to come home and she doesn't hear him. For the baby? Silly goon, there's no baby. And no reporters. No front pages. No Amos. Only three times nightly on the lesser vaudeville circuits in that double act with Velma Kelly ("Nowadays").

A CHORUS LINE

A MUSICAL by James Kirkwood and Nicholas Dante. Lyrics by Edward Kleban. Music by Marvin Hamlisch.

Produced at the Shubert Theatre, 25 July 1975, with Robert LuPone (Zach), Donna McKechnie (Cassie), Sammy Williams (Paul), Priscilla Lopez (Diana), Carole Bishop (Sheila), Wayne Cilento (Mike), and Pamela Blair (Val). Originally produced at the Public Theatre, New York, 15 April 1975, and transferred to the Newman Theatre, 21 May 1975.

A film version was produced by Embassy Films in 1985 with Michael Douglas, Alyson Reed, Cameron English, Yamil Borges, Vicki Frederick, Charles McGowan, and Audrey Landers.

CHARACTERS

Zach, the director/choreographer

Larry, his assistant

Cassie

Sheila

Val

Diana

Judy

Kristine

Maggie

Bebe

Connie

Mike

Richie

Don

Paul

Mark

Greg

Bobby

Al

Vicki, Tricia, Lois, Frank, Butch, Roy, Tom, etc.

Alone on a stage that was not long
since full of auditioning dancers,
Cassie (Donna McKechnie) gives herself to
"The Music and the Mirror."
Photograph © Martha Swope.

On the bare stage of a Broadway theatre, a chorus dancers' audition is taking place. The early stages of the call are over, and the mass of hopeful contestants for the few places in the chorus line of the new show have been thinned down to a final group of some two dozen boys and girls who are in the process of being taught a dance combination by the choreographer's assistant. The voice of the director, Zach, calls the beat from the darkness of the auditorium as the dancers perform the routine together. Then it is time for them to be looked at more individually. The group is broken down into sections of four dancers, each group to dance through the ballet steps separately. As they wait their turn, the young people's thoughts come across ("I Hope I Get It"). How many performers does he need for the chorus line? And, please oh please, may I be one of the fortunate ones chosen.

One by one, the groups of dancers perform the combination. Nerves are evident. One girl dances with her tongue anxiously following her movements, another overperforms and breaks from her place in the formation, and another, whose ballet is the least happy part of her dance repertoire, fails totally and has to step aside. Zach calls his corrective instructions from the theatre, and some of the artists are able to adjust their performance accordingly, but others find that their idiosyncrasies are not correctable. When the girls and boys have displayed their talent in ballet, a jazz combination follows and it is not necessarily the same dancers who shine. And many of the same errors are seen again. The boy who has been told to hold his head up persists through everything in looking at the ground.

When both combinations have been danced, it is time for a further thinning of the ranks. From the dance cards, Zach reads the numbers of the dancers who are to stay behind and audition further. There are eight girls, plus one called Cassie who is called out by name, and eight boys. Hearts are thumping: It looks as if an eight-and-eight lineup is needed, and it looks as though they have the job. But no. Zach asks for their photographs and biographies. It is not over yet. Lined up across the front of the stage, they are asked in turn to give their name, age, and hometown.

There are some nervous jokes over ages and real, as opposed to stage, names but the exercise performs its intended use. It shows up the personalities of the individuals and, most particularly, their hang-ups over age, race, and social background. Greg is Jewish; Connie is Chinese, four foot ten and thirty-two; Diana is from Puerto Rico; Bobby is from a wealthy neighborhood, Paul from Harlem; Sheila is approaching thirty and defensive about it; and Mark is twenty, inexperienced and enthusiastic. Cassie gets herself excused from taking part. Even then it is not over; Zach wants to know more. He wants them to talk about themselves, to find out what they are like as people, before making his final choice. It is Sheila who has the courage to ask how many dancers he needs, and the answer is four and four. Half of them.

Mike is first to be called forward, and, with a bit of prodding, he launches into the story of how he started dancing after watching his sister at dance class ("I Can Do That"). Bobby has no trouble talking—he's a practiced extrovert. Ignored by his bridge-playing, cocktail-drinking parents, he has developed a cocky manner and is equipped with a wad of extravagantly imagined stories about himself. As he rattles on, the other dancers are barely listening. They are lost in their own thoughts, searching their minds for amusing anecdotes with which to make an impression, or wondering whether it would be to their advantage to invent an interesting background ("And . . .").

Sheila is next, posing and performing the role of the wisecracking vamp she likes to pretend to be, in spite of Zach's efforts to get her to be natural. Sheila wanted to be a ballerina like her mother had almost been. She wanted to dance, like the lady in *The Red Shoes*. But what she really wanted to do, it finally emerges, is get out of an unloving home to that imaginary world of handsome princes and pretty girls in white ("At the Ballet"). Maggie, a child born to try to save a marriage, and Bebe, who was never pretty, went through the same thing and have similar stories. Kristine is really nervous and her husband, Al, who is also in the line, keeps defensively popping in a word or two to help her through her story. Kristine's hang-up isn't in her life or in her dancing, but she has a problem at auditions. She can't "Sing" at all.

Young Mark is scarcely old enough to have dancing memories. All his memories are of that momentous thing called puberty ("Hello Twelve"). Connie has spent all her life praying to grow beyond four foot ten so that she could be in the ballet. Diana wanted to be a serious actress and enrolled at the High School of the Performing Arts, but she couldn't get on the wavelength of a pretentious tutor called Karp and his improvisations, so she dropped out ("Nothing").

Don started at fifteen earning money dancing in strip-joints, Judy started performing to get her father's attention, and black, hyperactive Richie was training to be a kindergarten teacher when he realized he could get stuck there. One by one the stories and the thoughts mix with each other as the young people loosen up. Val has done something about her hang-up. She was plain and flat-chested. She could dance the other girls off the stage, but she never got jobs because she was plain and flat-chested ("Dance: Ten; Looks: Three"). So she went to a plastic surgeon and got herself fixed up with "tits and ass" and changed her life. Paul, on the other hand, clearly still has deep problems and he cannot even talk about them.

Zach gives the dancers a short break, but holds Cassie back. Once more she is to be given favored treatment, and it is soon evident why. Cassie has been through the chorus and gone beyond it. Years ago, Zach took her out of the chorus line and put her into a couple of featured parts, and he also took her into his home and his bed. The relationship ended and Cassie's career didn't progress. There were no more featured roles, and Hollywood didn't want her because, with all her advantages, Cassie couldn't cut it as an actress. What she did, she did magnificently, but that was it. Cassie is a dancer and now, after two years without work, she wants to go back and start over again where she was good: in the chorus line ("The Music and the Mirror").

When Cassie goes to join the other dancers to learn the song that they are to audition, Zach turns his attention to Paul and pries his story from him. Paul was always effeminate. When he saw the old movie musicals it was Cyd Charisse he wanted to imitate, not Fred Astaire, even though he knew it wasn't right. It wasn't being gay that bothered him, it was not knowing how to be male. When he left school, he went to dance in a drag show and they made a real girl out of him. Then one day his parents discovered what he did. He calls himself by an Italian name now, wiping out his Puerto Rican origin and his past, and he really can dance. Zach lets the boy regain some composure before calling the rest of the dancers back.

Now individual talent is not in question. What Zach is looking for is the ability to make oneself part of a team, to dance exactly like the person next to you as part of a background to a star. Together, the seventeen dancers perform the routine and the song they have learned ("One"). What shows up immediately is that Cassie is not a chorus dancer; she has special emphases to her dancing, an individual style, which does not belong in a chorus line. Zach continually corrects her. When she is corrected, however, she takes Zach's direction and performs just like everyone else. It breaks his heart to see her smothering her talent, but that is his problem, not hers.

They tap, they dance in pairs, and then, suddenly, Paul falls to the ground while doing a turn. His already damaged cartilage has given way and he has to be taken to hospital. The other dancers have just seen the end of a fellow dancer's life. Now they all have to think about what they will do when the day comes and they are obliged, for one reason or another, to give up dancing. Some want to stay in the theatre, as actors perhaps or on the production side, while others have other plans already worked out. But whatever they do, they will remember their days as dancers ("What I Did for Love").

Now Zach makes his final choice. Val, Diana, Judy, Cassie, Mike, Richie, Mark, and Bobby will be contracted for the show.

As a finale to the show, all the dancers, seen up till now only in their rehearsal clothes, parade across the stage in glittering top hats and tails to the strains of the hymn to every performer—"One."

1976

ANNIE

A MUSICAL IN TWO ACTS by Thomas Meehan based on the cartoon strip *Little Orphan Annie*. Lyrics by Martin Charnin. Music by Charles Strouse.

Produced at the Alvin Theatre, New York, 21 April 1977 with Dorothy Loudon (Miss Hannigan), Reid Shelton (Oliver Warbucks), and Andrea McArdle (Annie). Originally produced at the Goodspeed Opera House, Connecticut 10 August 1976, with Maggie Task, Shelton, and Kristin Vigard.

A film version was produced by Columbia Pictures in 1982 with Carol Burnett, Albert Finney, and Aileen Quinn.

Little Orphan Annie (Andrea McArdle)
gives the President of the United States some tips
on how to get the country back on the rails.
Photograph © Martha Swope.

CHARACTERS

Annie, *an orphan*

Molly, Pepper, Duffy, July, Tessie, Kate, *orphans*

Miss Hannigan

Oliver Warbucks

Grace Farrell, *his secretary*

Mrs. Pugh, *his housekeeper*

Drake, *his butler*

Rooster Hannigan

Lily St. Regis

Bert Healy

Bonnie, Connie, *and* Ronnie Boylan

FDR

Ickes, Howe, Morgenthau, Hull, Perkins, *his Brains Trust*

Bundles McCloskey, Lieutenant Ward, Harry, Sophie the Kettle, Cecille, Annette, Mrs. Greer, Fred McCracken, Jimmy Johnson, Justice Brandeis, etc.

Act 1

It is the middle of a 1933 night in the girls' dormitory at the New York City Municipal Orphanage, and little Molly has awakened from a sad dream with cries that have roused the rest of the girls from their sleep. Some of them react grumpily to Molly's distress, but little orphan Annie goes to comfort the child who has been dreaming of the mother she has never known. Annie is luckier than the other orphans; she knows that she really has a mother and a father, for she still has a note that they left when she was abandoned at the orphanage, and half a silver locket to which her parents hold the other part, waiting for the day when they can come to claim their child ("Maybe").

That all happened eleven years ago, and Annie decides that perhaps now it is time for her to take the initiative and go out and look for her family. She is on her way to the front door with her basket under her arm when all the lights go on. She is caught. Miss Hannigan, the raddled guardian of the orphanage, triumphantly hauls the child back to the dormitory and, as a punishment, sets all the orphans to work scrubbing the floor, even though it is 4 A.M. ("It's the Hard-Knock Life"). But Annie is not to be dissuaded. When the laundry man comes to take away the dirty linen, she hides in the laundry bag and effects her escape under Miss Hannigan's very nose.

Out on the streets of New York, Annie has to fend for herself and yet evade the pursuing city officials. Before long, she meets a kindred soul: a stray dog who is being pursued by the dog pound. She makes him her friend, names him Sandy, and shares with him her determination that everything will turn out all right in the end ("Tomorrow"). When night comes, Annie finds her way to the shelter of one of the city's Hoovervilles, a camp of down-and-outs who blame their fall from prosperity on the policies of President Hoover ("We'd Like to Thank You"). There she finds food and warmth, but the only reaction to her cheerful optimism is a sour suggestion that she ought to be in politics.

Back at the orphanage, Miss Hannigan's profession is getting her down. It is no way of life for someone who has an abiding loathing for "Little Girls." She has a moment of mean satisfaction when Annie, recaptured when the insanitary Hooverville was broken up by the police, is brought back. Miss Hannigan is taking out her frustrations on the unrepentant child when another visitor knocks at the door. This smart young woman is Grace Farrell, secretary to the well-known billionaire Oliver Warbucks. It appears that this gentleman, a former orphan himself, has decided to invite an orphan to share Christmas with him at his mansion, and Grace has been sent to the orphanage to select the lucky child. Annie's ears prick up delightedly and, after a swift exchange of winks, nods, and signals with the amused Grace, she succeeds in getting herself chosen for this wonderful adventure.

At the Warbucks house, Annie is happily fussed over by the staff and quickly decides "I Think I'm Going to Like It Here," but, when Warbucks returns, he is disappointed to find that Annie isn't a boy. He hadn't realized that orphans could be girls. What on earth does one do with a girl? Perhaps she would like to go to a movie and an ice-cream parlor and ride around Central Park in a cab. Annie is thrilled, but dashed when she finds that Warbucks isn't going to come with her. Some sad-eyed looks and a bit of mute infant pleading soon get him to change his mind, and corporation affairs are put aside as Warbucks takes Annie out to look at "NYC" from an unfamiliar angle.

Within a week, the billionaire and the orphan have become inseparable pals, and Grace is on her way back to see Miss Hannigan. Warbucks wants to adopt Annie and take her to live with him forever in the splendor of Fifth Avenue. Miss Hannigan is still privately screaming at the beastly injustice of it all when she gets some more unwelcome visitors: her rapscallion brother Rooster and his floosie, Lily St. Regis, who have come to scrounge a loan. The one consolation is that she has someone with whom to share her fury about Annie's promotion to "Easy Street."

Annie's promotion doesn't turn out to be as simple as it might have been. When Warbucks nervously tries to broach the subject of adoption and offers to exchange her old locket for a brand new one from Tiffany's, the little girl bursts into tears and tells him that she isn't an orphan. Out comes the story of the note and the locket and a heartfelt cry: All Annie wants in the world is to find her mother and father. Before long, Warbucks is on the phone to his pal J. Edgar Hoover, getting the FBI's finest put on to the case, and the whole Warbucks household is energetically assuring Annie "You Won't Be an Orphan for Long."

Act 2

The campaign to find Annie's family is soon massively under way. Warbucks goes on the nationwide Oxydent Hour of Smiles radio show ("You're Never Fully Dressed Without a Smile") to offer a $50,000 reward. The listening Miss Hannigan is grinding her teeth at all those zeroes when she gets a heart-lifting surprise: an unprepossessing pair called Ralph and Shirley Mudge turn up on her doorstep looking for their little daughter Annie. It is a fake, but a convincing one. Ralph and Shirley are none other than Rooster and Lily in disguise. They are

determined to win the $50,000, and, with Miss Hannigan's inside knowledge of the child's history, they reckon that they can carry off the deception successfully. Soon they will be on "Easy Street" too.

Little orphan Annie may have a problem but the country has problems too. President Roosevelt and his Brains Trust are in despair over the economic outlook. Warbucks calls to see his presidential friend, bringing advice and Annie with him, and the little girl soon has them all standing up and joining in an optimistic rendition of "Tomorrow." With the Brains Trust now thinking positively toward a new deal, Warbucks and Annie head back to New York, for Fifth Avenue is jammed with couples claiming to be Annie's parents. Surely one of them must be the real one.

Alas, Grace has established that they are all phonies. Not one of them knew about the locket; they were all just after the money. Annie is awfully disappointed, but she can take comfort from the loving Warbucks ("Something Was Missing") who is now more determined than ever to adopt her. Annie knows that, if she can't have her real mother and father, there's no one in the world she would rather have for her father than him ("I Don't Need Anything but You"). With that happy prospect in mind ("Annie"), Warbucks bundles Annie upstairs to get into her best red dress for their Christmas party.

No sooner has she returned to join Warbucks in the happiest night of their lives than the false Ralph and Shirley Mudge arrive. Primed by Miss Hannigan, they know all about Annie's locket and they have actually brought a matching half. The proof seems incontrovertible. They will return in the morning to collect Annie and the check. Everyone should be happy. After so much effort, Annie's parents have really been found. But, as Warbucks proposes a choked toast to little Annie Mudge, the heroine of the moment bolts upstairs in tears. Amid the ruins of Christmas Eve, the President arrives and, when Grace voices her suspicions that Mr. Mudge is not what he seems, the might of the nation is again put into action on the case of little orphan Annie.

When Annie descends the stairs early next morning with her little suitcase packed and ready to leave, she finds that the FBI has done its infallible work. Mr. and Mrs. Mudge are not her parents. Her parents were called David and Margaret and they are, alas, dead. Annie really is an orphan and that means that she can be "Daddy" Warbucks' little girl after all.

The only thing left outstanding is to find out who Ralph and Shirley Mudge are. After all, they knew about the locket and no one knew about the locket except Annie and Warbucks . . . and Miss Hannigan! Right on cue, Miss Hannigan turns up with the children from the orphanage to see Annie and her long-lost parents reunited. When the Mudges come to claim their little girl and their large check they walk into a trap. In front of the President himself, Rooster is unmasked, and he and Lily and Miss Hannigan are frogmarched off on charges of fraud, leaving Annie and her Daddy Warbucks, the President, and all the orphans to celebrate "A New Deal for Christmas."

The film score of *Annie* included four new songs: "Dumb Dog," "Let's Go to the Movies," "Sandy," and "Sign."

Two attempts at a musequel to *Annie*, *Annie 2* and *Annie Warbucks*, both folded without playing on Broadway.

1977

THE BEST LITTLE WHOREHOUSE IN TEXAS

A MUSICAL IN TWO ACTS by Larry L. King and Peter Masterson. Lyrics and music by Carol Hall.

Played at the Forty-Sixth Street Theatre, New York, from 19 June 1978, with Carlin Glynn (Mona), Henderson Forsythe (Sheriff), Clinton Allmon (Thorpe), Jay Garner (Governor), and Susan Mansur (Doatsey Mae). Played at the Eugene O'Neill Theatre, from 31 May 1982.

Originally produced at the Actors' Studio, New York, 20 October 1977, and produced subsequently at the Entermedia Theatre, New York, 17 April 1978.

A film version with additional songs by Dolly Parton was produced by Universal in 1982 with Parton, Burt Reynolds, Dom DeLuise, and Charles Durning.

Some first time customers:
the Aggie football team, stripped for action!
Ilene Jones, photographer.

CHARACTERS

Mona Stangley

Sheriff Ed Earl Dodd

Melvin P. Thorpe *of KTEX-TV*
"Watch Dog"

The Governor

Doatsey Mae, *a waitress*

Edsel Mackey, *editor of the local paper*

Mayor Rufus Poindexter

C. J. Scruggs, *President of the local Jaycees*

Senator Wingwoah

Jewel

Angel, Shy, Linda Lou, Dawn, Ginger, Beatrice, Taddy Jo, Ruby Rae,

Eloise, Durla, *girls at Miss Mona's*

Angelette Imogene Charlene, Aggies, etc.

Act 1   The Chicken Ranch was a kind of an institution in the little corner of Texas where it was situated. Under the rule of Miss Wulla Jean, it had become known as a practical, homely kind of whorehouse ("Twenty Fans") where things were made nice for first-time customers, where regulars were appreciated, and where, when times were hard, the management was happy to take payment in kind. In this part of the world that often meant in some sort of poultry, which was how The Chicken Ranch got its name. In the fullness of time, Miss Wulla Jean went to the big whorehouse in the sky, and her business was taken over by the most adept and long-serving of her girls, Miss Mona. Nothing changed. The Chicken Ranch stayed a nice "Lil' Ole Bitty Pissant Country Place" doing its bit for the community and not hurting anyone who didn't want to be hurt. Until its time came, one year, around Thanksgiving.

One day, two new aspirants to the Chicken Ranch's roster of working girls come to check in. One is clearly experienced in the worst of city whoring, the other looks as though she has come straight off the farm. Miss Mona's experience of girls and the world allows her to sum both girls up instantly and accurately. When she has removed the tarty blonde wig and sunglasses, and renamed her resistant first girl Angel, she has a fine candidate for the girl-next-door type. The other case is equally classic. Shy comes from a country family where she has been molested by her father. But she has made up her mind: she's determined to see it through as a whore, and since the sympathetic Miss Mona can see in her unpretentious attitude the makings of a woman and a worker ("Girl You're a Woman"), she agrees that Shy can stay.

At this selfsame time, Nemesis is preparing to go on the air. Nemesis is Melvin P. Thorpe, a broadcasting poseur fronting a frilled-up Watchdog program theoretically vowed to prevent social and commercial abuse but subjugated entirely to the greater glory and profit of the self-important Melvin himself. Last week he scored a triumph by proving that a peanut bar had less peanuts in it than advertised, and this week he has another great revelation for the listeners of KTEX-TV—"Texas Has a Whorehouse in It." In pious horror, Melvin declares to his audience, over the cooing of his backing singers, that this appalling thing called loveless copulation must be stopped, and he calls upon the Sheriff to take command and shut the whorehouse down.

Back at the Chicken Ranch, things are going on as normal. Angel is happily settled in to the homey atmosphere of her new job and is able to take time out to call her Mama. Mama looks after Angel's little boy who misses his mother but looks forward to the presents she'll be bringing him come Christmas. A wise Miss Mona overhears: Somehow Angel will have to have her period right on Christmas this year.

Jewel, Mona's maid, is having her day off today. She's off to see her feller for "Twenty-Four Hours of Lovin.'" She's going to give away free what the girls get paid for. But the girls have plenty to think about. The big football match is coming up, and the prize for the winning team is an evening out at Miss Mona's establishment. For that evening, Mona works up a special sort of Homecoming Dance ambiance with the girls dressed in 1950s style ball gowns (handily equipped with Velcro for easy removal).

The local Sheriff, Ed Earl Dodd, an old and dear friend of Miss Mona, comes by. He is annoyed over last night's television business, particularly as he was named. Mona is inclined to laugh it off. They have had moral crusaders before and they've survived. After all, most of the men around the district have been customers at the Chicken Ranch sometime in their lives. The Sheriff is not so sure. In the old days when all you had to do was crush some two-bit interfering "investigative" newspaperman it was easy, but these puffed-up television people have a much wider and more pernicious power.

He is right. Since nothing as important as a peanut bar holds his attention for the day, Melvin P. Thorpe (who surely has no other motive) is preparing to move in on the Chicken Ranch. Primping his profile before the cameras, he sets up his cameras in the main street of the little town of Gilbert, and gets ready to spread his message and reap his glory (Watch Dog Theme). But he has not counted on Sheriff Ed Earl. The Sheriff hits him with a bylaw and sends him packing with a mouthful of Texas invective unheard on television since its birth. For Ed Earl has forgotten the difference between a newspaperman and a television person: The latter has sound recording equipment and, oh my goodness, he is going to use it.

Ed Earl's performance, as relayed to the moral folks of Texas by KTEX-TV, doesn't do anything at all for the leading lights of Gilbert town. In fact, the sudden spotlight on their town makes them all decidedly nervous. But Ed Earl is unrepentant: He'd do it all a second time if that sawed-off little shit came around again. The plain, middle-aged waitress, Doatsey Mae, listens to the men's chatter, as she does every day, and goes off into a daydream about what it would be like—if she only dared—to step out of her innate respectability and be like the girls in the magazines ("Doatsey Mae"). But she contents herself with a small-town joke: Whatever happens in the football match, Miss Mona's the only one who's sure to be on a winner.

Down at the stadium, the ideal youth of America is preparing to throw itself into a life-or-death ball game. The Texas Aggies are supported by the Aggie Angelettes, a cheer team with obvious attributes ("Angelette March") and conditioned responses. When they have won the match, however, the boys have only one thing on their mind: Senator Wingwoah's promised night out at the Chicken Ranch (The Aggie Song).

The fact that the Senator was on KTEX-TV the night before denouncing the whole institution of whoredom is just one of those little political necessities.

He still gets taken care of, just like all the lads of the team, and while the folks are enjoying themselves in there, Miss Mona and Ed Earl are in the kitchen drinking coffee and chatting over old times. Then all Melvin breaks loose. Trespassing Thorpe and his little corps of photographers break into the house, flashing their torches and cameras, and soon all is chaos.

Act 2   The Senator is one of the prize catches. He talks a lot and is happy to hide behind the fast-stepping Governor of Texas as soon as he can. This Governor is a master of "The Side Step." He can talk for a week and say nothing in the finest-sounding platitudes you ever did hear. But he can't silence the maniacal, brownie-point-seeking Melvin P. Thorpe, who cuts into every speech with cries of what does the Governor propose to do about the Chicken Ranch? Finally, the Governor is obliged to give his nod to hypocrisy. He says that, of course, such a place must be closed down. With the squeezed-out authority of government to add to the God-granted charter of the "investigative journalist," Melvin goes to work, organizing protests and marches of the television generation faithful to parade outside Miss Mona's place until no customer dare come near.

Mona dispels them with a blast from a shotgun, but the situation looks bad. Ed Earl, it must be said, hasn't handled the business brilliantly, but Mona won't blame him. She's got memories of the young Ed Earl with whom she spent the Kennedy inauguration night in a hotel room down in Galveston. It would be too much to call it love, but it was a night she hasn't forgotten. Sadly, Ed Earl is way out of his territory. He's a fine small-town sheriff, but that doesn't mean he knows how to handle the megalomaniac Melvin P. Thorpes of the world. You couldn't expect him to. Mona certainly doesn't. She has no expectations of life. You take what comes to you and ask no questions. That way you get "No Lies."

The Chicken Ranch's rise to statewide fame has put an unaccustomed load on the town of Gilbert, and its chief citizens are getting tetchy. It really would make their lives easier if Miss Mona were simply shut down. Ed Earl refuses. Until the order comes from the Governor, he isn't moving. Then it does come and the sheriff has to pick up the phone and call Mona. He's sad to do it. She's a "Good Old Girl" and he feels a deep warmth for her and for the relationship they've comfortably created over the years, but there are some cats that just won't go back into a bag.

The girls are packing to go away. Quite where they'll go they aren't sure, but they're quick to assure each other they'll be fine ("Hard Candy Christmas").

Some will go up, some will go down. Angel is determined to go home and get a straight job and look after her boy; Shy looks happily for new pastures in the same game without even considering another way.

Ed Earl comes to say goodbye to Mona. He still isn't quite sure how it all got to this, he will never forget the way so-called friends ran away, and he just can't make himself say goodbye to Mona. He wants so very much for everything to be like it was before. She knows it can't be, but she makes one last try. Does he remember Kennedy's inauguration? He doesn't remember anything special about it. The assassinations he remembers fine and where he was and what he was doing when he heard about them, but not the inauguration. Some people remember one thing, others another. Mona's marvellous, remembered moment hasn't lived in Ed Earl's memory. Funny.

She says goodbye and, as he goes, she looks back along the life she has come through to get to this day ("The Bus from Amarillo"). The girls carry their suitcases off as she sings, and, somewhere in the glorious places of the town, the Governor is presenting Melvin P. Thorpe with a plaque in memory of his moral services to the state of Texas as Miss Mona steps out into the world, ready to start, somehow and somewhere, all over again.

A sequel, *The Best Little Whorehouse Goes Public*, was produced at the Lunt-Fontanne Theatre, 10 May 1994.

1978

On the Twentieth Century

A MUSICAL IN TWO ACTS by Betty Comden and Adolph Green based on *Twentieth Century* by Ben Hecht, Charles MacArthur, and Bruce Milholland. Lyrics by Betty Comden and Adolph Green. Music by Cy Coleman.

    Produced at the St. James Theatre, New York, 19 February 1978, with Madeleine Kahn (Lily), John Cullum (Oscar), Kevin Kline (Bruce), and Imogene Coca (Letitia).

A quartet of philosophical porters give the audience
time out from the hectic activity that's occuring aboard
the Twentieth Century.
Photograph © Martha Swope.

CHARACTERS

Lily Garland, *formerly Mildred Plotka*

Oscar Jaffee, *the high priest of the theatre*

Owen O'Malley, *his press agent*

Oliver Webb, *his business manager*

Letitia Primrose

Bruce Granit, *a damageable screen star*

Conductor Flanagan *of the Twentieth Century*

Dr. Johnson

Imelda Thornton, *a star*

Max Jacobs

Agnes, Congressman Lockwood, Maxwell Finch, Porters, Anita, etc.

Act 1

At a theatre in Chicago a play is disintegrating. The show is a failure, the audience is gone, the producer, Oscar Jaffee, is nowhere to be seen, and the actors haven't been paid ("Stranded Again"). The cast descend on the production's business manager, Oliver Webb, and press agent, Owen O'Malley, to no avail and storm off to find the culpable Jaffee. Then a suit of armor moves its mailed hand and passes a note to Owen. It reads, "Meet me on the Twentieth Century tomorrow—get me Drawing Room A." It is time to go ("Saddle Up the Horse").

At the Chicago railway station, the Twentieth Century waits at the platform, flanked by immaculate porters and conductors ready to receive its glamorous clientele. A sweet little old lady, Letitia Primrose, the head of the wealthy Primrose Restoria Pills family, boards the train and hard behind her come Owen and Oliver anxiously looking out for Oscar. They have little trouble securing Drawing Room A. It's a simple exercise involving ejecting a Congressman and his pretty secretary with a little bit of blackmail. But as the train moves off, it looks as if Oscar has not made it. Of course he has. Here he comes, outside the window, hand-over-handing from car to car. They're safely away, heading back to New York and a quarter-of-a-million dollar bankruptcy. But is Oscar depressed, deflated? Never. His is an unreasoning optimism undimmed by constant failure ("I Rise Again"). There are sixteen hours between Chicago and New York and the world can end—and begin again—in sixteen hours.

Now it is time for plans to be made. Oliver tentatively mentions an offer from the successful producer, Max Jacobs, for Oscar to direct a road company, and for the hundredth time in his years with Jaffee he gets the sack. Jacobs was once Oscar's office boy! And a road company? Never! Oscar's plans don't look downward. They head for the stars, and one of these is due to roll into their orbit at the train's first stop at Englewood.

There the famous film star Lily Garland will join the train. Lily is the girl whom Oscar raised from nothing to stage stardom before she walked out on him to begin her fabulous career on celluloid. She will return to the arms of her old mentor and lover, and, with her name on the bills of his new show, he will be able to name his own price on Broadway. Now do they understand why he had to have Drawing Room A? His spy system has told him that Lily is booked in the adjoining Drawing Room B. She will return to him. Max Jacobs? Bah!

The scene flashes back a reel of years to the stage of a theatre where Oscar is auditioning the starry Imelda Thornton for the lead of his new play. Since the piece requires Miss Thornton to sing, she has brought a pianist, a bumbling, breathless little girl called Mildred Plotka who spills the music all over the floor.

Miss Thornton is not an experienced singer and, when she goes a little astray in "The Indian Maiden's Lament," Miss Plotka does not hesitate to help her out. In fact, when Miss Thornton persistently gets it wrong, Miss Plotka finishes the song for her, cadenza and all. The star is burned up. She shrieks dismissal at her accompanist and gets rocked back on her heels when little Miss Plotka fires back on all cylinders, demanding her carfare in reimbursement for her time.

Oscar is thrilled. As the shattered Imelda is helped out, Mildred Plotka is offered the lead role in his new play. It is all there in her—the pixie, the eternal woman—and he will bring it out, mold it, make her a star. He woos her from her everyday thoughts with a vision of stardom and places the script in her hands. She begins to read the role. She is "Véronique," a French street singer, and, in a flash, there she is, on the stage, a new-born star surrounded by her marching cast of millions crying "vive la France!"

But that was all a long time ago. Mildred Plotka has been Lily Garland for a lot of her life now, and Oscar Jaffee has been out of it for as long as he was in it. Will she really give up Hollywood and return to where she started just for him? The conductor pops his head into the compartment to warn the occupants that there is apparently a religious maniac on the train. Someone has been sticking "Repent" stickers all over the place. He warns Mrs. Primrose too, and she, as she secretly slaps a sticker on him, nods in agreement. While he has Jaffee's attention, the conductor also just happens to mention that "I Have Written a Play." It is a phrase that dogs Oscar's life, and the conductor is quickly bundled out to announce Englewood and the arrival of Lily Garland on board the train ("Together").

Lily has a companion with her on the station, a chiseled beauty of the screen glorified under the name of Bruce Granit, but Bruce will not, she announces as she snuggles up to him for the benefit of the photographers, be joining her on the train. On the long journey to New York, she must travel alone. As soon as Bruce leaves the compartment, she declines into a boudoirful of broken-hearted loneliness, but her act is ruined when she finds that her escort has failed to get off the train in time. She is stuck with him all the way to New York. Her performance changes to one of a passionate desire to be alone, but Bruce takes her in his arms with celluloid style, and it is easier to succumb.

Their clinch is interrupted by Owen and Oliver, and Lily is delighted to see such old friends until she makes the connection—Oscar has to be around somewhere. Delight turns to venom as, bit by bit, she drags Oscar's plans from the duo. Come back to work for Oscar Jaffee? "Never!" Bruce is suspicious of anyone who can arouse all this passion in his woman. What is it about Oscar Jaffee and Lily? He accuses her petulantly of infidelity in retrospect, and she spits out a long list of lovers from which Jaffee is particularly excluded. She is, of course, lying. There have never been any other lovers. Just Oscar, all that time ago ("Our Private World").

In the meanwhile, Mrs. Primrose is causing her own kind of chaos in the train. Her stickers are turning up in the most unlikely places, and she is deliciously happy that her message is getting around—"Repent."

Amid the hurly-burly, Oscar is maturing his own plans. Lily will come back to him. Bruce Granit is no competition. He just needs a suitable piece of bait. Then the sight of the "Repent" stickers gives him a magnificent idea: Lily Garland as Mary Magdalen! A Mary Magdalen with every tub-thumping, heartrending, clothes-wearing scene an actress could desire. She will not be able to resist such a role just as, surely, she will not be able to resist Oscar himself. As he gazes in his mirror appreciatively, Bruce is gazing in the corresponding mirror in the next compartment. Both are sure within themselves that before the trip is over the lady will be "Mine."

Owen and Oliver have given up on Oscar and his plans and are getting pie-eyed in the bar when they get into conversation with Mrs. Primrose. It doesn't take long for them to discover her links with big business and religion. Both of these look very, very interesting. Mary Magdalen may have found a backer.

Meanwhile, Oscar has made his move. Mistily recalling their old love to Lily, he puts Bruce into a frenzy of jealous posturing, which ends with Lily throwing him painfully out of the compartment. Then she turns on Oscar. He can get out too: She doesn't want him, and she has proved she doesn't need him ("I've Got It All"). She asserts her stardom, he sneers at her celluloid career, and she trumps him by revealing that she knows all about his penniless condition. There is nothing he can do for her and there is nothing she will do for him.

For the moment, Oscar is defeated, but he will return as soon as he has strangled Oliver and Owen for betraying his poverty to her. However, the two lieutenants are soon back in favor for they have struck gold; they have Mrs. Primrose and her money to introduce to their boss. *Lux resurgit semper.*

Act 2 An entr'acte sung by four porters muses harmonically on the tenet that "Life Is Like a Train" before we get back to our story. Oscar, Owen, and Oliver are seen relieving Letitia of a check with a two and "Five Zeros" on it: $200,000 to bring their inspirational, devotional retelling of the scriptures alive in the theatre. Oscar is on line again, and, as if by fate, Lily's maid arrives at that moment to summon Oscar to her mistress's presence. Lily is playing the great and generous lady this evening and she has decided to make a beautiful gesture: She will settle a small annuity on Jaffee in gratitude for his help in her early career. She hands him a check for $35, and presto, he changes it into one for $200,000.

Lily cannot help but be interested in such an attractive sum, and, when he begins to describe the project and the part, she gets irresistibly caught up in the whole thing. Before long Oscar, Oliver, Owen, and Mrs. Primrose are all encouraging her to "Sign" a contract and crushing the bruised Bruce under every piece of furniture available as he tries to stop her.

But Lily feels something rising up in her that is stronger than mere desire for the money, the role, and the fame: She feels Oscar getting to her. She knows that she must not go back to him to be his puppet again. She must keep her hard-found freedom. She must not, she cannot, she dare not. . . . Then Oscar turns the knife. Why keep this project for the stage? It can be a film. Mrs. Primrose will be happy to finance it and it can be Lily's own personal production—free of the studios, free of everyone. . . .

At this vital moment in time, two asylum attendants are boarding the train. They have come for Mrs. Primrose. She is an escaped patient from the Benzinger clinic for the decidedly loopy. In fact, to put it kindly, "She's a Nut." As the news spreads, the jubilant Bruce heads straight for Lily and, at the crucial moment, snatches the pen from her signing fingers. Oscar Jaffee is defeated. Lily is livid at the trick she believes has been played on her. Then, right on cue, who should arrive on the train and in her very compartment but her loving producer, Max Jacobs. Lily flies furiously to him and his proffered new play as Oscar grinds his teeth with rage.

Lily is reading Max's play. It is by lovely, classy, sophisticated Somerset Maugham and Lily adores it. Only, something in the back of her mind keeps wondering if perhaps the classy, sophisticated heroine couldn't have just a little of the Mary Magdalen about her? A blinding revelation, perhaps? And the style, couldn't it maybe . . . ? Left alone, she imagines herself as Maugham's "Babette" but, as the play comes to life in her mind, the biblical keeps on intruding into its scenes. Oscar Jaffee keeps intruding. Lily fights back and finally she captures the character of Babette while keeping the Magdalen and Oscar at bay. Triumphant at her mastery of self and subject, she announces that she will do Jacobs's play.

Out in the club car, Oscar plays his last and greatest scene. He produces a gun and soulfully declares "The Legacy" he leaves to his nearest and dearest, before leaving the room. When they hear a shot Owen and Oliver are skeptical with the skepticism of years, but they are aghast when Mrs. Primrose gallops on brandishing a smoking revolver. She has shot Oscar! Oscar staggers on to collapse in the arms of his allies but, when a doctor is called, she diagnoses only a scratch. He is unharmed. But the doctor, like most people on this train, has apparently written a play ("I Have Written A Play") and, with a promise of making her a Broadway author, Oscar persuades her temporarily to alter her diagnosis.

Lily is brought in to take her place at the death bed and a lovingly tearful scene ensues ("Lily, Oscar"). As her last gift to him, he asks her to sign her name to the contract he once offered her and she weepingly obliges. When Max Jacobs rushes in, Oscar flings aside his pretense and leaps up to display his contract, but Lily has the last laugh. She has signed it all right, but she has signed it Peter Rabbit! The two shriek recriminations at each other hilariously until, with a gulping passion, they fall into each other's arms. Sixteen hours on the Twentieth Century were enough to set at least two lives to rights.

THEY'RE PLAYING OUR SONG

A MUSICAL COMEDY IN TWO ACTS by Neil Simon. Lyrics by Carol Bayer Sager. Music by Marvin Hamlisch.

Produced at the Imperial Theatre, New York, 11 February 1979, with Lucie Arnaz (Sonia) and Robert Klein (Vernon).

There's no bigger buzz for a songwriter than to hear that "They're Playing My Song!" Robert Klein as Vernon Gersch and Lucie Arnaz as Sonia Walsk.

Act 1 At thirty-four, Vernon Gersch, successful composer, has made it into lush living land, and he has two Grammies and an Oscar to display as landmarks on his rise to comfortable fame. He is attractive, sharp, he has been engaged to three different girls in the past twelve months, and he needs a new lyricist. Because of this—the lack of a lyricist, not the three broken engagements—he has made an appointment with Sonia Walsk. Sonia once wrote the words for a successful song but it didn't breed. She is extrovertly confident, nervous, in debt, and dresses in clothes from short-run theatre shows. They both go to psychiatrists in the same block Vernon lives in, but, after all they are New Yorkers, Jewish, and in the music business, so what else would you expect? Sonia would give her left ear to write songs with Vernon Gersch, and now he's read the pieces she's submitted to him and he's arranged an appointment, so she has dressed up in her best off-cast from *The Cherry Orchard* and arrived at his apartment twenty minutes late to meet him.

He really liked one of her lyrics. One? Well, part of one. He liked it enough to have set it straight off ("Fallin' "). To his confusion, she likes only half the result—but it's the lyrics she doesn't like. His music is too good for them and she feels a cold blast of inferiority down her back. Except, perhaps just the first eight bars of the music . . . ? And now she has to rush: She's having her hair cut right down, and when do they start work, and perhaps he could just look at those eight bars. And wasn't it a little draggy? Then she's gone and he's wondering what the hell was wrong with those eight bars. Out in the hall, Sonia makes a good resolution not to be late for their first work session, not to have her weekend away but to work, not. . . .

She is, in fact, a day late for their next meeting and doesn't seem to have noticed. She had a traumatic weekend breaking up with Leon, the boyfriend she broke up with on Thursday and got together with again on Friday, so yesterday sort of went. Anyway, she's here now and ready to work on a song. Vernon proposes "Workin' It Out." He likes the title, he's got the rhythm and a bit of tune, and she can put in the lyrics to it. But that would be too simple. Sonia doesn't work like that. She has to talk it out with the girls, the other Sonias.

The thought that there is more than one of her almost fells Vernon, until she explains that the other Sonias are her alter egos, inside her brain. Doesn't he have them too? So, while Vernon goes to work on the music, plotting the song with the aid of his boys, Sonia's brain is off mulling over her love life, Vernon's attitudes, his rejection of her original lyric, anything that means she doesn't have to get down to work. Perhaps they should get to know each other properly first. I mean, how can people work together if they don't know each other? She proposes that he take her to dinner. No, it's not a date; no it's not a business dinner—it's just dinner. Tomorrow she and Leon are seeing their psychiatrist, then the next night is Leon's birthday, but she can make tonight. He gives in and, while she goes off on to another cloud to muse what he'd think of her "If He Really Knew Me," he calls up the restaurant.

When she goes, he picks up her stream of thought. She's a handful, but she might be hit material and he needs a new hit. She's also an hour and a half late for dinner because she's had a scene with Leon who doesn't want to leave. He's hysterical and maybe she should go back. This looks like the third time they aren't going to get past the first five minutes of a meeting but, when Vernon mentions Natalie Klein, his last fiancée, Sonia gets interested. He's going to be personal, spill out his personality to her. But he doesn't. He gets ratty and goes to leave and then she's really caught. Here's a person coming out at last.

They dance and he can't, which makes her feel even better, especially as their eyes meet and something happens. Unfortunately that something makes her think guiltily about Leon, and she tells him that she'll have to go. But he isn't listening to her, he's listening to the music. It's his music. His first big hit ("They're Playing My Song") and suddenly he's all switched on and telling her all about Natalie Klein, only now she's not listening because they're playing her big number. Whatever, the ice is well and truly crushed now. They're both talking happily and Sonia hasn't thought about Leon for five whole minutes. Why don't they work right away, at her place. Only Leon's there. Vernon switches off and Sonia sees it. She tells him to come in an hour. She'll have Leon out by then. And she does.

When he turns up, she's finally done the deed, but she needs to talk about it. Will he pretend to be her psychiatrist for a little? So he does, and she talks and she talks, while he thinks about himself ("If She Really Knew Me") until she stops and asks if he wants a turn. But Vernon is into self-analysis, as he demonstrates at length, and Sonia's mind starts to wander into "If He Really Knew Me." The total result of the evening is a question: Do they try to work this week on those five songs Barbra needs, or do they go to his friends' beach house for a nonworking weekend? The beach house wins hands down and, as Vernon leaves, Sonia decides that this is all starting out "Right." Come the weekend, off they go and it still looks right. But it's a long drive and Sonia is worried that her plants will die because Leon isn't there to feed them. Then they get lost and the car engine floods and soon nothing is right.

They get to the beach, she breaks into the wrong house, and he is getting more neurotic by the minute, particularly when she insists on the thrill of making love in the wrong house on the wrong bed ("Just for Tonight"). But, just as they are about to get to grips with each other, the phone rings. Sonia had checked into her answering service with the number before she found out it was the wrong house and Leon is calling. While she calms her quivering ex, Vernon goes out to settle in to the right house. Sonia puts down the phone and follows him, making a great effort to ignore the phone as it once again starts to peal with distress.

Act 2

Back in New York, Vernon can't sleep. He's in love. And while he can't sleep, the doorbell rings. It's Sonia's suitcases. Leon has turned up at her apartment in a terrible state so she couldn't throw him out. On the other hand, after what happened between her and Vernon over the weekend she couldn't very well stay there with him. So she's suggesting that she moves in with Vernon. He is flabbergasted. Actually, he was going to ask her to move in so she's sort of short-circuited him. But he loves her ("When You're in My Arms") so why not?

Moving in at least means that Sonia isn't late any more. It also means that they spend day and night working, which wasn't her idea of how things were going to be, but it's all right. They don't go out, because everything they want is here. Then, one night at 2.45 A.M., the phone goes. It's Leon and he's having a big one. Sonia is distraught. She has to go to him. So, while Vernon climbs up the wall with fury, she borrows five dollars for the cab fare and sets off back to her old apartment.

She doesn't turn up at the hour appointed next morning to cut the demo for their new song, and, when she finally does arrive, the first part of the little bit of session time left turns into a debate on Leon. Vernon makes her promise in writing never to take a call from Leon again, which makes Sonia furious and suddenly they find themselves questioning their whole relationship, work and love. It isn't working. Maybe the working's working, but the whole thing isn't. It's time to call it off. Well, at least they got some songs out of it. And they may as well lay down the last one. It's called "I Still Believe in Love."

While the song climbs the charts, Vernon is in Los Angeles. To be precise he's in Cedars Sinai Hospital with a broken leg after being knocked down on Sunset Boulevard, and who should come to visit him but Sonia. It's a real coincidence. She only just heard about his accident and she was coming here anyhow because Leon is in the same hospital having his white cells counted. She's brought him a present—a little baby toy piano. They like seeing each other again and, when she goes, he wonders if she mightn't once again "Fill in the Words" to the tune he is playing on his little piano.

December comes and Sonia gets a call from Leon. It's a very odd call. He's got a job and he's calling to see if *she* is all right. With the New York snow comes Vernon. He's still walking with a stick, but he's whole and he's back in town. As it happens, he met Leon while they were in the hospital and they had a good talk. They talked about Sonia a lot, but they also talked about themselves and themselves in relation to Sonia. Leon has a girlfriend now and he has given Vernon permission to ring him at 3 A.M. if he feels the need.

Sonia is off to London the next day to meet some guy who is going to be the new Elton John. Vernon is going into analysis, as it seems to have done a lot for Leon. So they say goodbye. But he comes back. He has dropped his stick down a sewer and can't get home. Actually, he hasn't done anything of the sort, but he wanted an excuse to come back. Couldn't Sonia stay in New York and try writing with the new Vernon Gersch instead of going to Britain for the new Elton John? And couldn't he stay the night? Of course. If he'd tried to leave again, she'd have broken his other leg.

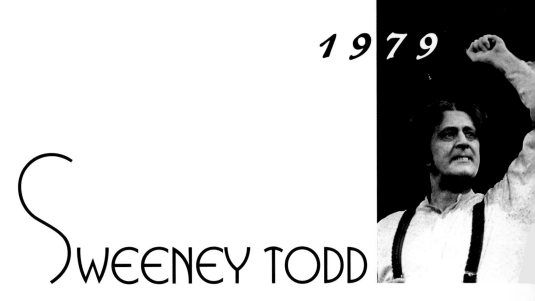

1979

Sweeney Todd

THE DEMON BARBER OF FLEET STREET. A MUSICAL THRILLER IN TWO ACTS by Hugh Wheeler based on a play by Chris Bond. Music and lyrics by Stephen Sondheim.

Produced at the Uris Theatre, New York, 1 March 1979, with Len Cariou (Sweeney Todd), Angela Lansbury (Mrs. Lovett), Victor Garber (Anthony), Sarah Rice (Johanna), and Edmund Lyndeck (Judge Turpin).

A television film was produced by RKO/Nederlander in 1982 with George Hearn, Lansbury, Cris Groenendaal, Betsy Joslyn, and Lyndeck.

. . . .

CHARACTERS

Sweeney Todd

Anthony Hope

Mrs. Lovett

A Beggar Woman

Judge Turpin

The Beadle

Johanna

Tobias Ragg

Pirelli

Jonas Fogg, etc.

An unwholesome alliance: the pie-making
Mrs. Lovett (Angela Lansbury) and
Sweeney Todd (Len Cariou), the demon barber
of Fleet Street, whose victims are madame's mincemeat.
Photograph © Martha Swope.

As a prelude to the action, "The Ballad of Sweeney Todd" introduces the famous tale of the demon barber of Fleet Street

Act 1   Down at the London docks, two men, newly arrived from across the sea, greet the city with different feelings ("There's No Place Like London"). For young Anthony Hope it is a welcome Britain after long travels abroad, but for Sweeney Todd the country and the city clearly have other and less kindly memories. As they take their leave of each other, the men are accosted by a crazy beggar woman who alternately begs miserable alms and crudely offers herself for sale. Todd harshly sends her on her way. Anthony, who has known him as a strong and kind man, is bewildered by his cruelty but Sweeney Todd is not the same man in London as he was at sea. To him, London is a great black pit inhabited by the vermin of the earth. In London there once took place the dreadful tale of "The Barber and His Wife"; he naïve, she young and beautiful and desired by a powerful man. It is a bad, sad story, and one without an end.

Todd makes his way toward Fleet Street. Looking about him, remembering, he marches on until he comes upon a certain shop where a beldam known as Mrs. Lovett sells what she admits are "The Worst Pies in London." He samples her pies and makes inquiries about the room above her shop. It is to let. No one wants it, for once a nasty thing happened there. There was a nice young barber with a little daughter and, above all, with a silly, pretty wife who took the fancy of a Judge and his Beadle ("Poor Thing"). The Judge and the Beadle arranged for the barber to be transported on a trumped-up charge and inveigled the pure, silly woman to a masked ball at the Judge's home. There she was raped and her child taken from her. The woman killed herself and the barber was never seen again, but the Judge still keeps the child, Johanna, as he has for fifteen years.

Before the tale is told, Mrs. Lovett has no doubts as to the identity of her visitor. He may have a different name, but it is the barber. Todd does not deny it. He has survived fifteen years of exile buoyed up by the hope of returning at last to his wife and child, and now the one is dead and the other alienated. Fifteen years of dashed hope merit a terrible revenge. Mrs. Lovett is cynical—how can a penniless ex-convict wreak revenge on the high and wealthy?—but she is also sympathetic and she can provide him, at least, with the means to keep himself alive. All those years ago, from the abandoned room she took the barber's razors and she has kept them close for the day of his return. Sweeney

Todd can go back to his old trade. Lovingly fingering the blades, Todd addresses them as "My Friends," while Mrs. Lovett simperingly impresses on him that she, too, is his friend.

From the uppermost window of Judge Turpin's house, lovely young Johanna sings to the birdseller's caged creatures ("Green Finch and Linnet Bird") below, and, as she sings, she is seen by Anthony who is passing by in the street. He is immediately taken by her beauty ("Ah, Miss"), and, when the beggar woman passes, he asks her who the girl is and whose the house. He buys a bird and offers it to the gentle Johanna who shyly descends to accept the gift, but the Judge catches her and threateningly warns the young man away from his "daughter." It is too late. Anthony has fallen in love, and he has made up his mind that he will steal "Johanna" from the Judge's clutches.

In St. Dunstan's Place, Sweeney Todd comes to make a reputation. There, a quasi-Italian barber, Pirelli by name, gives a fashionable shave while also purveying to a gullible crowd "Pirelli's Miracle Elixir." Todd mocks the properties of the elixir and turns the crowd against it and against Pirelli, and, when the mountebank tries to bluff his way back to favor, challenges him to a shaving and tooth-pulling contest.

Pirelli puts up a showy but inefficient performance (The Contest), but Todd quickly and cleanly completes both operations, winning the contest and the admiration of both the crowd and of Beadle Bamford who has been seconded to judge the match. All are invited to be shaved at Sweeney Todd's new establishment in Fleet Street. Already Todd's first hook is baited and the Beadle seems near to taking it, but he does not come to be shaved. Todd, though business is good, begins to fret. Mrs. Lovett has to keep him calm, advising him to "Wait." His chance for revenge will come.

One visitor who does come brings a surprise. It is Anthony and he is full of the story of the lovely maiden whom he intends to carry off from her cruel parent. When the name of Johanna falls from his lips, Todd does not blench, and he and Mrs. Lovett agree that Anthony may hide his love in the shop once she has been freed. The next to come to the barber's shop is Pirelli. While his little assistant, Tobias, waits in Mrs. Lovett's shop, the phoney Italian goes upstairs to try a little blackmail. He has recognized Todd and intends to profit from it. But he has underestimated his man. Whilst Mrs. Lovett feeds the simple Tobias on pies and gin, Todd strangles the blackmailer.

In the meanwhile, Judge Turpin has decided that he will marry the lovely young Johanna himself. The girl is distraught and, when Anthony manages to climb to her room, she pours out her heart to him. As he takes his fill of kisses ("Kiss Me") they decide to make their escape that night.

Turpin confides his marriage plan to the Beadle, who suggests that, for the girl's sake and ultimately his own satisfaction, the Judge should take care to look his best ("Ladies in Their Sensibilities") and recommends him to try the shop of

Sweeney Todd for a fine shave. Thus, while Johanna and Anthony are plotting to elope to the room above the pie shop, the Judge and the Beadle are heading to that selfsame room on professional business.

Pirelli's corpse is cooling in a chest when Turpin takes his seat in the barber's chair. He is in merry form and, to Sweeney Todd's echoing, he sings lecherously of "Pretty Women." But just as Todd is about to slice his razor through the Judge's throat, Anthony arrives crying the news of his plans. All is lost. The elopement is discovered and the Judge will now never return to the barber who is so obviously in league with this thieving boy.

Todd's chance of revenge is forever gone and in his dreadful disappointment he rages wildly at Mrs. Lovett ("Epiphany"). But, Judge or no Judge, there is still a present problem to be solved. Pirelli's body must be disposed of. Mrs. Lovett finds it almost a crime to bury so much nice, plump person. She really could use him, the price of meat being what it is. She giggles over the possibilities of her pies containing such ingredients ("A Little Priest") and Todd joins her song as he begins to plan a career supplying raw materials to her gruesome kitchen.

Act 2   Mrs. Lovett's trade has much improved and, with the aid of young Tobias, who has stayed with her since the mysterious disappearance of his master, she runs a moderately successful ale garden ("God, That's Good"). There is success upstairs too. The barbershop is booming and Sweeney Todd is able to afford to install an elaborate new barber's chair. From a trapdoor under the chair, a chute runs down to the basement where Mrs. Lovett's bakehouse produces the pies. It is quite a production line. Todd no longer kills only for revenge and safety, he kills for profit and, as he kills, he thinks of Johanna and takes revenge on the whole world for his and her sufferings. Anthony, too, thinks of Johanna and he wanders the streets of London looking for her, but the Judge has immured the child in an asylum and, when Anthony finally tracks her down, he comes up against Beadle Bamford who tries to have him arrested.

The beggar woman has not gone away. She has been seen hanging around Mrs. Lovett's shop and at night, as she watches the smoke coming from the bakehouse, she cries crazily of mischief ("City on Fire"). No one takes heed of her. No one knows that the crazy woman sees what goes on while sane folk sleep.

Mrs. Lovett's prosperity continues to grow. She sports ribbons and favors being flirtatious with Todd ("By the Sea"), but his mind dwells still on Judge

Turpin and revenge rots in his heart. He is full of venomous joy when Anthony brings the news of Johanna's whereabouts, and he plots for the boy to get her out by penetrating the gates of the madhouse disguised as a wigmaker sent to buy the hair of the madwomen. As soon as Anthony has gone to carry out the deed, Todd pens a letter to the Judge designed to lure him to the barber's shop. He writes that Anthony has abducted Johanna and is bringing her to his shop. There they may be caught red-handed.

So far, all the activities in Fleet Street have gone without a hitch, but a chink in the secret of Todd's work is about to appear. The boy Tobias has become foolishly fond of Mrs. Lovett and he fears for her ("No One's Going to Harm You") as he mistrusts Todd. His mistrust is deepened when he catches sight of Pirelli's purse, souvenired by Mrs. Lovett, and recalls that his former master disappeared in Todd's shop. His discovery makes Mrs. Lovett uneasy. She takes Tobias into the basement. For a treat she will let him make the pies. She shows him the big red oven and the meat grinder. As soon as a batch of meat comes in, he can begin to work. She leaves him to wait, and as she leaves she locks the door. Tobias will never come out again.

When she returns to her parlor, she finds she has a visitor. Beadle Bamford is sitting at her harmonium accompanying himself in some Parlor Songs. In between the songs he questions her. There have been complaints about the smell from her chimneys. He'll have to look at her bakehouse. She pretends that Todd has the key and is away, but when Todd returns unexpectedly she pointedly recommends that he give the Beadle a nice free shave.

Down in the bakehouse, Tobias has made an unusual discovery: A fingernail in a pie. He is fascinated by the chute, too, and very soon he discovers its purpose. As Mrs. Lovett pounds away on the harmonium, the slashed body of Beadle Bamford shoots down the chute and out onto the floor. Only now dares Mrs. Lovett tell Todd that their conspiracy has a new member, that Tobias is in on the whole affair, but Todd has no care for Tobias. At last his real revenge has begun: He has had the Beadle and the Judge will follow soon. At the madhouse, Anthony almost fumbles the plot. He drops his gun at the crucial moment, and it is the wretched Johanna who shoots down the proprietor of the asylum. As the lovers escape, the lunatics pour out onto the streets of London. Anthony and Johanna make their way to the barber's shop to find it empty, and Johanna waits there, disguised as a sailor boy, while Anthony runs off to find them a coach.

Todd has headed for the basement with Mrs. Lovett to deal with Tobias. But, outside the shop, the ever-watching beggar woman wanders about, calling for the Beadle. He went into the house and he didn't come out. Curious and crazy, she climbs the stairs to Todd's room and the frightened Johanna hides in the same chest that once sheltered Pirelli's body. The beggar woman looks about her. This room brings back the strangest memories. But she has little time to set her crazy thoughts in order for suddenly Todd is there and he is in an exulting haste. The

Judge is approaching. This madwoman cannot be allowed to foil his plan. The razor flies as he slits the poor creature's throat and tumbles her down the chute.

Now the hour of triumph comes. At last, Judge Turpin is in his room, puffed-up and proud, awaiting the girl he desires. Todd proffers a splash of bay rum, and the Judge takes the chair. As they sing together of "Pretty Women," Todd prepares his coup. Then it is time. He reveals himself to Turpin as the barber he so fiercely wronged and vengefully brings the blade down across the Judge's throat. Only when his revenge is complete and he is headed down the stairs does he remember Tobias. He returns to the barbershop for his razor and finds Johanna who, thinking him gone, has climbed out from the chest. Sweeney's eyes do not see his beloved daughter. They see only a young sailor, a young sailor who must have seen what happened. But as he seats the boy in the barber's chair he hears screams from below. It is Mrs. Lovett.

Rushing to the basement, he finds her caught in the grip of the hard-dying Turpin. Together they drag the bodies to the furnace, but Mrs. Lovett will not let him touch the beggar woman. Suddenly Todd knows who that demented crone was. She was his Lucy, his beautiful wife, and Mrs. Lovett had known it all along. It was his dear wife and, because Mrs. Lovett lied, he killed the one person in the world he really loved.

Mrs. Lovett defends herself frantically. Lucy did take poison, as she had said, but she did not die. She lived on with her wits gone. What use to anyone is a woman like that, compared to one such as herself. He can have her. Todd takes her in his arms and begins to dance and, when they dance past the oven, it takes only a twist of his strong arm to hurl Mrs. Lovett into the very furnace that baked her dreadful pies.

He turns back to the body of his Lucy, to cradle it in his arms, as little Tobias emerges from the shadows. What he has seen has taken the child's mind away, but he knows that Todd has harmed people and that he is bad. Lifting the razor from where Todd let it fall, he approaches the grieving man. Sweeney Todd is murdered with the same weapon with which he cut so many a throat. When Johanna and Anthony bring the police, they find the boy grinding away at the mincing machine. It is the end of the tale of Sweeney Todd.

1979

EVITA

A MUSICAL IN TWO ACTS by Tim Rice. Music by Andrew Lloyd Webber.

Produced at the Broadway Theatre, New York, 25 September 1979, with Patti LuPone (Eva), Mandy Patinkin (Che), Bob Gunton (Peron), Mark Syers (Magaldi), and Jane Ohringer (Mistress).

Originally produced at the Prince Edward Theatre, London, 21 June 1978.

On the balcony of the Casa Rosada, President Juan Peron (Bob Gunton) and his wife, Evita (Patti LuPone), celebrate their election victory before the people of Buenos Aires. Photograph © Martha Swope.

CHARACTERS

Eva Peron

Juan Peron

Che

Peron's mistress

Magaldi, *a tango singer*, etc.

Act 1

It is 26 July 1952. In a cinema in Buenos Aires, Argentina, a B-movie crawls groaningly to a halt and an announcement over the sound system informs the watching public that "Eva Peron, spiritual leader of the nation, entered immortality at 20.25 hours today." In silence, the audience leaves.

As the crowds gather for Eva's funeral, we are introduced to a man whom we will know as Che: a man who represents a combination of every feeling ever held against Eva Peron the politician and Eva Peron the woman. He mocks the funeral procession ("O What a Circus!"), jeering at its waste of pomp and feeling on behalf of a woman who was nothing but an actress, an actress who made the people believe her to be their Santa Evita when all the time she did nothing for them. He mocks, too, the poor people of Argentina who almost believed their Eva to be immortal and who, now that she is gone, are without guidance. Then he leads us back to the beginning of the life story of Eva Maria Duarte, later Peron and the Evita of millions.

It begins in a small Argentine town. Eva is fifteen when she meets a man whom Che glorifies with the title of "the first man to be of use to Eva Duarte." He is Agustin Magaldi, a tango singer ("On This Night of a Thousand Stars") from Buenos Aires. Eva has compliantly brightened up his provincial engagement and now she exacts her price: She wants to go back to the city with him. He warns her of the dangers of city life ("Eva, Beware of the City") but she is not daunted. The glamor of the city is what she wants, and she gets her way. Soon she arrives excitedly in "Buenos Aires."

It is not long before she disentangles herself from Magaldi. He has served his purpose and she is moving on ("Goodnight and Thank You"). Her moves onward are inevitably upward as she begins to make a small career as an actress, largely on the radio, but her big move is yet to come. Argentinian politics are in a parlous state. The time is ripe for change, and one of the foremost figures at the center of these changes is the increasingly powerful Juan Peron ("The Art of the Possible"). At a charity concert where Magaldi is performing and Peron speaking, Eva introduces herself with intent to the military-man-turned-politician. He is attracted, she is determined ("I'd Be Surprisingly Good for You") and they leave together.

Eva removes Peron's sixteen-year-old mistress from his bed with practiced ease ("Another Suitcase in Another Hall"), and installs herself in the girl's place. She is a strong and potentially powerful woman and a positive force in Peron's life and, as such, she is welcomed by neither Peron's army associates nor by the upper classes of Argentina ("Peron's Latest Flame"). Peron's position among the uncentered ruling military oligarchy is a key one, one that has allowed him to build up a following among the working classes, but one that has, equally, brought him many opponents ("Dice Are Rolling"). Eva pushes and persuades him toward taking supreme power with the support of the people to create "A New Argentina."

Act 2 By the time of the 1946 election, Eva Duarte has become Eva Peron and Evita to the admiring and loving people to whom she has tirelessly carried her husband's candidature. His victory and appointment as President of Argentina are announced "On the Balcony of the Casa Rosada." When he has spoken to the assembled crowds, Eva addresses them in her turn, emphasizing with consummate skill the Perons's position as the people's choice, taken from among the people themselves, and yet setting them up as unapproachable deities ("Don't Cry for Me, Argentina"). To an officer who reminds her that statesmanship is more than entertaining peasants, she replies, "We shall see, little man," before returning to the balcony to regale her people with promises of despoiling the aristocracy to give them all they could desire.

Soon, at the age of twenty-six, she is an important part of Argentina, a figurehead and a saint, "High Flying, Adored." She does not intend to stop there. She intends to take herself and Argentina to the world ("Rainbow High"). Equipped in style, Eva sets off for Europe ("Rainbow Tour"). Spain greets her with unbelievable enthusiasm, but from there on it is downhill. Even a beautiful woman cannot interest major nations in a government they consider either unimportant or unpleasant. The biggest snub comes from Britain, and Eva returns to Argentina in anger rather than triumph to take revenge on the British-centered aristocracy of Argentina ("The Actress Hasn't Learned the Lines You'd Like to Hear") under the pretense of encouraging democracy.

One part of this revenge is the creation of the Eva Peron Foundation, a charity to eclipse all other charities and their aristocratic patrons. By dint of persuasion, not necessarily gentle, the Foundation grows to enormous proportions ("And the Money Kept Rolling In") as Eva continues her work and her tireless quest for both personal success and the sort of cockeyed democracy she apparently believes in ("Santa Evita").

Che faces up to Eva ("Waltz for Eva and Che") to belittle both her work and her image. She replies, with what seems to be an attempt at honesty, that it is better to attempt to do something positive toward curing the world's ills than simply to stand aside and mock. But even in centuries she could not accomplish what she would want to, and she does not have centuries. She has very little time indeed, for she is a dying woman. Peron is not unaware that his wife is his greatest attribute ("She's a Diamond"), and that he will be in trouble without her.

Once again "Dice Are Rolling" and the political situation is on the move, but Eva is not yet ready to give up. She insists on becoming vice president, on having official political recognition, but Peron cannot make this happen. It would be far too dangerous politically and, besides, she could not physically manage it for she is desperately ill. But still she fights (Eva's Sonnet).

It is her last fight, however, and, as the jeering Che is only too happy to remind her, this time she has lost. The dying woman takes to the radio waves to turn down the offer of vice presidency that was never made (Eva's Last Broadcast) as, once again, she rolls out the loving phrases of her Casa Rosada speech: "Don't Cry for Me, Argentina." Thus Evita Peron dies, as fragments from the story of her life crowd around her (Montage). Her final words (Lament) express no regrets. She could have lived with less speed and less intensity and she might then have lived longer, but she chose otherwise. She hopes that those who follow her will understand what she did. For Eva Duarte longed to be remembered.

1980

42ND STREET

A MUSICAL IN TWO ACTS by Michael Stewart and Mark Bramble based on the screenplay and the novel by Bradford Ropes. Lyrics by Al Dubin. Music by Harry Warren.

Produced at the Winter Garden Theatre, New York, 25 August 1980, with Jerry Orbach (Julian Marsh), Lee Roy Reams (Billy), Wanda Richert (Peggy), and Tammy Grimes (Dorothy), and played from 30 March 1981 at the Majestic Theatre.

BROADS EET STATION

CHARACTERS

Andy Lee

Maggie Jones, *one of the authors of "Pretty Lady"*

Bert Barry, *her collaborator*

Billy Lawlor, *juvenile lead in "Pretty Lady"*

Peggy Sawyer

Lorraine, Phyllis, Annie, *chorus girls*

Julian Marsh, *Broadway producer*

Dorothy Brock, *a star*

Abner Dillon, *a manufacturer*

Pat Denning

Oscar, Mac, Doctor, etc.

The producer (Jerry Orbach), writers, and cast of Broadway's "Pretty Lady" woo chorine Peggy Sawyer (Claire Leach) back to the bright lights with a "Lullaby of Broadway." Photograph © Martha Swope.

Act 1

The word is round the gipsy cafés and dance classes of New York City that Julian Marsh is doing a new show. So it's out with your tap shoes and down to the 42nd Street Theatre where the auditions for *Pretty Lady* are taking place (Audition/"42nd Street").

The audition is over and the chorus girls and boys who have been selected are having their names taken when a young girl bursts onto the stage. Peggy Sawyer has come to audition but, because she couldn't pluck up the nerve to walk through the stage door till now, she's missed her chance. Or she would have, except that in her unusual entrance she has caught the eye of the show's young leading man, Billy Lawlor ("I'm Young and Healthy"). He is very taken with her and promises to help her catch the dance director's eye but, when he sets her singing, the response from the powers-that-hire is simply overworked irritation. Peggy is ordered from the theatre and, as she makes an exit as unorthodox as her entrance, she runs straight into the show's revered producer, Julian Marsh, who has come to give his prerehearsal pep talk to the boys and girls.

The star of the show is to be the experienced Dorothy Brock. Perhaps the word "experienced" is a bit kind; aging would be more to the point. But Brock's devoted admirer, kiddie-car magnate Abner Dillon, is the show's principal backer and therefore Brock is to be the star. When she arrives, it is evident that the star is a role she intends to play up to the hilt, but she has a tough opponent in Julian Marsh who, in spite of her open threats to walk out and take Dillon's cash with her, will not allow himself to be ordered about. Brock is handed a song to try and, sulkily, she starts "The Shadow Waltz." The rehearsals of *Pretty Lady* have begun.

In a break at rehearsals, Brock meets an old friend who is more than just an old friend. Pat Denning was her partner in vaudeville before she became famous. He was her lover then and she is still in love with him now, but she is not willing to risk losing Dillon and his money and the opportunity to star again in *Pretty Lady*, so Pat has to be kept out of the way. They can only arrange snatched meetings at times when Dillon is not around.

In the same break, Peggy Sawyer comes back. In her hurried exit that morning she left her purse behind. Kindly Maggie Jones, the author of the show, has found it and has noticed how little is in it so, as she returns the purse, she invites Peggy to join her and some of the other girls for a dancer's lunch at the nearby tearoom. Peggy is only too happy to accept. To get their dancer's lunch from Maggie, those girls have to dance their way to the tea rooms. Wisecracking Annie leads off and is stunned when little Peggy Sawyer manages to accomplish even the most difficult steps with bravura. She's good!

When lunch is done and the girls spill back out on to 42nd Street, they're dancing again ("Go into Your Dance") and Peggy is winning admiring looks all around until Julian Marsh hustles his chorus back to rehearsal. But wait! Something has gone wrong. The chorus is one girl short. What can be done? There is the big Boardwalk number to set this very afternoon and Mr. Marsh doesn't have a full company. He has a good mind to take the first girl who walks along the street. Peggy, about to wander off into unemployment and disenchantment, fortunately has good hearing. She makes darned sure that she is the first girl who walks by. Can she dance? Can she *dance*? She can do every tap step ever invented and, just to prove it, she does, right there in the middle of the street. So Peggy Sawyer is hired for *Pretty Lady* after all.

At the afternoon rehearsal, Brock plays a love scene with Billy under the inhibiting eye of Dillon and then goes into her song "You're Getting to Be a Habit with Me." Peggy has been hurried into the number without sufficient preparation and she goes disastrously wrong in the dance break, fraying the star's already ragged temper badly, but she escapes the consequences when she faints as a result of her efforts and has to be carried into Brock's dressing room to recover.

Pat Denning is there, awaiting a rendezvous with Dorothy, and he helps out by carrying the inanimate girl to a daybed, but it doesn't do anything to calm Brock's feelings when she walks in to find him bending over the recovering Peggy. A scene is averted, but then Dillon bursts in and Denning has to be passed off as Peggy's boyfriend while Dorothy is sent off to be sweet to the money man. The situation is worrying. Too much is riding on *Pretty Lady* for the show to be put at risk by Brock playing around with a vaudeville fellow. Brock won't promise not to see Pat Denning, so Julian takes the only way out. He telephones a friendly gangster. If Denning won't stay away, he must be scared away. Pat takes the point quickly and suddenly finds that he has an urgent job in Philadelphia. Without even waiting to say goodbye to Dorothy, he leaves. What Pat doesn't know is that the out-of-town tryout of *Pretty Lady* has been rescheduled. Instead of opening in Atlantic City, the show is going to make its bow at the Arch Street Theatre in Philadelphia ("Getting Out of Town").

At the final rehearsal ("Dames"), Brock throws a tantrum. Since she can't dance, she has been fairly obviously left out of the big production number and, her nerves on edge over the Pat Denning affair, she takes the dance arrangement as a personal insult. At the party that evening, she drinks too much and tells Dillon what she thinks of him, causing a chaos that can only be assuaged by the attentions of Maggie and every available chorus girl.

Dorothy rushes to her room to start ringing all around town trying to find Pat. She cannot be allowed to find him. Once again, Julian gets on the phone to gangsterland, but this time he is overheard by Peggy who hurries to Dorothy's room to pass on a warning. When she gets there, Pat has already arrived and the jealous Dorothy sees in Peggy's well-meant attentions the signs of something more. She drunkenly orders both of them out of her room before collapsing into a love song ("I Know Now").

Somehow, everyone makes it to the opening night ("I Know Now"/"We're in the Money"), and, as the show progresses, *Pretty Lady* seems certain to be a hit. Then, as Dorothy launches into "42nd Street," a dancer stumbles and pushes Peggy into her path. The star, unable to avoid the girl, falls and does not get up. The curtain comes down and, as a furious Julian Marsh fires the offending Peggy on the spot, an announcement goes out to the front-of-house that Dorothy Brock will not be able to continue. The performance has been abandoned.

Act 2 It is soon clear that it is not only that performance but the whole production that will have to be abandoned. Brock's injury is a broken ankle, and there is no way that she will be able to take her part in *Pretty Lady*. The kids are out of a job, but busy convincing themselves that "There's a Sunny Side to Every Situation," when Annie comes up with an idea. Why close? Why not just replace Brock? Why, right here in the company they have someone who sings a storm, is as pretty as paint, and could dance rings around Brock even when her ankle wasn't broken: Peggy Sawyer!

Annie leads a deputation to Julian Marsh and it doesn't take too long before he is convinced. It is worth a try. They will close down in Philadelphia and head right back to New York to revamp the show as a vehicle for Peggy. The only thing is that she's gone. He sacked her. Well, in that case it's up to him to get her back.

Julian Marsh dons his hat and heads for Broad Street Station and there he finds Peggy, sitting on her suitcase on the platform. All the fire has gone out of her. She is going back to Allentown and forgetting all about show business. Julian takes it on himself to relight the fire with visions of Broadway ("Lullaby of Broadway"), which are soon echoed by the whole company until Peggy, suddenly in love with it all again, agrees. She will do it. She will be the star of *Pretty Lady* on Broadway.

Now begins the slog, the learning of the new songs and the new dances under the unyielding direction of Julian Marsh until the girl is almost falling apart with tiredness. Finally, the big day comes, and, as Peggy prepares herself for the performance, she receives an unexpected visitor, Dorothy Brock. Brock has been watching the rehearsal and she has been able to see Peggy's talent shining out. She has come to wish her good luck and to give her a little tip about the singing of the last but one number ("About a Quarter to Nine"). She can afford to be generous for the broken ankle has turned out to be a blessing in disguise: It made her realize that stardom was not as important as love, and that morning she has married Pat Denning.

With the chorus kids willing her on and Julian Marsh's words ringing behind her—"You're going out there a youngster, but you've got to come back a star!"—Peggy Sawyer goes on to the stage at the 42nd Street Theatre with the whole of *Pretty Lady* riding on her aching back (Overture/"Shuffle Off to Buffalo"). The performance comes to a climax with the performance of the "42nd Street" scena and the curtain falls on a triumph. *Pretty Lady* is a smash and Peggy Sawyer is a star. She is invited to a big party at the Ritz to celebrate but, as everyone hurries off, she remains on stage to thank the man who made it all possible, Julian Marsh. Now that she is a star, can she do what she wants? Of course she can. In that case she isn't going to the Ritz, she's going to the chorus kids' party. And perhaps he might come too? Perhaps he might. Anything can happen in this crazy world of the theatre on "42nd Street."

The songs in the Broadway stage version of *42nd Street* include, apart from those from the film version, Warren/Dubin material from *Go into Your Dance, Gold Diggers of 1933, Dames, The Singing Marine*, and *Hard to Get*.

DREAMGIRLS

A MUSICAL IN TWO ACTS by Tom Eyen. Music by Henry Krieger.

Produced at the Imperial Theatre, New York, 20 December 1981, with Jennifer Holliday (Effie), Sheryl Lee Ralph (Deena), Loretta Devine (Lorrell), Ben Harney (Curtis Taylor, Jr.), and Cleavant Derricks (Early). Played at the Ambassador Theatre, 28 June 1987, with Lillias White, Alisa Gyse, Arnetta Walker, Weyman Thompson, and Herbert L. Rawlings, Jr.

The dollified Dreams are on their way to fame, but, when the dollifying goes too far, oversized Effie (Jennifer Holliday, left) gets the chop.
Photograph © Martha Swope.

Act 1

Somewhere in the United States of America, in 1967, there is a talent contest taking place. Not a kiddie show, but a contest among a bunch of acts verging on the payable who are providing a nice cheap program for the manager of the Apollo Theatre, as a support to his real, professional topbiller, James "Thunder" Early. But Early is in a small stew. He's been fiddling around with his backing girls again, and they've had enough. They're walking out, right now, in the middle of the contest, ten minutes before Jimmy's due to go on, and just days before he starts a ten-weeks' tour.

In the middle of this drama, as the sounds of the contesting acts drift through to backstage, the group that should have been on number two, but didn't show, rushes in. Three girls who've trained all the way from Chicago and a hometown contest win to try to move up that last huge step to show business proper: Beautiful, bubbly Deena, baby Lorrell, and belligerently powerful Effie, the lead singer of the trio. They've even brought along Effie's brother, C. C., who writes their songs for them.

A little interference from the bystanding Curtis Taylor, Jr., who seems to carry weight with the MC, gets the girls a reschedule to last spot on the contest program, but Early's manager, Marty, cares nothing for the contest. He sees just one thing. Here are some instant backing singers for his star. Only it's not that easy. Although Deena and Lorrell are thrilled at the idea of singing the oohs and aahs behind James "Thunder" Early, Effie won't hear of it. They don't like doing backing. And, anyway, after they win this contest, they'll be far too busy doing their own act.

The girls knock out their number in style ("Move [You're Steppin' on My Heart]"), but they aren't going to win. That's already been arranged; Curtis Taylor, Jr. has slipped the MC $50 just to make sure. "Don't worry" he assures the worried Marty. The girls are under his exclusive management, and they'll do Early's backing.

When the contest result comes through, Effie is furious. They are getting right back on the train. But Taylor moves in quickly, with an offer of money to sing behind Early tonight and much more money to sing behind Early for ten weeks on the road. When Effie still proves unmovable, he takes her aside and ladles out the soft soap and the I'll-make-you-a-star talk. He wins. And in minutes the girls are on stage again, doing those oohs and aahs that make the harmonies in Early's "Fake Your Way to the Top."

The girls go fine, but Early's not happy with his reception. His material's worn through. He needs new stuff. Taylor is happy to oblige. He slips C. C. into the picture. This boy wrote the song the girls just sang. When Early shows that he might be impressed, Taylor moves swiftly into his act, selling the songwriter with all the patter of a slick salesman ("Cadillac Car").

So C. C. goes along with the girls and Early when the show goes on the road, and pretty soon they are putting down one of his numbers on record ("Cadillac Car"). It does all right. In fact, Early and his new girls are up to Number 27 on the charts when a better-known group covers the number and wipes them out. What went wrong? Why weren't they protected? Curtis swears it'll never happen again, even if he has to "get to know" every deejay from one side of America to the other personally. Marty reckons he's mad. He'll never do it. But apparently he does. When Jimmy Early and the Dreamettes come out with "Steppin' to the Bad Side" it gets played everywhere, and reaches Number 1.

Curtis is wheeling and dealing at a speed and on a level that is way beyond Marty. He's even talking about getting Jimmy and the girls into the Miami Atlantic Hotel. A black act in there? He has to be joking! And while he's wheeling and dealing, he's romancing Effie, just like Jimmy's romancing Lorrell. Everything seems to be rolling on oil, and before they know where they are, Miami's a go! ("Baby, Baby, Please").

While they're playing Miami, rumors start the round. Curtis has got Jimmy into the Americana in New York, but there's something about Cleveland. The girls are going to Cleveland? It's true. Curtis is breaking up the group. The girls are going out as an act on their own: the Dreams. Effie is full of happiness. Her man has done what he promised her. Now they're really on their way. But her happiness is short-lived. The lead singer of the Dreams isn't going to be Effie, it's going to be beautiful Deena. Curtis has it all worked out—a new sound, a new look.

Effie can't turn anywhere for support. Only the apparently powerless Marty seems to be on her side. It's all been worked out. Even C. C. was in on it. If they want to break into that mainstream pop field where the big dollars are, they need to change. They need a lighter tone than Effie's deep soul singing, and they need a more glamorous look. Her turn will come, C. C. promises, but right now it has to be someone else's turn. For the good of them all. But Effie's no good at thinking about the good of the "Family." She only knows that she's the best and she's the one who should be out front.

When the Dreams open at the Cleveland Crystal Room, Deena is out front and Effie is back with Lorrell ("Dreamgirls"). The act, and in particular, its beautiful and charming leading girl, make a huge success. Curtis is delighted. He was right. Now he'll make Deena into a huge star. And Effie's endless cries of "What about me?" go less and less heeded.

Before too long, Effie starts playing unprofessional. And one day, in the course of a television recording ("Heavy") she even walks off the set. Deena turns on her angrily, and Effie comes back in a rage: Deena's stolen her spot and she's stolen her man too. She knows what's going on between Deena and Curtis. The quarrels get more and more frequent, and worse and worse. As weeks go on, Effie takes to crying off sick, and at last in Las Vegas things come to a head. She rolls in late, on the night that Jimmy has chosen to pop in and catch the act, and right behind her comes Curtis in the company of a beautiful young woman. Effie is being replaced.

The accusations and rantings fly, but Effie hasn't a leg to stand on nor a friend left. She's alienated everyone. And anything and everything she might say can no longer make any difference. She tears her heart out in an impassioned plea to Curtis to love her ("And I am Telling You I'm Not Going"), but he turns his back on her and walks away. It's all over. And Deena Jones and the Dreams, without Effie White, go on to fame and fortune.

Act 2   It's 1972, and the Dreams and Deena are still at the top, with a bigger, glitzier, slicker act than ever. Back in Chicago, Marty is trying to get a job—any job—for Effie. It's not easy, because Effie went to pieces the last time she was given a chance to start over. And when Marty does finally get an old friend just to listen to her, she starts all over again with her pickiness and her grand airs: "I want." Even Marty finally hits back. Maybe Curtis was right—she's more of a pain than her talent justifies coping with. That finally pulls Effie up short. She'll try. She really will ("I am Changing").

At the top of the heap, however, all is not hunky dory. Curtis has got a fresh bit of image remaking all worked out, but this time he's got more than just an Effie White in disaccord. Curtis's new plan involves a change in the group's sound, and he's had their latest song arranged accordingly. But C. C. doesn't like it. It's his number, and he didn't write it to sound like that. And Deena, Mrs. Curtis Taylor, Jr., is not happy either. She's been offered a film role, and she'd like to take it. But that's not in Curtis's plans either. He tries to convince his hottest bit of property ("You're My Dream") and its seems that, for the moment at least, everything will be all right.

The Dreams and Jimmy Early meet up when they share a platform at a political fund-raising program, and Lorrell puts the hard word on Jimmy. Seven years now they've been a couple. When will he divorce his wife and marry her? ("Ain't No Party"). He won't. He can't. And he's got a song to go on and sing ("I Meant You No Harm").

Now the falling apart starts. First of all, C. C. decides to make the break. If Curtis won't let his song be sung the way he wrote it, he knows someone who will. Then Jimmy, more and more on the downward track and more and more discontented with the style of music he's being made to sing, throws a wild number into his program and drops his trousers on stage. He's out (The Firing of Jimmy); he's finished. And Lorrell is gone, because she's got a song to go on and sing.

C. C. goes to Effie and, with the path smoothed by Marty, the reconciliation is made. Effie records the number that was the cause of C. C.'s quarrel with Curtis ("One Night Only") and soon she's on the come-backwards trail. Effie's record starts to climb the charts, and Curtis sees red. He gets out his arrangement of "One Night Only" and has it recorded by Deena and the Dreams. As Deena's record starts to climb the charts, Effie's starts to tumble.

When the Dreams visit Chicago, Curtis Taylor gets an unwanted caller backstage. Or, rather, a group of callers—C. C., Marty, Effie, and one Mr. Morgan, a lawyer. They have documents to prove that Curtis has been cheating. The payola, bribing disc jockeys to play Deena's record and, above all, not to play Effie's. Its a jail-worthy crime.

By the time they have all finished with him, Curtis Taylor, Jr., has lost everything, even Deena, poor innocent Deena who never knew what tactics her husband had been using to bolster her career. She's not only walking off to her film job and leaving the Dreams but she's walking out of their marriage, too. But they let him save face. He's there in New York to present the last Dreams concert ("Its Hard to Say Goodbye My Love"). Then each of the girls goes off to make her own way in the next part of her professional and private lifes. Dreams don't last forever.

CATS

A MUSICAL based on *Old Possum's Book of Practical Cats* by T. S. Eliot. Music by Andrew Lloyd Webber.

Produced at the Winter Garden Theatre, New York, 7 October 1982, with Betty Buckley (Grizabella), Terrence V. Mann (Rum Tum Tugger), Stephen Hanan (Asparagus), Timothy Scott (Mr. Mistoffolees), Ken Page (Deuteronomy), Reed Jones (Skimbleshanks), Bonnie Simmons (Griddlebone), Christine Langner (Rumpleteazer), Rene Clemente (Mungojerrie), and Harry Groener (Munkustrap).

Originally produced at the New London Theatre, London, 11 May 1981.

Cats, cats, cats, and more cats.
Cats that go on forever.
Photograph © Martha Swope.

CHARACTERS

Asparagus/Growltiger

Bombalurina

Bustopher Jones

Demeter

Deuteronomy

Grizabella

Jellylorum

Griddlebone

Jennyanydots

Jemima

Macavity

Munkustrap

Mungojerrie

Mr. Mistoffolees

Rumpleteazer

Rumpus Cat

Rum Tum Tugger

Skimbleshanks

Victoria

Admetus, Alonzo, Carbucketty,
Cassandra, Coricopat, George,
Tantomile, Victor, Etcetera, Bill
Bailey, Tumblebrutus, Silabub,
Pouncival, Plato, Quaxo, etc.

Act 1

The playing area represents a gigantesque rubbish heap, here a supersized tin can, there a piece of Brobdignagian newspaper, a Titan's tire or the hood of an abandoned automobile made for someone much bigger than you or I. It looks just like an ordinary, if oversized, trash tip when the light of day is on it, but no sooner does darkness descend than this piece of ground comes alive. As the lights go down and the music begins, the twinkling eyes of numberless creatures can be seen on all sides and, around the rubbish dump, around your feet, rustle dark, slinking creatures with glittering eyes, moving lightly and quickly, to the accompaniment of strange yowling sounds. Then they freeze as a noise is heard and the headlights of a passing car send the animals fleeing back to the hiding places of the rubbish heap.

They are cats, these quiet, eagerly shining beasts who haunt the open spaces and the rubbish heaps of the world. Cats of all shapes, all sizes, and kinds, but every one a Jellicle (Prologue: "Jellicle Songs for Jellicle Cats"), members of that mysterious fraternity that can see in the dark, of that celebrated family that accompanied Dick Whittington, the Pied Piper, and every witch that ever rode a broomstick, of that feline family that always falls on its feet. There are inconveniences of course. When the brotherhood sings too loudly, someone is liable to throw an old boot at them, but it isn't long before they are back at their singing and dancing.

But wait a minute! Did we hear someone say that they don't know what a Jellicle Cat is? Well, perhaps a little explanation is due about a very private and personal (perhaps one should say cat-onal) subject—"The Naming of Cats." You might call your cat by a perfectly ordinary name but, underneath, every cat has another, special name; a name that is his and only his, and that name—which a human can never discover—is what makes him himself. So when you see a cat sitting, gazing into space, don't think he's mindlessly wasting his nine lives. He's actually reflecting on his name.

On the empty piece of ground amid the rubbish, one little white kitten (Victoria) stretches herself into some pretty, balletic poses, until the announcement comes: Tonight is the Jellicle Ball and every Jellicle cat is invited. There the Jellicle leader will lead the ball and make the annual Jellicle choice. One selected cat will be allowed to ascend to the Heaviside layer, there to be given the chance to live another life, for better or for worse. Which will it be? Which of the many cats whom we will now meet will be chosen for this rebirth?

The first personality—oh dear, cat-onality—we meet is "The Old Gumbie Cat." From under the rusting car bonnet emerges a plump little bundle of tabby-striped-spotted fur, spread into jolly rolls of wrinkles by too many days lazing in the sun or the firelight. Jennyanydots, for that is her real name, is not as lazy as it may seem. At night, when everyone is asleep, she gives self-improvement courses to the mice and cockroaches, and dances a mean tap-dance at the head of her forces. Then, because a little black and white pussy called Quaxo needs to show off his versatility, she abandons the jolly cockroaches and indulges in a tap competition with him before waving us goodbye.

Our next visitor is "The Rum Tum Tugger," a swaggering, pop-pussy who bursts through the back-cloth to set all the kittens off into ecstasies of squealing with his sexy prowl and Presley-ish cadenzas. He is a contrary cat, a fellow who always wants what he hasn't got, a fellow who doesn't even like a cuddle. What sort of a cat is that? Curious, but ooooh, what a cat.

The cavalcade of jolly cats halts as a stranger breaks through the party. It is "Grizabella, the Glamor Cat." Once a beauty, her alley-cat life has brought her down until she is nothing but a torn and stained outcast from whom the kittens shrink in dismay. She passes by, for she cannot stop in such an unfriendly place. But all places are equally unfriendly to Grizabella.

"Bustopher Jones" is much more the sort of cat we like. He is the cat of London's clubland; a sleek, overfed fellow with a bright white bib and shiny spats glistening on his smooth black coat; quite the gentleman, with his well-oiled whiskers and a carnation sprouting from his buttonhole. He is a total contrast to "Mungojerrie and Rumpleteazer" whose arrival is appropriately heralded by the siren of a police car. This bouncing duo are a couple of sneak-thieves—"knockabout clowns, quick-change comedians, tight-rope walkers, and acrobats"—the sort of cats who get into anything, anywhere, no matter how well you think you've locked up. Here is a real team of rascally cat burglars.

Now it is time to welcome the grand master of the cat lodge, the vast, placid, impressive "Old Deuteronomy" who takes his ponderous place at the center of affairs as the entertainment continues. This time we have a little story: Munkustrap's relating of "The Awefull Battle of the Pekes and the Pollicles," a fight among dogs that was settled (and its combatants set to flight) by the intervention of the great Rumpus Cat. As the story unfolds, the pekes with their little sacklike faces challenge the pollicles with their boxlike feet, and the slipper-headed pugs and the curly-wigged poms join in to make it a regular dog fight until, shooting forth from what seems to be the depths of the earth, comes the black, flailing figure of the frightful, red-eyed Rumpus Cat to end both the fight and the tale.

When the story is done the rumor goes nervously around that Macavity is nearby, but nothing happens and the fearful cats emerge from their hiding places to join in "The Song of the Jellicles," and a whispering, multicolored set of dances, which is "The Jellicle Ball." As the cats disport themselves, Grizabella watches painfully from a distance until she is chased off, leaving the other cats to dance the night away under the autumn colors of the moon while she has only a "Memory" of happiness left to her.

Act 2

The cats' evening continues as Deuteronomy muses on "The Moments of Happiness," and an old cat is led by a kindly helpmate to watch the festivities. This is Asparagus, otherwise known as Gus, and he is— or, rather, was—a theatre cat ("Gus, the Theatre Cat"). It is a career that has left him with a wealth of memories that he is only too pleased to recount to the younger generation. The great days of the theatre are gone; there is nothing now like the theatrical world under Irving and Tree, the world of which he was a part, where he trod the boards and had the distinction of understudying Dick Whittington's cat, and, best of all, of once appearing as Growltiger.

The story of "Growltiger's Last Stand," the heroic but desperate history of the piratical cat done to death by the beastly Siamese, is a dramatic one. The valiant Growltiger and his paramour, the Lady Griddlebone, were indulging in a private paroxysm of Italianate romance ("In una tepida notte") when the cowardly Easterners crept up on them. Alas, they did what no Englishman would do and attacked a man while he was making love. They took the lordly Growltiger prisoner and forced him to walk the plank, and, though his demise made a sad if salutory story, it made a wonderful, theatrical role. Not like the namby pamby parts cats get today.

Our next illustration is "Skimbleshanks, the Railway Cat." A bundle of cat-friends sing the story of his happy life on the railways of Britain as they drag items from the rubbish heap to build an imitation train, but their rollicking is ended by another strange, crashing noise and a hollow laugh. This time, surely, it is the dreaded Macavity. There he is! No . . . no . . . he's there! Over on the other side!

As the cats scatter, Demeter and Bombalurina hold their ground warily to sing about "Macavity, the Mystery Cat." He's surely to blame for many a cat crime, but you'll never catch him at it. Whenever the price of crime is to be paid, Macavity's not there. And, surely enough, he isn't. Just when you think you saw him scuttle off in one direction . . . there he is, laughing at you from the other side. And when you think you know that that bundle of elderly fur is Old Deuteronomy, you really shouldn't be surprised to see the fur coat pulled aside to reveal Macavity.

But if that is not Deuteronomy, where is he? There is one way to find out, you must ask the magical "Mister Mistoffolees." Here he comes, flying in from above, his black coat glittering with lights and flashpots at his fingertips, producing ribbons from an empty tin, flipping spots off a scarf, and throwing off fouettés as if he'd come from the Royal Ballet with the sole intention of displaying his repertoire of steps in one comprehensive dance spot. When he is done, he flings a red scarf over a kitten and, whipping it away, produces his magic. There stands Old Deuteronomy.

Now daylight is coming. It is time for the Jellicle Ball to end and for Deuteronomy to announce the name of the cat chosen to have a second chance, another set of lives. Grizabella walks on; she pours out the "Memory" that overflows from her sad heart and, having done so, she prepares to carry on, to leave this unsympathetic world. But the little white kitten stops her. Slowly she brings the sad, tattered cat back, and, as she leads Grizabella toward Deuteronomy, some of the other cats join her. For Grizabella is the cat who has been chosen. She will have another opportunity.

Deuteronomy takes her by the hand and leads her to an old tire, and, when they step together onto the punctured pneumatic, it begins to rise into the air. As they float above the ground, the sky opens, a staircase descends, and Grizabella steps on to it in a swirl of mist. Up, up she climbs and then she is gone. The tire returns to its place and Deuteronomy rounds off the proceedings with a little lecture on "The Addressing of Cats" as all the characters whom we have met during the evening crowd around to sing us farewell.

Joseph and the Amazing Technicolor Dreamcoat

A MUSICAL by Tim Rice. Music by Andrew Lloyd Webber.

Produced at the Royale Theatre, 27 January 1982, with Bill Hutton (Joseph), Laurie Beechman (Narrator), and Tom Carter (Pharaoh). Produced at the Minskoff Theatre, 9 November 1993, with Michael Damian, Kelli Rabke, and Robert Torti.

First performed at the Colet Court School, London, 1 March 1968. Produced in a theatre version at the Edinburgh Festival as part of *Bible One: Two Looks at the Book of Genesis*, 21 August 1972. Subsequently produced in a series of revised versions.

First American production at Cathedral College, Douglaston, Long Island, 3 October 1969. First produced on the American professional stage at the Brooklyn Academy of Music, 22 December 1976. The Broadway production was first mounted at the Entermedia Theatre, New York, 18 November 1981.

CHARACTERS

Jacob

Joseph, *his son*

Reuben, Simeon, Levi, Napthali, Isaachar, Asher, Dan, Zebulum, Gad, Judah, Benjamin, *his other sons*

Pharaoh

Potiphar, *a well-off Egyptian*,
Potiphar's wife,

Butler, Baker, etc.

"Close every door to me." Joseph at rock bottom: His amazing technicolor dreamcoat has been confiscated and he's been thrown in jail. But Jacob's little boy has some dreamy tricks up his very short sleeve. Photograph © Martha Swope.

The story begins in the land of Canaan, somewhere back near the beginning of the bible. A founding farmer called Jacob had a dozen sons ("Jacob and Sons") but he had an especially soft spot for one called Joseph, who reminded him of his favorite wife. This favoritism didn't make Joseph very popular with the other members of the family, and their antipathy toward their spoiled brother grew even stronger when their father gave a fantastic new coat to his number-one son. No more dowdy sheepskin like his brothers: Joseph's coat was a rainbow affair ("Joseph's Coat") and he stood out among his drably clad family like a happy bruise.

Unfortunately, Joseph had more ways of getting on his brothers' nerves than just showing off his gaudy topcoat. He had a habit of relating his dreams to them which would have been really boring if the dreams hadn't been quite so infuriatingly self-aggrandizing ("Joseph's Dreams"). The first one was about wheat. Safe enough? No. In this dream all the brothers have stooked their wheat at harvest time, and what happens but all their stooks start bowing to his one. Then they are all stars, only his star gets homage from all the rest, not to mention the sun and the moon. If you believed him and his dreams, it was clear that one day Joseph was going to have them all under his thumb. This would make life (and Joseph) even more unbearable than it and he were already, so the brothers decided there was only one answer and that was fratricide. They took Joseph out to a nice, distant place, ripped up his rotten coat, and tipped him into a pit to perish.

But fate was still on Joseph's side. At that moment some hairy Ishmaelites came jogging by on their donkeys and the brothers saw the chance to make a bit of cash on the side. Joseph was hitched up out of the pit and sold off as an Ishmaelite slave ("Poor, Poor Joseph"). A passing goat was slaughtered to provide some corroborating blood to sprinkle on the shreds of his coat, and the brothers went back to Jacob to squeeze out a few crocodile tears in support of their tale of brother Joseph's sad demise ("One More Angel in Heaven").

The Ishmaelites sold Joseph at a good profit to an Egyptian property magnate called "Potiphar." Joseph, with his talent for getting on, quickly managed to please his new master and was soon promoted to the top of the household. He also succeeded in pleasing Mrs. Potiphar but that made Potiphar much less pleased. Joseph got double quick demotion and ended up in prison ("Close Every Door").

He wasn't the only servant of Egypt to have fallen. He shared his cell with a couple of Pharaoh's minions who had committed some royal misdemeanors and went in fear of their lives, a fear which gave them really bad dreams. Here was the opportunity for Joseph to start his dream-reading business again, in spite of the trouble it had got him into in Canaan. To one man he prophesied doom, but to the other he promised a return to his position as the Pharaoh's butler. As for himself, well, he still had his old Canaan dreams to fall back on ("Go, Go, Go Joseph"), and he was right.

"Pharaoh" was the biggest thing in Egypt, but Pharaoh was also having bad dreams. So what more natural than he should call on this chap in jail who had correctly forecast his butler's restoration to favor? Joseph was brought to court and Pharaoh poured out his dreams (Pharaoh's Story): meaningful charades involving fat cows and thin cows and ripe and rotten corn. Joseph was able to translate this on his ear. The dreams were a long-range weather forecast. They prophesied seven years of super-cereal crops followed by seven years of drought. Therefore, they were a warning to Pharaoh on agricultural policy. He must stockpile foodstuffs frantically during the good years to enable his country to get through the bad ones (Pharaoh's Dream Explained).

Pharaoh didn't wait to test this plausible explanation ("Well Stone the Crows"). He had Joseph's chains chopped off and promoted him to Minister of Agriculture on the spot. Of course, in the irritating manner that had characterized his whole life, Joseph was right and he organized the whole thing so that there was no crisis in the Egyptian markets throughout the famine years. Not so in Canaan where, because of the fraternal susceptibilities in Jacob's family, they didn't have anyone to give them forecasts. Canaan was hard hit ("Those Canaan Days") and Jacob and his wives and eleven surviving sons grew thin and sick. Finally, the brothers decided to head for Egypt to see if they could get in on the immigrant labor market and thus fill their needs.

When they reached Egypt (The Brothers Come to Egypt), they pleaded for food handouts to Joseph in his capacity as the Minister of Agriculture. He recognized them right away in spite of their scrawniness, but they didn't recognize him nor realize the irony of their bowing before him just as his early dream had predicted ("Grovel, Grovel"). Joseph, who wasn't quite the paragon of virtue you might have thought, had a tiny vindictive streak in him, so he tried a little plot. He gave the brothers the sacks of food they desired but, in the bottom of one sack, he hid a precious goblet. As they were leaving, he cried out "Who's the Thief?," and had them all searched. The goblet was found in the sack of little brother Benjamin.

Benjamin obviously didn't have any annoying potential. He was very popular with his family, and the other brothers all got down on their knees for another grovel, begging Joseph not to give Benjamin a criminal record (Benjamin Calypso). Joseph thought this showed that his brothers had been improved by a bit of starvation and were no longer the sort to throw helpful brothers into pits or sell their family off to hairy Ishmaelites, so he decided the time had come to make himself known ("Joseph All the Time").

And so there was a happy ending after all. Joseph used his position in the government to get visas for all his family to come and live in Egypt and partake of the plentiful food (Jacob in Egypt), and they all lived happily ever after ("Any Dream Will Do").

Joseph and the Amazing Technicolor Dreamcoat began as a fifteen-minute cantata and was lengthened for subsequent concert and stage productions until it was sufficiently substantial to fill a full evening's program.

1983

LA CAGE AUX FOLLES

A MUSICAL IN TWO ACTS by Harvey Fierstein based on the play by Jean Poiret. Lyrics and music by Jerry Herman.

Produced at the Palace Theatre, New York, 21 August 1983, with Gene Barry (Georges) and George Hearn (Albin).

CHARACTERS

Georges

Jean-Michel, *his son*

Albin

Jacob

Francis

Edouard Dindon

Madame Dindon

Anne, *their daughter*

Jacqueline

Monsieur Renaud

Chantal, Monique, Dermah, Nicole, Hanna, Mercedes, Bitelle, Lo Singh, Odette, Angélique, Phaedra, Clo-Clo, *Les Cagelles* Madame Renaud, Paulette, Hercule, Étienne, Babette, Colette, Tabarro, Pepé, etc.

"A Little More Mascara." Albin (George Hearn) by day, he becomes the fabulous Zaza of the Côte d'azur nightspot La Cage aux Folles by night. Photograph © Martha Swope.

Act 1

At the famous St. Tropez nightclub, La Cage aux Folles, Georges, our host for the evening, introduces the "girls" of the revue ("We Are What We Are")—Chantal the carolling songstress, Hanna from Hamburg with her whip, and the enigmatic Phaedra whose talent lies in her tongue. The girls in this club are, however, boys, for La Cage aux Folles is the Riviera's mecca of drag.

Tonight, when the girls finish their number and crowd off into the wings to take off their high heels, they are shoved back on to the stage. The show's star, Zaza, isn't ready and they have to do their number again. There are grumbles: Zaza is clearly not being temperamental for the first time.

Zaza—otherwise Albin, Georges's lover, helpmate, and star of twenty years—is having a monumental sulk, and not without cause. Having slaved lovingly over a complicated lunch for Georges, he waited and waited and waited. No Georges, no explanation, so no show. Zaza is still in her bathrobe with not a sequin in sight, and five hundred people are waiting in a packed nightclub for the star to appear. A little scene is played, Albin gets his moment of genuine remorse and love from Georges, and, when he has got it, Zaza is in business again. Albin sits down at his dressing table and, with the addition of makeup, wig, and gown transforms himself into Zaza ("A Little More Mascara").

The evening, which has begun so dramatically, still has another surprise in store. Jacob, the black "maid" of the household, unveils a dashing young lad. He is Jean-Michel, the son of the family. Biologically, of course, he is only Georges's son, but Albin has been his mother for twenty years. Jean-Michel is back home and he has some wonderful news. He's getting married. Her name is Anne and her father is Édouard Dindon, the deputy general of the Tradition, Family, and Morality Party who has pledged as part of his platform to close down the drag clubs of the coast.

The second bit of good news is that Dindon and his wife are coming here to meet Jean-Michel's family. Jean-Michel has not exactly told the truth about his family: Georges has been described as a retired diplomat and Albin hasn't been described at all. Jean-Michel simply asks that he not be around.

Georges is mortified. How can the boy treat the mother who has loved him so dearly in such an ungrateful and cavalier fashion? But Jean-Michel is truly in love ("With Anne on My Arm"), with all the selfishness of youth, and he is unaware of the hurt he offers elsewhere. There is worse to come, too. When Anne's parents visit, he wants them to meet his real mother. It's not that he wants to see her himself—she hasn't put in an appearance since he was a baby—but the Dindons expect a mother, so a mother there must be. Weakly, Georges agrees to try, but who is to tell Albin?

News travels fast, and an outraged Albin flies on to the scene, awash with horror at the thought of wedding bells for his son. Georges lovingly encourages him to a little walk in the evening air ("With You on My Arm"). It will be easier to break the rest of the news away from home. On "The Promenade," Jean-Michel has met Anne who is all aglow at the thought of meeting her beloved's family, but he forces her into a hurried exit when Georges and Albin appear on the horizon.

Georges gradually starts to get down to details. Sybil first; the mother. Albin merely threatens murder if she is allowed in the house. But that's the easy bit. The rest is almost impossible. There is a moon out and love is in Georges's heart ("Song on the Sand") as Albin softens. He withdraws the murder threat. Sybil can come. But, just as Georges has braced himself for the hard bit, the clock chimes and they have to flee back to the club for the second show.

While they have been away, Jean-Michel has taken Georges's courage and Albin's acquiescence for granted and he has started shifting out the more extravagant furniture and homophile *objets d'art* from the apartment. Georges has to cover up and, to make sure the boy realizes the enormity of what he is asking his father to do, he makes him stand and watch Albin, the one person solely responsible for his upbringing and comfort, as he performs "La Cage aux Folles" to a packed house. But as Albin comes to change his costume in the wings, Jean-Michel passes too blatantly close with an armful of gowns taken from Albin's cupboard, and Albin demands to know what is going on.

While Albin changes costume behind a screen, Georges, more able to do the deed now that he doesn't have to look him in the eye, attempts jokingly to put forward the plan. When Albin emerges his face shows his devastation. He walks whitely to the stage to perform "We Are What We Are" but, after a few lines, he sends the other girls scurrying from the stage and delivers his ultimatum to Georges and the world ("I Am What I Am"). When he has finished, he tears his wig from his head, flings it to the floor, and walks out of the club.

Act 2   It is morning when Georges tracks Albin down in the town. He explains that Jean-Michel has acted with the foolishness of love, and, as for himself, he too acted foolishly, but is none the less equally in love ("Song on the Sand"). Albin cannot stay too angry very long, especially as Georges has devised a plan for bringing him back into the ménage. If he can just butch his act up a bit he can pass off as Uncle Al. It is a hideously distasteful charade for a lady and a star but, since he is quite sure they will mess the whole thing up if he is not there, Albin agrees and is made to suffer a crash course in "Masculinity."

Jean-Michel has stripped the apartment and decorated it in a style reminiscent of a medieval chapel. It is deeply and religiously camp, and Jacob's effort to be a butler, instead of a maid, under a powdered wig is nothing short of desperately unconvincing. Albin's Uncle Al at least has the merit of genuine effort behind it. While the nervous preparations go on, Albin takes delivery of a telegram and, when he reads it, he goes quiet.

There is no quiet in the rest of the room: Jean-Michel's nervousness has surfaced in a great resentment that Georges has allowed Albin to be present and to threaten the exercise. This time Georges will not give way: The boy has no right to such ingratitude ("Look Over There"). Jean-Michel knows he is in the wrong, but the conflict of feelings in him is too much and he rushes out. Then Albin shows Georges the telegram: it is from Sybil and she isn't coming. There will be no mother for the Dindons. Then the doorbell rings. While Jacob rushes to the door and Jean-Michel tries to organize his failing spirits, Albin rushes, petrified, into his room.

The introduction of the Dindons gets off to a shaky start when the Cage aux Folles creeps dangerously into the conversation in the first seconds, wobbles again when Georges forgets his allotted identity and poses as a legionnaire instead of a diplomat, and totters, worst of all, when Jacob serves the hors d'oeuvres on plates decorated with erotic classical Greek motifs (Cocktail Counterpoint). And, of course, there is no mother. Until, that is, the bedroom door opens and a buxom fortyish mother emerges. It is Albin, nattily dressed in a smart two-piece and all a-twitter with joyful conversation.

Before the Dindons can gather their thoughts, mother is quick to score a point. Jacob has burned the dinner, so they must all go to a restaurant. They must go to Chez Jacqueline. Madame Dindon is thrilled, for Chez Jacqueline is the most exclusive place in town and you have to book months ahead. Dindon is sceptical, but Albin picks up the phone, calls his dear friend Jacqueline, and *voilà, c'est fait*. In a twinkling they are Chez Jacqueline, being greeted by the hostess herself, happy to return a favor to Zaza who paid such delicious attentions to her special customers at La Cage the previous night.

Unfortunately, no one has warned Jacqueline of the ins and outs of the occasion and, when she introduces Zaza as a celebrity and begs for a song, Jean-Michel collapses inside. Goodbye, wedding! Pushed by a delighted Madame Dindon, Zaza obliges and soon the whole restaurant is joining in "The Best of Times." But, carried away on the élan of her song, Zaza forgets that she is not at La Cage aux Folles and, reaching the final chord she ritually pulls her wig from her head. Pandemonium breaks loose.

Back at the apartment, Dindon indulges in a feast of moral outrage prior to staging what he intends to be an effective exit, but his exit is spoiled when Anne refuses to go with him. She loves Jean-Michel and, whatever her parents may say, she also likes Georges and Albin. After the events of the evening, Jean-Michel has also been restored to his senses. He has an apology to make, not to Dindon but to Albin and to Georges ("Look Over There") who are very much more real people than the Dindons will ever be.

When Dindon goes to sweep out on a puff of moral indignation, he is greeted at the door by Jacqueline, and Jacqueline has brought a Press cameraman or two. How remiss of her to have had the famous Deputy Dindon at her restaurant and to have let him escape without even a photograph. Now he, the most famous antihomosexual of the coast, simply must have his photo taken dining with the most famous homosexuals of St. Tropez. Dindon is cooked. Bravo Jacqueline! Then Albin and Georges intervene. They have a plan. First of all, the children must be allowed to wed and Anne must, of course, have her dowry. When that is agreed, then they will help Dindon to escape the Press.

The finale of the first show is playing at the adjacent Cage aux Folles. As Georges announces the artists, they descend the staircase one by one—the girls of the show followed by Anne, dapper in tails, Jacob glittering in sequins and making the entrance he has dreamed of all his life only to trip on his train and tumble all the way down, Madame Dindon looking sensational and moving every portion just as it should be moved, and, finally, Dindon himself, all dolled up as the ugliest woman imaginable. As they parade down the stage of La Cage aux Folles, Jacqueline takes revenge on behalf of mankind. She brings in the Press, their cameras flashing ravenously. While Georges hurries the Dindons out, Jean-Michel and Anne escape in a different direction and soon the whole singing, dancing company vanishes into the distance.

Alone, under the Mediterranean night sky, Albin and Georges walk toward each other and meet ("Song on the Sand") as the curtain falls.

Sunday in the Park with George

A MUSICAL IN TWO ACTS by James Lapine. Lyrics and music by Stephen Sondheim. Produced at the Booth Theatre, New York, 2 May 1984, with Mandy Patinkin (George) and Bernadette Peters (Dot/Marie).

The result of George's Sundays in the park, Seruat's
"Un dimanche d'été à l'île de la Grande Jatte"
brought to still-life in the finale to Act I.
Photograph © Martha Swope.

CHARACTERS

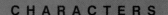

Act 1	Act 2
George, *an artist*	George, *an artist*
Dot, *his mistress*	Marie, *his grandmother*
Old Lady	Dennis, *a technician*
Her Nurse	Robert Greenberg, *the museum director*
Jules, *another artist*	Naomi Eisen, *a composer*
Yvonne, *his wife*	Harriet Pawling, *a patron of the arts*
Louise, *daughter of Jules and Yvonne*	Billy Webster, *her friend*
A Boatman	Charles Redmond, *a visiting curator*
Franz, *servant to Jules and Yvonne*	Alex, *an artist*
Frieda, *cook for Jules and Yvonne, wife to Franz*	Betty, *an artist*
A Soldier	Lee Randolph, *the museum's publicist*
Mr. and Mrs., *an American couple*	Blair Daniels, *an art critic*
Louis, *a baker*	Elaine, *George's former wife*
Celeste 1, *a shopgirl*	A Photographer, a Museum Assistant, a Waitress
Celeste 2, *another shopgirl*	
Other people in the park	

Act 1

The place is Paris, France, the year is 1884 (insofar that either consideration matters). They matter only in that one of the people we are about to meet actually does have a basis in fact and time and place. Here he is called George. His factual *sosie* was called Georges, Georges Seurat, the *pointilliste* painter who, during his very short life, played a part in the late nineteenth-century breakaway from the breakaway from the classic style of representational art. Today, Seurat is remembered—when he is remembered by anyone who's not an art student or scholar—for his waterside pictures *"Une baignade Asnières"* and *"Un dimanche d'été à l'île de la Grande Jatte."* But enough of the once-real Georges, and back to our George. George is an artist. He wears a black beard and a felt hat and says that he finds an empty piece of paper "a challenge." He will bring order to what he calls "the whole"—he announces—by Composition, Balance, Light, and Harmony.

Right now, far too early in the morning, he is out on an island in the Seine, and he is doing a fresh-light figure study of a young woman in a bustled gown. She is his mistress, Dot, and she's neither very keen nor very comfortable nor very able to concentrate on holding her position while the self-indulgent artist sketches her ("Sunday in the Park with George").

Other people are also out in the early morning light. There is a crotchety old lady with her nurse, a nurse who is being chatted up by a German coachman. And there is a group of boys bathing on the other side of the water under the noncommital eyes of a youngish man. The youngsters are shouting what they hope might be insults across the water at the artist, but when—with a firm motion of the hand—he fixes them on canvas in the image of *"Une baignade Asnières,"* they come out with all the look of youthful angels.

While the frozen tableau of *"Une baignade Asnières"* is on the stage, a well-dressed couple wander by. They are Jules, an established artist of the old school, and Yvonne, his wife, who has trained herself to say big, bad, and even sometimes comprehensible critical words about any art that isn't her husband's. They, of course, have nothing but scathe and scorn for George's work. It has "No Life." But they are kind enough to make insincere conversation with the young artist.

George has promised to take Dot out for the evening, and as the time gets near she is seen at her table, painting and powdering and preening. George is painting and preening too, but his efforts are going into his picture. With order, design, composition, tone, form, symmetry, balance . . . and "Color and Light." When Dot has done her dolling up and the time comes for them to go out, he cancels. There's no question of him going out. He has to finish painting the hat that he's working on.

The next time we see George out on Grande Jatte on a Sunday afternoon, he is drawing a common boatman. And he is without Dot. Dot has had enough. She's left him, and—to the surprise of some of the regulars—she's walking arm in arm with Louis, the baker. That's good grist for a great deal of the kind of "Gossip" that people like the two trawling shopgirls—who are both called Céleste—specialize in.

The mocking Yvonne and the all-but mocking Jules are there too, with their revolting child, Louise, being condescending, as usual, but the common boatman, who's learned to say curiously trendy words like "overprivileged" somewhere along his lifeline, sneers more generally. The whole world isn't worthy of him and his mangy dog. Dot is the only one around who seems to have any kind of a positive thought in her. She's sitting with a little, red book, trying to teach herself reading and writing, until Louis arrives with a tin of her favorite creampuffs.

George is deep in his painting. He concentrates on sketching the boatman's dog, and he invents a dog's-life monologue for the beast ("The Day Off") as he draws him. George's everyday thoughts are clearly a bit less sophisticated than his art theory, for the words he makes up for Spot the dog and the lapdog Fifi who comes along to join him, descend steadily toward the bathroom floor.

Meanwhile, Dot is having a dilemma. Should she return to George? "Everybody loves Louis," including her. Louis is kind and simple and loving and bakes wonderful cakes and is rotten in bed. George, on the other hand. . . . At the peak of her aria, Louis turns up with a *pâtisserie*. That's the end of the dilemma. It has to be Louis. Louis's *pâtisseries* also go down decidedly well with a caricatural pair of American Southerners. They hate Paris, but they just love its cakes.

The two Célestes finally pick themselves up a couple of odd-seeming soldiers and disappear, leaving George alone. It is the perfect moment for a soliloquy and George doesn't disappoint. He uses the opportunity to put forth his case over his apparently callous treatment of Dot. He'd thought she'd understood that his urge for creativity came before all his other urges. "Finishing the Hat" will and would always be more important to an artist than anything or anyone else.

The new, big painting George has been putting together is in a sufficient state for George to invite Jules to come and see it. He comes, and he barges in on a conversation between George and Dot. She's come to ask him for a painting he did of her, as a souvenir, and to say goodbye. She and Louis and her child, who is of course also George's child, are going to make pastries in America.

While Yvonne takes Dot aside and talks to her in terms that are almost human, George shows Jules his painting, the painting of la Grande Jatte with its novel stippled light effects. Jules finds it unbearably calculated and calculating. It is clear there is no way he is going to use his influence to help George get it accepted for the next Salon. The artist is disappointed. And, on top of that, Dot is going ("We Do Not Belong Together"). It's one of those days.

Now there is just George and his painting. A painting that is not the uplifting reality that Jules would have appreciated, but reality as rearranged and improved on by George, in accordance with his list of catchwords ("Beautiful").

Reality can, of course, always be improved on. Down on la Grande Jatte we once again meet the people whom George has sketched for his painting, but now they are in rather different situations. Dot and her child are ready to leave France, the Célestes have quarreled over the soldiers and are getting ready to quarrel some more, Jules is looking for some tall grass in which to enjoy Frieda, and Yvonne—put wise by the ghastly Louise—is looking for Jules. And when all the participants in this pleasant French afternoon come face to face, things boil up into a real screaming match. But George is not interested in this disorder. He can improve on this uncivilized mess. Order, design, tension, balance, harmony, and all the rest of it, all those things that don't coincide neatly in real life, can coincide under the artist's brush. The brawling characters are pulled apart, and set, each one, in his or her destined place in the scheme of things. And, when George is done, there is a living tableau of "*Un dimanche d'été à l'île de la Grande Jatte*" on which to bring down the curtain. After the artist, as a final touch, has taken off the hideous Louise's spectacles.

Act 2

The Act opens with the picture as we last saw it. The people in the picture are uncomfortable ("It's Hot Up Here") and complaining. When they have finished, George appears, and delivers a little speech on his fascination with light. Then he's gone. Georges Seurat died at the age of thirty-two. The characters descend from the painting and depart with varying words of valediction.

Then it's 1984, and we are in an American museum. The American museum where "*Un dimanche d'été à l'île de la Grande Jatte*"—its characters, of course, intact and in place—is now enshrined.

Now we meet another George, who is also an artist, and who is the grandson of Marie, the baby Dot bore to George in Act I. Although—with no real proof to hand—he's always been a bit dubious about the truth of that fact. This George has been commissioned by the museum to turn out a work of art to celebrate the centenary of George the first's painting. What he has come up with is a Chromolume, a piece of mechanical performance art—to put it politely—of which he's already manufactured a half-dozen, and he's brought his historically useful grandmother along with him to add verisimiltude and a smidgin of relevance to its unveiling. Unfortunately, when the machine is set going, it blows something electrical, but art is eventually restarted with the help of an ex-NASA scientist, and the guests are able to watch a display of whirling laser beams that's something between a computerized magic-lantern show and an updated glitterball.

Then it's over, and everyone goes off to the reception that is the real heart of the day's entertainment. At the reception, they can exchange pretentious chunks of fine flannel art-talk that make the striving Yvonne's first-act sneers sound positively intelligent. But the reception has a more important purpose than providing the opportunity for a bit of peacocking. It is the place where you can get to know or know better all those useful, useless people who make the art world, with its millions of dollars of mindless giveaways, go round: where you have your chance to persuade a trustee that he should entrust you and your newest gimmick or style with what's been entrusted to him. What tomorrow's public is to be made to believe is the latest state of art, who's in and what's out, can be decided over the cocktails and chatter of an art gallery reception.

Here is where George shows of what his artistry is really made ("Putting It Together"). You're only as good as your next commission, your next foundation, and your next lot of trustees. And George has the talent of apparently being in ten places at once as he chats his chat, slings his lines, and, playing the game with practiced expertise, lines himself up the next bit of his artistic future. And if one critic dares to say that she finds his work getting a bit too repetitive, he's also got the know-how to brush her under the carpet. In a system that perpetuates both mediocrity and trendiness, George is a master artist when it comes to getting commissions from foundations. Money. So, who cares what he turns out for his commission, as long as it leads to another commission?

Ninety-eight-year-old grandmother Marie has had lucid and less lucid moments during the course of the proceedings, but she apparently likes George's laserball machines. And she thinks that Dot would have liked them too. All that color and light. And she has this theory, that "Children and Art"—of any quality—are really the only two worthwhile things a person can leave behind them.

It has been arranged by the international art fraternity that the Chromolume will give a performance on la Grande Jatte, and George and his NASA scientist go to Paris to organize the show. For some incomprehensible reason, George has turned down his next commission. He's decided that he wants to do something different. So this will be his last Chromolume jaunt, presented on a la Grande Jatte that is not much like the one George the first painted a century back.

Marie has died since the first presentation, and George has inherited the little red book that she had from her mother, in which Dot wrote down her grammar exercises as she sat in the park of la Grande Jatte while George sketched. Reading it now, almost on the spot where it was written ("Lesson number 8"), George is moved to the conclusion that he's finished as an artist. He's outgrown what he can do. But as he sits there, despondent, a good fairy comes to him. It is the shade of Dot, with good advice to give ("Move On"): Order, Design, Tension, Composition, Balance, Light, Harmony.

Then the music rises and all the people from the painting appear, ready for the finale ("Sunday"). When they've finished, George seems to have got over his artist's block. Quite where he's going from his blank page we don't yet know, but at least there'll be no more Chromolumes.

1985

BIG RIVER

THE ADVENTURES OF HUCKLEBERRY FINN. A MUSICAL IN TWO ACTS, based on *The Adventures of Huckleberry Finn* by Mark Twain, by William Hauptman. Lyrics and music by Roger Miller.

Originally produced at the La Jolla Playhouse and at the American Repertory Theatre, Cambridge, Mass., 17 February 1984. Produced at the Eugene O'Neill Theatre, New York, 25 April 1985, with Daniel Jenkins (Huck), Ron Richardson (Jim), John Short (Tom), Bob Gunton (King), and Rene Auberjonois (Duke).

Huckleberry Finn (Daniel Jenkins) and slave Jim (Ron Richardson) set off together down the Mississippi River for two acts of adventure and song.
Photograph © Martha Swope.

CHARACTERS

Huckleberry Finn

Tom Sawyer

Widow Douglas

Miss Watson

Jim

Pap Finn

Judge Thatcher

The King

The Duke

Maryjane Wilkes

Harvey Wilkes

Sheriff Bell

Sally Phelps

Silas Phelps

Doctor

A Young Fool

Mark Twain, Ben Rogers, Jo Harper, Simon, Dick, Woman in Shanty, Men on a Skiff, Hank, Andy, Lafe, Susan Wilkes, Joanna Wilkes, Bill, Counselor Robinson, Alice, Alice's daughter, et al.

Everybody who was ever a child knows the story of Tom Sawyer and
Huckleberry Finn, and how they set murderous Missouri wrong to right and
happy-ended up with a hidden treasure all their own. Well, if you don't, it's never
too late. You'd better dip into Mark Twain's novel *The Adventures of Tom Sawyer*.
This musical—and the novel that it came from—are a sort of a sequel to that one.
The vast wealth that Tom and Huck discovered has been put neatly into the
hands of a gentleman Judge who knows about such things, and—in these days
before currency speculation became a legal international pastime—they're
earning a nice regular little return on their capital. But that doesn't change life
too much down in St. Petersburg, Missouri. Tom is back at school, leading a
nice, almost middle-class life with his Aunt Polly and—in spite of his past
adventures—dreaming of pirates and highwaymen and rape and pillage and all
the other good things a young lad's library teaches him to long for. Huck is
supposed to be at school too, but he plays hooky. And he's supposed to be being
almost middle-class too, under the narrowly kindly eye of the sisters Miss
Watson and Widow Douglas. But unlike Tom, Huck wasn't born to school and
almost middle-classness. He's the son of a drunken and lawless hobo, brought
up barefoot and wild as the williwaw, and he's finding it mighty hard to change
his ways, and mighty hard to act like a boy with a big bank balance.

Act 1   Huckleberry Finn has skipped school
and gone fishing, yet again, and Widow Douglas
and Miss Watson are worried that he's going to
end up as worthless and as godless as his late
father ("Do You Want to Go to Heaven?"). They
do their best to tell the boy off. They even
whip him a little. But it's all to no avail. When
he's supposed to have been put to bed in
disgrace, he shimmies down the drainpipe
and runs off with Tom Sawyer and his little
friends to play gangs in the caves ("The Boys"). But for all
the big talk that Tom and the other boys deal in, Huck knows that
they'll be back at school the next day. Not even Tom—who talks the biggest
and wildest of all—would be really ready to come off on a real adventure
with him ("Waitin' for the Light to Shine").

Adventure of a not wholly welcome kind soon comes Huck's way. When
he gets back to the Widow Douglas's house, he finds his father there. Pap Finn
isn't dead at all, but gruesomely alive. It's soon obvious why he's come back
from the safely dead; he's heard about Huck's money and he wants it for
himself. On $300 a year, he—and Huck of course—can live like kings. The

Judge is unable to stop the boy's father from taking him away from his new home, and soon the pair of them are back in the woods living in Pap Finn's filthy shack. Huck is little better than a skivvy to his father who is permanently bottled on raw whiskey, and permanently sputtering out foul-mouthed gibberish about the authority that's trying to trick him out of the money and his boy. The boy and his money. The money. ("Guv'ment"). When the drink is on him really badly, he sees snakes where there are none; one night, he even attacks Huck with his hunting knife. Huck can't stay. Next day, when his pap's away, he cuts the throat of a hog, spatters the shack with its blood, fits himself out with a little survival gear, and paddles off in his canoe to hide out on Jackson's Island, in the middle of the Mississippi River. ("Hand for the Hog").

While Huck is lying low on the island, he hears the folk of St. Petersburg out searching for him, but he stays hidden. He's just getting to like being on his own ("I, Huckleberry, Me") when he meets up with a friend. Like Huck, Jim is a runaway, but a very different kind of runaway, because Jim is Miss Watson's slave. He heard that Miss Watson was being persuaded to sell him to the South, so there was nothing left for him to do but light out. He's got himself a raft and he's going to float down the Mississippi river to the free states on the first stage of a trip to find his wife and his children. Huck's found himself a partner in adventure; in spite of all the trouble he might get into for harboring a runaway slave, he's going down the river too.

Before they set out, Huck can't resist sneaking back into St. Petersburg to find out just what folks are saying about his disappearance. To his horror and surprise, he finds that the story that's doing the rounds is that he's been done in! Who was it killed Huck Finn? Not his drunken pappy, but runaway slave Jim. So Jim's not just wanted as a runaway, he's wanted for murder! Huck hurries back to the hideout with the news. There's no time to delay. They have to push off right away ("Muddy Waters").

The river is still flooded, and as the raft drifts downstream, it passes all kinds of flotsam—even a dead body. That one's too much, and Jim won't let the boy look at it, but Huck Finn soon shows that he can cope with life on the run. He knows how to catch a catfish and how to steal a chicken. So the two of them don't go hungry.

The days and the towns drift by, and they get closer and closer to that fork in the river that will set them on their right way to the free states. On the way they meet the occasional fellow traveller—a boatload of slaves "Crossing Over" from St. Louis, a pair of of law-abiding men out looking for runaways ("River in the Rain"), and finally a curious couple of refugees who try to convince Jim and Huck that they are the Duke of Bridgewater and the Dauphin, son of the last King of France. They're actually a pair of escaped convicts. Huck and Jim soon see through their act, but the pair are running away, just like them, and they see no reason not to let them ride along.

Act 2

The Duke and the King soon get together a scam. They will be actors ("When the Sun Goes Down in the East"). As they float down through Tennessee, they put themselves together a show, and when they get to Bricktown, Arkansas, they're ready to pull in their first gullible, all-male public to see the Duke's patchwork of Shakespeare and the fabulous female creature called "The Nonesuch." The King is dressed up to represent the Nonesuch, but even Bricktown, Arkansas isn't dumb enough to fall for such an act, and soon the team are on their way again.

They don't move on with quite the same genial feeling among them, though. The Duke and the King have insisted that Jim stay chained up, just so there's no mistaking his position, but Huck isn't happy with that. In fact, he's all for a parting of the ways with their traveling companions. He'd be happier continuing the journey as they began it, just he and Jim ("Worlds Apart"). But the King and the Duke aren't having that. Either Huck sticks with them or they'll denounce him for helping a runaway slave.

The raft next calls in at Hillsboro, where fate hands the runaways a scam on a platter. They meet a young halfwit ("Arkansas") who lets them know that the unknown brother of the recently deceased Peter Wilkes is expected. Where there's a grave, there's a will, and the King and the Duke are swift to follow up. They find the mourning in full flow ("How Blest We Are"), and the daughters of the dead man unsuspecting of a trick. Soon the King has bamboozled the eldest Wilkes daughter, Maryjane, into handing over all the family money to him for safekeeping and investment.

Huck quickly develops a soft spot for the genuinely grieving Maryjane ("You Ought to Be Here with Me"), and he determines that the King sha'n't hornswoggle such a pretty girl out of her rightful inheritance. He succeeds in stealing the bag of gold from the King's room, but is forced to hide it in the dead man's own coffin. The next day—after the King has delivered a high-flown but meaningless funeral oration—he watches helpless as the Wilkes family fortune is lowered into father Wilkes's grave.

The service is not long done when the skein of lies the crooks have woven start to unravel. The King has started cashing in by selling two of the household slaves, and Maryjane is aghast. Huck can't bear to see her upset, so—as he gets ready to go—he tells her that the two shysters are impostors. But her money is safe. ("Leaving's Not the Only Way to Go"). Then the Sheriff arrives, and with him comes the real brother Wilkes. The King faces out the situation with practiced ease, but finally the real Wilkes comes up with a proof. His late brother had a tattoo on his chest—the men who laid him out will have seen it—

let the King say what it represents. The King takes a flying guess. It's a wrong one, but he's saved when the local men admit they didn't notice any tattoo at all. There is only one way to settle the claims. Peter Wilkes will have to be dug up.

By the time the coffin is opened, and the bag of gold discovered sitting on the corpse's chest, Huck Finn is halfway down the road to the river and the raft. But when he gets there, Jim is gone. He waits anxiously for him to come back, but the only person who appears is the Duke, in a pitiful state. He's been tarred and feathered by the furious townsfolk. The Duke's responsible for Jim's absence; he sold him to a local farmer called Phelps for a few extra dollars. Huck doesn't know what to do. He thinks of writing to Miss Watson to come and fetch Jim home. But then he knows he can't do that. He's got to go and find the slave and help him to get away, to the wife and children he'd been so longing to see ("Waitin' for the Light to Shine").

And so, Huck arrives at the Phelps farm only to find himself welcomed as . . . Tom Sawyer! The Phelpses are Tom's Aunt and Uncle and they're expecting young Tom any minute. When the real Tom arrives, he eagerly offers to join in the adventure of helping Jim escape. Only Tom isn't interested in a simple, effective plan. He wants one that's full of danger and drama. Jim could do without the frills. He just wants to be "Free at Last."

The escape would have gone off quite easily had it not been for Tom. To get some drama into the situation, he forewarned farmer Phelps. And to get really involved in the drama, he offered to be the one to distract the farmer when the time came. His reward is one of Farmer Phelps's bullets in his leg. When Huck goes to get a doctor to help his seriously hurt friend, the escape is aborted and Jim's hopes of freedom are down the drain. At least so it seems. But bit by bit the truth comes out. Tom admits to being Tom, and admits too that Jim is a free man. Miss Watson has died and in her will she set the slave free. Tom knew that before all the "escape" was set up, but he couldn't miss out on the chance for an adventure. He had all sorts of other adventures set up too, if they'd got away. So perhaps Jim and Huck should be glad they got caught.

But now the adventure is over, and it's time for the men who took part in it to go on to the next part of their lives. Tom will stay to convalesce with his family. Jim will head North to try to find his wife and children. And Huck? Huck doesn't know. He can't go back to St. Petersburg, because sure as shrimps his Pap would find him again, and things would go back to being like they were before. Now, and only now, does Jim tell him. That corpse they passed floating down the river as they made their escape from Jackson's Island . . . it was Huck's Pap, drunken drowned. So maybe Huck can go home. Maybe he will go home. Or maybe he won't. Because everywhere he goes folks seem to want to civilize him. And Huck Finn hasn't got no intention of getting civilized.

THE MYSTERY OF EDWIN DROOD

A MUSICAL IN TWO ACTS by Rupert Holmes suggested by Charles Dickens's uncompleted novel of the same title.

Originally produced at the Delacorte Theatre, New York, 21 August 1985. Produced at the Imperial Theatre, New York, 2 December 1985, with Betty Buckley (Edwin Drood), Howard McGillin (John Jasper), Patti Cohenour (Rosa), George Rose (Chairman), and Cleo Laine (Puffer).

The Chairman of the Royale Music Hall (George Rose)
invites his audience's opinion. Who do *you* think is
behind *The Mystery of Edwin Drood*?
Photograph © Martha Swope.

CHARACTERS

Mayor Thomas Sapsea (William Cartwright, Chairman of the Royale Music Hall)

John Jasper (Mr. Clive Paget)

The Reverend Mr. Crisparkle (Mr. Cedric Moncrieffe)

Edwin Drood (Miss Alice Nutting)

Rosa Bud (Miss Deirdre Peregrine)

Helena Landless (Miss Janet Conover)

Neville Landless (Mr. Victor Grinstead)

Durdles (Mr. Nick Cricker)

Deputy (Master Nick Cricker)

The Princess Puffer (Miss Angela Prysock)

Bazzard (Mr. Phillip Bax)

Alice, Beatrice, Shade of Jasper, Shade of Drood, Harold, Julian, Horace, et al.

Once upon a time, back in the nineteenth century, a gentleman called Mr. Charles Dickens made a large part of his living as an author by writing soap-operatic serials for magazines. Like their modern-day radio and television equivalents, these serials followed the melodramatic fortunes of their characters through apparently endless series of more-or-less probable romantic and dramatic episodes, before ultimately bringing them tidily to their better or worse ends in the last episode of the series.

Unfortunately for the characters of his final serial, *The Mystery of Edwin Drood*, Mr. Charles Dickens came to his own end before he had arranged theirs, and so they were left suspended in middrama for what one might have thought would be eternity. But it wasn't. Putting an ending to Mr. Dickens's unended tale became a favorite literary and dramatic pastime in the last century, with various scholars or writers plumping—usually rather unimaginatively—for one outcome or another. It was left for Mr. Rupert Holmes to come up with the only really satisfactory answer in what he calls a "solve-it-yourself Broadway musical." That answer is: make up your own mind.

Act 1 Tonight, we're sitting in the padded-plush, smoke-stained purlieus of the rather less than top-notch Royale Music Hall in suburban London in the year of her Majesty's reign 1873. We're getting ready to wallow merrily in a lusty evening's entertainment from our old (and, especially, our young) favorites of the Royale company under the gavel of Chairman William Cartwright ("There We Are"). Tonight, it seems, we're going to see something rather outside the usual line of songs and acts. A musicale with dramatic interludes? What's the fellow talking about? With a plot that hasn't got an end? We have to what? Vote? Oh get on with it. Let's see the girls. And the comics. And the girls.

Mr. Cartwright begins by introducing us to the principal artists who are to appear in Mr. Dickens's story. Top of the bill comes dandy Clive Paget, the Royale's leading man, who plays John Jasper, choirmaster, composer, vocal instructor, and organist at rural Cloisterham Cathedral. John Jasper is not, however, the virtuous young tenor-singing hero we might have expected. There are times when—if we knew what the word meant—we might suspect that this Cloisterham Apollo was little short of schizophrenic. In his more frigidly lucid moments, John Jasper is not unaware of the fact that he is tottering on the brink of sanity ("A Man Could Go Quite Mad"). The way he is behaving, the Reverend

Septimus Crisparkle—played by your very own Mr. Cedric Moncrieffe—will soon be nursing doubts as well.

In fact, John Jasper is not our piece's hero. That honor falls to the gentleman of the serial's and the show's title, Jasper's nephew, Edwin Drood. Mr. Paget is not playing the hero's role because, in the best tradition of the Victorian burlesque theatre, Drood is a travesty role. It is therefore taken by the Royale's principal "boy," the leggy and sometimes lovely Miss Alice Nutting. Edwin Drood is betrothed—and has been since earliest childhood—to the purer-than-possible and ever-so-orphaned Miss Rosa Bud. Soon he will wed her and the two will leave Cloisterham for the sandier air of Egypt, where Edwin is planning to make his fortune by inflicting horrible, colonizing things like roads on the defenseless locals. Uncle John Jasper has Edwin's portrait of Rosa hung on the wall of his study, and it is noticeable that he does seem to get curiously twitchy when the child's name and the forthcoming wedding are mentioned. Edwin is most concerned at this twitchiness, and Jasper has to admit to a little ill-health— sufficient, in fact, that he has to make regular trips to London for treatment.

Uncle and nephew indulge in a hand-on-hand-on-breast duo of extravagant loyalty ("Two Kinsman"), and then the time arrives for us to meet our heroine, Miss Rosa Bud, as portrayed by the Royale's ingénue, the virginal-looking Miss Deirdre Peregrine. Since today is Rosa's birthday, Jasper—by way of a gift—has written a song for his preferred pupil to sing ("Moonfall"). It is a song that plumbs the heights of her winsome soprano range, but which—to her blushing horror—expresses sentiments that lie ill on the lips of a modest maiden.

Two exotic newcomers arrive in Cloisterham, who have a distinctly unpinnable accent and a tinge of the permanently tanned in their features. Helena Landless and her brother, Neville, have come from Ceylon, and they too are orphans, though of a slightly more recent date than Rosa Bud. Neville is a young man given to violent and threatening words, and Helena is no ingénue but a perspicacious and purposeful young woman; their presence can be counted on to deepen the mystery we are about to become involved in. For we must never forget, as this story unrolls, that we are in a mystery—anywhere and everywhere, a clue to the melting down of that mystery may be hidden or half-hidden. So we must always be on our wits' wings, listening to every word that is spoken for that fleeting clue.

The comedians of the evening's entertainment are three. Nick Cricker and his young son play Durdles, the boozy churchyard worker, and his Deputy, and the third is . . . well, unfortunately the Royale's third comedian got too thirsty too early this evening, so Chairman Cartwright is obliged to step down from his table and himself take the role of Cloisterham's Mayor Sapsea. As it happens, Mayor Sapsea has business with Durdles, father and son, for they have just completed the interment of Mrs. Sapsea, oversplendidly entombed as befits her husband's position in the community.

When a few dead-body jokes have been exchanged, Mayor Sapsea turns back into our evening's Chairman and, with a few words, transfers the scene from Cloisterham to London, to a sinister opium den, run by a hag called the Princess Puffer ("The Wages of Sin"). There, we find none other than John Jasper, swilling laudanum-laced wine, and living the lascivious dreams the drugs provoke (Dance: Jasper's Vision). As he dreams, however, he cries out the name of Rosa Bud, and the eyes of the haggard Princess light up with frenzied curiosity. Who is this customer who cries out the name of? . . . (note, this is definitely a clue).

Back at Cloisterham, Edwin Drood has made the acquaintance of Helena and Neville Landless, and—given Edwin's penchant for condescending remarks, and Neville's for fiery reactions—the making has not been wholly cordial ("Ceylon"). Jasper is quick to notice the friction, and to point it out to Mayor Sapsea. The two may seem like young gentlemen, but there are two sides to everything and everyone—he knows—and he sees danger in Neville Landless ("Both Sides of the Coin").

The Chairman waves a word, and suddenly we are in the crypt of Cloisterham Cathedral. Jasper has drugged Durdles with a little of his "special" wine, and has been doing something down in Mrs. Sapsea's spacious tomb . . . only, what? What? Shall we ever know? (Actually, we never will.) Surely this *must* be a clue . . .

Christmastime approaches, and it is time for a few more twists in the tale. First of all comes a real surprise: Drood and Rosa break off their engagement. It is not that they have faltered in their affections, but they have been engaged for so very, very long that they really cannot say for sure whether they truly love each other. They have to become "Perfect Strangers" before they can find out. But Rosa, who is apparently not as ingenuous as she seems, insists that Edwin's uncle be not informed of their newly disengaged state.

The principals of our story have been invited to Christmas dinner at the home of John Jasper. It is a vile night, and, as the meal stumbles on, Jasper frequently encourages his guests to partake of the special, warming wine that he has prepared to a recipe brought back from London. Drood is ruder than ever to Neville, and soon the atmosphere deteriorates even more alarmingly than the weather ("No Good Can Come from Bad"). All in all, it is not the best of Christmas dinners. But when the evening comes to an end, and it is time for each to go to his home, all seems to have been patched up. Edwin insists, in spite of the weather, on walking home, and Neville insists on accompanying him. Jasper, at the last minute, insists that Edwin take his heavy, hooded coat as protection against the weather.

And that was the last anyone ever saw of Edwin Drood. Only Jasper's coat was found, the next day, bloodied and torn, under a rock by the river. The coat is found by Bazzard, a municipal worker, who is played by the Royale's Mr. Bax. This is just about the only function that Bazzard (and Mr. Bax) have in the show, something that strikes our Chairman as somewhat curious. About Bazzard that is, for it is reasonably clear why Mr. Bax has not been given a larger role. But Bazzard? Why did Dickens invent him if it was just for this one moment? Was Bazzard to have had a key role in the unwritten part of the mystery? But tonight Mr. Cartwright is feeling kindly—just for this one night, Mr. Bax shall be allowed to give an interpolated number. The thrilled actor takes his big moment in a song in which he dreams that one night he'll be called on to play a starring role ("Never the Luck"). When his song is done, he bows and is bundled offstage. His moment is over.

Now, events move briskly on. Neville Landless is accused of the murder of Edwin Drood, and—with Edwin out of the way—John Jasper declares his love to Rosa. She rejects him bitterly ("The Name of Love") in what serves as a dramatico-musical curtain to the first act.

Act 2   Mr. Cartwright drags his audience back from the bars and the company of those habituées of what obviously counts as a Promenade at the Royale, to continue the entertainment. Following the tragic events at Cloisterham, two strangers arrive in town ("Settling Up the Score"). One is the Princess Puffer, the other a curious, bearded fellow called Dick Datchery.

When the company has finished singing the Royale's interpolated-into-everything theme song, "Off to the Races," the two newcomers are allowed to get involved in the action. Puffer runs into Rosa, and Puffer's thoughts and fears are confirmed. She is, indeed, the Rosa Bud that Puffer feared and thought she might have been. Things are becoming clearer. She (and Datchery) must press on with their inquiries ("Don't Quit While You're Ahead"). . . .

What those inquiries were, we shall never know, for this is the point where Mr. Dickens departed this life, and left Rosa, Puffer, Jasper, Crisparkle, Neville, Helena, and the rest of the characters to wither away unshriven and unannealed. But at the Royale Music Hall they don't go in for withering. Mr. Cartwright intends to have a button on this evening's entertainment, and on his Musicale with Dramatic Interludes. So he takes charge.

The first thing, of course, that has to be decided is "is Edwin Drood really dead?" Being a democratic (or indecisive) fellow, the Chairman asks for a popular vote. The result is unanimous. Obviously Miss Alice Nutting is not a well-liked member of the company; all her colleagues vote her "dead." There will be no more numbers from Alice tonight. Miss Nutting flings out an oath and storms off in a fury.

The second question to be answered is, "Who is Dick Datchery?" Well, that beard and costume, they were quite clearly a disguise. Who is it who is loitering in Cloisterham in such a disguise with the intent of uncovering the mystery of Edwin Drood? And why? Mr. Cartwright summarizes the clues and motives that have been proffered during the evening for the benefit of those who weren't paying attention, and the audience is asked to vote as to the identity of the sleuth.

Then, it's on to more serious things. Drood has been deemed dead. Therefore, someone must have killed him. Who? This time the voting is much more serious, and it takes long enough for the whole company to give a reprise of "Settling Up the Score." Finally the result comes through. The murderer of Edwin Drood was. . . . Well, it was whoever the audience voted for, of course, give or take a bit of adept miscounting by a chairman who has been dropped a fiver by an artist anxious to have a star role in the next part of the entertainment.

That part of the entertainment is the Conclusion, and it goes like this: Early in the morning, Rosa Bud is fleeing toward Cloisterham Station to catch the London train when she is waylaid by the Princess Puffer. Does the child not know her? Puffer is no other than her old nurse, the woman who brought her up from the age of two and the sad death of her mother, till the age of six and the arrival in Puffer's life of a too-attractive man. Alas, the man proved faithless and Puffer began the descent down "The Garden Path to Hell." Then came that fatal day when a drugged man in her den cried out the name of Rosa Bud in his dreams. So the Princess set out to follow the man and find again the child she had abandoned. Only she, herself, was followed by this strange man Datchery. And he was none other than. . . . Well, of course, he was whoever the audience (and the chairman) voted for. But each of the principals is provided with a tale to suit the occasion, and all the tales point fatally to but one man: John Jasper!

His face lit with maniacal glee, John Jasper confesses. But—unless, of course, the audience has voted Jasper as the murderous criminal—there is now utter confusion! For, when the confessing is done, the addled Durdles speaks up. And what does he have to say? Why, quite simply that John Jasper did not murder Edwin Drood. While sheltering from the Noellic storms that fatal night, he saw Edwin Drood meet his doom, strangled just outside Jasper's door. And—thanks to a convenient flash of lightning—he saw who did it. Then he saw Jasper discover the body, carry it to the churchyard, and haul it into Mrs. Sapsea's tomb. He saw Jasper plant the torn and bloodied cape. All this he did, but John Jasper did not murder Edwin Drood. The murderer was. . . .

Well, if you didn't know who it was, you do now. And when the murderer has delivered his final aria of guilt ("Confession") the mystery of Edwin Drood is no longer a mystery.

But a night at the Royale Music Hall cannot end on murder and guilt, even murder uncovered and guilt attributed. The Royale Music Hall prefers Happy

Endings. So the audience is put to work one more time. For a Happy Ending they shall have a romance between two of the remaining characters.

But, that's not all. We have yet another surprise in store for us. When the evening's lovers have been paired off according to the (sometimes perverse) voting of the audience, there is a further Happy Ending to come. Mrs. Sapsea's tomb heaves into view, flies open, and out comes . . . Edwin Drood. Miss Alice Nutter has had the last word. And here she is with not only an explanation—she was only stunned, not killed—but with a number ("The Writing on the Wall") to bring the evening's proceedings to an end.

1987

Les misérables

A MUSICAL TRAGEDY by Alain Boublil and Jean-Marc Natel based on the novel by Victor Hugo. Music by Claude-Michel Schönberg.

Produced at the Broadway Theatre, 12 March 1987, with Colm Wilkinson (Valjean), Terrence V. Mann (Javert), David Bryant (Marius), Leo Burmester (Thénardier), Frances Ruffelle (Eponine), Judy Kuhn (Cosette), Randy Graff (Fantine), and Jennifer Butt (Mme. Thénardier). Played at the Imperial Theatre from 19 October 1990. Originally produced at the Palais des Sports, Paris, 17 September 1980.

First produced in its revised, English-language version by Herbert Kretzmer at the Barbican Theatre, London, 30 September 1985, and at the Palace Theatre, London, 4 December 1985.

With words of youthful idealism,
Enjolras (Michael McGuire) encourages
his street-fighting friends into risking their
lives on the barricades.
Photograph by Michael Le Poer/Bob Marshak.

CHARACTERS

Jean Valjean

Javert

Fantine

Cosette, *her daughter*

Thénardier

Madame Thénardier

Éponine, *their daughter*

Marius

Montparnasse, Babet, Brujon, Claquesous, *Thénardier's gang*

Enjolras

Combeferre, Feuilly, Courfeyrac, Joly, Grantaire, Lèsgles, Jean Prouvaire, *students*

Bishop of Digne

Gavroche

Farmer, Laborer, Innkeeper, Innkeeper's wife, Foreman, Factory Girl, Old Woman, Crone, Pimp, Batambois, Fauchelevent, etc.

Act 1

Nearly twenty years ago, Jean Valjean was arrested for stealing a loaf of bread, and, his guilt established and his reasons unexplored, he was sent to prison for five years. Had he lived out his sentence under man's law resignedly, he would have been freed at the end of the five years, but Valjean's mind and heart revolted against his imprisonment and he attempted to escape. He was caught and his sentence increased and it was not until nineteen years had passed that Prisoner 24601 finally reached the day when he was eligible for parole from the fetters of the chain gang (Prologue: "Look Down, Look Down").

Parole is not the same as freedom. Valjean is a ticket-of-leave man, and, wherever he goes, honest folk shy away from him, refusing him work and shelter, until the good Bishop of Digne takes pity on him and offers him food and bed. Valjean returns the Bishop's kindliness by robbing him of his silver, silver that he might sell for the sort of money that can place him out of reach of those who scorn him, but the law that has ruled his life is not ready yet to let him go, and the thief is arrested.

The Bishop, however, will not bear witness against him and even claims before the constables that he gave the silver to Valjean as a gift, adding, in corroboration, two valuable candlesticks to the bewildered man's hoard. With this silver Valjean may, nay must, start a new and honest life. The Bishop has bought his soul for God (Soliloquy: "What Have I Done?") and his life must begin anew.

Eight years pass and Valjean, having broken his parole, has created himself a new life and a new identity under the name of Madeleine in the small town of Montreuil. There he has become both a wealthy factory owner and mayor of the town. The folk of his town and those who work in his factory are no better off than he was in his young days ("At the End of the Day") and one who finds life particularly hard is the young Fantine. She has not only to support herself but also to send money to support her illegitimate daughter who is being brought up by foster parents in the country. Nevertheless, she will not yield to the sexual advances of Valjean's foreman to help alleviate her troubles.

When Valjean sees her fighting with another factory girl over a letter about her daughter, he pauses only long enough to order the girls brought to book and not to inquire into the reasons for their brawl. Fantine's secret is exposed, and the foreman revengefully dismisses her. With no job, Fantine is in despair ("I Dreamed a Dream") and finally, desperate for money to send to the ever-demanding foster parents to ensure her daughter's well-being, she sells her locket, her hair, and, finally herself, joining the "Lovely Ladies" who hawk their bodies along the docks.

Although her body is subjugated, Fantine's mind refuses to give in. One day, she rejects the advances of a particularly distasteful client and attacks him with her fingernails. The man is an important citizen, and Fantine finds herself brought before Inspector Javert, the self-same representative of the law who, so many years before, had paroled Valjean. Fantine is on the verge of being arrested when the Mayor arrives on the scene and orders that she be sent not to jail but to a doctor.

Javert does not recognize the flourishing citizen of Montreuil as the missing convict but, when Valjean uses his unusual physical strength to lift a runaway cart from the leg of a trapped man, Javert's mind is stirred into remembrance. Only one other man he has known could have accomplished such a feat of strength. He was a convict, a fugitive whom Javert has been tracking for years with the relentless regard for the letter of the law that drives him. But that man has just been recaptured.

Hearing that an innocent man is about to take his place in prison, Valjean is torn between the desire to remain free and his duty to innocence ("Who Am I?"). Finally, before the bar of the court, he tears open his shirt to expose his convict's brand and declares himself as Valjean.

Javert sets out to arrest his man, who has made his way to the hospital where Fantine lies dying ("Come to Me"). Valjean promises the woman, whose death he has partly caused by his lack of care, that he will atone for his neglect by being responsible for her daughter, but, before he can make his escape, the Inspector is upon him, armed for his arrest. Valjean pleads for a short reprive, just time enough to allow him to find the child, Cosette, and make provision for her safety and her future, but Javert is not willing to accept the word of a man who has proved himself a thief and a liar and he stands his ground. Valjean then uses his strength. He attacks Javert physically and, knocking the man of the law to the ground, he disappears into the night.

The little Cosette has not been cared for as her mother believed ("A Castle on a Cloud"). The foster-parents, a worthless inkeeper called Thénardier and his slatternly wife ("Master of the House"), have used the money Fantine sent for their own purposes and for the benefit of their spoiled daughter, Éponine, while treating Cosette as nothing better than a servant. When Valjean arrives to take her away, they wring as much cash from him as possible (Thénardier Waltz) before letting the child depart.

Ten years later, in 1832, both Valjean and Javert, still yearning for the day when he may recapture the man whose freedom stands before him as an insult both to the law and to himself as its unquestioning representative, are in Paris. Javert is still a policeman and Valjean is once again a prosperous gentleman, living a quiet and private life with the teenage Cosette whom he has raised as his own daughter. The Thénardiers, too, are in Paris but in a very different area. They inhabit the slums of the town where they lead a gang of street ruffians of which Éponine is a useful member. As for their young son Gavroche, he makes his friends among the beggars and whores of Paris (Beggars' Chorus).

Éponine has turned out a streetwise but decent child, in spite of her parents, and her sordid life is given its sunshine by a secret love that she carries for the student, Marius Pontmercy. Marius is fond of the youngster, but he is taken by a *coup de foudre* when he sees Cosette one day in the street. Their meeting is a brief one, for Javert happens upon the spot and Valjean swiftly disappears, hurrying the girl with him.

Thénardier arouses Javert's suspicions about the gentleman who had such a seeming fear of the law, and all the Inspector's old feelings rise obsessively up in him. Surely, with the right that is behind him, God will not let him be bested by this man ("Stars in Your Multitudes"). Eponine realizes that the girl Marius has fallen for is the very child with whom she was brought up and she bravely looks at the difference in their positions now, as Marius begs her to help him find Cosette once again.

General Lamarque, the sole member of the ruling government in whom the poor people of Paris have trust, is dying, and there is great unrest in the town. A group of students gather at a café to talk of revolution ("Red and Black"), and, when the news of Lamarque's death arrives, they rush out into the street, inflamed by wine and by the diatribes of Enjolras, one of the most dramatically idealistic of their group, to take up arms in the cause of what he and they envisage as freedom ("Do You Hear the People Sing").

Éponine leads Marius to the home of Valjean and Cosette, sheltered from the world behind high walls, and the boy climbs the wall to meet the girl he loves ("In My Life"/"A Heart Full of Love"). While Éponine waits outside, she sees the rest of Thénardier's gang approaching. They too have spied out the house of the prosperous gentleman and they are planning to rob it. Éponine, desperate to protect Marius, and afraid he may believe that she led the gang there from jealousy, braves her father's wrath and screams. The gang flee, but the fracas leaves Valjean convinced that Javert is again on his track, and, as Paris begins to boil with unrest, he swears to leave France altogether and take Cosette away once again ("One Day More").

Act 2   In the streets of Paris, the students and their allies set up barricades made from the debris of the city. Behind them they will conduct their battle against the government's troops ("Here Upon These Stones"). Marius has joined Enjolras's band and Éponine has braved the barricades to be by his side. The greatest service she can render him is to take a letter to Cosette, a letter expressing his love and his prayer that he will survive the coming battle so that he may once again be with her. Éponine stifles her own feelings and takes the letter, delivering it to Valjean who opens it and reads the young man's cry of love and hopeless hope. Her mission completed, Éponine determines to return to the barricades and the man she loves ("On My Own").

The students are already face to face with the army at the barricades when little Gavroche turns up a surprise. Javert has masqueraded as a revolutionary and infiltrated the students' camp as a spy, but the lad, who goes everywhere and sees everything, recognizes him and Javert is taken prisoner, defiantly predicting the fall of this foolish and illegal rebellion. The battle has already begun when Éponine returns, creeping through the flying bullets toward Marius, but her insistence on returning has been her bane; she is hit and she finds happiness only as she dies in Marius's arms ("A Little Drop of Rain").

Valjean makes his way to the barricades more successfully. He will fight on the rebels' side, but that is a secondary consideration. He has come to find Marius, to watch over his safety in the fighting, and to make sure he is protected and preserved for the sake of Cosette. In the course of events, he is given the opportunity to kill the imprisoned Javert but, declaring that he has nothing against a man who has done nothing but follow his duty, he instead slips the policeman's bonds and lets him go free. The amazed and uncomprehending Javert hurries away with a warning that Valjean's action changes nothing in his determination to render him some day up to the justice he has so long flouted.

As night falls, the students take rest and wine before the new day's fighting ("Drink with Me"), and Valjean sends up a quiet prayer that his mission to save Marius may succeed ("Bring Him Home"). But, when the next day comes, casualties mount quickly. Little Gavroche falls the first, collecting live ammunition from the corpses of fallen soldiers, and one by one the others follow, until it seems that Valjean alone is left alive behind the barricade.

Determinedly he searches out Marius and finds him, badly wounded but living. Making use of his great strength, he lifts the cover of a sewerage manhole and, as the army closes in on the barricades, he disappears into the network of tunnels that run under the Paris streets, carrying the unconscious boy over his back.

The sewers of the city have also become the lair of the foul Thénardier who brings there the bodies of the fallen to despoil them at his leisure ("Dog Eats Dog"). When Valjean falls unconscious under his efforts, Thénardier steals a ring from the unconscious Marius's hand, but he hurries away when he recognizes Valjean's face. Finally, Valjean emerges from the sewers with his burden and runs straight into Javert. This time there is no escape and he seeks none. He asks for time only to deliver Marius into the hands of a doctor, then he will return and Javert can do with him as he wishes.

Javert, barely knowing his own mind, agrees, and, when Valjean has departed he interrogates his soul (Soliloquy: "Who Is This Man?") as to the rights and wrongs, the legal and the moral necessities in his life and in Jean Valjean's. Nothing tallies. Nothing makes sense. Everything he believed in so firmly for so long he now doubts. Inspector Javert has come to the end of his quest and he has found only unbearable uncertitude. It is too much for him and he throws himself from a city bridge to his death in the waters of the Seine.

As the women of Paris bewail the foolish waste of life the fighting has caused ("Turning"), the recovering Marius brokenly looks at the empty café where his friends once flaunted their ideals ("Empty Chairs at Empty Tables"). That is all gone now. He is part of another world, a world in which Cosette is beside him and where he grows daily stronger, looking toward the day when they may be wed. To the boy, Valjean admits what he cannot say to Cosette: He is Jean Valjean, a criminal, and his tale might one day bring shame and disgrace on the child he has loved. As soon as she is safely married, he will leave them forever.

The wedding is celebrated magnificently (Wedding Chorale), and the Thénardiers turn up, masquerading unconvincingly as aristocrats, with the intention of blackmailing the bridegroom. Jean Valjean is a murderer and unless Marius pays them off they will reveal what Thénardier saw in the sewers the night the barricades fell—Valjean with a body over his shoulder. Thénardier brings out in evidence the ring he took from the victim's hand, and Marius recognizes it as his own.

Now he knows that he owes his life to Valjean, that it was he who carried him from the barricades to safety. As the Thénardiers mockingly carry on their charade of aristocracy ("Beggars at the Feast"), Marius and Cosette hurry to find Valjean. He is alone in his room and his life is dripping away. Already he can hear the voice of Fantine calling to him from the world beyond and, as he retails to Cosette her true history, the spirits of the dead crowd around him. At last, surrounded by love, he dies.

This synopsis is based on the revised, English language version of the show as produced first in England, and subsequently on Broadway.

1987

INTO THE WOODS

A MUSICAL IN TWO ACTS by James Lapine. Lyrics and music by Stephen Sondheim. Produced at the Old Globe Theatre, San Diego, December 1986.

Produced at the Martin Beck Theatre, New York, 5 November 1987, with Kim Crosby (Cinderella), Chip Zien (Baker), Joanna Gleason (Baker's Wife), Danielle Ferland (Little Red Riding-Hood), Bernadette Peters (Witch), and Robert Westenberg (Cinderella's Prince).

You never know what will happen if you venture *Into the Woods.* You can meet all sorts of folk from fairy tales other than your own, and . . . look out for giants! Photograph © Martha Swope

CHARACTERS

Narrator

Cinderella

Jack

Jack's Mother

Baker

Baker's Wife

Cinderella's Stepmother

Cinderella's Father

Cinderella's Mother

Florinds

Lucinda

Little Red Riding-Hood

Witch

Mysterious Man

Wolf

Granny

Rapunzel

Rapunzel's Prince

Cinderella's Prince

Steward

Giant

Snow White

Sleeping Beauty

Once upon a time, in the eighteenth-century heyday of the brand-spanking new fairy tale, the authors of such tales had the habit of equipping their work with a Moral. In its simplest form, it was, of course, there in the action for all who were interested to read or listen to, but if the author thought it seemly, she also dropped in a little—or not so little—essay, an improving homily, as a forepiece or afterpiece to her history of princes and princesses and the latest variation of the forces of evil. *Into the Woods* is a late twentieth-century fairy tale—for all that it borrows a number of characters from those earlier works— and that necessarily means its characters aren't satisfied to let you off with just an optional homily. In between the more normal activities of a fairy tale, such as dropping slippers and killing giants, these folk talk. And talk. And analyse. There are no psychiatrists in fairyland, you see. And *Into the Woods* is a fairy tale for the Age of the Psychiatrist.

Act 1 The folk of our fairy tale are discontented. Most of them, that is. Half-witted, thatch-topped Jack is in the dumps because his cow Milky-White seems to have given up producing milk. His mother is down because she has a fool of a son who doesn't know a male cow from a female one, and because she's a sluttish housekeeper who hasn't got any money nor the prospect of any. The Baker and his wife are sad and frustrated because Mrs. Baker doesn't seem to be able to conceive a child, and they want to be parents. And Cinderella, a smut-nosed slavey to her horrid stepmother and florid stepsisters, just wants to get out of the house. You know she will. She'll go to the ball and marry the prince. But, hang on, you aren't face to face with the usual Cinderella here. You can tell, the moment she opens her mouth. Where other, reasonably normal Cinderellas want to go to the ball, this one tells us that "I Wish To Go To the Festival." She wishes. They all wish. They all wish one thing or another. That something in their lives was changed. And if it were changed, why they'd each and every one be so much happier.

The action of our tale begins with the appearance of Little Red Riding-Hood. She's off into the woods to visit her granny, and so she's called by the Baker's house to beg a loaf of bread, not to mention some buns and pies, all of which are pretty unlikely to make it to granny's house. For Little Red Riding-Hood has gluttonous appetites ("Into the Woods"). Now is perhaps the moment—before we get too deeply in—to say that these woods that she's off into aren't just woods. You know, trees and grass and a nice little windy path trimmed with daisies. They're Highly Significant Woods. Woods with a Deeper Meaning. They represent Life. Just as you never know what you're going to run into in the next moment of your life, so you never know what's lurking round the next tree. So look out. You've been warned.

Little Red Riding-Hood isn't the only one who ends up the opening number ready to go off into the woods. Jack's mother has had enough of the milkless cow—especially since Jack's been pumping its useless udder in her living room—and she sends the boy off to sell the beast for no less than five pounds (sterling is apparently currency in fairyland). The way to market lies through the woods.

The Baker and his wife have had an unsolicited visit from the ugly witch next door. She's apparently come for no other reason than to gloat, and she's got a horrid story to tell. The reason the couple are childless is that she has put a barren spell on them. Once upon a time, when the Baker's mother was with child, his father went out to gather greens to staunch her pregnant cravings. Unfortunately, he stole them from his neighbor's extraspecial heirloom of a garden. This is not the kind of thing you should do to anyone's vegetables, and it's certainly not a thing you can do with impunity to the vegetables of an influential fairy. When the witch discovered that the Baker's father had even stolen some of her most magic beans she was wand-waving furious. She not only confiscated their new-born child, and watched its mother die of despair, but she cursed the whole house with childlessness forever. Well, almost forever.

You see, the witch wasn't always hideous. She was young and pretty. It wasn't until the beans her mother had willed to her were carried off by the Baker that an ancestral fury fell upon her and she became the gnarled and horrid creature you now see. So even the witch isn't exempt from the general sentiment of wanting something: She wants to be young and pretty again. And there's a way. Someone has to bring her four ingredients: a cow as white as milk, a cape as red as blood, hair as yellow as corn, and a slipper as pure as gold. So if the Baker and his wife want the curse taken off them, they'd better get smartly off into the woods a-looking for the cow, the cape, the hair, and the footwear. They've got three days. The Baker is very macho and insists on going alone. Only he can't remember the list of things half the time. So his wife decides to go into the woods, too, at a distance.

Cinderella has been ripped-off. Her stepmother said she could go to the Festival (it's not just one ball, you see, it's three: one on each of the successive nights leading up to the witch's deadly deadline) if she got a bundle of beans cleared out of the ashes. She cheated, and got her bird friends to peck them out, but she did it. Then her stepmother said she didn't have a decent frock or coiffure and wouldn't take her anyhow. So while the rest of the family trundle off to the palace, Cinderella heads into the woods to sit by her mother's grave. She can have a good weep and, with any luck, a touch of magic might drum her up a passable outfit.

Oddly enough, all these folk who are setting out into the woods think they'll be home before it gets dark. Cinderella gets served first and most uncomplicatedly. She clearly knew what she was doing. Her mother speaks to her from beyond the grave, turns on a bit of magic, and presto, she's decked out in a lovely gold and silver dress and golden slippers. Cinderella sets out to cover on foot the journey to the palace that her sisters made by coach.

Little Red Riding-Hood has a less magical but more eventful time. She's skipping along the path grannywards when she encounters a Wolf ("Hello, Little Girl"). The Wolf tries to encourage her to slow down and be companionable, to try something new in the way of little-girlish experience, but Red Riding-Hood remembers her mother's instructions and speeds on her way. Not only one pair of covetous eyes follows her. For if the wolf has culinary plans for those plump little thighs, the Baker has his eyes on that red cape: Item One in his Quest.

Unlike the Wolf, however, the Baker has qualms. You can't strip a little girl of her outermost garment just like that. He pauses, and his pause means his wife catches up with him. It seems as if they are going to start arguing rights and wrongs all over again, when they suddenly spot Jack coming through the wood, with the cow: Item Two.

Jack isn't very happy ("I Guess This Is Goodbye"). And he's confused. He's met a Mysterious Man who's told him he won't ever get five pounds for his cow. He'll be lucky to swap it for a bag of beans. So when he meets the Baker and his wife and they offer him the handful of "magic" beans found in the Baker's father's old jacket in exchange for Milky-White, he unenthusiastically agrees. Maybe he can buy her back later.

The Baker is taken aback to find that they've little better than fiddled the boy, but his wife is more pragmatic. They need the cow. And anyway they only told a little lie about those old beans ("Maybe They're Magic"). She sets off homeward with the cow while her husband goes after the cape. He catches up with Red Riding-Hood and his moral compunctions aren't put too sadly to the test. After he's rescued her and her granny from the wolf's stomach, she actually gives him the cape as a thank-you present ("I Know Things Now").

The Baker's Wife meets Cinderella running home through the trees, with one heck of a tale about being at a ball and dancing with the Prince ("A Very Nice Prince"). Then she sees the escaping lady's shoes. Gold ones: Item Three. Mrs. Baker very much needs one of those shoes. But while she's chasing Cinderella's footwear, the cow gets away; then one of the "magic" beans that Jack's angry mother had thrown away shoots a beanstalk skyward.

When we next see Jack, he's been up the beanstalk ("There Are Giants in the Sky"). He's had a really nice time with some really nice giants, but he got homesick so he's filched a sack of his new friends' gold and climbed down home. Now he can go and give the Baker the money and get Milky-White back. But the Baker has no intention of giving back the cow. And even if he did, he couldn't. The Baker's Wife has lost it!

In another part of the forest, two Princes meet. One is the one from the ball, and he's looking for Cinderella. The other one is his brother, who's seen this damsel called Rapunzel up in a tower and fallen for her. He climbs her long hair to get up to her, but he can't get her down. Both Princes are in a delicious, unconnubial fit of "Agony" at not being able to have what they want.

Their duet is overheard by the Baker's Wife and, although she's not disinterested in Princes, what really catches her interest is the mention of Rapunzel's hair. Item Four. The last one (providing they can get the cow back and Cinderella's shoe off). She heads for the tower, fools the girl into flopping her braids over the windowsill, and tugs sharply. She's got her hands full of tresses when Cinderella comes pounding past, just like the previous night. This time the goodwife grabs for the all-important shoe. But the Prince and Cinderella's family are close behind and their prey lurches to escape as they arrive pantingly on the scene, closely followed by the Baker, who has found the cow!

Now the questing pair have three items. Actually, the Baker's Wife is finding this new adventuring spirit in her husband quite pleasing. He, in his turn, is finding that husband-and-wife teamwork is a good thing ("It Takes Two"). Then suddenly Jack rushes on, chasing a hen that lays golden eggs. It lays one in the delighted baker's hand, but when Jack demands his cow back in return, trouble bubbles up. And at the height of the arguing, the cow drops dead.

Two midnights gone, and now they need a new cow and they still haven't got that jolly shoe. The Baker is a little less nice about his methods now as the nitty-gritty nighs. Especially as he has just one bean left to get a cow with while his wife does something about Cinderella's footwear.

The Bakers are, however, not the only folk in these woods to have problems. The witch is having a real tantrum. She's discovered that Rapunzel's elevating trick with the hair isn't being used to get just the witch she calls mother up to the top of her tower but a nasty, randy Prince as well. After all her efforts to keep her child away from the ills and evils of the world, the little brat seems keen to go and dabble in it all ("Stay with Me").

The third night is getting to its mid, and so Cinderella—who's been out on a third night's fairy-tale cockteasing—pretty soon puts in an appearance. But tonight she's in quite a state. The Prince had covered the palace steps with pitch, and when she tried to do her nightly flit, she got stuck. She's had to leave a perfectly good shoe behind ("On the Steps of the Palace"). The Baker's Wife swaps her two ordinary slip-ons for the remaining gold one, just as the Baker turns up with a white cow. They've done it!

Even an amazing jolt and thump, and Jack's Mother screaming that a giant has fallen into their back garden, cannot stop the anxious questers from getting their magic to the witch. But when the cow is brought forth it turns out to be a fake: The Baker has covered an ordinary cow with flour! The witch is furious and orders everyone to get down and dig up the dead Milky-White. She will bring the beast back to life. And so, with the four necessary items, the magic is made. The witch drinks down the glass of magical milk produced by the revived Milky-White, and as the last stroke of midnight tolls . . . it is done! The witch is young and beautiful again. Soon, Jack has money and his slightly bilious cow back, the Baker and his wife are uncursed, and Cinderella and Rapunzel have been united with a Prince apiece. As they all sing their happy ending there is barely a cloud in the sky. Except that the witch has, with her regained youth, lost her power and her daughter, and Cinderella's sisters, whose vanities have all been blown away, are blind. Their eyes have been pecked out by the birds in revenge for their past nastiness. Nothing's perfect. Even "Ever After."

Act 2

Act 2 begins as Act 1 did. Even in happily-ever-afterdom, people still have wants. Wishes. But by and large they're "So Happy." Until, one day, the Baker's roof falls in and the witch's garden is trampled down. Terror is abroad, and it's back "Into the Woods" again. But the woods have suffered too, and it soon becomes clear that, horror!, there's a giant abroad in fairyland.

The two blissfully unaware Princes, however, have other preoccupations. Now that they're happily married, they miss the exquisite striving for the impossible that they knew before. But happily one's discovered Snow White and the other Sleeping Beauty, both waiting to be rescued from their traditional predicaments ("Agony"). So, life still holds some delicious yearning for them.

But this little amorous predicament is nothing to the fix the whole of fairyland is in. The giant that's abroad is the wife of the one that fell down the beanstalk when Jack cut the thing down at the end of Act 1. She's the giant who welcomed Jack to their land in the skies before he robbed them of their gold, their hen, and their harp, and finally slew her husband. Now she wants revenge. The magicless witch is quite happy to give the boy up, but not everyone will agree, and dissension begins to blow up among the happy-ever-afterers.

The only person for whom no one seems to have any affection is the Narrator who's been doing an Edgar Lustgarten sort of commentary from the side of the stage at intervals in the evening when a bit of story needed explaining. He is pushed sacrificially into the Giant's murderous clutches, but even though the creature is thoroughly nearsighted she is not fooled. As the Narrator splatters to the ground, she comes on, demanding that Jack be brought to her. Jack's mother shrieks her defiance at the monster, and is fatally felled by Cinderella's Prince's Steward, then Rapunzel gets in the way of the forty-foot feet and perishes in her turn. The witch has lost her child. Why didn't she stay safe in the nice tower she built for her? (Lament).

The obvious thing to do now is find Jack. Maybe he can apologize. So the slightly depleted band spread out and start pacing the forest. The Baker's Wife runs into Cinderella's Prince and finds out what it's like to be chatted up, deep-grassed, and elegantly dumped by a real, live one-night-stander of a Prince ("Any Moment"/"Moments in the Wood"). It's quite an experience. But it's her last. As she gets up to continue her search, the trees crash down in front of her, and then comes the forty-foot foot.

At the same time that the Baker's Wife is being seduced for the last time, the witch finds Jack, and drags him back to the meeting place in the wood. Now he's got to make reparation for all the trouble he's caused. But was it his fault? Depending on how you look at it, it was just about anybody's fault ("Your Fault"), and just about anyone can blame anyone else. Except—hang on—who produced those troublemaking beans in the first place. The witch! It's all *her* fault.

The witch is up to her ears with it all ("The Last Midnight"). Her fault! That's fine, coming from this bunch of liars and cheats and thieves. All willing to do anything at all to get their hands on what they wanted in life. Well, she's had enough. She scatters handfuls of beans around her, throwing them away in defiance of the same law that brought age and ugliness on her before. She doesn't care. It's the end. She's going. And they can all get on with the world and the woods on their own.

The despairing Baker is about to leave his motherless baby with Cinderella and set out into a new life, but a duet ("No More") with the Mysterious Man—who is none other than his bean-stealing father, still loitering in the woods to do a little good—restiffens his courage, and he returns to join the other survivors in a philosophical ensemble encouraging each other to believe "No-One Is Alone." Then the Baker and Jack set out to trap the Giant, with the aid of some of Cinderella's Prince's pitch, and Cinderella's eye-pecking birds. Their plan works. The Giant is trapped, blinded, and falls.

As the evening's action winds down, everyone looks to the future. Little Red Riding-Hood (whose mother got splattered as well) will take the place in Jack's life previously held by his mother. Since they have no house left, they'll move in with the Baker. And since Cinderella has no intention of returning to the faithless Prince and his far-too-fairy-tale castle, she'll come and do the housework.

All the dead and departed come back to life for one last number, full of homily. It ends with a happily ever after, but as the music ends, Cinderella's voice can be heard—as it was at the opening—mooning "I wish . . . "

The Phantom of the Opéra

A MUSICAL IN A PROLOGUE AND TWO ACTS based on the novel by Gaston Leroux. Book by Andrew Lloyd Webber and Richard Stilgoe. Lyrics by Charles Hart. Additional lyrics by Richard Stilgoe. Music by Andrew Lloyd Webber.

      Produced at the Majestic Theatre, New York, 26 January 1988, with Michael Crawford (Phantom), Sarah Brightman/Patti Cohenour (Christine), Judy Kaye (Carlotta), Steve Barton (Raoul), Nick Wyman (Firmin), and Cris Groenendaal (André). Originally produced at Her Majesty's Theatre, London, 9 October 1986.

The Phantom (Michael Crawford) might look as if he's about to take a bite out o of Christine Daaé (Sarah Brightman), but he's only singing to her "The Music of Photograph by Clive Barda.

Prologue

On the stage of the Opéra de Paris in 1905, an auction sale of properties, ephemera, and other articles exhumed from the theatre's vaults is taking place. Several lots are sold to an elderly gentleman who is named as Raoul, Vicomte de Chagny, among them an oriental musical box in the form of a monkey and barrel organ. It is a piece that clearly has a relevance to the story of the old gentleman's life. The auctioneer brings forward the reassembled fragments of a giant chandelier, recalling its connection with the strange and still incompletely explained tale of the Phantom of the Opéra, which had caused such excitement in Paris nearly half a century earlier. As the working portion of the chandelier is relit, the overture begins. Gradually, the chandelier grows from a fragment to full size and finally rises to the center of the house to hang in its former position as the stage of the Opéra returns to 1861.

Act 1

A dress rehearsal for the opera *Hannibal* is in progress with the portly tenor Ubaldo Phangi in the title role and the soprano Carlotta Giudicelli in the florid star role of Elissa, when the proprietor of the Opéra, Monsieur Lefèvre, interrupts the proceedings to introduce to the company his successors. Messrs Firmin and André are to take over the running of the theatre under the patronage of the young Vicomte de Chagny. The gentlemen watch the rehearsal as Carlotta displays her art in flights of coloratura, and Phangi performs a decidedly hefty Hannibal. At their request, the prima donna obliges with an out-of-context rendition of the aria "Think of Me."

As she sings, there is a crash and the backdrop tumbles down dangerously near to her head. The chorus and ballet girls cry out aloud—it is the Phantom of the Opéra. Carlotta stalks furiously from the stage, leaving Lefèvre to brush aside an incident that might alarm the new owners. His task is not made easier when the ballet mistress, Madame Giry, brings a message that she says has come from the Phantom himself. It is addressed to André and Firmin and reminds them of his requirements. Box Five shall be left unsold, as it was under Lefèvre's management, for the private use of the Phantom, and his monthly salary shall be punctually paid.

In the meanwhile, the Opéra is without a prima donna. Carlotta is refusing to perform in *Hannibal* that evening and there is no understudy. Madame Giry's little daughter, Meg, who is performing in the Opéra ballet, puts forward the seemingly ridiculous idea that one of her fellow dancers, Christine Daaé, should tackle the extremely technical and difficult role. Firmin and André are properly sceptical at the idea of a ballet girl becoming a prima donna but, having no other answer, they permit Christine to sing for them. The girl obliges with "Think of Me," and, as she sings, the scene changes to the evening performance in which she is appearing in the role of Elissa.

Watching from their box, Firmin and André are delighted with their discovery, but the Vicomte de Chagny is even more thrilled for he recognizes in the new prima donna a childhood acquaintance, a little girl whose scarf he once rescued from the sea and whose face and friendship have remained ever since in his mind.

As Christine returns to her dressing room at the end of the performance, the sound of a strange voice echoes in her ears, "bravi, bravi, bravissimi." It is a voice that, she confides to Meg, she knows well. She has a mysterious teacher whom she has never seen and whom she believes to be the "Angel of Music." When Christine's musician father lay dying, he comforted her by telling her that he would send the angel of music to guard over her in her loneliness. His promise has come true for, alone in her dressing room, she is visited by a disembodied voice that has encouraged and trained her in her singing until her lovely young voice has attained sufficient scope to allow her to perform a role such as Elissa.

The managers hurry backstage to lavish their congratulations on the new prima donna, but Raoul de Chagny orders them away as, alone with Christine, he happily recalls their childish days and the song they sang together about the angel of music ("Little Lotte"). Christine earnestly tells Raoul that she has truly been visited by that angel. Not taking her literally, he laughingly agrees and asks her to supper.

No sooner has he left to allow her to change than Christine's angel comes to her, his voice full of anger at Raoul's familiarity with his pupil. He has decided the time has come when she shall know his face and he commands her to look into her mirror. There, in the glass before Christine's eyes, stands a cloaked and masked figure, calling to her to come to him. Waiting outside the room, Raoul becomes alarmed at the sound of conversation but he cannot open the locked door. When, at last, the door opens of its own accord, he finds that Christine is no longer there. She has disappeared through the mirror.

The Phantom—for Christine's angel is he—leads his pupil through the secret passageways behind the mirror down into the caverns and underground waterways deep below the Opéra, ferrying her by boat through a subterranean lake, which seems to be lit by innumerable candelabra, as her mind tries to reconcile her old thoughts of an angel with what is all too clearly a man ("The Phantom of the Opéra").

The Phantom takes Christine to his home, a set of richly furnished rooms hidden beyond the lake and far under the streets of Paris. He has brought her there to sing for him, to be his creature and his inspiration. Under his influence she will sing like no one has ever sung before ("The Music of the Night"). He caresses her and she loses her fear of him sufficiently to touch the strange mask that covers his face, as he removes a dust sheet to display a waxen image of Christine herself dressed in a bridal gown and veil. As Christine stares at the model, amazed, it moves toward her and she faints.

When she awakens the next morning it is to find the Phantom at work at a gigantic organ, composing his music. Beside her, a little Persian music box is tinkling out a melody as she attempts to bring back the strange, dreamlike events of the previous night ("I Remember"). But it is no dream. The man is there. Approaching him quietly, she whisks away his mask to reveal a hideously deformed face. The Phantom turns on her furiously. Now that she has seen his real face she will think of him always as a physically deformed creature rather than one whose mind and skills can produce beauty ("Stranger Than You Dreamt It"). Reluctantly, too, he knows he must return her to the theatre before her absence causes a search. She will return to the Opéra and carry out the plans that he has made for her.

Backstage in the theatre, Joseph Buquet, a stagehand, is frightening the chorus girls with tales of the Phantom and the ghastly Punjab knot, a seemingly magical piece of rope with which the ghostly creature has been known to strangle his victims ("Magical Lasso"). At the same time, up in the managers' office, Firmin and André are finding that Christine's triumph and the mystery of her disappearance are potent box-office attractions, but, nevertheless, they have problems.

The Phantom has sent a series of "Notes" to the personnel of the Opéra: a critique of the performance to André, a reminder to Firmin that his salary is still unpaid, a threat to Raoul that he must not attempt to make further contact with Christine, and another to Carlotta telling her that should she attempt to resume her place as prima donna a dreadful fate will befall her. Finally, there is one for Madame Giry detailing the Phantom's plans for the Opéra. The next opera to be presented will be *Il Muto* in which Christine shall be given the leading role of the Countess while Carlotta plays the nonsinging role of the page boy. Carlotta is furious, and André and Firmin have to beg her to return with the assurance that the casting will be exactly the reverse ("Prima Donna").

When *Il Muto* is staged ("Poor Fool He Makes Me Laugh"), the Phantom takes his revenge. In the middle of the performance, he causes Carlotta to croak like a toad, and, when she tries to continue, he causes the chandelier to tremble so violently that the prima donna breaks down and cannot carry on. The managers hurriedly bring the curtain down and announce that the opera will be resumed shortly. A ballet is rushed on to fill the gap but, as the scenery parts, the body of Joseph Buquet is spied dangling hideously from a Punjab knot.

Christine hurries Raoul up on to the roof of the theatre. There, at least, they will be far from the secret passageways of the theatre and safe from the Phantom's all-seeing eyes ("Why Have You Brought Me Here?"). She pours out to the incredulous Raoul the frightful and frightening tale of her underground journey with the Phantom ("Raoul, I've Been There") and he comforts her with words that soon turn to words of love ("All I Ask of You"). As they kiss, a shadowy figure is seen behind the huge winged statue crowning the pediment of the building: The Phantom is there, he has seen them, and in his heart he is betrayed.

Christine returns to the stage to complete the opera in Carlotta's place, but, as she steps forward to take her curtain call, there is a terrible volley of laughter and the great chandelier topples from its moorings and crashes to the stage at Christine's feet. The Phantom has delivered his warning.

Act 2

It is New Year's Eve, and the Opéra is host to a great masked ball ("Masquerade"). Six months have passed since the episode of the chandelier and, to everyone's relief, there has been no further evidence of the infamous Phantom. Raoul and Christine have become secretly engaged and she wears his ring on a chain around her neck, but she cannot bring herself to wear it openly for deep inside her the fear of the Phantom still stirs. She is right still to fear for, at the height of the ball, he appears splendidly dressed with a death's-head mask glittering appallingly where his usual mask should be ("Why So Silent?").

His long silence is now explained. He has brought them the score of an opera he has composed, *Don Juan Triumphant*, and commands that the Opéra shall stage it or risk even worse events than the harmless smashing of a chandelier. Approaching Christine, he seizes the chain around her neck and tears the ring from it. She is his, and no ring nor chain can alter that. Before the terrified girl can reply, he vanishes, seemingly into nothing, leaving his garments in a heap on the floor.

Raoul will not accept a supernatural explanation and sets out to discover more about this Phantom. He has noticed enough to know where to begin his questioning: Madame Giry clearly has information that she has not revealed. Under his questioning she tells her tale. Many years ago, in a low Paris fair, she saw a freak on display. It was a man, a dreadfully deformed creature, but a man with a prodigious mind and great talents who, it was said, had built for a Persian monarch a dreadful torture-chamber in the form of an inhuman maze of mirrors. The creature escaped from his exhibitor and vanished, no one knew where, and it was soon afterward that the strange happenings began at the Opéra. If it were this man with his amazingly inventive mechanical mind and his deadly Persian noose who had been causing the seemingly inexplicable happenings of the past years in the theatre, perhaps they would not then be quite so inexplicable.

André and Firmin are appalled by *Don Juan Triumphant*. It is certainly not Meyerbeer, Bellini, Mozart, or even Rameau. It is full of strange unmelodious music, which they would not dream of presenting on their stage, but they are too frightened to refuse and, out of fear, they submit to the insulting "Notes" by which the Phantom organizes and directs the preparations for the production. Carlotta is cast in a minor role, while the prima donna role goes to Christine who, it is emphasized, must return to her "angel" for further tuition.

Christine is unwilling to play the part written for her, but Raoul insists that *Don Juan Triumphant* must be performed. The Phantom will be sure to come to his box to watch the performance and then he can be arrested. Christine does not know what to do ("Twisted Every Way"). Can she lead to his death the man who was once her angel, and can she bear to perform this opera knowing how and why it was written?

Don Juan Triumphant is put into rehearsal and Phangi finds it impossible to cope with the untraditional intervals of the Phantom's music, turning the concerted music into a shambles. Christine is still prey to mixed fears and longings. Asleep and awake, she can hear the Phantom coaxing her voice from her, the angel of music her father promised her, yet surely no angel. At her father's grave she opens her heart ("Wishing You Were Somehow Here Again"), but, in reply, she hears only the voice of the Phantom as the figures of father and guiding angel become strangely mixed in her mind ("Wandering Child"). But the Phantom is actually there. He has dared to issue forth from his labyrinth, and from among the gravestones he is attempting to woo the girl to him. He is foiled by the appearance of Raoul, who breaks the spell and carries Christine to safety under the furious imprecations of the Phantom ("Bravo, Monsieur").

On the night of the première of *Don Juan Triumphant*, marksmen are strategically placed in the auditorium of the Opéra, but the Phantom plays his voice around the theatre distractingly, unnerving the soldiers completely. When the opera starts, Phangi plays the role of Don Juan up to the last scenes in which he lays siege to the chastity of the peasant girl, Aminta, played by Christine. Taking his servant's cloak, Don Juan disguises himself and hides to await the approach of Aminta. But as Phangi steps into the shadows, he falls victim to the Punjab knot, and, when Don Juan emerges, it is the cloaked Phantom himself who faces Christine ("The Point of No Return").

As he sings, the passion in his words builds beyond the confines of the role. He pours forth his love and, giving her his ring, begs Christine to save him from his dreadful solitude. As he reaches his final plea, the girl steps forward and pulls away his cloak—the Phantom is revealed to the whole world in his deformed state. With a howl, he vanishes, bearing Christine with him, as the marksmen rush to the stage to discover only the lifeless body of Phangi. Once again, Christine is forced down into the underways of Paris ("Down Once More") with the theatre staff and a troop of armed men hurrying in pursuit ("Track Down This Murderer").

In the Phantom's abode, Christine faces up to the man who would be her lover, this man who thinks himself persecuted because of his dreadful appearance. His actions belie his words. His face means nothing to her. She can see beyond it not to a tortured soul but to an evil one, and she can have no pity for him. If she cannot feel pity she can never feel love. Raoul, meanwhile, has succeeded in following their tracks through the labyrinth and he appears at the grill masking the Phantom's home from the lake outside. The Phantom laughingly lets him enter and, from nowhere, the dreaded Punjab knot appears, snaking around the young man's neck and choking the life from him as the Phantom bids Christine make her choice: Give her love to him or see Raoul die.

Finally Christine steps toward the creature and kisses him long on the lips. His appearance does not daunt her; he need not be alone. The kiss breaks something inside the Phantom. When she moves away, he releases the rope from Raoul's neck and, as the voices of the pursuing mob are heard in the distance, bids them go. While the music box plays, Christine returns his ring and, as he whispers "Christine, I love you," she and Raoul step into the boat to cross the lake and return to their freedom. Then the Phantom covers himself under his cloak and, when the mob invade his home and the cloak is torn aside, he has vanished. Only his mask remains.

CITY OF ANGELS

A MUSICAL IN TWO ACTS by Larry Gelbart. Lyrics by David Zippel. Music by Cy Coleman.
Produced at the Virginia Theatre, New York, 11 December 1989, with James Naughton (Stone), Gregg Edelmann (Stine), Randy Graff (Oolie/Donna), Kay McClelland (Gabby/Bobbi), Dee Hoty (Alaura/Carla), and Rene Auberjonois (Fidler/Irwin).

Author Stine (Gregg Edelman), his wife (Kay McLelland), and hero Stone (James Naughton) soar above the soapy remains of Stone's screenplay at the final curtain of *City of Angels*. Photograph © Martha Swope.

CHARACTERS

Stine, *a writer of fiction*

Gabby, *his wife*

Buddy Fidler, *a movie director-producer*

Donna, *his secretary*

Carla Haywood, *his wife*

Jimmy Powers

Avril Raines, *a starlet*

Pancho Varga, *an actor*

Del Dacosta, *a songwriter*

Angel City 4, Gilbert, Anna, Shoeshine boy, Studio Engineer, Gerald Pierce, Werner Krieger, Stand-in, Cinematographer, Prop Man, Gene, Buddy's nephew, Soundman, Clapperboy, Studio cops, Hairdresser

People in the Movie

Stone, *a private eye*

Oolie, *Stone's secretary*

Alaura Kingsley, *a femme fatale*

Peter Kingsley, *her stepson*

Mallory Kingsley, *her stepdaughter*

Luther Kingsley, *her husband*

Big Six, *a thug*

Sonny, *a smaller thug*

Jimmy Powers, *a movie crooner*

Lieutenant Munoz, *a police detective*

Bobbi, *Stone's ex-fiancée*

Irwin S. Irving, *a movie mogul*

Dr. Sebastian Mandril

The Angel City Four, hospital orderlies, Man in a phone booth, Margaret, Butler, Man with a camera, Mahoney, Harlan Yamoto, Gaines, Guard, Girl, Margie, Bootsie

City of Angels takes place in two places: in real life, and on the movie screens that exist in the minds of Stine, the author of the screenplay that is to become the film *City of Angels*, and of his producer Buddy Fidler. The action of the musical swings backward and forward between reality and soon-to-be-celluloid, with the same actors filling the real-life supporting roles around author Stine and the screen ones around his film hero, Stone. In a stage production, the switch from reality into film mode is signified by a bit of color coding. Real life takes place in full color; the film scenes are played in black and white.

Act 1   One, two, three shots ring out. An ambulance siren shrieks. And a voice is heard— one of those wry, darkness-filled voices whose duty it was to narrate the events and thoughts of the private eye films of the 1930s—telling us, in pure gumshoe lingo, at whom those shots were aimed. They were aimed at the man who is now a body on the hospital trolley that's coming toward us. And that body is—or was?—Stone, a private dick in the ironically named City of Angels—Los Angeles. So what happened?

Flashback seven days. We're in Stone's office and he has a visitor. A devastatingly glamorous dame who, after some unconvincing finessing, admits that she is the extraordinarily wealthy Mrs. Alaura Kingsley. And she's in trouble. Her luscious teenaged stepdaughter is missing. As he looks at Mrs. Kingsley and looks at the photo of missing Mallory, as he listens to his visitor's beautifully proportioned "Double Talk," every drop of whiskey in Stone's veins cries out that there's a nasty curve hidden somewhere in this affair, though it's not visible to the slavering eye. When a check for $100 goes on the table, the slavering eye moves like lightning. In less time than it takes to say "hard cash," Stone is hired. Then, as Mrs. Kingsley starts to leave, the action grinds to a halt. And goes into reverse.

Author Stine is erasing his last few lines. But he's no sooner got the scene going forward again than the phone rings. His characters and their doings go into limbo as he takes a call from his producer, Buddy Fidler. Now it's Stine's turn to listen to some "Double Talk" in the bits of conversation that are directed at him between Buddy's other telephone calls. It seems that Buddy doesn't like the flashback opening. It has to go. Stone shrugs—for the kind of money he's being paid he can do without his opening scene. And at least his producer seems interested in the film, even if he's a bit tart in his comments. He goes back to work, and his characters take up where he and they left off.

Stone sends his faithful secretary Oolie out to cash the $100 dollar check, and starts thinking about where to start looking for Mallory Kingsley. Then. . . .

Stine is watching his wife packing. Gabby's an editor for a New York publishing house, and she's going back east for some meetings. Mrs. Stine is an unusual lady. She's into integrity, and in more ways than one. She hates her husband's zero-loaded contract with the film studio, for example, because she sees it as him prostituting his talents. She's also suspicious—with past proofs on her side—of his ability to keep his pants on when she's not around. But life has to go on. He goes off to a studio showing. She goes for her plane. And, as both sides of the action take a pause, we hear Gabby Stine and Oolie, Stone's secretary, duetting in the direction of their husband and employer respectively "What You Don't Know about Women."

Stone has begun his search for Mallory by checking into a motel. But he soon has a visitor, two visitors. They turn up the radio nice and loud, and while superstar crooner Jimmy Powers and his Angel City Four musically warn "Ya Gotta Look Out for Yourself," they take Stone to pieces.

Buddy Fidler loves that bit. Except for the words. Writers. They always use too many words. But he'll fix it. Like he always fixes it. That's "The Buddy System."

The mangling of Stone is investigated by the local police, headed by one Lieutenant Munoz. Now Munoz was once a colleague of Stone's when Stone was a policeman himself, and it's his guess that, if Stone's in trouble, there's a woman in the case. Just like last time. . . .

Last time was years back. Stone was in love with a nightclub chantoosie called Bobbi Edwards ("With Every Breath I Take") and wanted her to marry him. But Bobbi had dreams of stardom, and she wouldn't take that step into matrimony until the greatly influential Hollywood producer Irwin S. Irving had been by her act. Only trouble was, Irwin wanted a different kind of act out of her, and Stone walked in while the performance was on. And emptied a couple of cartridges into Mr. Hollywood.

Stine is exchanging longing transcontinental words with Gabby when Donna, Buddy's secretary, turns up. She wants to break the latest bit of bad news to him gently. Buddy doesn't like that bit, the bit where Irwin gets shot. Donna smiles. Surely Stine realizes that the producer must see himself in the character. Stine isn't so sure. Does Donna see herself in Oolie? She doesn't, but she's free to take dinner that night with a temporarily womanless writer.

Up at the Kingsley mansion, overlooming the Arroyo Seco Canyon on the top of Paso Robles Drive, Alaura Kingsley is having her ready-for-tennis upper thigh deeply oiled by her stepson, when Stone puts in an appearance. He is going to drop the case. But Alaura will have none of it. To convince her private eye how much she needs him, she introduces Stone to her husband, Luther Kingsley, warplane maker and multibillionaire. Luther lives in an iron lung, his well-being cared for by the omming Doctor Sebastian Mandril. He is also, apparently, willing to pay $10,000 for his daughter's recovery. Zeroes spell danger, but they also spell game, set, and match to Mrs. Kingsley ("Tennis Song").

Stone starts his search for Mallory at the bottom, among the city's lowest forms of life ("Everybody's Gotta Be Somewhere"). It's dirty work, and at the first day's end he is ready for his bed. Only it's occupied, by a naked woman. He knows from her photograph that his search is over ("Lost and Found"). But then Mallory starts to untie his tie. . . .

Back in real life, Donna is tying up Stine's. Gabby was right. Keeping his pants on isn't one of her husband's greater talents.

Stone is better at it. He likes to talk first. Or, rather, he wants Mallory to talk. She comes up with a not very original but not unconvincing tale of blackmail, at the end of which she pins the weary dick to the bed just long enough for a camera to flash. The story of Stone's life: another dame, another gun, another flashback.

This one takes him back to the moment when Irwin's corpse was rolled into the morgue. When the coroner allowed that—in spite of the bullet holes in his ribs and kidney—the movie mogul had died of natural causes. When Bobbi walked away. And Mexican Lieutenant Munoz—blazing with fury that his white-skinned colleague had been allowed to get away with murder—vowed that one day, one day he'd get him, somehow and for something, that would take him to the electric chair he ought to have gone to. That he would have gone to if he'd been a brownskin like Munoz.

"Munoz," "White-skinned"? What's all this racial-social crap? Cut it. And Irwin, dead, in the morgue? No, no, no. None of that. You've got a perfectly good corpse later on, after Dr. Mandril gets shot on the edge of the looming cliffs at Paso Roble. Anything you need to say or do in a morgue, you can say it or do it then. OK? But no social crap and no dead Irwin. And there's a list of no-no words, too. . . . You can't say things like Jesus Christ. Buddy is still fixing.

Rewrite. The confrontation between Munoz and Stone is now tacked into the scene following the murder of Dr. Mandril. Munoz has a song, and Stine has dropped the occasional Hispanic word into its lyrics with all the daring of a little boy trying out his first four letter words ("All Ya Have to Do Is Wait"). Then he tries to ease Buddy's newest idea into the script. Buddy's motive—to replace all that social crap—for Munoz's jealousy of Stone. Munoz had the hots for Bobbi, too. Stine tries his best, but, as the unconvincing dialogue pecks out of his typewriter, he meets a bit of unexpected resistance. Stone thinks it stinks, and he says so, right to his author's face. The two end up in a slanging match ("You're Nothing Without Me"), but Stine has the ultimate power. Fingers to his typewriter, he types "Munoz punches Stone hard in the stomach." And as his hero gasps at his creator's betrayal, the author types "fade out" and brings down the act curtain.

Act 2

The second act opens to Jimmy Powers and his backing group crooning "Stay with Me" along the airwaves. Airwaves that lead right to the Bel-Air bedroom of Mr. and Mrs. Buddy Fidler. Mrs. Fidler is actress Carla Haywood and she is to play Alaura in the film.

Stone is in jail, bagged by Munoz on suspicion of the murder of Dr. Mandril. Since he's in jail, he can't do much about finding out who ought to be in jail instead of him. Good old reliable Oolie promises to do her best, but right now it's her bedtime ("You Can Always Count on Me").

Stine wakes up in the real-life equivalent of that bed. Donna is alongside him. She tells him how well his rewrites work, while he lacerates himself enjoyably thinking of the scorn Gabby would pour on his endless compromising. And Donna takes up Oolie's tune as she puts herself down cleverly and come-onishly with her version of "You Can Always Count on Me."

Stine climbs out of bed and goes off to Buddy's top people's party. It's one of those showbiz parties where everybody is busy sizing-up or sneering over everyone else. The whole occasion swims in a cream-cheese-thick swell of soft soap. Stine doesn't have too good a time. He calls Gabby on Buddy's phone, only to find she'd called his lodging and got Donna. And Gabby may have loads of real integrity, but stupid she isn't. She hangs up on him. Then he gets cornered by the starlet who's been hired to play Mallory. She's ready to go down on her knees to him to have Mallory not get killed off before the dénouement. It's what she's obviously intending to do while she's down on her knees that has Stine—still suffering from Gabby's dropped-dead phone—lathered up.

A conversation with Carla also turns to script problems, most of them caused by Buddy's disembowelling of the original draft. But Stine has got into the Buddy swing now, and he's quite capable of coming up with a piece of old-fashioned train-on-the-tracks hokum involving a load of explosives and a tricked-up phone to get from one "fixed-up" fragment of his plot to the next.

Carla is sidetracked when music strikes up outside. Jimmy Powers is about to deliver. She's clearly quite used to Jimmy delivering. Curious that Buddy, who normally doesn't miss a trick, doesn't see what they're up to.

Stone is out of jail. His bail was mysteriously paid. By whom? You'd never guess. No, not one of the Kingsleys. It was the two bashemup boys from Act 1! But why? Because they needed to have a another even more painful and terminal interview with our hero. You see, Dr. Mandril had paid them in advance to avenge any untimely end he might come to, and being honorable men they're going to do it. But the business with the explosives and the tricked-up phone they organize goes painfully wrong. The hoods are exploded, Stone escapes, and, late that night, he suddenly appears at Alaura's bedroom window.

Stone wants explanations, Alaura has plenty. It appears that the whole thing was a put-up job organized by stepson Peter and by Mallory, and Stone was the fall guy. Alaura also has ways and means of stopping a fellow getting on with his job. And Stone isn't going to waste the opportunity.

Stine, on the other hand, looks as if he's going to throw every opportunity that's been opened to him out the window. He's leaving Hollywood for New York. He's going to find Gabby and convince her to come back to him. The only trouble is, she doesn't believe a word of his carefully worded explanation and she tells him so ("It Needs Work").

Stone, having apparently finished his business in Mrs. Kingsley's bedroom, has set off to dig out Peter Kingsley from the whorehouse that he frequents. He buys time to talk to the girl Peter visits regularly and finds . . . Bobbi, the girl for whose act of murder he carried the bag and took the sack. For what? For this ("With Every Breath I Take"). But now the pieces of the puzzle are starting to fit together. And a call from Oolie adds a vital squiggly bit. . . .

When Stone shows up that night at the Kingsley house, in the middle of a very picturesque storm, he finds Mrs. Kingsley spoonfeeding the head in the iron lung. The tale Stone has to reveal would make even an iron lung spew up its supper, especially when it is revealed that the supper is being served to him by the former Mrs. William Lloyd Drexel. Mrs. Drexel was a nurse who married her aged invalid husband and stood all ready to collect his millions when he finally died of lovingly administered slow poison. Unfortunately, Mrs. Drexel had forgotten about state-of-the-art autopsies, and so she had to give up her inheritance rather than be prosecuted by the Drexel children for murder.

Next time, with the botched rehearsal behind her, the former Mrs. Drexel, now Mrs. Kingsley, wasn't going to make the same mistake. Peter, Mallory, and the interfering Dr. Mandril all had to be disposed of, and who better than a cloddish private eye—especially one with a record for murder—to carry any cans that needed carrying. And, as the icing on her plan, that same dumb dick is now at the end of Mrs. Drexel/Kingsley's gun, about to pull out the plug that supplies electricity to the ineffably wealthy iron lung. Mallory is already dead, murdered by Peter who thinks himself his stepmother's ally. But Peter will never live to tell, for the brakes of his car have been. . . .

Then Peter rushes in. Followed by Mallory. It's all gone wrong! And it's time for the big confrontation. Body pressed to body, the villainess's gun squeezed bulkily between them, Alaura Drexel-Kingsley and Stone struggle toward the climax of the plot. Then one, two, three shots ring out. And Stone falls to the floor. Alaura's face is suffused with victory. Then she goes all red somewhere under her expressively shaped left breast. And, seconds later, she too hits the floor. It is the end.

It may be the end, but it's not the end as Stine wrote it. We might have known, when we saw Mallory there. Who has succumbed to the ingénue with the lips? Need we ask? While Stine was off in New York trying to tack his marriage back together, Buddy "fixed" the ending. Stine is livid. This is utter crap. And it soon becomes obvious that not only Buddy but Donna—and probably the shoeshine boy, the hairdresser, and the ingénue with the lips—have had a hand in it as well. Donna, who he'd thought was on his side! "Funny."

It is the first day of the shooting of Buddy Fidler's new film *City of Angels*. Everyone is there. Including Stine, who's in for a shock or two. The first comes when he sees the screenplay credit: "by Buddy Fidler and. . . ." His second when Stone appears. Because it isn't the Stone we all know, the Stone of Stine's movie in the mind. It's megacrooner Jimmy Powers. Now we know why Buddy didn't notice his wife's affair, her affair with all that drawing-power. He probably arranged it!

The actors begin their scene, but after a few lines have been "murdered," a voice cries "cut." Buddy's gluteals slam shut. No one, but no one calls "cut" on set but him. What is this profanity? It's Stine. He's finally got his integrity up. He takes the script and throws it at Buddy. It's all his. Stine's quitting and going back to fiction between covers. Buddy shrieks for his heavy men, but as they attack the writer, Stone comes to the defense. He goes to the typewriter and starts erasing the text . . . back . . . back . . . back to the moment when Stine threw the script at Buddy. Everyone freezes . . .

Stine and Stone reprise a gleeful "I'm Nothing Without You," and then Stone types a little more. Gabby appears from out of nowhere to stand alongside her husband and his creation, and the three of them sail up on a stage crane to a fantastical ending high above the chorus. Well, every show has to have a Hollywood—not to mention a Broadway—ending. Even if it's not one that's been fixed by Buddy Fidler.

1990

Aspects of Love

A MUSICAL IN TWO ACTS by Charles Hart and Don Black based on the novel of the same title by David Garnett. Music by Andrew Lloyd Webber.

Produced at the Broadhurst Theatre, 8 April 1990, with Kevin Colson (George), Ann Crumb (Rose), and Michael Ball (Alex).

Originally produced at the Prince of Wales Theatre, London, 17 April 1989.

Love-struck Alex (Michael Ball) gets to know actress
Rose Vibert (Ann Crumb) over a post-show glass of
barely affordable armagnac in a Montpellier café.
Photograph © Joan Marcus.

CHARACTERS

Alex Dillingham, *a young
Englishman*

George Dillingham, *his uncle, an
English painter*

Rose Vibert, *an actress*

Marcel Richard, *an
actor–manager*

Giulietta Trapani, *an Italian
sculptress*

Elizabeth, *George's housekeeper*

Hugo le Meunier, *Rose's admirer*

Jenny Dillingham, *daughter of
George and Rose*

Jerome, Fairground Barker,
Hotelier, Doctor, Hotel Cashier,
Pharmacist, Gondolier, Registrar,
et al.

Act 1   A not-so-very young man stands center stage, pouring out his heart in song ("Love Changes Everything") to a shadowy, unidentifiable figure, or—more truthfully—to the world in general. His life has been made—or been marred—by one overwhelming love. He will never, can never be the same man again. And yet there is the future to go on into. But we, we shall go back into the past, to the beginning of this terrible love story. It all started seventeen years ago, in the year 1947, in a theatre in Montpellier.

A producer called Marcel Richard has had the curious idea of taking a production of Ibsen's *The Master Builder* into the French provinces. It has, scarcely surprisingly, not been a success, and leading lady Rose Vibert is in a terrible temper when the Saturday night curtain comes down. It's been a dreadful, audienceless week, and now she has to face a fortnight out, unpaid and unlodged, before the company plays its next date in Lyon.

Rose pours her temper all over Marcel, and in pure self-defense the poor franc-stripped producer tries to distract her by presenting her with an admirer. Alex Dillingham is English, a teenage boy who has been captivated by the actress. He has come back to the play each and every night of the week, and he even threw her flowers. Didn't she notice?

Rose is mollified by this touch of calf-adoration, and she permits her young admirer to squire her to the café for an after-show drink ("Parlez-vous français?"). There, with little thought for his young pocket, she orders a cavalier armagnac and then a second, but gradually the worst of her mood passes and in the end she is able to make fairly civil conversation. Now Alex, breathless with excitement, makes his big play. She has two weeks out and nowhere to go, so why doesn't she come to his villa down south? Rose sizes up the situation and the boy, and she accepts.

The Rose Vibert who turns up on Montpellier station later that night isn't so much the twenty-five-year-old provincial leading lady of earlier in the evening as a teenaged girl, off on an adventure, an adventure that starts with a kiss, even before the journey starts. As the train steams south through the night, the lovers-to-be doze on each other's shoulder ("Seeing Is Believing"). Alex is in love with all the fierceness of his seventeen years. Rose, with eight years more wisdom, or at least more experience, is off on what could be an enjoyable fortnight's break.

The shine has rather gone off her enjoyment by the time they reach the city of Pau and the promised villa. Alex, who had no key, has had to break into the house, and she has torn her best dress as a result. It's not his place at all; it belongs to his Uncle George, a rich, dilettante artist. But Rose decides there's no use making a scene. After all, there is no one to see it.

Courtesy of a gardener who knows how to send a telegram, news of his nephew's escapade soon reaches Uncle George, and he is not pleased. He is sufficiently displeased—and intrigued—to quit his Parisian flat and a pleasant little sexual idyll with sculptress Giulietta Trapani, and head for Pau. In the meantime, the young people are enjoying themselves. They race through the cupboards and attics of the villa, dragging out George's supplies of exotic foods to make their meals, and making merry with the pictures and clothes they find. Most of George's own pictures are copies of famous originals, but one—the best—is a portrait of his late wife, dressed in a beautiful ball-gown. Rose even finds the ball-gown itself, packed away in a chest, still as fresh and welcoming as the day that George painted his lovely wife wearing it.

In the evening, they dress up in some masquerade costumes and act out scenes from *Cyrano de Bergerac*, so that when George arrives on the scene he is confronted by a Cyrano and a Roxane rapidly reaching the climax of the play. Rostand rattles to a halt in embarrassment.

Embarrassment, however, does not last long. George is soon being charming to Rose, and congratulating Alex on his choice of a companion. Rose is duly charmed, but Alex is terrified. His uncle is not taking him seriously. He cannot, or he will not see that this is not just a casual affair of the kind that George has so often lived through. Does he not understand that this is the great love of Alex's life? Please, don't spoil it; please, go away.

Rose has taken off her play-acting costume and changed into a more suitable dress, one that will make her look her best. When she returns to the men's company, George almost collapses. She is wearing his wife's ball-gown, the ball-gown of the picture. And, for one moment there, George thought . . . Rose is deeply penitent and, to Alex's despair, she devotes herself wholly to George until the end of the evening.

George quits the villa, and the city, and the two young people are again left to themselves. But it is not the same. Alex suffers from nightmares that Rose is gone, and, indeed, a few days later a telegram comes from Marcel, summoning her back to work. It is not until she is gone that Alex realizes Marcel had no idea where Rose was. The telegram was a fake; she wanted to go.

Two years have passed. Alex is in the army and in Paris ("If You Reach for the Moon"). Not unnaturally, he goes to visit his Uncle George at his flat, and he finds Rose there. Rose, whom he has dreamed of finding once again since the day she left Pau. But not here. Not like this. Not as his uncle's . . . what? Wife? Mistress? Bitterly, he accuses her of betraying their love for the comforts of the older man's money, and, in spite of her denials, he cannot bring himself to understand that George might be able to offer Rose something, anything that he cannot, excepting money.

Rose is George's mistress. She has been for some time, and she has been faithful to him, which is more than he has been to her. But she did love the desperate Alex once, and—she assures him—nothing says that she may not love him again. Alex is not slow to seize his chance.

When he climbs out of George's bed the next morning, Rose is already gone, and she has left tart instructions for him to get out of the place. George is due to return, and she doesn't want him upset by some silly scene. Alex goes wild at hearing George's well-being put before his own. What was last night all about then? When Rose returns, he pulls his gun on her, threatening that if he cannot have her, no one will. The response is not quite what he expects. Enraged by this bit of melodrama, Rose picks up a candlestick and hurls it at the boy. The gun goes off, the bullet hits Rose in the arm, and George walks in.

The situation clearly needs to be talked over ("She'd Be Far Better Off with You"). Alex is repentant, George generous, and their interview ends with George packing his bags to go and visit Venice and Giulietta Trapani, leaving Alex and Rose to work their relationship out. He is, perhaps, aware of what will happen. The moment he is gone, Rose sends Alex packing. She may love him, but George comes first. And now she is going on a little trip to Venice.

George and Giulietta are having a companionable time together. He is making a fine heroic story for himself out of the episode of Alex and Rose and the gun, and she is using him as a model ("Time and Light Are Fading"). But their peaceful existence is soon broken into. Rose arrives, suffering badly from her bullet wound and pursued by a posse of people with whom she has apparently succeeded in running up debts since she left Paris for Venice. George and Giulietta take care of the debts, and then of Rose, and by the time two convalescent weeks have passed, the women have become firm friends. But, beyond the merry amorality in which they all like to think they can live together, Giulietta can see the strength of the bond that exists between the other two.

One day, the happy little triangular party comes to an end, for George has discovered suddenly that he is no longer rich. His money has been entirely lost in a bad investment. Now Rose feels able to ask him to marry her. They are married at a registry office in Venice, with Giulietta as best man. And George can still raise a delightedly titivated twinkle at the sight of his "best man" kissing the bride.

The news of the marriage, and of Rose's subsequent pregnancy, reaches Alex deep in the jungle. It changes nothing ("Love Changes Everything").

Act 2 In the twelve years since her marriage, Rose Vibert has become a star of stage and screen. Nowadays Marcel Richard's productions are mounted not in the provinces but in Paris, and right now Rose is starring for him in Turgenev's *A Month in the Country* ("The Perfect Leading Lady"). As often as she can, however, the family cake-winner goes down to Pau where George lives with their little daughter, Jenny. But she has a young admirer, Hugo, on hand in Paris for amusement and exercise.

Tonight she has another visitor, Alex. No longer the seventeen year-old Alex she first met, or the nineteen-year-old Alex whom she threw out of George's home all those years ago, but an Alex of thirty. Rose is delighted. He must come down to Pau and see George. And meet Jenny.

Jenny is a pretty and lively twelve-year-old, and George dotes on her. She is the best thing that has ever happened to him ("Other Pleasures"), and George is wholly happy. Especially when Rose comes home, and particularly when Rose comes home bringing Alex. One person, however, is not so happy. Giulietta has cancelled the visit that she had planned for this weekend, suffering from heartache ("There Is More to Love"). Alex will not meet her just yet.

Alex finds that the villa and the wonderful panorama of the Pyrenees awaken all sorts of old longings and passions in him. If, that is, they had ever really been asleep. But he puts those passions aside and, instead, finds simple pleasure in the friendship of little Jenny ("I am a Mermaid"). It's a friendship that blooms over the next couple of years, as Alex becomes a regular visitor at the villa in Pau, but his situation vis-à-vis Rose does not change. She loves George. She can sleep with Hugo because he means nothing to her and cannot threaten that love, but she can have nothing but a chaste, loving friendship for Alex, because to have anything more would be dangerous. He means too much to her.

If things do not change much in the lives and ways of older folk, they change with great rapidity in the young. Jenny is fourteen and she is growing up. One night she puts on the ball gown that Rose had worn to such effect the first night she met George, and comes down to dinner in it. Rose and Alex, remembering the terrible shock it caused all those years ago, are aghast, but George seems not even to notice. He is happy just to take Jenny is his arms for her first grown-up dance ("The First Man You Remember").

George is Jenny's first partner, but at the evening's end, when George has been long in bed, her last partner is Alex. He didn't ask her, so she asked him. And when their dance is done, Jenny is in love. She can confide in her mother that, for the first time in her life, she feels like a woman. Rose is not exactly pleased, but she believes Alex when he tells her that he could never let himself fall in love with Jenny. George is very much unhappier and very much less trusting, especially after he sees the child kiss Alex one day out in the country. He works himself up into quite a state over the thought that his beloved child is being stolen from him.

Things come to a peak on Jenny's fifteenth birthday. As a birthday treat, they have all gone to the circus in Paris. Alex and Jenny get called down to take part in the jollity going on in the ring, and George—excluded from the foolish romp—finds himself twisted up with jealousy. He causes a scene that only the adults understand.

George, Rose, Alex, and Jenny: four people in love. And it is doing them little good ("Older than the Stars").

Alex has promised to see Jenny to her birthday bed, but it proves to be a promise fraught with dangers in the fulfillment. Jenny, who has never had the passions of others hidden from her, knows what she feels for Alex. She knows what she wants. And Alex knows that, in spite of what he may feel, he must never, ever give in. He will not give in. As for George, all he knows is that Alex is upstairs in Jenny's bedroom, and that can only mean one thing. Strenuously, he starts up the stairs to interrupt their lovemaking, but he does not ever find out that his suspicions were unfair. As he reaches Jenny's bedroom door he collapses. His heart, that much overused organ, has given out.

George willed that his funeral should be a gay, lively affair with music and dancing. He willed that his eulogy be given by Giulietta Trapani, and that it should be a celebration of the principle of "live-for-today, without afterthought" that he had espoused for all but the last minutes of his life ("Hand Me the Wine and the Dice"). In the dancing that follows the eulogy, Alex and Giulietta meet. Soon after, they are missing from the festivities. And, as the evening draws to an end, Alex returns to the house with an announcement: He is leaving. For good.

First he tells Jenny. She is in despair; doesn't he love her? Is three years too much to wait? Or is it Giulietta? She saw them together earlier in the evening. Is that it? Alex is spared having to go into too many details by the appearance of Rose. Rose tries to say goodbye to him in a civilized fashion, but in the end her emotion bursts from her ("Anything but Lonely"). George is gone. Alex cannot go as well. She cannot and must not be left alone!

But Alex is going. Not without a great deal of pain and heartache, but he is going. The not-so-very-young man whom we saw at the evening's opening, singing out his heart over the terrible power of love, was thirty-four-year-old Alex. The shadowy figure who stood alongside him is shadowy no longer; it is Giulietta, and she is offering him the chance to try George's philosophy of life: "The Wine and the Dice." Why not? Time enough to think about tomorrow tomorrow.

This synopsis is taken from the revised version that played on tour in Britain in 1993. Several scenes have been added or subtracted since the original production, and a considerable number of lyrics and lines modified.

1991

MISS SAIGON

A MUSICAL IN TWO ACTS by Alain Boublil based on the libretto *Madama Butterfly* by Luigi Ilica and Giuseppe Giaocosa and its sources. Lyrics by Alain Boublil and Richard Maltby, Jr. Music by Claude-Michel Schönberg.

Produced at the Broadway Theatre, 11 April 1991, with Lea Salonga (Kim), Willy Falk (Chris), and Jonathan Pryce (The Engineer).

Originally produced at the Theatre Royal, Drury Lane, London 20 September 1989.

GI with heart (Willy Falk) meets
tyro tart (Lea Salonga)
without view to marriage.
Photograph © Joan Marcus.

CHARACTERS

Kim, *a Vietnamese bar-girl*

Gigi, *another*

Chris, *an American soldier*

John, *another*

Ellen, *Chris's wife*

Tran van Dinh, *known as* The Engineer, *a pimp*

Thuy

Tam, *Kim's child*

Owner of "Le Moulin Rouge," Schmaltz, Harrison, Travis, Weber, Estevez, Allott, Marine Sergeant, Phan, Huynh, Mimi, Yvonne, Yvette, Mama San, Bar-girls, American marines, Reporters, South Vietnamese officers, Bar customers, Conference delegates and hall-staff, et al.

Act 1   It's a Friday night in Saigon, Vietnam, in April 1975, and we are in a drab city nightclub-cum-brothel called Dreamland, run by a half-caste brute who likes to be called "The Engineer." His real name is the more prosaic Tran van Dinh. But Tran likes to make American. The American soldiers who've been in Vietnam over the years have, of course, been a fabulous source of income for Tran. But now they offer the chance of something more. Now that it seems that the glory days of whore profiteering are coming to an end in Saigon, they can offer escape. That all-important little U.S. visa that will allow a girl with an American husband or child, or a man with enough guile and influence, to get out of Saigon and across to the land of everything-for-nothing: the United States of America.

Tonight, Tran has brought along a new recruit to freshen up the tawdry group of shagged-out girls who staff his club. She's called Kim. She'll parade about with the rest, selling drinks and herself, and take part in the grotesque election of Miss Saigon. A Miss Saigon is crowned each Friday night, chosen by the popular applause of the customers, and she goes as a prize to the winner of a raffle draw.

Tonight, among the crowd of soldiers—American and local—and civilians who gather at the club ("The Heat Is on in Saigon"), are U.S. Embassy clerk John and his friend Chris. For some reason, John's got this idea that Chris should get himself laid tonight, even with the kind of tart that's on view at Dreamland. But Chris isn't keen. Once he used to be a real man, drugging and screwing his way around the town like real men do, but then it all went sour on him. But then he sees new girl Kim, and his manhood revives.

The "contest" is won by Gigi, a sluttish, dirty-mouthed child, whose first words to the marine who wins her are "You take me to America?" No more than the others does she know what "America" really is. She just knows it's not Saigon. It's movies and ice cream and dollar bills ("The Movie in My Mind"); it's fairyland.

Tran's activities these days are all aimed in one obsessive direction. He wants, he needs that American visa in his passport. He has to get to America, where he can practice his profession among seemingly unlimited amounts of money and lust and money. It's all there, just waiting for him. He approaches John with a small bribe. But John isn't getting mixed up with Tran the Engineer. No further, anyhow, than overpaying him for a night's worth of Kim as a gift to his buddy.

Chris doesn't say "no," and the pair quickly leave the club for Kim's shack and some sex. Later in the night, Chris climbs out of bed. He looks out the window ("Why, God, Why?"), he looks at Kim, then, leaving some money on the table, he goes out. But he doesn't get far. He goes back, she wakes up, and love blossoms in the space of a duet ("Sun and Moon").

When he comes up for breath, Chris calls John (Telephone Song). He wants to take all his leave allowance at one time, so that he can carry on being in love nonstop. John tells him to get back to the Embassy. Things are happening, and they are happening fast. Chris wins himself a short respite and hurries off to deal with Kim's very short-term employer, the Engineer. Tran tries to barter Kim for the all-important visa, but Chris only gives him money (The Deal). It's a lot of money, but it's not what Tran wanted.

Kim moves in with Chris. The other, less lucky bar-girls—even though they knew Kim only for a matter of minutes before she was whisked away—all come around to help. Cinderella's got her Prince. One of them will be getting out of Saigon. When Chris turns up, the girls sing the young pair a wedding song ("Diu vui vai"). Then the door flies open, and a Vietnamese man walks in. He is Thuy, Kim's cousin and the husband arranged for her by her parents before their deaths. He has come to claim his bride ("Who Is This Man?"). When Kim refuses to abandon Chris, Thuy curses her and leaves her in tears in the arms of her American ("The Last Night of the World").

Suddenly we move three years on in time. It is the third year of the reunification of Vietnam, and the people are in the street celebrating ("The Morning of the Dragon"). Tran the Engineer has spent those years being brainwashed and planting rice in the outback, but now he has been brought back to what is no longer Saigon but Ho Chi Minh City. Since he had almost no brain to wash, he is still the same conniving, repulsive Faginesque creature as ever. So why this return? Someone has use for him, and that someone is Thuy, now promoted to a high position in the new régime. He orders Tran to find Kim.

Where is Kim? Kim is living in a shared room with a number of other women. And she is still dreaming of Chris ("I Still Believe"). But where is Chris who, when we last saw him, was sharing an everlasting love duet with her? Chris is in America. And he is married to a woman called Ellen. But he has bad dreams, and Ellen knows that he has not shared all of his past with her ("I Still Believe"). So what happened? What happened?

Tran doesn't have too much trouble tracking Kim down ("Coo Coo Princess, Look Who's Here"), and he brings Thuy to her home. Once again the virulent man tries every way he knows to persuade Kim to honor their families' pact of marriage, but Kim will not. As far as she is concerned, she is already married. He threatens her with a touch of the "reeducation" suffered by Tran for her past as a whore, but Kim finally produces her answer to all: a two-year-old child, Chris's son. This act of bravado does not quite have the effect counted on. Thuy draws his knife and goes to cut the baby down, and Kim, in retaliation, draws Chris's army pistol and guns her cousin down.

Outside in the square, the populace hail a new Vietnam and raise a statue to Ho Chi Minh. Elsewhere in the city, Tran the Engineer is making his way back to what remains of his old club. He is sitting there, picking through a boxful of hidden treasures, reviewing his situation ("If You Want to Die in Bed"), when the fleeing Kim turns up, her child in her arms. Quite why she ran to the traitorous Tran is a puzzle, but as soon as Tran finds out who that baby is, he sees how he can turn the situation to his advantage ("Let Me See His Western Nose"). The baby is the son of an American. The girl is the wife—give or take a ceremony—of an American. And he will be the brother of that wife. They will all go to America and have ice cream and pimp profitably on the streets of New York. As Tran goes off to start his latest bit of engineering, Kim sings to her baby ("I'd Give My Life for You"). At the last, we see Kim and Tran and the baby joining the exodus from Vietnam.

Act 2

When John got back to America, after the war was done, he got involved with a humanitarian organization trying to clean up some of the human mess that the American retreat had left behind it. He gives lectures and shows devastating slides of wretched children ("Bui-Doi") as part of his presentation. Today Chris is at his lecture, for John has apparently got something to say to him. It must be about Kim.

It is. When she and Tran came to register themselves and the child for emigration, the details found their way to John's organization. He knows Kim is alive, working as a bar-girl in Bangkok, and that she has a child, Chris's child. Chris is stunned. He also has to face telling the whole truth of his Vietnamese life to his wife.

Kim, Tran, and the baby have indeed got as far as Bangkok, after a month struggling to Thailand on a boat from Vietnam. But it hasn't done them much good. Tran is working at his old trade, selling one night in Bangkok to indiscriminately randy tourists, but now for someone else's benefit rather than his own ("What a Waste"). Kim is part of the package. Then John turns up. Kim longs for news of Chris ("Please"), and when she hears that her "husband" is actually in Bangkok she believes that all her waiting has come to an end. Tran is anxious that the fish—so near now—should not get off the hook. What will Chris's reaction be when he hears of the baby? He may run. Kim must get to him first. Tran will find out at which hotel he is staying.

Left alone, Kim sleeps and, as she sleeps, the nightmares come. The murdered Thuy ("Did You Think I'd Gone Away?") appears. And then the night that she and Chris were torn apart. At the "Fall of Saigon," as the last American Embassy personnel were helicoptered out, she was unable to get through the crowds and the wire to reach her "husband." So that's what happened.

Tran has found out where Chris is, and Kim sets off for the hotel. But when she gets there she finds not Chris, but Ellen. And Ellen tells her everything, in a nice way, but with her territory firmly marked out. Chris and Ellen have their own life, and, though they are of course willing to help, there can be no question of their life actually being mixed with Kim's. And no question of their taking Kim's baby to live with them in America. Kim will not believe what she hears from Ellen's lips. She cannot believe that Chris would abandon his child and deny him movies and ice cream and dollars. He must come to her himself and tell her, or she will not believe it.

Ellen has just time to work herself up into a dramatic state of mind ("Her or Me") before Chris and John return from their fruitless search for Kim. And Chris, as if he wasn't in deep enough emotions, has to face up to an Ellen who wants to talk about it (The Confrontation). Kim, for her part, has to face up to Tran, who is interested in only one thing: Has she got the papers? When do they leave? How long before he can wallow in "The American Dream"?

In her room backstage at the club, Kim dresses her child in his best ("Tam, Tam, Little God of My Heart") and waits for Chris. Then, as she sees him approaching, she pulls out the pistol he left her and shoots herself. Now he will have to take his orphaned child to America. Ice cream. Movies. Dollars. Pimps.

1992

FALSETTOS

TWO MUSICALS IN ONE ACT by William Finn and James Lapine.

Produced at the John Golden Theatre. New York, 29 April 1992, with Michael Rupert (Marvin), Stephen Bogardus (Whizzer), Chip Zien (Mendel), and Barbara Walsh (Trina).

March of the Falsettos was originally produced at Playwrights Horizons, New York, 1 April 1981.

Falsettoland was originally produced at Playwrights Horizons, 28 June 1990, and at the Lucille Lortel Theatre, New York, 14 September 1990.

There's nothing like a boy's baseball game for getting all the family on the same side. For once.
Photograph © Martha Swope.

CHARACTERS

Marvin

Trina, *his exwife*

Jason, *his son*

Whizzer Brown, *his lover*

Mendel, *his psychiatrist*

Doctor Charlotte

Cordelia

March of the Falsettos

Marvin, Jason (age 11), Mendel, and Whizzer Brown are Jews. Not just Jews, but New York Jews. And not just New York Jews, but New York Jews of the 1970s. The sort of 1970s New York Jews that need psychiatrists. The sort of New York Jews that make you think there aren't any other sort of New York Jews except ones who need psychiatrists. Even though Mendel is one. A psychiatrist, that is. Marvin, Jason (age 11), Mendel, and Whizzer Brown are not really very original or outstanding or interesting people. In fact, they're pretty much clichés. They are just four neurotic 1970s New York Jews, whose main preoccupation in life is not their job, the money in the bank, or even the Blooms and the Bernsteins next door. It's Love and How to Get It ("Four Jews in a Room Bitching").

Quite honestly, up to now, they've all made a bit of a mess of it. Or had it messed up for them. You see, once upon a time Marvin married Trina. Trina was Jewish, attractive enough, and had a father who was keen to see her married. She cooked and baked and cleaned and screwed nicely enough (the result of this last, in particular, being Jason now aged 11) to keep Marvin reasonably happy, and to help him keep up the illusion that he was a loved and loving man. Only, one day Marvin met somebody else. Somebody who was only half-Jewish, but even more attractive, who cooked and baked and cleaned only intermittently, but who screwed a treat. So he went off with him. He went to live with Whizzer Brown, and divorced Trina. But Marvin was unwilling to altogether leave behind the comfortable life his exwife had made for him. Marvin wanted to eat his bagel and still have it: wife, son, and lover ("A Tight Knit Family").

Now, Marvin—psychoanalyzable neurotic though he is—is used to getting and having what he wants. After all, even though we never see him going to work, he apparently does, and as a result of whatever he does he's apparently getting-on-for-rich. So he mostly gets what he wants. But this one he's going to have to work hard for. Because, for a starter, Trina is finding the whole wife-lover-son thing a bit hard to take. In fact, she's headed straight for the Mr. Mendel the psychiatrist ("Love Is Blind"). Mr. Mendel the psychiatrist is soothing and he is also more taken by the distraught and probably (eventually) available divorcée than would seem in line with his professional position.

Marvin and Whizzer have been together now for nine or ten months (depending on whose counting you rely). The "Thrill of First Love" has given way to a rumbustious kind of bickering, bitching, and bed relationship that seems to suit them both. Except, of course, that Marvin wants to be loved. And he's by no means given up visiting Mr. Mendel the psychiatrist. Because half the fun of it all is talking about it, even at Mr. Mendel's prices. The only trouble is, Mendel seems more interested in asking intimate questions about Trina's life and sex life than in listening to Marvin's maunderings ("Marvin at the Psychiatrist").

Jason is really more interested in chess than sex, particularly other people's, but being a good little up-top-date boy, he's au fait with the situation ("My Father's a Homo"), and it doesn't bother him too much. Trina and Marvin, however, can't take the fact that it doesn't bother him much. They are deeply concerned that their child isn't deeply concerned over what's happening in his family, and they try everything they can think of to coerce him into joining the family trek to the shrink (Everyone Tells Jason to See a Psychiatrist). It's tough going, and Jason finally agrees to go only when Whizzer, arm-twisted by Trina and Marvin, suggests it mightn't be a bad idea.

Marvin, meanwhile, is making a mess of his life with Whizzer. He clearly expects the same kind of servicing for his money that he got from Trina. He wants to be fed and he wants to be bedded. And he wants a good fight, so he can threaten to call the whole things off every so often. And, of course, in between times and all of the time, he must be loved. And meanwhile Mendel is still raking in the ex-family's money as both Marvin and Trina call for their periodic rant ("This Had Better Come to a Stop").

Trina isn't sure she's not cracking up over all this ("I'm Breaking Down"), but even if she is, she's finding out some surprising things. Sometimes she thinks she actually likes Marvin's boyfriend. And she definitely likes Marvin's psychoanalyst. But her family's breaking up, and she's breaking down. And what if Jason turned out like Marvin? Trina calls Mendel and asks him to come and have a talk to her son ("Please Come to My House"). So Mendel comes, and lectures the boy on feeling good (Jason's Therapy), while Trina goes out to the kitchen and does what she's always done: makes food. By the fifth session, the psychoanalyzing seems to have shifted camp. Jason's perfectly aware that Mendel—who seems to have been making himself more and more at home in this house—has ambitions in the direction of his mother, and it's he who hands out the advice. Soon, Mendel is doing the proper thing ("A Marriage Proposal").

Marvin didn't really intend his "Tight-Knit Family" to include his shrink, and he's very peeved over the now obvious affair that's going on between the pair. But Trina knows what she's letting herself in for (Trina's Song): another man who's never grown beyond being a boy. And the four ungrown-up men who started the evening off, their genitalia glowing grossly, and piping their voices falsetto in imitation of prepubertal days, march up and down to the "March of the Falsettos."

Marvin tries to teach Whizzer to play chess (The Chess Game) but the evening ends in the same bickering and the same threats to call it all off that most of their evenings seem to end in. And at the same time that Mendel and Trina are

"Making a Home" in preparation for their Big Day, Whizzer is looking clearly—and without the aid of a psychoanalyst—at his tempestuous and only maybe worthwhile life and what-might-be-love with Marvin ("The Games I Play").

Then Marvin gets the invitation to Trina and Mendel's wedding. He's livid. He gets the two of them over to his place, starts to bitch and bawl in his usual spoiled brat fashion, and, unable to produce the effect he wants, ends up slapping Trina in the face ("Marvin Hits Trina"). After which the word "love" gets spilled around an awful lot, among a whole bunch of folk who don't really seem to have too much idea what it means ("I Never Wanted to Love You").

Marvin is allowed a kind of a reprieve as this evening of narcissism, foolishness, and squabbling draws to an end. He's left alone with his son. He tells him he loves him. And he wishes him good fortune along the road to the kind of adulthood that he's never managed to achieve himself.

Falsettoland

It's 1981, two years since we abandoned Marvin doing his pasteover job on his life. And we're still in what's now called Falsettoland, that hothouse of the immature and unfulfilled. The cast has been joined by the Mendel's neighbors, the hospital intern Dr. Charlotte, and her girlfriend Cordelia, who does interesting nouvelle-cuisiny things with kosher cooking. But it's still Marvin's show. He's come to cordial terms with Trina and her new husband, sees Jason on weekends, has split up with Whizzer, and still has less *savoir vivre* and emotional security than his twelve-and-a-half year-old son.

Unfortunately for all concerned, Trina and Marvin are going to have to spend some time together, because it's just about time for Jason to be bar mitzvahed ("The Year of the Child"). A bar mitzvah, of course, is bound to provoke all kinds of problems, especially when the Marvins of this world are involved. Trina and Marvin fall into quarrels almost immediately, and Jason is left with the problem of whom he's going to invite. What girls that is. Because the ones he fancies aren't the ones with the right credentials for his family ("The Miracle of Judaism").

The boy's parents also see each other at Jason's baseball game. Baseball isn't quite the game for Jewish boys. And Jason's hopeless (The Baseball Game). Both parents get a bit of a surprise when Whizzer turns up. It seems Jason invited him, so he came. There's still a strong feeling—which might even be a touch more than lust—between him and Marvin, and for a moment there it seems they might even start to talk about starting to get back together. But at the psychological moment, Jason does the impossible. He actually hits the ball. And he's so stunned he doesn't even think to run.

Things occasionally look as if they might have arranged themselves for a pale imitation of the best, but contentment never reigns long in Falsettoland ("A Day in Falsettoland"). Mendel is depressed by his work, and that has an effect on his sexual frequency. Trina is irked about the off-and-on affair between Whizzer and Marvin, even though she knows it's none of her business, and she has to remind herself that she's got a lovely son and a nice, if less frequent, husband and that she shouldn't be feeling down. But she is. As for Cordelia next door, who spends all day experimenting with her nouvelle kosher food, she also spends all day petrified that when Dr. Charlotte comes home after a day saving lives she won't like it. Whizzer and Marvin play raquetball, which the younger man naturally wins, and bicker.

Over all of this hangs the shadow of Jason's bar mitzvah, which the kid pretty soon realizes isn't being run for his benefit at all, and is in any case going to be hellish ("The Fight"). So he decides he won't have one. If Mendel weren't a psychiatrist, the family would certainly call one in now. But Mendel does his best anyway, delivering a nice little bit of New York Jewish folklore with practiced sincerity ("Everyone Hates His Parents").

Actually, sometimes Marvin has moments when things seem really good. Like in the early morning, with the sleeping Whizzer lying alongside him ("What More Can I Say?"). But they won't stay good for long, and this time, for once, the trouble isn't of Marvin's making. Dr. Charlotte spots it ("Something Bad Is Happening"). And then Whizzer collapses during a game of raquetball.

Now Whizzer is in hospital. He has AIDS. He is going to die. It is all beyond Trina's understanding. There used to be days when you knew where you were. If you played by the rules the results came out right. Not any more. Nothing goes by the rules any more ("Holding to the Ground").

Everyone visits Whizzer. Marvin supplies encouragement ("Days Like This I Almost Believe in God"). Cordelia supplies chicken soup. Mendel tries to supply a laugh. Jason brings the chess board. This strange family seems as if it is actually taking strength from the adversity that's hit it. There is even talk of "Canceling the Bar Mitzvah." Marvin and Whizzer seem closer than ever ("Unlikely Lovers"), but the end is clearly nigh. Jason knows it, and he prays for "Another Miracle of Judaism," while Dr. Charlotte reiterates "Something Bad Is Happening," and Whizzer simply wishes to himself that he'll have the courage to go decently when the time comes ("You Gotta Die Sometime").

The bar mitzvah does take place. Jason finally solves his dilemma. His entry into adult life takes place in the room where Whizzer is just about to leave his behind. The family descend on the hospital room bringing with them all the paraphernalia of the feast ("Jason's Bar Mitzvah"), and a rather original version of the ceremony leaps into action. But then Whizzer can take no more.

The others depart, and Marvin and Whizzer are left alone. To talk and think only about themselves, about what has become of them, about the regrets that they say they don't have ("What Would I Do?"). And then Whizzer is gone. Mendel closes the evening with a welcome to Falsettoland as we leave it—or, at least, this picture of it—behind.

1994

Sunset Boulevard

A MUSICAL IN TWO ACTS by Don Black and Christopher Hampton based on the screenplay by Billy Wilder, Charles Brackett, and D.M. Marsham, Jr. Music by Andrew Lloyd Webber.

Produced at the Minskoff Theatre, New York, 17 November 1994, with Glenn Close (Norma Desmond), Alan Campbell (Joe Gillis), George Hearn (Max von Mayerling), Alice Ripley (Betty Schaefer), Alan Oppenheimer (Cecil B. DeMille), and Vincent Tumeo (Artie Green)

Originally produced at the Adelphi Theatre, London, 12 July 1993.

First produced in America at the Shubert Theatre, Los Angeles, 9 December 1993.

"With one look I can break your heart."
Norman Desmond (Glenn Close)
sings of the power of her art.
Joan Marcus, photographer.

CHARACTERS

Norma Desmond

Joe Gillis

Betty Schaefer

Max von Meyerling

Cecil B. DeMille

Artie Green

Myron, Mary, Joanna, Sheldrake, Jonesy, Morino, Manfred, Hog-Eye, Sammy, Heather, Financemen, Salesmen, Party Guests, Film folk, et al.

Act 1

Sunset Boulevard. It's one of those once magical names. Like Golgotha only greater. Like Babylon but grander. Like Paris in springtime, but oozing more glamor and romance than ever came out of the whole of France put together at no matter what time of the year. Once.

Sunset Boulevard was where those Kings and Queens of the early twentieth century— the celluloid stars of the heyday of Hollywood—had their homes. Vast, extravagant mansions now, too often, like this one, allowed to go as shabby as an old piece of scenery left over from the movies their owners inhabited. Today, however, this particular Sunset Boulevard mansion has a particularity. In its swimming pool, there floats a corpse—the corpse of a young man. And another young man—or is it the same young man?—is offering to tell us the story of what happened. Not the newspaper version; the truth.

The story begins six months previously. Joe Gillis, a small-time movie writer, is down at the Paramount studios trying to dredge himself up some work in a city and an industry overloaded with wannabes, done-a-bits, and people who lunch. Or talk about lunching. As if lunching ever got anyone anywhere even if and when you did do it.

This time around, Joe is really on his uppers. He's even been pursued to the studio by a pair of brokers' men, determined to repossess his unpaid-for car. And he's low enough to accept $20 from old friend Artie Green. But work? Mr. Sheldrake, who can give or withhold the work that means survival in sprockethole city, doesn't even come up with a bit of leftovers. Worse, even his secretary rubbishes Joe's latest effort. So there's nothing left for Joe to do except run that hundred-mile studio gauntlet of lets have lunches all the way back to the gates.

He's on the way out, wondering how to get past the lurking brokers' men, when Sheldrake's secretary puts in an appearance. For a secretary, she seems to have a lot of opinions, but this time one of them seems to be in his favor. She's read a magazine story he once wrote and she thinks it could make up into a film. She'll sell the idea to Sheldrake if he'll work on it. Will he meet her at Schwab's on Thursday night to talk about it? Well, will he? Right now, for Joe, a more important question is "will she distract those broker's men while he makes his escape with his car?" She will if he will. It's a deal.

So, while Betty Schaefer tricks the pair of repossessors away from their posts with the hint that they might get a glimpse of Hedy Lamarr, Joe Gillis and his car make a getaway. Well, it's not really a getaway, more of what you might call a head start. Soon Joe is racing through the streets of Los Angeles with a pair of brokers' men up his exhaust pipe and little but painful prospects. The car chase looks like it will have a splatty ending when Joe's vehicle blows a tire down on Sunset Boulevard, but he manages to steer himself into an open driveway. And at the end of that driveway is a big, open, empty garage. It looks as if fate has been kind.

As it happens, the garage isn't empty. It's got an old automobile in it. One of those ones you used to see in silent movies, or see silent movie stars riding in. A limousine lavish and luxurious up to—and even beyond—the point of ridiculousness. It soon turns out that the apparently abandoned mansion isn't empty either. First, Joe hears a woman's voice, and then he is confronted by what seems to be a caricature of a Continental butler. Before he knows it, he's being ushered into a huge, lavish, shadowy living room decorated with the memorabilia of the Hollywood past that it's clearly been part of. And the butler is talking about a coffin.

Then she makes her entrance: A bizarre-looking, yet undeniably magnetic woman of middle age, encased in dark glasses. She makes her entrance at the top of the stairs, and then makes it again all the way down them. And she's talking about burying someone, or something. Sweeping past Joe, she makes her way to a table at the back of the room and leans over what could just be the draped body of a child. She has delivered a soulful farewell to the bundle in her arms ("No More Wars to Fight") when it becomes evident that the object of her sorrow is the corpse of a chimpanzee. Joe has been mistaken for the pet undertaker. But he's made no mistake about the lady. She is Norma Desmond. She used to be in pictures, and she used to be big.

Norma Desmond has just one answer to that. She is still big. It's the pictures that got small. In the world before words, when acting was an expression that meant something, she was the greatest ("With One Look"). And she is going to be great again. She is planning a comeback. Joe is just about to leave when she calls him back. In one of the few phrases he's managed to edge in to her wild, wordy torrent of the past half hour he mentioned that he was a writer. Norma Desmond can use a writer. She has prepared a screenplay for her return to the pictures. She will play Salomé. He will read it.

Joe has nothing to lose. He settles down with the vast pile of script that is Norma's screenplay, and, refuelled regularly with sweet champagne, he reads, and reads, and reads. It is, of course, quite impossible stuff. Nothing more than a hugely overwritten and incoherent vehicle for its aging author in the role of the sixteen-year-old biblical temptress. But as he reads, Joe gets ideas. And those ideas make him kind. "It's extremely good for a beginner," he proffers, but maybe it could take just a few cuts, some trimming, some editing? And who will do this? Why, Joe Gillis. At a price.

Norma Desmond does not worry about price. As long as she gets what she pays for. He will, of course, move in here. There is a room over the garage that he can have. Max, the butler, made the bed up several hours ago. Even though he thinks he's in charge, Joe can't fail to be a bit impressed. She's quite a character, this Norma Desmond. Max wouldn't put it that way. To him, she is, quite simply "The Greatest Star of All."

At Schwab's drugstore, come evening, you find all those little people who you previously saw trying their luck down at the studios in the morning. As well as some who actually have jobs. Joe goes there to fulfill his promise to Betty Schaefer and runs into good old Artie. Good old Artie, it turns out, is engaged to Betty Schaefer. Betty is really anxious to talk about Joe's old story, and she's more than a bit taken aback when Joe simply makes her a present of it. That wasn't what she'd wanted at all. Her idea was that they'd work on it together. She isn't to know that Joe's got richer food on his menu.

Joe goes to work on Norma's script and quickly finds that a brisk scissors-and-paste job is not what the lady has in mind. His period of employment is going to last for weeks, not days. Weeks of Salomé, weeks of the room over the garage, weeks of spending the evenings watching reruns of Madame's old movies. But it's a job, so why argue? Why hurt her? And when Joe watches Norma watching her old movies, happily reliving her glory days ("New Ways to Dream"), he even experiences a sad kind of fondness for this foolish, faded star.

Finally the day has to come. The remake of the script is finished and Norma's astrologer has pronounced the day propitious for its delivery to Cecil B. DeMille. Max is to take out the limousine and drive Norma's dream-film to the studio. And Joe? Well, it's time for him to return to the real world. Isn't it? No, it isn't. The idea of Joe's departure puts Norma into a state of raw panic. There is so much more work to do. There must be. He must stay. On full salary of course. So Joe stays.

Joe stays, and Norma comes alive as she lavishes attentions and money and new clothes ("The Lady's Paying") on him. And she arranges a grand party for the New Years' Eve that he'd promised to spend with Artie and Betty and his old friends. Only when New Year's Eve comes, there are no guests. Just Norma, dressed up like he's never seen her before, champagne, a gold cigarette case, and a Palm Court orchestra playing for just two to dance to ("The Perfect Year"). Then comes first a playful kiss, then a more intentioned one, and finally Norma's confession of love.

Joe panics. He knew what he was doing. He always knew what he was doing, but now he's feeling cut off at the knees. Being the boy of a wealthy woman is one thing, but listening to Norma Desmond telling him she's in love with him. . . . Before he can reassess, it's too late. The lover vanishes, and the star returns. And it is the star who slaps his face and rushes up the stairs.

Joe goes out. He goes to Artie and Betty's party still dressed in his tuxedo and vicuna coat and looks and feels out of place among the young people all joyfully looking forward to the undoubted success that will be theirs "This Time Next Year." Finally he picks up the phone and calls Norma's house. He gets Max. Norma has slashed her wrists.

Joe rushes back to find a pale, unsteady, bandaged Norma under Max's care. The recriminations end in a kiss, but this time it's Joe who kisses Norma. It is Norma, however, who pulls Joe down on to the couch as the curtain falls.

Act 2   Joe is loafing alongside the pool, slinging himself some disabused filmland clichés ("Sunset Boulevard") when Norma delivers the big news. DeMille loves the script. Some assistant of his called. Still, since he didn't call himself, she'll take her time going to see him.

Time ends up being three days. The limousine is taken out of its garage again, and Max drives Norma and Joe to Paramount Studios. Thanks to an old-time security man who recognizes her, embarrassment is avoided at the gates, and DeMille is forewarned of her coming. When she arrives on the soundstage, the director does not tell her the truth, that her script is appalling and that he never asked to see her. He is kind and he is gentlemanly. Then one of the elderly lighting men, way up in the grid, realizes who it is down there. Deliberately he turns a large spotlight on to her. And there she stands: Norma Desmond, back on the scene of her greatest triumphs ("Everything's As If We Never Said Goodbye").

While Norma has been having her moment, the two men have also had encounters. Joe runs into Betty who's been wondering where he'd disappeared to. Max meets the person from Paramount who'd rung the house. It wasn't "some assistant," it was Sheldrake, and he didn't ring to talk about Norma or the screenplay, he rang to see if he could use the limousine in a picture. Max is devastated. Norma must never, never know. For right now she is flying on a cloud, as she leaves her studio, squired gently by DeMille, and convinced that any day now she will be back at work.

Joe does get back to work—with Betty. While Norma spends her time getting herself into massaged and beautified form for her comeback, and while Artie is out of town on location, the pair begin seriously to get their screenplay into shape. But Norma is watching, and soon the question comes, "Who is Betty Schaefer?". Betty Schaefer is nothing a kiss can't blow away. But it doesn't stay that way. On the night the two write the words "the end" at the bottom of their project, they put a beginning on another. They kiss, and Norma and Artie are both forgotten, because they're just "Too Much in Love to Care."

The one who knows, the one who always knows, is Max. Max doesn't say "don't," he merely asks for caution. Madame must not be allowed to know.

Madame must never be hurt. But Joe knows that she must be. It's not a case of "if," but one of "when." Eventually, for starters, she will have to know that DeMille has no intention of making her film. But Max says otherwise. He made her a star, and he will never let her be destroyed. Joe frowns. Max made Norma Desmond a star? Yes. He was Max von Mayerling, the director of all Norma's early films, and later her husband ("New Ways to Dream"). Now, years on, he is still wholly and utterly devoted to keeping alive what he created.

Norma may not know about DeMille, but she knows about Betty Schaefer. Maybe not everything, but she knows that Joe spends time with the girl, and that is enough. So she picks up the telephone and calls Betty Schaefer. She's going to tell her what Joe is. Where Joe is. But halfway through the conversation the receiver is taken from her hand. Joe has walked in behind her. He takes up where Norma had left off—that's right, if Betty wants to know what and where he is, she'd better come right over. 10,086 Sunset. Before his look of loathing, Norma rushes up the stairs to her room. It is the beginning of the end.

Betty arrives to find out what's happening, and it is not long before she realizes whose house she's in. She also realizes the situation she's in. And, to her horror, she hears Joe telling her that he's not going to leave this rich life behind. He's staying. Betty rushes out, and Norma—who has been listening to every word from behind the balustrades of the staircase—starts down the stairs toward him, full of relief and hope. But those sentiments aren't allowed to survive for long. In spite of what he said, Joe is not staying. He's giving back everything Norma ever gave him, and he's giving her something extra—the truth. One by one, he strips away all the comfortable lies with which Max has padded her existence for so many years. The studio doesn't want her script, they don't want her, they only wanted her car. The fan letters that come each day are letters that have been written by Max. And, finally, goodbye.

Joe Gillis hadn't counted on one thing. Norma Desmond knows how to play a scene with a gun. The hammer falls, and Joe Gillis falls too.

We are back where we started at the beginning of the evening. Joe Gillis's body is floating in the swimming pool, and the place is full of newspuppies, yapping hungrily for their picture or their phrase.

Then, unexpectedly, Norma appears at the top of her staircase. She's dressed in a strange costume that might be a mock-up of Salomé and she still has the gun that killed Joe in her hand. Odd, disconnected phrases from the past fall from her lips. Her mind has gone. Max stops the police from approaching her, and moves to her side. He calls for "Lights!," "Cameras!," and "Action!," and, as Norma hears those familiar words, hears the whir of the reporters' cameras, and sees and feels the flashbulbs flashing, she begins to dance her way down the stairs. She pauses only to deliver a few words of happiness and gratitude to Mr. DeMille, to tell him and everyone else how happy she is to be back making a picture, and then she continues down to the bottom of the stairs, to the waiting police and the end.

APPENDIX OF COMPACT DISC RECORDINGS

Recordings of stage productions and stage-related studio cast recordings. Film and television recordings are not included.

H.M.S. PINAFORE (1879)

D'Oyly Carte Opera Company, 1930 (Arabesque/Pro Arte CDD 598)
D'Oyly Carte Opera Company, 1960 (Decca 414 283-2LM2)
"Glyndebourne"/Sir Malcolm Sargent recording with *Trial by Jury* (EMI CMS7 64397-2)
New Sadler's Wells Opera Company (CDTER2 1150)
Archive compilation with *The Mikado* (Cedar CDHD 253-4)
Welsh National Opera Company (Telarc DC-80374)

THE PIRATES OF PENZANCE (1880)

D'Oyly Carte Opera Company, 1929 (Arabesque/Pro Arte CDD 597)
"Glyndebourne"/Sir Malcolm Sargent recording (EMI CMS7 64409-2)
D'Oyly Carte Opera Company, 1968 (Decca 425 196-2LM2)
D'Oyly Carte Opera Company, 1990 (TER CDTER2 1177)
Welsh National Opera Company (Telarc CD 80353)
Archive compilation with *Ruddigore* (Cedar CDHD 255-6)

THE MIKADO (1885)

"Glyndebourne"/Sir Malcolm Sargent recording (EMI CMS7 64403-2)
Sadler's Wells Opera cast recording with *Iolanthe* (excerpts) (EMI CD-CFPD 4730)
D'Oyly Carte Opera Company, 1973 (London 417 296-2)
D'Oyly Carte Opera Company, 1990 (TER CDTER2 1178)
English National Opera Company (TER CDTER 1121)
Welsh National Opera (Telarc CD-80284)
Archive compilation (with *H.M.S. Pinafore*) (Cedar CDHD 253-4)

NO, NO, NANETTE (1925)

Broadway revival cast (Columbia CK 30563)
London cast recording (Sony West end SMK 66173)

THE STUDENT PRINCE (1924)

Studio cast with Marilyn Hill Smith (TER CDTER2 1172, highlights on TER CDTER 1005)
German cast recording (in English) (Bayer BR150 004 CD)

LADY, BE GOOD (1924)

Studio cast recording with Lara Teeter and Ann Morrison (Electra
    Nonesuch 79308-2)

OH, KAY! (1926)

Off-Broadway revival cast (DRG Stet 15017) (with *Leave It to Jane*)
Studio cast with Dawn Upshaw (Nonesuch 79361-2)

THE DESERT SONG (1926)

London cast recording (Pearl GEMM CD 9100)
Studio recording with Gordon MacRae (EMI Angel CDM 7 69052-2)
French studio cast recording (TLP C-35105)

SHOW BOAT (1927)

London cast recordings (Pearl GEMM CD 9105)
Broadway revival cast, 1946 (Sony Broadway SK 53330)
Lincoln Center production, 1966 (RCA Victor 09026-61182-2)
London cast recording 1971 (Stanyan STZ 107-2)
Canadian production 1994 (LIVENT RSPD 257)
Archive compilation (CBS Special Products A55)
Studio recording with John Raitt (Columbia CK2220)
Studio recording with Jason Howard (TER CDTER 2 1199)
Studio recording with Jerry Hadley (EMI Angel A2-49108, highlights on
    EMI Angel CDC 49847-2)
Studio recording with Denis Quilley (Pickwick PWKS 4161)

OF THEE I SING (1931)

Broadway revival cast, 1952 (Broadway Angel ZDM 2435 65025 2 9)
Concert production (with *Let 'em Eat Cake*) (CBS M2K 42522)

ANYTHING GOES (1934)

Off-Broadway revival (revised version) cast recording with Eileen
    Rodgers (Epic EK 15100)
Broadway revival cast recording with Patti LuPone (new revised version)
    (RCA Red Seal 7769-2-RC)
London revival cast recording with Elaine Paige (new revised version)
    (First Night CAST CD18)
Australian revival cast recording with Geraldine Turner (new revised
    version) (EMI CDP 792103)
Studio cast recording (EMI Angel 49848-2)

ON YOUR TOES (1936)

Broadway revival cast (TER CDTER 1063) (two versions)

PAL JOEY (1940)

Studio cast recording with revival stars (Columbia CK 4364)

Broadway cast recording with Jane Froman (Broadway Angel ZDM 0777 7 64696 2 1)

London revival cast recording (TER CDTER 1005)

OKLAHOMA! (1943)

Original cast recording (MCA Classics/Broadway Gold MCAD-10046), reissued with additional material in *Rodgers and Hammerstein 50th Anniversary* set (MCAD-10798)

London cast recording (Laserlight 12 450)

Broadway revival cast recording (RCA RCD-1-3572)

London revival cast, 1980 (TER CDTER 1208)

Studio cast recording with John Raitt (CBS Special Products AK 44060)

Studio cast recording with Nelson Eddy (Sony SK 53326)

ON THE TOWN (1944)

Studio recording with John Reardon and original cast members (Columbia CK 2038)

Studio recording (Deutsche Grammaphon 437516-2)

Studio recording with original cast members (MCA MCAD 10280)

CAROUSEL (1945)

Original cast recording (MCA Classics/Broadway Gold MCAD 10048), reissued in *Rodgers and Hammerstein 50th Anniversary Collection* with additional material (MCAD 10799)

London revival cast recording (First Night CAST CD40)

Lincoln Center production with John Raitt (RCA Red Seal 6395-2-RC)

Broadway revival cast recording 1994 (Angel CDQ 7243 5 55199 2 4)

Studio cast recording with Samuel Ramey (MCA DMCG 6028)

Studio cast recording with Dave Willetts (Pickwick PWKS 4144)

ANNIE GET YOUR GUN (1946)

Original cast recording (MCA MCAD 10047)

London cast recording (Laserlight 12 449)

Lincoln Center production (revised version) with Ethel Merman (RCA Victor 1124-2-RG)

London revival cast recording with Suzi Quatro (First Night CAST CD4)

Swedish cast recording (Sonet SLPCD 2832)

Studio cast recording with K. Criswell (EMI CDC 7 54206-2)

BRIGADOON (1947)

Original cast recording (RCA Victor 1001-2-RG)

British revival cast recording (First Night CAST CD16)

Studio cast recording with Rebecca Luker and Brent Barrett (Angel 0777 7 54481 2 2)

KISS ME, KATE (1947)

Original cast recording (Columbia CK4140)
Original cast stereo rerecording (Broadway Angel ZDM 0777 7 64760 2 5)
London revival cast (First Night CAST CD10)
Studio recording with Josephine Barstow (EMI Angel CDS 7 54033.2)

SOUTH PACIFIC (1949)

Original cast recording (Columbia CK 32604, reissued on Sony Broadway
    SK 53327)
London revival cast recording (First Night CAST CD11)
Studio cast recording with David Kernan (Pickwick PWKS 4162)

GUYS AND DOLLS (1950)

Original cast recording (MCA Classics/Broadway Gold MCAD-10301)
Broadway revival (revised version) (Motown MOTD-5277)
London revival cast (Chrysalis CCDD-1388, reissued on MFP [EMI]
    0946 3 21388 2 8)
Broadway revival cast (RCA Victor 09026-61317-2)
Studio recording with Frank Sinatra (Reprise 9 45014-2)

THE KING AND I (1951)

Original cast recording (MCA Classics/Broadway Gold MCAD-10049)
Lincoln Center production with Barbara Cook (Sony Broadway SK 53328)
Broadway revival cast with Constance Towers (RCA Red Seal RCD1-2610)
Studio cast with June Bronhill (EMI AXIS 701672.2)
Studio cast with Julie Andrews (Philips 438 007-2)

DAMN YANKEES (1955)

Original cast recording (RCA Victor 3948-2-RG)
Broadway revival (revised version) cast recording (Mercury 314 522 396-2)

MY FAIR LADY (1956)

Original cast recording (Columbia CK 5090)
London cast recording (Columbia CK 2015)
German cast recording (Philips 822 651-2)
Danish cast recording (Fanfare FANCD 8703)
Studio cast recording with Jeremy Brett (London 421-200-2)
Studio cast recording with Alec McCowen (TER CDTER2 1121)
Studio cast recording with Denis Quilley (Pickwick PWKS 4174)

CANDIDE (1956)

Original cast recording (CBS Masterworks MK38732, reissued on Sony
  Broadway SK 48017)
New York City Opera version (New World NW 340/341-2)
Scottish Opera version (TER CDTER 1156, highlights on CDTEO 1106)
Studio cast conducted by Bernstein (Deutsche Grammaphon 429734-2)

THE MUSIC MAN (1957)

Original cast recording (Capitol CDP 7 46633 2, reissued on Broadway
  Angel ZDM 7 64663 2 3)
London cast recording (Laserlight 12 447)
Studio recording with Timothy Noble (Tel Arc CD-80276)

WEST SIDE STORY (1957)

Original cast recording (Columbia CK 32603)
Studio recording with Kiri te Kanawa (Deutsche Grammaphon 415 253-
  2, highlights on 415 963-2)
Studio recording with members of Leicester Haymarket Theatre cast
  (TER CDTER2 1197)
Studio recording with Barbara Bonney (IMG CD 1801)

THE SOUND OF MUSIC (1959)

Original cast recording (Columbia CK 32601, reissued on Sony Broadway
  SK 53327)
London cast recording (Laserlight 12 448)
Studio recording with Frederica von Stade (Telarc CD-80162)
Studio recording with Liz Robertson (Pickwick PWKS 4145)

GYPSY (1959)

Original cast recording (Columbia CK 32607)
London cast recording with Angela Lansbury (RCA Victor 69571-2-RG)
Broadway revival cast recording with Tyne Daly (Electra Nonesuch 9 79239-2)

BYE BYE BIRDIE (1960)

Original cast recording (Columbia CK 2025)

CAMELOT (1960)

Original cast recording (Columbia CK 32602)
London revival cast recording with Richard Harris (TER CDTER 1030)

HOW TO SUCCEED IN BUSINESS WITHOUT REALLY TRYING (1961)

Original cast recording (RCA Victor 60352-2-RG)

LITTLE ME (1962)

Original cast recording (RCA Victor 09026-61482-2)
London cast recording (DRG 13111)

A FUNNY THING HAPPENED ON THE WAY TO THE FORUM (1962)
Original cast recording (Bay Cities BCD 3002)
London cast recording (West End Angel 07777 89060 2 5)

SHE LOVES ME (1963)
Original cast recording (Polydor 831 968-2)
London cast recording (West End Angel 7243 8 28595 2 9)
Broadway revival cast recording (Varese Sarabande VSD-5464)
London revival cast recording (First Night CAST CD44)

FUNNY GIRL (1964)
Original cast recording (Capitol CDP 7 46634 2 reissued on Broadway
    Angel ZDM 7 64661 2 5)

HELLO, DOLLY! (1964)
Original cast recording with Carol Channing (RCA Victor 3814-2-RG)
Original production cast-change recording with Pearl Bailey (RCA Victor
    1147-2-RG)
Revival cast 1994 (Varese Sarabande VSD 5557)

FIDDLER ON THE ROOF (1964)
Original cast recording (RCA Red Seal RCD1-7060)
London cast recording with Topol (Columbia CK30742)

MAN OF LA MANCHA (1965)
Original cast recording (MCA MCAD-1672)
French cast recording (Barclay 839 585-2)
Canadian cast recording (MPD 9329)

SWEET CHARITY (1966)
Original cast recording (Columbia CK 2900)
Broadway revival cast recording (EMI America CDP 7 466562 2)
London cast recording (Sony West End SMK 66172)
Dutch revival cast recording 1989 (Disky DCD 5126)

CABARET (1966)
Original cast recording (Columbia CK 3040)
London cast recording with Judi Dench (Sony West End SMK 53494)
London revival cast recording with Kelly Hunter (Relativity/First Night
    88561-8259-2)
Dutch revival cast recording (Disky DCD 5125)
Austrian cast recording (Spectrum 521 577-2)

HAIR (1967)

Original Broadway cast recording (RCA Victor 1150-2-RC)
Original London cast recording (Polydor 519 973-2)
London revival, 1993, cast recording (EMI 7243 8 281010 2 2)
Australian revival, 1992, cast recording (Boulevard D30816)
German cast recording (Polydor 833 103-2)
German revival cast recording (Polydor 521 322-2)

COMPANY (1970)

Original cast recording (Columbia CK 3550)
London cast recording (Sony West End SMK 53496)

GODSPELL (1971)

Original cast recording (Arista ARCD-8304)
Australian cast recording (EMI-Regal 157262-2)
Australian revival cast recording (1992) (Etcetera ETC001)
Studio cast recording (TER CDTER 1204)

JESUS CHRIST SUPERSTAR (1971)

Original concept recording (MCA DMCX 501)
London cast recording (MCA DMCF 2503)
Australian revival cast (1992) (Polydor 513 713 2)
New Zealand revival cast recording (1993) (Polydor 521 589 2)
Twentieth Anniversary Album (First Night Encore CD7, highlights on
    CAST CD 31)

GREASE (1972)

Original cast recording (Polydor 827 548-2)
London revival cast recording (Epic 474 632 2)
Broadway revival cast recording, 1994 (RCA 09026 62703-2)
Broadway revival cast with Brooke Shields (RCA 09026 62703-2)
Studio cast with John Barrowman (TER CDTER 1220)
Studio cast with Carl Wayne (Pickwick PWKS 4176)

A LITTLE NIGHT MUSIC (1973)

Original cast recording (Columbia CK32265)
London cast recording (RCA Victor GD 85090)
Studio cast with Susan Hampshire (TER CDTER 1179)

CHICAGO (1975)

Original cast recording (Bay Cities BCD 3003)

A CHORUS LINE (1975)

Original cast recording (Columbia CK 33581)
Australian cast recording (Polydor 835 485-2)
Japanese cast recording (Pony Canyon PCCHH 0005)
Italian cast recording (Carisch CL 36)

ANNIE (1976)
Original cast recording (Columbia CK 34712)
Norwegian cast recording (Polydor 511 816-2)

ON THE TWENTIETH CENTURY (1978)
Original cast recording (Sony Broadway SK 35330)

THEY'RE PLAYING OUR SONG (1979)
Original cast recording (PolyGram Casablanca 826 240—2-M-1)
London cast recording (TER CDTER 1035)

SWEENEY TODD (1979)
Original cast recording (RCA Red Seal 3379-2-RC, highlights on RCD1-5033)

EVITA (1979)
Preproduction recording with Julie Covington (MCA MDCX 503)
Original cast recording (MCA DMCG 3527)
Broadway cast recording (MCA MCAD 2-11007)
Korean cast recording (DRG 13104)
European touring company recording (Polydor 839 247-2)
Brazilian cast recording (Epic 752.006/2)

42ND STREET (1980)
Original cast recording (RCA Red Seal RCD1-3891)
Australian cast recording (RCA Red Seal VRCD 0812)

DREAMGIRLS (1981)
Original cast recording (Geffen 2007-2)

CATS (1982)
Original cast recording (Polydor 817-810-2, highlights on Polydor 839 415-2)
Broadway cast recording (Geffen 2031-2, highlights on Geffen 9 2026-2)
Japanese cast recording (Pony/Canyon D50H 0013-1/2)
French cast recording (Polydor 839 449-2)
Dutch cast recording (Mercury 832 694-2)
German cast recording (Polydor 817 365-2)
Mexican cast recording (Polydor CDNPM 1416)

JOSEPH AND THE AMAZING TECHNICOLOR DREAMCOAT (1982)

Studio recording with Gary Bond (MCA DMCL 1906)

Broadway cast recording (1982) (Chrysalis F2 21387)

Studio cast recording with Tim Rice (EMI Compacts for Pleasure CC242)

London revival cast recording with Jason Donovan (Polydor 511 130-2)

Broadway revival cast recording with Michael Damian (Polydor 314 519 352-2)

Canadian revival cast recording with Donny Osmond (Polydor 314 517 266-2)

Australian recording with David Dixon (Polydor 861 965-2) (4 songs)

Studio recording with Robin Cousins (Pickwick PWKS 4163)

LA CAGE AUX FOLLES (1983)

Original cast recording (RCA Red Seal BD 84824)

German cast recording (Polydor 829 646-2)

Austrian cast recording (Reverso 660 803)

Italian cast recording (Carisch CL39)

SUNDAY IN THE PARK WITH GEORGE (1984)

Original cast recording (RCA Red Seal RD85042)

BIG RIVER (1985)

Original cast recording (MCA MCAD 6147)

Australian cast recording (Rich River Records BRR 1989)

THE MYSTERY OF EDWIN DROOD (1985)

Original cast recording (Polydor G827 969-2 Y-1), reissued on Varese Sarabande VSD-5597

LES MISÉRABLES (1987)

Original concept recording (First Night Encore CD6)

London cast recording (new version) (First Night Encore CD1)

Broadway cast recording (Geffen 9 21151 2)

French cast recording (Tréma 710 369/370)

"Symphonic" version studio recording (First Night MIZ CD1 and highlights on CAST CD20)

Manchester cast recording (First Night SCORE CD34)

Swedish cast recording (CBS 467870-2)

French cast recording EP (Trema 7455549)

Dutch cast recording (Mercury 848 597-2)

Austrian cast recording (Polydor 837 770-2)

Hungarian cast recording (Bonton 71 0096-2)

Studio recording with Dave Willetts (Pickwick PWKS 4175)

INTO THE WOODS (1987)
Original cast recording (RCA Victor 6796-2-RC)
London cast recording (RCA Victor RD 60 752)

PHANTOM OF THE OPÉRA (1988)
Original cast recording (Polydor 831 273-2, highlights on 831 563 2)
Canadian cast recording (Polydor 847 689-2)
Austrian cast recording (Polydor 839 206-2)
German cast recording (Polydor 847 514-2)
Japanese cast recording (Pony/Canyon D50H 0009)
Dutch cast recording (Polydor 314 521 205-2)
Swedish cast recording (Polydor)
Studio recording with Graham Bickley (TER CDTEM 1207)

CITY OF ANGELS (1989)
Original cast recording (Columbia CK 46067)
London cast recording (First Night CAST CD34)

ASPECTS OF LOVE (1990)
Original cast recording (Polydor 841126-2)

MISS SAIGON (1991)
Original cast recording (Geffen 7599-24271-2, highlights on Geffen
   GEFD 24621-2)
Japanese cast recording (Toshiba TOTC 8008-09/2, highlights on Toshiba
   TOTC 6432)

FALSETTOS (1992)
March of the Falsettos original cast recording (DRG CDSBL 12581)
Falsettoland original cast recording (DRG CDSBL 12601)
Reissued together on DRG 22600.

SUNSET BOULEVARD (1994)
Original cast recording (Polydor 519 767-2)
American cast recording (Polydor 31452 3507 2)

SONG AND NAME INDEX